STREET GRIMOIRE

MW01097442

CATALYST
game labs

© 2014-16 The Topps Company, Inc. All Rights Reserved. Shadowrun, Matrix, and Street Grimoire are registered trademarks and/or trademarks of The Topps Company, Inc., in the United States and/or other countries. No part of this work may be reproduced, stored in a retrieval system, or transmitted in any form or by any means, without the prior permission in writing of the Copyright Owner, nor be otherwise circulated in any form other than that in which it is published. Catalyst Game Labs and the Catalyst Game Labs logo are trademarks of InMediaRes Productions, LLC.

Second Printing by Catalyst Game Labs, an imprint of InMediaRes Productions, LLC
PMB 202 • 303 -91st Ave. NE, E-502
Lake Stevens, WA 98258

Find us online:
info@shadowruntabletop.com
   (*Shadowrun* questions)
http://www.shadowruntabletop.com
   (Catalyst *Shadowrun* website)
http://www.shadowrun.com
   (official *Shadowrun Universe* website)
http://www.catalystgamelabs.com
   (Catalyst website)
http://shop.catalystgamelabs.com
   (Catalyst/Shadowrun orders)

INTRODUCTION

Awakened individuals in the Sixth World are coveted, feared, and targeted. They need to keep building their powers not just so they can make a few nuyen successfully completing runs, but so they can stay fend off their rivals and keep themselves alive. We all love Stunballs, but if they're the only weapon in your magical arsenal, it won't be long before you're over-powered, blown away, and eventually fed to one of the critters of the Sixth World that has developed a taste for Awakened blood. There is a whole spectrum of power out there; *Street Grimoire* is here to help you access it.

This book exists to give Awakened characters—and the Awakened NPCs the gamemaster wants to throw in their way—a full range of powers, giving them a chance to get their work done however they see fit. They can go in loud or quiet, covert or overt, or however they want to get the job done. More specifically, here's the information and tools this book holds:

Surviving Magic talks about what it is to be Awakened in the Sixth World, how manifesting the Talent can be both a blessing and a curse, and what any magically talented person should know to get by.

Magic in the World talks about the various magical phenomena Sixth World residents encounter, including voids, mana storms, ley lines, and more. Knowing how to use them—or avoid them when necessary—can give Awakened characters a much-needed edge.

Magic Traditions covers the different ways of looking at magic talent in the world and provides guidelines for building characters who fit in those traditions.

Magical Societies covers some of the various organizations that host Awakened individuals, discussing the benefits and possible difficulties that come from being a member.

Dark Magic provides some of the reasons people of the Sixth World find magic scary. Bug spirits, shedim, shadow spirits, and more—if you want to throw something especially nerve-wracking into your game, or if you want to know just what kinds of threats are out there, this chapter needs to be reviewed.

Expanded Grimoire is especially for the spellslingers, as it lists dozens of additional spells with a wide range of effects, greatly expanding on how spellcasters can go out into the world and take care of business.

If the Expanded Grimoire doesn't provide enough options, then check out **Shadow Rituals**, which offers several new spellcasting rituals for groups of mages looking to wreak havoc in the world.

Secrets of the Initiates talks about the ways of expanding your magical power and the benefits available from those who choose to walk difficult paths.

Physical Magic is there to make sure the adepts have plenty of toys to play with, including a host of new powers and new qualities, which give adepts the chance to follow a certain Way, building their talents in a particular area to maximize their power.

The Immaterial Touch dives into the mysterious and wild world of spirits, including details of new types of spirits the Awakened can conjure to do their bidding.

Turning Lead into Nuyen shines the spotlight on the alchemists of the Sixth World, providing new recipes and compounds for them to cook up.

Lastly, **The Life of a Talismonger** is there for the enchanters and reagent hunters, providing advanced rules addressing customizing foci and using different qualities of reagents in enchanting work.

So whatever your brand of magic may be, *Street Grimoire* has resources for you. Nothing left to do now but dive in!

STREET GRIMOIRE CREDITS

Writing: Jason Andrew, Peter M. Andrew, Jr., Mark Dynna, Jason M. Hardy, Adam Large, Philip A. Lee, Scott Schletz, R.J. Thomas, Malik Toms, Michael Wich

Editing: Kevin Killiany, Philip A. Lee

Art Direction: Brent Evans

Cover Art: Victor Manuel Leza Moreno

Cover Layout: Matt Heerdt

Iconography: Nigel Sade

Interior Art: Gordon Bennetto, Joel Biske, Echo Chernik, Daniel Comerci, Victor Perez Corbella, Peter Dora, Homeros Gilani, David Hovey, Igor Kieryluk, Miklós Ligeti, Melanie Maier, Victor Manuel Leza Moreno, Alessandra Pissano, Mark Poole, Michael Rookard, Rob Ruffolo, Andreas "AAS" Schroth, Bryan Syme, Christophe Swal, and Damon Westenhofer

Interior Layout: Matt "Wrath" Heerdt

Shadowrun Line Developer: Jason M. Hardy

Playtesting & Proofing: Ghislain Bonnotte, Jackson Bruntsing, Derek Dokter, Mike Gearman, Tim Gray, Lars Wagner Hansen, Mason Hart, Pete Houtekier, Kendall Jung, Matt Riley, CZ Wright, and Leland Zavadil.

WHERE FEW
DARE TO TREAD

Every shadowrunner on the planet has three things that every other runner has, whether she chooses to acknowledge them or not. Aleksandra Severnaya, ThD, had no problem admitting the first thing—her birth name—because it appeared on her business cards. Not until she received the strange request from unusual channels did she remember the other two.

Everyone, from SINners to SINless, from mundanes to Awakened, has a mother. And everyone, whether a homeless vagrant or well-to-do corp man, has a home. Not necessarily a "where I sleep at night" home or "where I feel safe" home, but somewhere they come from. Once Sandra got a call from an unknown number in the opposite hemisphere, she remembered her real home, the place where she was born.

"Sashka," the caller had said when Sandra played the voicemail in her Atlanta office.

Only a select few had her commcode; fewer still knew her well enough to use that name. No matter how much she had tried to forget, no matter how much noise from the distant Matrix connection garbled the audio, her Uncle Grigoriy's husky, accent-laden voice was unmistakable.

"Your mother and many others here have taken ill," the voicemail continued. "Doctors are not sure what is wrong. She keeps asking for you. If you want to see her before she takes a turn for the worse, I would suggest coming home as soon as possible. Perhaps—perhaps maybe you can find out what is wrong."

There was more to the message, but Sandra stopped listening about halfway through. She hadn't been home in more than a decade, mostly because she wanted to forget where she came from. For years, her busy life in the CAS capital pushed any recollections of Pripyat, Ukraine, out of her head. But unless she was mistaken, Uncle Grigoriy had been fighting off a good cry while recording that message.

What to do? she thought.

You want my opinion? Judah volunteered in her head. Sandra's ally spirit was hovering nearby in astral space, doing whatever it did when she didn't have any active tasks for it. She liked to imagine it was sitting in the corner chair of her office, licking its giant, golden paws and cleaning its fur and mane like the big cat that it resembled when materialized.

Always, she replied, turning her astral gaze on the spirit, whose fiery, leonine aura blazed with golds and oranges and reds.

The spirit stared right back with an eerily level gaze. *If you don't get a chance to say goodbye, I guarantee you will regret it later. I know you don't like going back home, but it's more than just your mother who's sick. And what is it your scriptures say? "Whatever you've done for the least of my brethren, you have done also for me." Something like that.*

Sandra turned away from the spirit.

Plus, Judah added, *it might be fun to get away from Hotlanta for awhile.*

She closed her eyes and conjured images of her mother and her hometown, as she'd last seen them ten years ago. How many

PHILIP A. LEE

people were barely scratching out a living over there while some mysterious sickness ravaged through the town?

Sandra bit her lip and shook her head. Judah was right.

Go wake up Miles, she told the spirit. *And tell him to pack for an international flight.*

As far as the rest of the world was concerned, the Master of Thaumaturgical Arts degree that Sandra's elven assistant Michael "Miles" Dorchester got from Texas A&M&M was on the level. Only Sandra and a few facilitators knew his degree was a forgery, but she knew no one who needed occult investigation services would take her seriously if they knew her assistant only had a bachelor's from Georgia Tech. The rumor was that his nickname came from his initiatory ordeal, where he had to walk barefoot for untold kilometers out in the Mojave Desert, but this was not actually the case. She once got him drunk enough to learn that he was called "Miles" because of a childhood prank involving some Robert Frost poem about snow. Of course, once she stepped off the semiballistic at Boryspil Airport, no one in the whole Ukraine gave a devil rat's ass what kind of magical degree her assistant had or where his nickname had come from.

Back in the Confederated States, Sandra would hand out AR business cards at the drop of a hat—"SEVERNAYA SPIRITUAL INVESTIGATIONS: WE KNOW WHAT HAUNTS YOU"—but here, everything felt different and detached, even in Kiev. The whole landscape of the city held a somber tone, as though some kind of intangible storm had blown through and sucked up all traces of life and color. This was not the Ukraine she remembered. Her childhood home had never been the lap of luxury, but seeing it like this pricked her insides with an icy spike of unreality.

"What a *dump*," Miles said, absently scratching the tip of his pointed ear as they waited for a taxi. "You *sure* this is where you grew up?"

Am I remembering this place wrong? Sandra thought.

No, Judah replied. The spirit hovered about in astral space, prowling around like a caged circus animal. Puffs of annoyed breath fumed from its catlike nostrils. *It's not just you. There's something wrong out there. I can feel it.*

Sandra shuddered. *Go see what you can find. And be careful.*

Judah grinned, his astral form revealing sharp canines that would have frightened just about anyone else but her. Then the spirit vanished.

"Pripyat, please," Sandra said in Ukranian after sliding into the next available airport taxi. She had spent so long in the States that she had to deliberately remind herself to add a little native touch to her accent.

The ball-cap-wearing ork taxi driver turned pale, as though she'd just asked him to drive over his own grave. "Not a chance," he growled with an accent far more convincing than her own. "I can take you as far as the Exclusion Zone perimeter, but if you want further than that, you're on your own."

Sandra frowned and glanced sideways at Miles in the seat next to her. "What's wrong with Pripyat?" she asked the cabbie.

"No one goes to Pripyat anymore. Not since the outbreak."

Uncle Grigoriy had said some people were sick, but his message didn't sound like there was a full-on epidemic going on. And the newsnets never mentioned any problems in the region. "Outbreak? What outbreak?"

"You know as much as I do. If the feds say 'You can't enter the Exclusion Zone,' then I can't enter the Exclusion Zone, paying passengers or not. Simple as that." He turned around in the driver's seat and fixed her with an inquisitive stare. "Why you wanna go to Pripyat anyway? There's a ton of Kiev landmarks I could take you to instead."

"I grew up there," she replied.

"My condolences," said the cabbie. "Now, unless you want me to take you somewhere else around the city, get the hell out of my cab."

Uncle Grigoriy's voicemail replayed in her head. How much longer did her mother have? Sandra knew that unless she took some shortcut, she might never get a chance to say goodbye. She and Miles could probably slip into Pripyat by themselves, but time was running out. Wheels would help speed things up.

She fiddled around in her pockets and then reached at the back of her neck to unclasp her necklace. "I've got a better proposition," she said. "You take me and my partner here to Pripyat, and I'll give you this necklace as payment." The shimmering, orange-gold charm on the reinforced golden chain was an Eastern Orthodox cross, with a smaller crossbeam at the top and a slanted cross beam near the bottom. Every millimeter of the cross was inscribed with scripture passages in enameled, red Cyrillic text.

The glint of greed reared its head in the cabbie's eyes. "How—how much is it worth?"

Sandra shrugged. "I haven't gotten it appraised, but it's made out of solid orichalcum. The metal alone should be worth several thousand *hryvni* to the right buyer."

The cabbie licked the corner of his lips. "And how do you expect me to get you past the quarantine checkpoint? You got another one of those trinkets to bribe security?"

"Let's say I've got a few aces up my sleeve," she said with a smirk.

The ork looked her up and down. "All right. I'll take it."

Sandra clasped her hands around the cross to dissolve the enchantment on it before handing it over. The necklace had been a minor spell focus—no big loss, all things told. She could always make another, but she couldn't make a second chance to bring her mother back from the brink.

"Name's Petro," the cabbie said. He readjusted his cap and faced the steering wheel. "Okay, let's do this before I change my mind."

Years before Sandra was born, the Chernobyl Exclusion Zone created by the infamous nuclear reactor disaster of 1986 had been deemed safe for human habitation. Both Chernobyl and Pripyat had slowly repopulated in the years since, and Sandra and all of her childhood friends had grown up without any trace of mutations that the Exclusion Zone naysayers had warned would happen. Now, as Petro's taxi approached the Exclusion Zone border, she saw something completely unexpected. A guardhouse with an electronically controlled chain-link gate, electrified razor-wire fences, drone patrols whizzing about overhead, and dozens of armed guards who were more security than she had ever seen in the area.

Under the cover of Sandra's sustained invisibility spell and Miles' silence spell, the taxi followed right on the heels of an official government truck that pulled up to the checkpoint. Once the truck cleared, Petro floored the taxi and followed the truck through the gate before the guards could close it. While security was present, they were either unobservant or lax; none of them noticed the maneuver or cared about it.

Beyond the gate, the landscape Sandra had grown up with felt completely foreign to her. Grey everywhere—grey tree trunks, grey earth, grey sky, grey buildings—as though the whole physical plane had been photographed in monochrome.

"Everything looks ... dead," Sandra said with a shiver.

"Yeah," Miles said. "Anything from ol' Jude?"

"No. He's still scouting ahead, but—" She shook her head slowly. "I don't like this one bit. This is more than an epidemic."

"Almost looks like an aspected domain," Miles said. And he would know. His bachelor's thesis dealt with that very thing.

They say you can't go home again, and Sandra saw the truth of this firsthand as Petro drove through Pripyat. Her old stomping grounds had fallen victim to the ravages of decay. Collapsed fences, dilapidated buildings, and wilting vegetation ruled each block of the street Uncle Grigoriy's message had mentioned. Not even the worst Atlanta ghetto looked this bad.

Petro parked in front of an ancient-looking hospital that Sandra knew had been built before she emigrated from the country. The few staff she saw milling about were green around the gills—dark, sunken eyes and pale, clammy skin.

Grigoriy was waiting for her in the somber reception area and gave her a fierce bear hug. His haggard face looked no different than those of the hospital staff. Sandra didn't need a degree in medicine to know her uncle had also contracted the contagion.

"What happened here?" she asked.

"They say it's radiation sickness," he said, coughing. "But that's impossible. The Exclusion Zone has been radiation free for decades. Government doesn't want to cause a panic, so we're all stuck here until they find out what's making everybody sick."

"Something in the water, maybe," Miles mused.

Sandra's quick dip into astral space revealed how wrong her assistant was. Grigoriy's aura was muddled with blacks and greys of what was likely radiation sickness, but it carried a faint astral signature too, which was not at all normal. Trying to assense the signature set her stomach doing backflips, and she suppressed the urge to throw up.

But the urge won. All over Miles' thousand-nuyen deathrattle-leather wingtips.

"You all right, Sashka?" Grigoriy asked.

Sandra wiped her mouth with the back of her hand. "No," she said. "But I think I know why everyone's sick."

She felt the floor wiggle underfoot, as though someone heavy was walking too hard nearby. Then the ground shook beneath her, *hard*, nearly knocking her to the ground. Miles stumbled to his knees; Sandra braced herself against the wall

Another tremor followed it, then another. Something of incredible mass was heading toward the hospital.

Judah's ghostly feline face suddenly appeared in front of her, his auburn mane rippling in the air. Grigoriy and the nearby hospital staff gasped at the manifested spirit. "Sandy, Miles," Judah said, "we've got incoming. Better get outside now, or it's going to follow me in here."

Sandra snapped into operating mode. "Uncle, keep these people inside and make sure my mother is safe! Miles, follow me!"

Between earthquakes, she burst through the front doors into stark daylight and saw something that turned her blood to ice. A massive wolf, larger than anything imaginable, loped down the street, crushing—no, rusting—whole cars beneath its massive paws. Its hide was a knotted tangle of mange and bloated, mutated pustules. Chipped and broken fangs dripped a ghostly green saliva, as though the wolf had been chewing radioactive rocks. One of its eyes was ghosted over with a cataract; the other was crusted closed and leaking vitreous fluid.

Sandra had no doubts the wolf could still see her. On the astral, the spirit was just as twisted as its exterior. Its aura radiated a dizzying swirl of browns, greys, and blacks that made her want to throw up again. A shimmering astral tendril connected the spirit to its nearby summoner.

This diseased and mutated spirit had to have been summoned by a toxic magician, a path few sane magicians dared to tread. Sandra had faced a toxic spirit before, but never one like this, never one so powerful that its radioactive energy aura had polluted the whole landscape. Just looking at the spirit in meat space made her feel weak in the knees—and, once again, in the stomach. But she had no time for nausea.

She coughed hard into a fist. Her hand came away bloody.

"Miles!" she shouted. "The summoner! Take out the summoner!"

"On it!"

Her assistant ran down the street to avoid the incoming monstrosity, but it was too fast. The wolf spirit lunged forward and swatted Miles aside. Its giant paw struck him so hard that one of his wingtips was left where he'd been standing. Miles hit the side of the nearest building, fell down, and didn't rise. The vibrant colors of his aura meant he was still alive—for now—but he wouldn't be able to help her.

Chips of concrete rattled free from nearby buildings with each of the monster's steps. Sandra readied as many spells as she could to try stopping this monstrosity, but it was too close. Fireballs barely singed the mutated hide. Other magical distractions only seemed to anger it. It stood above her. Toxic waste dripped from its teeth. Its waiting jaws exuded a storm of heated air laced with the stink of burning metal.

A massive current of mana flooded to her fingertips. Before the toxic wolf could bite her in two, Sandra was ready to blast it with a spell powerful enough to incapacitate or kill her. Better her own magic kill her than something so twisted.

As if from nowhere, a reddish-gold blur slammed into the wolf's side and crushed the beast against the building across the street. When the bricks and dust settled, Sandra saw a gargantuan lion the same size as the wolf grappling with the spirit. Judah reared back on his hind legs and swatted at the wolf with both paws. Her materialized ally's mouth was open in a snarling rictus of hatred.

Better late than never, Judah said. *At least that toxic summoner won't be causing us any problems for awhile.*

Sandra let her spell fizzle. She could only watch in awe, spellbound as Judah ripped the toxic spirit apart, one swipe at a time. But he was paying the price. Huge patches of the lion's coat were falling out. Misshapen tumors formed across his face and hide.

Another bloody cough wracked Sandra. Dizziness swept over her, and she fell down to her knees, unable to focus her vision. She knew the radiation was quickly killing her.

Banish it, Sandy! Judah shouted in her brain. *Now! It's our only chance!*

Sandra propped herself up on one knee and shifted her focus to the astral plane to home in on the gossamer tendrils connecting the wolf spirit to its incapacitated summoner. She envisioned herself slashing through the cords with a sword made solely out of wind. The strands were slick and oily. Just grazing them made Sandra empty her stomach again; blood and bile splattered the pavement. In her lightheadedness, a sense of euphoria mixed with a sickening sensation. Vileness mixed with a cloying, heady stench.

Come now, the wolf spoke directly into her head. *You know you want a little taste of corruption.*

She could barely keep her eyes open. Her limbs felt heavier than shipping containers. To buy herself more time, she abandoned her doomed meat body and freed herself from fleshly constraints. No matter what happened, she couldn't let this monster destroy her mother or her home.

Go to Hell! she commanded the spirit. With the last of her willpower, her astral form shattered the bond between spirit and summoner.

The wolf's tortured howl reverberated throughout astral space. With nothing to anchor it to the physical plane, the spirit vanished and departed for whatever twisted metaplane it called home.

Judah's astral form drew up alongside hers as she sat down next to her meat body. His aura was weak and tainted with strands of brown and black, but he would eventually recover. Her own body, bruised and bloody from severe radiation poisoning, would not.

I'm sorry, Judah said, rubbing his muzzle against her astral shoulder. *I wish there was a way to fix you.*

In astral form, she found it impossible to cry. *Keep an eye on Miles for me, will you?* she said. *He's an idiot, but he means well.*

Shall I stay with you until you go? the lion asked.

With her meat body close to death—or already gone, for all she knew—Sandra felt her astral form already beginning to slip away. *Go chase down that summoner,* she said. *There's something I have to do.*

Judah nodded. *You've been good to me, Sandy. I won't forget you.*

At a loss for words, she merely smiled and wandered off into the hospital. Her astral form drifted from room to room, searching. Even after all these years apart, she still recognized her mother's aura when she found it. It was faint, just like her own, but Aneta Severnaya was a fighter, and now that the source of radiation was gone, she and all of these radiation sufferers would likely recover.

Sandra didn't even have the strength to manifest. Instead she sat by the bedside and touched her mother's aura, which was strengthening by the moment.

Goodbye, Mother, her astral form whispered. It was all she had left.

SURVIVING MAGIC

No. The corner of Ayana's "Brackhaven For President" poster curled beneath blue flames beside her pink four-post bed. A thin scent of plastic drifted towards her.

"This isn't real," she said in a choked whisper. If it were real, she could control it. She could call it forth at will. But she couldn't could she?

Anya snatched her Maria Mercurial doll off her bed. She concentrated on the silver hair. With a sound like a zipper closing, the doll's hair drew together. There was a hint of smoke and the hair began to glow ember red. Then it was ash.

No. This wasn't supposed to be happening. Didn't she have enough to deal with? Fat and blonde, Ayana had too much working against her social status. Acne scars pitted her face. The boys called her Ork, and the orks laughed alongside them.

She called up her playlist in AR and spun the music dial until her favorite Latch-Key Kids song flared up. Music blared from tinny wall speakers, *Kids don't bother to love, because love has nothing on drugs.* She wished she could dive into the music, go away, be anywhere else but here right now. Here was not safe.

A commlink sparkled and buzzed on the desk against the far wall, her mom calling her down for dinner.

One last meal? The thought brought a teary-eyed smile to her face. Yeah, that worked. She'd go downstairs and eat with her drekhead of a little brother. With any luck her ability could go off again and set her brother on fire. Wouldn't that be wiz?

No. They would test again in the fall. Maybe by then she could find a way to beat the test. She could run away. Bobby Paine ran away from his parents back in the fifth grade, after the test. Everyone thought it was because he failed, but he said it wasn't. Nobody believed him. Nobody would believe her either.

The pink bed squeaked as she stood.

Her father still used a straight-edge razor. He kept it in the bathroom on an old tin tray. She went there now, careful to avoid the planks of the old wood floor that could give her away. Ayana didn't know if her father would be angry with her or proud for doing this, but one thing was certain—she would do it. The dishonor of her curse was worse than anything spilt blood could produce.

She saw it first out of the corner of her eye, a flame like the ones she was cursed to make. It started as a candle's flicker and grew until it was as round and full as a grapefruit. Ayana wanted to run or scream, but she was too afraid to do anything. The thing hovered inches away from her. It had no eyes or mouth, only the candlelight flicker of its form. All at once a voice came out of it, like that of a young girl. It said, "Stop."

Ayana gulped hard and stepped back, half falling unto the bed.

"Stop, girl. It isn't your turn to go yet."

"Wha-what are you?"

"You'll learn one day. If you let yourself."

"My family—"

"Will never understand what you are or what you are meant to become."

The tears came now, cutting dirty rivulets down her pocked face. She sobbed and could not talk.

"Continue to pretend. I will continue to protect you, and when the time is right I will come for you. Do you understand?"

Ayana looked up at the light and nodded. The candlelight orb flickered twice and it was gone.

Outside, winter rain pattered off the roof of a black Hyundai Shin-Hyung. Sandman moved his hands through the air, working the ant-sized AROs that danced above his steering wheel. He sighed and stretched, rolling his neck from left to right. A form materialized in the leather seat beside him. It held the shape of a ball and flickered like a candle.

Sandman said, "Is it done?"

The spirit shimmered slightly, "The girl believes."

"Good." He tapped on an ARO and it spun upward, shifting from red to join a second green ARO hovering just below the roof of the car. The rest remained red. Sandman yawned, but shook it off quickly. Two more stops on the list before he could finally sleep.

○ I'd like to say I came up in the shadows, but you all called bullshit on that backstory a long time ago. There is a difference between being raised in an environment where magic is praised and growing up where casting a spell can get you killed. That is the harsh reality most of us deal with every day, and who better to walk us through it than Man-Of-Many-Names. In spite of his often-cryptic postings, he has some straight facts to share about magic and the way things work in the Sixth World. Pay attention and I'll bet you learn something.

○ Frosty

BORN AWAKENED

I was not born into a world of magic. I came from a family who believed that magic was something that happened to other people. My father used to tell us, as many still do, that magic was another scientifically definable resource so limited as to be negligible. I believed him. When my father saw Daniel Howling Coyote dance he turned away, oblivious to what the moment meant for our people. He was a nuclear engineer. He wanted magic to represent just a fraction of what the future held for us, and he worried our people would suffer if we put all our faith in magic.

We *Dineh* (Navajo) call those who possess magic *Haatalii*. When I was young, children pretended to be rich with magic and tradition. We didn't pretend to be the Indians of old. We were the native people of a world with plenty of riches, and when the cowboys attacked in our games we hit them back, hard, with the ferocity of spirits. My father didn't like us playing this way. He kept doubting magic, and I kept believing him. When the *Haatalii* came to my school to test our potential, I refused to participate. I thought that might make my father happy. Instead it made me an outcast from my own people. Simply put, people thought I was weird and picked on me. Some things don't change much over the years.

I discovered my ability at the age of 15. I had no idea what happened at the time, but now I recognize it as Astral Perception. I'd been shielded from magic and tucked away in private schools that favored data over dreamcatchers, so my first impression was that I'd gone blind,

even insane. It wasn't that I didn't know how to turn it off. I could see that trigger deep in my mind, but I didn't *want* to turn it off. The astral world is beautiful contrast to our normal world of stone and steel. For the Awakened, the physical world is a skin we can peel away to see what lies beneath.

There was no one in my life who could tell me what I could do, or at least not anyone I trusted. I attempted to discover the Ways for myself and floundered until Wolf found me and showed me the Path. Once I knew what I was, I learned to hide my magic. The teachers wanted us to be *Haatalii* to earn the bonuses the schools offered for finding people like us. Gangs wanted us as evidence of their power. The military wanted us to project the Native strength Howling Coyote forged.

I thought my story was an isolated incident until I walked in the greater world. I was lucky. Others never live long enough to enjoy the gifts of the Awakening. Across the globe the Awakened are honored, revered, feared, or persecuted according to the rules of their culture. In some dark places even gender affects how magic use is perceived. Women born with the gift can be seen as cursed, and their lives end once that curse is discovered.

○ There is real money in the business of locating and extracting girls like this. I'm not in the biz for feel good stories, but once in a hunter's moon I get to do a job that benefits more than the corp I'm pushing mana for. When I get a chance to rescue kids from people who don't understand magic—folks like the Human Brigade—I feel like maybe I'm earning a bit of karma for some of the fucked-up shit that goes down the rest of the time.

○ Ma'Fan

○ But who are you extracting them for? These girls are probably looking at a life of serving corporate masters, beholden to the group that saved them and earning a minimum wage for their loyal service.

○ Mika

○ That isn't my problem, omae.

○ Ma'Fan

- After the initial investment, the washouts end up in experimental programs or just dumped back out on the streets where they bleed into the shadows. A few can handle it and become shadowrunners or even stable members of the society, but most end up the property of gangs.
- Jimmy No

Magic is a curse. Magic is a gift. Magic is a choice—all depending upon where you are born. Since the Awakening we've been trying to make sense of who becomes Awakened and who doesn't. For a time scientists assumed that to be goblinized or born of the elven breed made you more susceptible to having magical ability. Despite what science is capable of, there is no scientific way to determine whether a child is born with magic until magic decides to show its face. Likewise there is no scientific procedure to guarantee your child can wield mana or what style of magic that child will manifest.

As Ehran the Scribe said, "Magic is the purest expression of the relationship between man and the spirit world. There is something in our DNA that opens the door to that other place. However, it is the paradigms that we adopt that allow us to step through."

Believing in Wolf is a paradigm, or system of understanding, that allows me to use my magical potential. The Christian priests believe their power comes from God, and they pray to manifest their abilities. Magicians write complex algorithms, Wujen manipulate *qi* to produce magical effects, and so on. As a magic user your paradigm can be nearly anything. The way you interact with magic determines how the world interacts with you.

- I heard a story back in Germany about doctors kidnapping women of child-bearing age who had magical potential. They would inseminate them with the seed of a magically active male and try to birth a child with the potential.
- Red Anya

- I believe it—people will try a lot of things to get magic to appear. I was hired once to deliver a medical package to a lab in Amazonia. I snooped, of course—you don't waltz into Amazonia without understanding exactly what the frag you're getting into. I learned the package came from somewhere in Boston and was the 'male product' of an imprisoned shapeshifter. I don't want to know what Mr. Johnson was planning for that specimen, but it sounds a lot like Red Anya's story.
- Lyran

MAGIC IN POPULAR CULTURE

Sukie Redflower 5 is an abomination. Thanks to the power of organizations like Horizon, the popular perception of shamans is that they're either beautiful NAN princesses or weathered Amerind men wearing feathers and smoking peyote. Granted, there are some people like that out there, but the stereotypes do harm in the expectations they create. The media portrayal of magic is fundamentally flawed. Magic is normally an invisible process to the non-Awakened. A normal can no more discern the casting of a spell than a casual shopper can read the coding behind a sales algorithm directed against them. But this invisibility doesn't look great on camera, so media outlets find ways to portray spellcasters as different and readily identifiable. Shamans are reduced to old men dressed in outdated tribal gear and mages return to the robes of Tolkien fantasy.

In rare cases we can see the physical effects of magic, and this is the type of magic the media tends to like. The portrayal of magic in the Sixth World leads to a strange separation from the reality of what it means to be Awakened and how the Awakened are viewed by the average person. Thing number one to remember is that magic is extremely rare. The average citizen is more likely to encounter a shadowrunner than they are to encounter a spellslinger. In fact, if they actually encountered an Awakened individual, it's unlikely they would even know it. Nevertheless magic insinuates itself into daily life, acting as either the carrot or the stick. It carries with it a certain promise of wealth, with all those high-end medical clinics that promise magical healing. The top security firms all claim to offer protection packages that include a personal mage—as long as you pay a hefty

WORD ON THE STREET

HOW DO YOU FEEL ABOUT MAGIC?
(Asked at The Galleria, Dallas-Ft. Worth Metroplex)

Mark Tucker, 64, business owner: It ought to be regulated better. I mean, how do I know the guy I'm trying to hire isn't casting a spell on me and making me hire him, so he can take over my business?

Samantha Epstein, 15, student: The books never got it right. Gandalf the Grey? Harry freaking Potter? No way, man. Mages are nuclear. One time I saw this cop step into the road and smash a getaway car just by pointing her finger. Now that's some wiz stuff right there.

Peter Duncan, 28, unemployed: It's not at all what people think. That power has to come from somewhere, and not some drekking manasphere. Where was that power all this time? And what about the dragons? The more people use that mojo, the stronger Dragons get. I'm telling you there's a connection!

Kevin Hardaway, 47, political lobbyist: The idea that one person can wield that kind of unregulated power is terrifying. They need to be registered, and if they threaten society, they need to be put down.

premium. At the other end of the spectrum, parents still remind their children that the bogeyman is real and he haunts the night waiting to cast spells on naughty children. Folklore and cultural mores are teeming with examples of what can come from magic, both good and bad—from the fairy godmother who will get you to the ball to the devil who will gladly buy your soul. So, even if no one really experiences it, the stories of what magic is and does shape the culture around us, affecting what mundanes think we can actually do.

MAGIC IN ETHNIC CULTURES

Few cultures initially greeted magic with exuberance. Many fell into the old prejudices. Fear drove those in power to seek control over the Awakened, and what they could not control, they destroyed. In parts of Africa, Eastern Europe, and deep within the CAS there remain pockets of denial where being a mage is punishable by death. Kids work hard to hide their abilities and sometimes are driven to suicide when they discover their talent in order to avoid the ridicule and disgrace the family would face for producing a spellcaster.

This prejudice resonates on a national level, fundamentally as a result of media perceptions. You've heard it all before: Tír na nÓg is crawling with druids, Chinese magic users are all Wujen, and if someone looks like they come from Aztlan, they probably want to tap your vein for their next spell. This isn't what everyone in a particular place believes, but enough do that it can effect how you are perceived. The NAN is open about this. Shamanism is seen as the traditional path, and those who call themselves magicians or otherwise are still viewed as outsiders. A handful of Sixth World cultures are notable for their treatment of the Awakened.

ASAMANDO

Several metahuman nations sprouted up just after the awakening. Each handled the legalities of magic differently. In Asamando, the country's laws were designed with magic in mind. Nearly thirty percent of the citizens are magicians from various traditions, but because they are also ghouls very few outsiders dare to venture inside the borders to learn what Asamandians have to offer. With a population that hovers around ninety-five percent HMHVV-infected, Asamando is known as the Ghoul Homeland. A nation of ghouls is a guaranteed draw for the attention of the Awakened. In addition to all the ghouls, Asamando boasts a sizable population of free spirits, which led to laws against spirit binding in certain parts of the country.

- Corporations won't openly speak about the recruitment and research they do in Asamando. They are extremely interested in the high concentration of magic in the region. Yet they are afraid that the senseless bigotry that forces my people to live in the shadows may affect their bottom line.
- Hannibelle

- Senseless bigotry? Let's not forget that ghouls eat flesh. But anyway, Asamando's not the only metahuman nation in Africa causing a stir. If you're a round-ear, avoid going down continent to Azania where the Zulu elves are extremely worried about losing their grip on the nation and have been making that fact known to outsiders.
- Turbo Bunny

- Mujaji's absentee leadership in that part of the world has led to a great deal of instability. The Trans-Swazi federation has even gone so far to reach out to other nations, including Asamando, for help with the growing crime problem in Cape Town. So far the only sorts willing to help have been mercenaries and shadowrunners.
- Frosty

ARABIAN CALIPHATE

Sharia law is rarely a constant throughout the Caliphate, where magic is considered to be against the teachings of Allah. The faithful treat magic as one of the seven deadly acts and openly oppose its practice within the Arabian Caliphate. Any use of magic within the Caliphate is outlawed. Meanwhile, the Islamic leadership itself is quick to differentiate between magic use and "gifts" handed down to the faithful by Allah. The *Sufi,* or Islamic mystics, are not magic users. In Caliphate thinking and terminology, they have received the gifts of Allah and use those gifts to advance His word.

This distinction can be political as well, as shown through Islam's acceptance of Ibn Eisa, leader of the Islamic Unity Movement, who was assassinated in 2061 only to rise from the grave and continue leading his order without challenge, even after he was outed as a shedim in 2064.

PHILIPPINES

The Philippines makes this list for two reasons: Yomi Island and the Huk. Yomi Island, or Lagu Lagu as the natives call it, remains a hotbed of spirit and metahuman activity. Despite the island being liberated from Japanese rule in '61, Japanese intelligence keeps records of everyone coming and going from the Island. Smugglers who know the waters earn a decent living moving people to and from Lagu Lagu in secret.

Smugglers can also earn some nuyen smuggling magically active teens out of the country before the Huk government can sink their claws into them. The Huk government came under fire in 2073 when a Horizon reporter exposed a connection between a rash of kidnappings in Marawi and the Huk government. The report proved that members of the government's military branch hired guerrillas to kidnap children known to have magical potential, possibly to recruit into the army or for other as yet unknown purposes. The government denied this program existed, but the kidnappings continue to this day. The problem has gotten so bad that children are refusing to be tested for the talent in fear that it could lead to them being snatched from their homes in the middle of the night.

- Try broad daylight. The Huks are using former guerrilla warriors who refused to go straight after the Huks seized control of the country. It has created a huge political backlash for a government that is still struggling to maintain legitimacy with the UN. If another link to government-sanctioned kidnappings can be uncovered, it would cause a lot of trouble for the Huk.
- Kay St. Irregular

ITALIAN CONFEDERATION

Nowhere else is magic so clearly a gift and a curse as in the Italian Confederation. The power of the Catholic Church stretches into every household of the nation. The mandate of the Church to locate and recruit Awakened children drives action. The Church considers a magical child a gift of God and pushes them to orders and societies where they are indoctrinated into Catholic traditions and ways of magic.

The Church runs aptitude testing throughout the Confederation. It is embedded as part of weekly worship and teachings. If any child suspects they have been chosen by God to receive the talent, they are told to self-report. Most reporters have little to no magical aptitude and only do so for the increased social standing reporting gives their family.

TÍR NA NÓG

Being born behind the veil means starting life in a place where everything is shifting beneath your feat—literally. Tír na nÓg is controlled by magic, and those born with the gift are seen as heralds of this improved, Awakened world. While citizens with the talent are treated well by the rich, the poor and downtrodden don't see Awakened kids as instant shoe-ins to the Seelie court. They know fame and wealth is a distinct possibility for an Awakened child, but they also know that exploitation, strange metaplanar journeys, and madness can also be part of the equation.

ATHABASKAN COUNCIL

The tribes of this region languish in the enduring lie of "rugged individualism." You are free to practice any sort of magic you want, so long as it is shamanism. Those who don't follow tribal tradition are shunned as outcasts. Most power sites are closed to all but shamans, and even then sites are often restricted to particular totem followers. As a result non-shamanic traditions tend to practice their magic in secret or simulate the tribal wear and ritual in order to pass.

- ⊚ Council leaders are aware of this, and they regularly have spirits sweeping the nation and reading auras to see if they find anyone practicing anything besides shamanism. Those people are reported to local authorities. So if you're a non-shaman in Athabaskan territory, make sure your astral overwatch is up to snuff.
- ⊚ Jimmy No

AZTLAN

To understand the cultural impact of Aztlan you have to recognize that the president also serves as the emperor of the national religion while holding a high rank within Aztechnology. This close relationship between state, church, and corporation fuels everything from international relations to the country's criminalization of unsanctioned magic.

Prior to the Awakening, eighty percent of the people living in the region practiced Catholicism. As magic returned, so did worship of the old Aztec Gods. Today Catholicism, along with all other non-native religions, are banned within Aztlan, severely limiting the number of traditions that can be legally practiced there. As with the Athabaskan Council, spellcasters born to other paths than the shamanic traditions hide their abilities or mask them in the garb of the Aztec gods. The people stand by the Path of the Sun. There is an ingrained sense of cultural value in the word of the church, so much so that mothers will turn in their children for practicing unsanctioned religions.

- ⊚ If you don't understand the general fanaticism of the Aztlan people, you have no business running there.
- ⊚ Marcos

- ⊚ If you don't understand how to undermine that fanaticism and use it against the citizens, you also have no business running there.
- ⊚ Traveler Jones

HAWAI'I

The islands of Hawai'i are notable in that Fifth World prejudices were only strengthened by the Awakening. Hawai'i remains one thing to tourists and something else entirely to natives, only now the law reflects this divergence. *Haole*, which covers both visitors and non-natives, are forbidden from practicing magic without a license. Getting a license is a multiple-day affair that requires the petitioner to have a native sponsor who is willing to take legal responsibility for the applicants actions as if they were their guardian. The datastores of paperwork reduced the number of *haoles* practicing magic legally to a handful of university professors and corporate researchers. More practice magically illegally, using forged permits and occasionally corporate writs.

AMAZONIA

It would be a joke to call the Amazonian government anything more than the puppet of the dragons who nest there. With those dragons recovering from wars against Aztlan and each other, the Awakened are high-value assets, both to assist in that recovery and replace what was lost. The Department of Amazonian Intelligence and Security (DISA) tries to keep a file on all the Awakened entities in the country. DISA utilizes an intricate network of informants to uncover the newly Awakened and visiting magicians alike. The spy organization falls short in some of the ghettos, but it is best to believe that if you've been tested, then the dragon has a file on you.

- ⊚ Which dragon? Hualpa? Boiuna? Possibly even M'boi or another Lindworm? It's been a free-for-all down there lately since the multiple blows Hualpa and the nation have taken.
- ⊚ Winterhawk

MAGIC IN THE K-12 SYSTEM

Media interpretations of magic ripple across all the institutes of socialization. Schools must answer to parents, and parents (bless their hearts) are afraid of everything. In public and private institutions across the world, testing for magical aptitude falls under the category of standardized testing. Some school systems begin testing as early as third grade, while others wait until fifth grade to see if your child displays magical aptitude. Testing continues annually into the high school years. Puberty is widely accepted as the point where Awakened abilities begin to manifest, so testing is mandated by the end of your freshman year of high school. Scientists suspect that the timing has to do with hormone levels, so research has largely focused on the relationship between genetic markers and the key chemical indicators of puberty. However, no one has been able to isolate a specific gene as the cause of magical ability. The fact that children of Awakened are very frequently not Awakened seems to argue against a strict genetic explanation for magic.

Once tagged as having magical potential, children are tracked by the school system. In some cases, such as school systems in Aztlan and many Southeast Asian nations, kids are separated out into classes where their abilities can be monitored. School districts say the reasoning behind this is to help the child reach their potential, but more often the separation is about security.

- Whose security? The kids? The schools? The separation is more about putting the magic kid in a bubble so authorities can keep a closer eye on how those powers develop in order to take advantage of them one day. It is no secret that K-12 schools sell database records to universities and corporations. Data miners troll through school records in order to identify recruitment targets. The more people get recruited from your school, the more notoriety your school gains, the more nuyen ends up in your pocket.
- Nephrine

- All it takes is one kid accidentally falling off a jungle gym and everyone's screaming about how the magic kid used her powers to push him. Short of erecting expensive detection wards, schools can't track who is using magic on that level. Kids can get away with that "his abilities make me feel unsafe" drek. The fact is the magic kid is going to be the target of bullying a hell of a lot more than being the bully. Powers are extremely unpredictable at that age, and most kids are too terrified to actually use them.
- Lyran

The pre-high school magical testing process is optional in most of the world. Surprisingly, few students opt out of the testing. A 2068 Awakened World Research study found that elves refused testing at a significantly higher rate than other racial groups. The study suggested refusing the test tends to do more with the social stigma of refusing than it does any fear of being found out as Awakened. This doesn't hold true for elves, who reported that the refusal had more to do with being outed as *not* having abilities.

- Well that's simply terrifying. Imagine being an awkward teenage girl just trying to fit in. Now throw in trying to hide the fact that you have the barely controllable magical potential to go nuclear and powerball the entire freshman class.
- Sunshine

- Gives a new meaning to Teenage Wasteland.
- Snopes

COLLEGE LIFE

Awakened life is a very different experience in college than in K-12. Academia did not get around to pledging support to magic until about five years after the Awakening. Now magic as a field of study draws in more grant and contract dollars than any other field save for nanotechnology. UCLA claims to be the first university to have conferred a Doctorate of Thaumaturgy, but before such things had names Oxford and the University of Oslo were offering courses of study in Magical Awareness. Still, MIT&T is the most well-known program and one of a handful to offer magical degrees to non-Awakened individuals.

- Wait, what? How can you give a magical degree to someone who can't wield magic?
- Snopes

- Undergraduate courses fund day-to-day university operations. Course competencies are designed to provide maximum access in order to generate maximum revenue. So, if you have the nuyen to take the classes, you can feasibly earn an undergraduate degree in magic without ever casting a spell. It's rare, but non-spellslingers can still play at graduate level where degree paths diverge into Research/Philosophy and Application-styled tracks.
- Elijah

- The Magical Studies Undergraduate Program at MIT&T is more about understanding how magic works than honing your individual abilities. The courses are especially useful when you're running with a crew that doesn't have a mage. They tell you how to know when magic is working against you.
- /dev/grrl

Universities present the most consistent career path for magicians, but they create a problem because magicians often end up with the same flavor as their university, taking away from the individuality of the form. Overall there are Associate, Bachelors, Masters, and Doctoral level degrees conferred in Thaumaturgy. The organization of Thaumaturgy colleges has sparked debate how magic should be taught. Traditionally speaking, Thaumaturgy is considered a science at the university level. Magicians construct spell formulae and follow traditions rooted in reason. Newer programs relate magic more closely to schools of art, treating the traditions as individual art forms and conferring Thaumaturgic Arts degrees at the Bachelors and Masters levels.

- The American Association for the Advancement of Thaumaturgy (AAAT) and other academic governing bodies live with the political nightmare of deciding what does and does not count as academic magic. These bodies hold a conference every year in Marseille hosted by the DIMR. AAAT leans towards defining magic as an academic science, which is why hermetic initiations often involve a thesis. The 2069 conference finally accepted Shamanastic Studies as a ThD degree path.
- Jimmy No

- The debate between defining magic as Thaumaturgic Arts or Thaumaturgic Sciences is mired in political quicksand. No shadowrunner cares if you have a M.M. or ThD, but it affects payscale at the university level and within corporations. Universities and corporations pay you more if you hold a doctoral degree. That thinking even filters down to the Johnson hiring you to pull a job. The fact is, having the degree can affect the quality of work you get and how much the client is willing to pay.
- Winterhawk

Slowly other paradigms are being accepting and cultivated based on their benefit to the supporting institution. Wellesley College outside of Boston began recruiting physical adepts and training them to harness their abilities through forms of dance. Local corporations quickly glommed on to the potential of this art-based methodology, so it is becoming more common in trade schools and specialized corporate schooling. In these types of programs, the degree conferred is a Masters of Applied Magic, M.M.

- I'm surprised at how often I'm contacted by Doctoral students looking for help running down a particular reagent, background data on some obscure magical order, and what not. Getting the Doctorate requires a tremendous amount of specialized knowledge that can be hard to come by without the help of those connected to the shadows.
- Elijah

For those who follow the path of shamanism there is little a university degree can offer. Shamanic studies are mentor based and some (including myself) work with the totem spirit and develop that relationship. This is preferable to training from an individual, because an individual will teach you all that he feels is useful to function in the Awakened world, as refracted through their biases and sensibilities. Your totem spirit is the truest reflection of your tradition and capabilities, so the learning you receive accentuates what you can do. More importantly it leads you to the path you are meant to follow. I serve Wolf, and from Wolf I learn all I need to in order to fulfill my total potential as a shaman. I have studied with others on occasion, but no training helped me to find my way in the same manner as Wolf.

In recent years there has been a spike in the number of community colleges that cater to the Awakened. Administrators found that so many Awakened were overlooked in the early days of magic that there currently is a marketable number of middle-aged students returning to the classroom to discover what they can do. The majority of them lack the discipline for university training or have so little magical potential that a two-year focused program is enough to maximize their abilities.

AMERICAN ASSOC. FOR THE ADVANCEMENT OF THAUMATURGY LIST OF AWAKENED DEGREE FIELDS

Arcanoarchaeology	Artificing
Astral Studies	Attunement
Centering	Cleansing
Divination	Feng Shui
Forensic Magic	Geomancy
Metaphysics	Metaplanar Studies
Occult Studies	Practical Conjuration
Psychometry	Somatics
Shamanistic Studies	Talismongering
Applied Thaumaturgy	Theoretical Magic

Additionally, the community-based nature of two-year colleges lends itself better to non-traditional pathways. Universities focus on the science of Thaumaturgy, while CCs remain dedicated to the curriculum needs of the community. So it would be easier to find a class on Druidic history at the CC down near Boston's Irish quarter than it would be, say a class on Westphelian Theurgists.

- The CC system is a safer bet than universities for the SINless, given that the CCs are locally funded, meaning they supposedly won't be selling information about their students to the corps and major universities.
- Glitch

- Mayor Jonathan Blake, who happens to own the multinational Centurion Services Group, backs Bellevue Community College. Likewise, the Northridge CC program down in Austin, CAS is wholly backed by Lone Star. Many other CCs and private colleges are funded by anonymous donors, which raises questions about the true purpose of the donations.
- Mr. Bonds

WORKING FOR THE MAN

It pains me to admit that magic owes a great debt to the corporations. Wagemasters were among the first to embrace magic in the Sixth World. Though spellcasters and adepts are barely a fractional portion of the world population, the power we wield makes us extreme security risks. Corporations first sought to understand how magic worked and moved quickly to find ways to exploit it—and us. Early spellcasters profited much in the same way as pioneers of social media. The newness of invisible power allowed those savvy enough to step into the void and provide a much-desired service. The first spellcasters set their own rates. A few even parlayed that into corporate ownership and remain players in the corporate game.

- Man-Of-Many-Names paints a few pretty brushstrokes of the relationship between spellslingers and corps, but he isn't telling you that he's covering over several years of outright abuse perpetrated by these same corporations. In the early days the Japanacorps would kidnap magically active individuals and experiment on them, trying to find out what made them special.
- Mihoshi Oni

- Aztechnology collects ritual samples of its mages as a security precaution to ensure they can be located if abducted. This is the same reasoning used to collect samples of top execs.
- Hard Exit

- Every corporation with the means to do so takes ritual samples. The real question you ought to be asking is: Who controls the samples?
- Mr. Bonds

- The Jaguar Guard controls the samples and stores them in secured facilities throughout Amazonia. I know because I tried to hit one. I couldn't break through—the ju ju they have down there is beyond lethal.
- Ma'Fan

- It sounds like instead of going to work for a mega, you might be better off working for the smaller outfits better chance for promotions and notoriety. That is until you get poached by one of the bigger houses.
- Kia

The choice to sell yourself to a corporation is dangerous and some might say asinine, however the benefits hold enough allure to sway even the most radical of us. Corporations hire freelancers because they fill a skillset that would otherwise be unavailable to them. As such, hiring corporations continue pay top nuyen for specialized magic users, even going so far as to put up with our eccentricities. The smaller the corporation, the more they are willing to offer, in order to avoid seeing magical talent lured away.

Those born to in corporations have an entirely separate path. Corporate control starts at a young age, and individuals are specialized and tracked, almost from birth. This is as much a function of the corporate family as of the corporation itself. Having Awakened children means instant advancement for the parents. It moves them to another echelon, and the only cost is subjecting their children to the rigors of corporate training.

Working for the corps can mean access to resources you won't find elsewhere. The cost of that access is that everything you do for a corporation is recorded some-where. Even off-book or 'black' jobs are logged by Mr. Johnson, and occasionally their superiors, in order to see if the operator is corporate material.

- I don't know how much corporate work you do, but the line of drek you're feeding us here makes you smell like a n00b. The file corps keep on magical operatives has more to do with ensnaring that person than checking to see if they are reliable. Wuxing got real unpopular with local Wujen after a runner caught them sending a clean-up crew to the op site in order to recover enough material to constitute a ritual sample.
- Snopes

Every corporation takes a slightly different stance on how they pursue and ultimately utilize magic. It is worth your nuyen to increase your understanding of at least the a handful of major magic players.

WUXING

Wuxing is a rising power that deserves attention but doesn't get it. Sometimes the most overlooked of the Big Ten, Wuxing gained prominence after being gifted two hundred million nuyen and two mysterious magical items in Dunkelzahn's will. Chief among Wuxing's assets in the magic field is Ming Solutions, a magical asset integration company. Ming works closely with Wuxing's construction arm to ensure that all new construction is designed around the principles of Feng Shui. If your field is geomancy or the pursuit of *qi*, working with Wuxing can provide the opportunity to advance your craft.

MITSUHAMA

MCT is a world leader in magical goods. Their Thaumaturgical Research Division operates a magical research database favored by top universities. The gem of the Mitsuhama magical empire, Pentacle Distribution, is the number two telesma corporation in the world. They would do well to remember that just because you're the emperor it doesn't mean the crown is safe. In London, Glendower Export Associates trying to muscle into Pentacle Distribution turf, and there is a lot of money to be had as a soldier in that war.

ARES MACROTECHNOLOGY

Despite what they advertise, Ares is a military solutions company first. Ares Firewatch is considered the UCAS' first line of defense against insect spirits, locating and destroying hives before they become a problem. Scouting out suspected bug hives tends to be contracted out to shadowrunner teams who have a better understanding of whatever local environment might be hosting the hive. Ares isn't just trying to wage war against the bugs on our plane either. Several Ares subsidiaries are engaged in researching how to strike at the bugs before they reach us.

The real cutting-edge extraplanar research has been happening at Institut Thaumaturgique du Québec. Ares contracts out some of the institute work to specialists with extensive experience exploring the metaplanes.

- Ares acquired Institut Thaumaturgique du Québec when CatCo crumbled. Instead of merging the research corp with Xerxes Positive Research, Ares held it at a distance at the behest of Damian Knight himself. The move turned out to be a smart one. ITQ barely survived a hostile takeover by a conglomerate of companies a year after its acquisition. Most of those companies listed in the takeover bid were indirectly connected to the Draco Foundation, including MechAnima, Libra Holdings, and Centurion Financial, strengthening the claim that it was a bid orchestrated by Nadja Daviar.
- Mr. Bonds

AZTECHNOLOGY

Aztech is known for its perversions, specifically the blood magic that is commonplace there, but it is more than that. The corp is very much interested in druidic magic, for example. The earth-centric rituals of Druidism would lend power to their expansion into Amazonia and give them something of a defense against the jungle itself.

SUICHINI MAGICAL MECHANICS

A dragon owning a corporation is nothing new, but Ryumyo hasn't shown the profit-based instincts of his kind when it comes to this corporation. Eighty-five percent of corporate profits are put back into the corporation in order to fund magical research.

- The other fifteen percent are washed, dried, and shipped out to various Yakuza interests, often as a payoff for services rendered. Occasionally Suichini capital ends up funding shadowruns against the Vory. Recently I've met with a lot of private contractors who are being paid through shell companies shared by Suichini and the Yakuza to explore the West Siberian Plains.
- Mihoshi Oni

WORKING FOR THE CHURCH

Once major religions stopped shouting "Demon!" and holding crosses to the foreheads of spellcasters, they figured out that magic could be a helpful recruiting tool. Religion is based on the premise of believing in things that cannot be seen, but it must account for the things that can be seen. This is more easily accomplished when the folks doing the casting are sitting in the pew beside you praying to the same God.

Therein lies the problem. To truly gain mastery of the

TRANS-UNION INTERCORP SEARCHNET

Search Parameters: Top Magical Goods and Services Labels
Search Results: Multinational results listed ...

ARCANE SERVICE PROVIDERS

Manadyne	Parashield
Ares Firewatch	Mysticks and Magicks
HermeTech Associates	Ming Solutions
Elementals' Services	Rees Arcana
Centurion Applied Magicks	
(*Formerly Cross Applied Magicks*)	
Kami Consulting	Farsight

MAGICAL GOODS MANUFACTURERS

Pyramid Arcane Supplies	Pentacle Distribution
The Arcanum	TalisPoint
Magicknet	Manadyne Manufacturing

LORE STORES

Ipissumus	Lore Stores Inc.
MageWerks	Yin and Yang
Pentacles	Pentagrams

MAGICAL IMPRINTS & PUBLICATIONS

Pentacle Press	Ambrosius Publications
Pentagram Publishing	MagicMind
LoreNet	

craft, especially at the higher levels of initiation, a magician must become aware that the paradigms are just that—age-old traditions we use in order to manifest the mysteries of the magical world. That understanding exposes a truth about belief that often contrasts with the realities of the Sixth World.

Most world religions are predicated on the belief that their word is the one true word. The existence of magic and the metaplanes suggests there may be more than one manifest faith. I can believe the slice of stone wall dividing my kitchen from my living space is a higher power and pray to that for guidance, but unless there are others who share my beliefs it isn't a faith. In the sense that faith is shared belief, even a cult can become an organized faith. Through that faith Awakened members of a church can gain the ability to initiate and grow their abilities.

- The Church of Scientology, once recognized as a fad cult and tax shelter for the rich, crossed the threshold to faith in the late forties when its members began manifesting magical abilities and formed an order within the ranks of the church. This order now oversees auditing of new members, the process by which members uncover their spiritual awareness.
- Elijah

Religion is about membership as much as it is about faith. Religions need people in order to flourish, and as pre-Christian religions gained sudden prominence following the Awakening, the big three recognized the threat for what it was. Christianity, Judaism, and Islam united for one flickering moment, though with the limited purpose of labeling these new religions as neopaganism and denouncing them. Neopaganism lumps together a number of polytheistic texts, cobbling the mythos of Wicca, Druidism, Asatru, Native American worship to name a few. The labeling was brief and managed only to slightly limit the number of followers the big three lost to the newer (or older, from some points of view) faiths.

- ◉ The intentions behind the denouncement neopaganism were far more insidious than that. If it were just about preserving membership, they would have called out Hinduism and Taoism as well. All I can say is the churches play the long game nearly as well as dragons do.
- ◉ Frosty

The battle to be the true word is far from over. Many of faith have turned to the shadows to find the talent they need to pursue their goals. Take note of these potential employers:

THE CATHOLIC CHURCH

The power of the Vatican reaches across the world like rays of sunlight to some, like polluting smog to others. They had the potential to make a smooth transition to a magical world, as the structure for the acceptance of magic was already in place, laid out by the Congregation for the Causes of the Saints. Acts of magic in the Fifth World were deemed miracles or relegated as the work of the devil, but they were acknowledged as something that existed in the world. Negative reactions to new metatypes and magic by the highest officials of the church, however, slowed their acceptance of magic as a whole after the Awakening. The climate has thawed, though, and today all but the most conservative congregations incorporate magic into their theological worldview. They distinguish between good magic and bad based on whether or not you are practicing your craft in service of the Church and in accordance with a tradition the Church accepts. This last part is not absolute; the Church will hire the Awakened regardless of tradition so long as the have the skills to complete the needed work.

ISLAM

It can be an extremely difficult road for a child of Allah who discovers they have magical potential. Islamic law outlaws the practice of magic—that is, unless it doesn't. Within Islam the fine line between being an outlawed spellcaster and a herald of the Islamic faith often comes down to who you know and how well you are respected. There are other loopholes as well. Countless Muslims who believe they are blessed with potential or have family members that may be blessed turn to the *sufi* mystics. Sufism is considered to be the will of Allah, and thus exempt from the ban on magic use.

HINDU

Given the number of people India, the Hindu faith is relevant on size alone. Proponents of Hinduism continue to believe they practiced magic prior to the Awakening. I've heard some describe practicing their *brahmanas* pre-Awakening as a turning on a faucet before the water actually flows to the house. Once it flowed it came out with such force as to wash away all doubt about the Vedic Texts. Specifically, the *Atharva-Veda Samhita* has developed a large following. This Vedic text speaks of the spells, charms, and magical formulae of the religion.

WITCHCRAFT

Wicca regained prominence in the post-Awakening world almost as swiftly as my own Native American traditions did. Without the flash and thunder of the Great Ghost Dance, Wicca was able to stay off the public radar for years, slowly gaining an informal structure that morphed into a network of initiate groups. Unlike most large religions, there is not a central organizing body to determine what is or isn't Wicca, a fact which allows many groups to practice forms of neo-paganism under the guise of Wicca.

The "do no harm" principles inherent in the religion are largely forgotten in the public misinterpretation of Wicca. At the core of the religion is a principle that comes from the Wiccan Rede, "An Ye Harm None, Do What Ye Will." However, when people think of Wicca they still see green witches and the spectacle of Halloween. Unfortunately, that longstanding tradition colors what many think of magic. Many of the Wiccan faith feel it is their duty to change the perception.

VODOU

Vodou, or Sèvis Gine as it is known in most of Africa, is not one religion but many, all of which center around the Iwa-yo, a collection of spirits that are presumed to exist on the metaplanes. Vodou is closely entangled with Catholicism, and often Catholic prayers and rituals will be used as part of the process to invoke loa.

Vodou is extremely popular amongst the pirate clans that roam the Carib League. Even non-practitioners continue to 'practice' rituals, be it an extension of their faith, or as habit learned from their parents.

- ◉ Vodou is a way of life in the Carib league. Everybody believes in Vodou and is both scared and respectful of it. Vodou priests are treated like simstars on the islands, the reason being you don't want one of them throwing some juju on your rig to make you disappear beneath the waves.
- ◉ Kane

MAGIC IN THE SHADOWS

The most dangerous path we of magic can choose is to walk in the shadows. You may read my words and question why one would choose a life in the shadows when so many other options exist. The answer is simple: freedom. Though we are beholden to others, even in the shadows, the puppet strings are much longer, affording us a control over our actions that corporate, academic, religious, and other forms of SINner life cannot.

The shadows represent the greatest freedom for Awakened individuals, but this also comes with risks. Foremost amongst those risks is the isolation. A wage mage or even an academic has the backing of a cohort of like-minded professionals who have some responsibility to support what their paymasters are trying to achieve. Those of us who live in the shadows tend to operate without a coven or some other organization to support us. It exposes us to more risk to work alone, but it also means we are beholden to no one but the Great Spirit.

You can survive the shadows, so long as you understand the rules.

RULE #1: GEEK THE MAGE

The first thing a combat mage needs to understand is they are the primary target in any combat situation. As such you have to take steps to not be so easily identifiable. Holding an AK-98 marks you as a warrior. Standing there empty handed marks you as the one who gets geeked first.

* Makes perfect sense. Combat is about recognizing the variables and controlling what you can. A magic user is an uncontrollable variable. By the time you figure out what they are capable of, the fight is over, generally with you strapped in the back of a DocWagon extraction vehicle. So you geek the mage before she makes your stomach explode and deal with the bullets later. The same holds true for physical adepts. In close-quarters combat a physad is the most dangerous force in the room.
* Black Mamba

Fear can be your greatest advantage. Your enemy doesn't know what you are capable of, so until you cast you are capable of anything. This principle carries over to interrogations, negotiations, and even social settings where people know you are a spellcaster or social adept. The threat of a lie-detection spell or magically heightened charm is often enough to keep people honest.

RULE #2: THERE IS MUCH MORE TO FEAR THAN FEAR ITSELF

When I discovered my ability I was naïve. I followed spirits believing they were honest about their intentions to aid my learning. I once encountered an entity

that claimed to be willing to teach me advanced techniques. But something felt wrong about the encounter. It was too eager to share what it knew for nothing in return. I refused the teaching and set about finding out where the spirit came from. I learned the entity was not what it claimed to be but instead a toxic form that had already claimed the lives of three shamans.

We spellcasters and adepts represent a fraction of the entities roaming the magical realms. Some are here to help us understand the gift of mana. Most have darker intentions. Don't trust any being you don't know unless you can vet it through sources you trust.

- The old-timey runners used to kick around stories about an entity named Tutor. Nobody quite knew what it was, but they knew it was trouble. Tutor never went away. I've heard the name as recently as last year associated with some of the twisted magic coming out of Chicago.
- Axis Mundi

- What do you all know about The Smoking Mirror? The name came up in my research on a little-known metaplane tied to the Aztec God, Tezcatlipoca. I'm not sure if the mirror is an artifact, ritual, or something else, but it seems to be the only way to access knowledge about this plane of existence.
- Ethernaut

- Think about what you're asking, omae. These are reckless energies that have motives and power far beyond your understanding. Getting involved with them is not only dangerous but also extremely foolish.
- Frosty

- I have my big boy pants on, Frosty. I know what I'm doing.
- Ethernaut

RULE #3: KNOWLEDGE IS NUYEN

Ehran the Scribe tells us the more obscure your tradition, the harder it is to find someone to light your path. The other side of that maxim is if you have the knowledge to teach others, someone out there is willing to pay for it. Let's face facts; the problem with the shadows is that you don't have a deep-pocket connection to university donors or corporate interests. Harvard is not going to bankroll your efforts to acquire reagents. Pentacle isn't going to hand over the latest formulae for a Ball Lightning spell.

A shadowrunner needs to develop a strong network of contacts that allow him to stay connected to people who he needs and people who need him. What surprises me about runners is how quickly they forget their value outside the run. The Awakened can operate in a variety of roles. It is the sole area where the media helps

our lives. Martial arts students, for example, are drawn to adepts and eager to pay for lessons from a true master of the craft. The same is true of shamans who can manage a good living dusting sage around wageslave's homes to ward off evil spirits.

- Formulae are in especially high demand for nascent magicians. There is a good amount of nuyen to be made by creating spell formulae and selling them on the black market.
- Jimmy No

Pre-existing networks of contacts are there if you can find them. Lore stores rarely offer anything more than basic fetishes, so gaining access to people with real knowledge of local magic means tracking down a legitimate talismonger (I'm told the **Magical Societies** part of this posting might have useful information about contacting talismongers). Another option is to scan the local Matrix. Private usenet groups are crammed with people offering services. Usenets are difficult to breach, requiring an invite much like our JackPoint. Membership is often restricted to individuals who benefit the group, be it through knowledge, skill, or connections. If you cannot work your contacts for a link to a private usenet, try the colleges. Major university programs operate accessible networks that help them understand what's going on with magic off the grid. It is a good place to find basic contacts.

RULE #4: YOU ARE THE COMMODITY

No offense to my good friend Netcat, but the spellcaster is always the most valuable player on a runner team. We execute a skill set that no one else on the team can learn to replace. Take care of yourself and get the nuyen you're owed for a job, especially when you think you're owed more than those around you. Your costs are higher, so the cut should reflect that.

- That's bullshit and you know it. Hackers are just as irreplaceable. It isn't just about the numbers. I know hackers outnumber the Awakened a thousand to one or some shit like that. Finding people you can work with who also have the specific skills to complement other members of your team is hard. Once you start messing around with the payday, feelings are going to get hurt and it doesn't end well.
- Netcat

- I ran a quick maintenance cost breakdown between mages, hackers, and samurai and the numbers come out fairly even. The needle did not move until I factored in equipment upgrades. Bioware, cyberware and some weapon costs are comparable to magical foci costs.

MAGIC USENET GROUPS

The Matrix can be a treasure trove of magical knowledge if you know where to look. Private usenet hosts around the globe are key repositories of information about local magical happenings. These hosts represent a way to connect to others practicing or dealing in the magical ways. They also represent a recruitment tool for magical societies trolling for talent. Though the majority of these groups are too small to mention, a handful have grown large enough to gain recognition.

MAGESTONE
London

Magestone is a breakaway from a larger forum started by Oxford University. It began as a way for ThD students to maintain contact with the shadows for research. It grew into an information network drawing together talismongers, fences, university researchers, freelance spellcasters, and even corporate contacts. There are two stages of membership. Stage one means being invited in by an existing member. At this stage access is limited to the forums and datastores. Once a panel of administrators has vetted a new member, that member is granted stage two clearance, which gives full access to all of the information on the host. Rumors abound of a third clearance level that gives high-ranking members of the forum access to a private host.

THE EYE
Confederate American States

The Eye started as a content aggregator. Hackers would raid university datastores and repost the information to The Eye with changes to reflect what they knew vs. what the mainstream wanted people to know. It has since developed into a depository of files about all forms of magic in the Sixth World. The only way to gain membership is to bring in a new datastore either of the edited and updated variety or pure paydata gleaned from a private source.

SE LIGA MACUMBA
Amazonia

Born out of the favelas, Liga, as it is known to locals, is one part research network and two parts smuggling network. Liga plays host to Amazonia's extensive magical black market, serving as a contact point between talisleggers looking to move fauna around and even out of the country. The network is constantly hiding from Amazonia authorities, leading it to be invite-only.

THE EMERALD PALACE
Seattle

Tucked away in a corner of ShadowSEA is Seattle's premier magical information network. The host is managed by a trio of spellcasters and serves as a place where academic, corporate, and private interests merge. The Emerald Palace boasts a direct information link to Mitsuhama and MIT&T research. However, the main draw is its extensive magical groups database. Potential Emerald Palace users go through a rigorous background check before being offered membership. Members insist the network is crowdsourced, though rumors persist that the host is funded through DIMR interests.

KOWLOON_MK
Hong Kong

The Walled City is known for its mysterious magic, but in the Matrix Kowloon_MK is where you go to get mysteries solved. The host is notable for its collection of information on magical items and locations, especially data concerning Dragon Lines. The Kowloon host is purposefully designed to resemble the walled city in Matrix space. Specific locations within the host are overlaid on the walled city in AR, meaning you need to understand how to navigate the city itself in order to navigate the host.

However, formulae and lodge costs far outpace a samurai's upkeep.

The disparity between magic and hacking technology is closer. Once you factor in the cost of purchasing and fitting rigger drones, you find it is more expensive to be a vehicle hacker than it is to be a mage.

- Mr. Bonds

- I stand by my words.
- Man-of-Many-Names

Our rarity makes us targets, not just in terms of combat, but for extraction as well. There are corporations that will hire you to a run, just to see what sort of magic you are capable of. Be aware of the runs you sign on for; it might be that someone is setting you up to take you for your magic.

RULE #5: NEVER DIE ALONE

The shamans I know are the single magical operator on their respective teams. We come together monthly to share our stories, give tribute to our respective totems, and to remember we aren't alone. Magic is a lonely profession. So few of us have the talent that it is rare to see multiple magic users operating in the same runner team.

Find other spellcasters or adepts with this shared understanding can help keep you grounded. Already you are separate from the team you work with because they can never see the world as you do. As hard as it is to find someone to trust, it is doubly hard to find one with skills significantly more advanced than your own to the point where they can teach you, even after more than half a century of magic in our world. Even if you cannot find someone skilled enough to help you better your craft, at least find someone who understands what you go through.

MAGIC IN THE WORLD

It's been a hot few months, but this last week paid out. Sylvester and his team chased rumors of blue sand through the Rub'al Khali desert before finding some sort of remains of a temple. In the depths, some ten meters down, they found cuneiform script and the bones of the previous inhabitants.

"So what does it say?" asked Sylvester as he brought K-rations over to a balding dwarf at a makeshift table within the ruins.

"Well, you're right. The jade planisphere is here, or at least it was brought here by these blokes." Rustbucket waved toward two mummified remains sitting upright in alcoves. "Dax says there's a chamber below this one. I'm betting that it's full of this blue sand."

"Good work." Sylvester then switched to his commlink, "Dax! Knotingham! Get down here, time to dig."

With Rustbucket's directions and Dax's radar imagery, Sylvester managed to open up the ancient door to a stairway below. Blue sand followed their steps as they descended, Knotingham in front with an electric torch. The room below was slightly larger than the one above, with dozens of pottery containers scattered around the floor. In the center was a stone table. Knotingham's light revealed six disks of jade mixed in sparkling dust.

"Gold?" asked Knotingham.

"Even better," replied Sylvester as he put his fingers in the dust. "Orichalcum." He picked up one of the disks and spun it in the light. "Rustbucket, what do you make of the markings."

Rustbucket scanned the disk into his commlink to check the marks. "Sorry boss, this is beyond my library. My guess is that maybe it's a derivative of Or'zet."

"Or'zet? Bullshit," Dax said as he followed the rest into the chamber.

"Bullshit or not, Dax, check this out." Knotingham reached into one of the containers and pulled out what looks like a human skull with large canine teeth filed into sharp points.

Sylvester was still at the table with the orchalicum dust, scrolling his finger through it. There was a flash from the table, and the electric torches dimmed.

"What the ... ?!" Rustbucket yelled. Then said nothing more as a blade was thrust through his neck. Knotinghan and Dax whirled, saw who had stabbed him and froze in place. Sylvester held a bloody dagger, and his grin and eyes were both full of madness. Knotingham couldn't believe what he was seeing; when his training kicked in, it was too late. He reached for his gun, but before he touched it Sylvester shot a bolt of lightning from his hand. Knotingham fell to the ground with a shower of blue sand and shattered pottery. Dax fired his pistol, wounding Sylvester's arm. This didn't faze Sylvester. He shot Dax a hard stare that came with fire, erupting around Dax and consuming him.

There was darkness for a long time, even after Knotingham woke. He blinked several times and saw no difference between his eyes being opened or shut.

"Still alive?" said a voice in the darkness

"Who are you?" asked Knotingham. He reached for his pistol, fighting the ache that had soaked into every last muscle.

A faint glow appeared. He was still in the room where Sylvester had gone crazy. The bodies of Das and Rustbucket were still there, and the table was empty of jade disks and orichalcum. He could not see a source for the light, or who had caused it to appear.

"Who I am is not important," the dark voice said. "All that matters is a simple question: Do you wish revenge?"

Knotingham struggled to one knee, the pain of each movement only making him angrier. When he was up, panting from exhaustion, he nodded curtly.

"Good. Follow my orders and you will survive to complete such a task."

The glow started moving. Knotingham heaved himself to his feet and struggled after it, following it out of the temple and into the moonlight. The camp was gone, but a dark shadowy figure stood next to a pair of horses.

In Knotingham's mind, the voice spoke to him again, "Come Knotingham. We travel west."

POSTED BY: WINTERHAWK

We say it all the time, even if we do not quite know what we are saying. When did the Sixth World start? When magic came back into the world. We know that event happened because its effects are everywhere, plain to see. Dragons, elves, dwarfs, trolls, orks, and more walk among us. Adepts punch through steel with their bare hands. Spellslingers summon fire and lightning out of nothing. And spirits silently whisper hidden secrets into our ears.

We know what magic can do, but there is still a wide disagreement about what magic *is*. We know how magic changed the world, but we don't know why it decided to come back, or how it enables the Awakened to do the things they do. We seize power from something that is, at heart, a mystery.

So if so much is uncertain, how much do we actually know about this force that fuels so many plots, plans, schemes, and shadowruns? What is magic, and how do we design a place for it in our world? Let's take a look.

LAWS OF MAGIC

Scholars can argue about magic all day, all night, and through the rest of time if you let them. Yet despite the contentious disagreement, there are some things generally agreed upon to be true. So let's start there.

MAGIC IS LIFE

The first thing any student of the arcane should understand is that the magic that can be drawn from the aether for spells and powers is all around us, and it has a connection to all life. This has been established as fact, as magic cannot be performed outside the gaiasphere, and it has been further proven with space stations creating biospheres that allow the practice of magic. This relational concept is exploited by twisted magicians through blood magic (discussed more on p. 89). Now, thinking about life on earth, you can see that just as life is not evenly distributed across the planet, so would mana. Life being as stubborn as it is, there are places on the planet where mana may be quite low, but very seldom is it entirely absent. Places with low amounts of magic are called *mana ebbs*. Some of these places are so low on mana that they are called *voids*. Without mana, magic is difficult to use; it can even be dangerous, as once you start toying with the flow of life in such of spot, you cannot always be sure how your own life force will flow and if it will stay safely contained in your body, or if it will backfire on you and cause all manner of strange distortions to your casting.

MAGIC IS SENSITIVE

Mana is very sensitive to metahumanity; our emotions and exploits can disrupt the accessibility of magic. Mana can be affected by a wide range of events, from a rock concert to a violent robbery, or from from toxic waste to smog. Mana becomes what is called "psychoactively charged" by these events. This charge creates a positive background count (detailed more on p. 30) on the astral plane and it's called **aspected**. If the aspected mana carries some emotional or psychological significance, it's called a **domain**. Cathedrals and monasteries are domains aspected toward a religious tradition. A toxic waste dump is aligned, predictably, toward pollution.

Aspected mana is difficult to use; in some cases, it may shut down an Awakened person's powers entirely. Unless, of course, they are **aligned** or **acclimated** (p. 30) with the aspect. Magicians have learned to occasionally use this to their advantage, aligning the mana towards their tradition through **geomancy** (p. 143).

MAGIC IS UNPREDICTABLE

Mana is unpredictable and dynamic, and mana energies flow back and forth. Some mana ebbs and aspected mana changes are temporary, fading back into the normal background gradually after the triggering event concludes. Other, more permanent changes can cause **mana surges** or **mana storms** depending on various things like a difference in background count on the astral plane. This unpredictability causes physical and astral chaos on top of making a magician's practice of magic difficult.

MAGIC IS POWERFUL

Yes, I know, that does not qualify as a shocking statement. It you have been in the shadows for any length of time, you have seen what it can do. It's strong enough to bring creatures from far-away astral places, turn people into animals (or goo), and bring down lighting on a target many kilometers away, provided the magician can see it. There are domains so great that an unprepared mage could be knocked unconscious by their sheer power, and there are great flaring bursts of mana called **mana warps**, which are more powerful than even the most powerful of domains.

MAGIC DOESN'T BELIEVE IN RULES

This is a fact that drives my academically minded colleagues batty. They study and study, poring over obscure books and test results, reviewing the latest formulae designed by brilliant and/or insane thaumaturgists, trying to fit everything into a clear and unified system. And then they see a passage, or a result, or something that does not fit in with their scheme, and it all falls apart.

The simple thing to do is not be like them. Don't think you understand magic. Don't think that magic is understandable. You may be lucky enough to be able to channel mana without burning up, but stay humble. One day magic will rear up and surprise you, and you can only hope to walk away from such an encounter alive. and castrate you.

Despite what I've just said, there appear to be limits to what magic can do. It cannot be used to alter the space-time continuum, raise the dead, or teleport your physical body from one place to another. Skills do not cross over from area to area—sorcery skills cannot summon spirits, and conjuring cannot be used to enchant items. Beyond those areas, though, I would be hardpressed to speak in absolutes.

THE RULES WE IMPOSE

Magic may not be willing to follow rules, but many metahumans tend to be fond of orderly systems, especially when they are attempting control over large groups of people. Megacorporations and nations have varied and detailed sets of laws governing how magic can be used, which reflect both their desire for order and their fear of what magic can do.

In most of the civilized world, killing someone with a spell automatically raises it to murder one, as the fact that you had to go to the time and mental effort to cast a spell makes them presume premeditation. There are, of course, allowances for self-defense, but those tend to be in place to provide cover to the rich and powerful; it's far more difficult for the poor and SINless to find shelter in these laws.

- What about preparations?
- Netcat

- It's a little hazy, but many jurisdictions treat them the same as spells. They figure if you went to the trouble of making a dangerous preparation, then you need to be responsible for controlling what they can do. If you didn't, well, then they put you on the same plane as a spellcaster who killed someone, meaning murder one.
- Haze

Adept powers are another tricky area of jurisprudence. Unlike spells, many adept powers are intrinsic, meaning they take no thought to activate. These cases have a chance of being classified as manslaughter if things go badly, but this is not always the case. The fact that some adept powers do, in fact, require activation often leads authorities to make a presumption of guilt against them. In other words, if they cannot definitively show otherwise, they will be presumed to have acted with premeditation.

Spirits are perhaps even more difficult to deal with. If you lose control of your spirit and it goes on a rampage, in most places, the spirit is considered your responsibility, and therefore you'll face charges. The trick, of course, is proving who had control of a spirit in the first place.

Some places, such as Tír na nÓg, give spirits more legal rights. This can in some ways be difficult for summoners, as spirit abuse may be punishable by law. On the positive side, spirits are viewed as legal entities, and thus they may receive the greater punishment for their actions, with the summoning magician only facing accessory charges.

Since the Awakening, mundane and Awkened alike have become aware of unsavory practices of magic requiring human sacrifice and summoning earthly spirits, twisted by pollution. These include blood magic, dark, and toxic arts (further discussed on p. 79). So potentially dangerous are these arts that many organizations place bounties on blood and toxic Awakened. This is not without its problems, as dark practitioners don't really stand out from other mages and are difficult to identify. This has occasionally led to a witch hunt-like atmosphere, with those who practice necromancy being particularly likely to be targeted.

Beyond the laws covering murder and such, there is the frequent requirement that Awakened people be registered. This has two purposes—keeping track of those who might add value to a nation or corporation, and keeping track of potential troublemakers. Using magic without the appropriate licenses will usually get the attention of whatever law enforcement is in the area, so be prepared to cast carefully and move quickly.

Along with the practice of magic, doing business in magical areas also requires the appropriate licenses and permits. If you are teaching magic, selling reagents, or crafting magic-related paraphernalia, you must report what you do to the relevant authority. Some organizations take this further than others. The NANs respect Awakened and treat their business activities like any other, while the CAS and UCAS see magic material in

the same boat as handguns and hazardous material and give it similar restrictions. Ironically talisleggers (those who transport illegal magical goods) are penalized more in the NAN than in the CAS, as the NAN respect the land and frown upon those who would strip its resources.

It's illegal to sell magic items to an unregistered Awakened in many nations, as is the selling of magic items without a license due to the possibility of fake or dangerous items. It's also illegal in most jurisdictions to offer false services of magic; quack healers using drug-imbued oils and other tricks to give the impression of magical healing are most common, especially with those avoiding the law or are SINless needing such help.

There's one more area that has some variable coverage in the law, but it's not as severe as the others. The gist of it is, be careful when you are astrally perceiving someone. Some privacy-oriented areas have laws against looking at someone's aura without their permission. In other places there is no law in place, but the practice is considered rude. So be certain to understand the laws and customs of wherever you may find yourself.

MAGIC INCARCERATED

Awakened individuals make law enforcement nervous, as it's difficult to confine someone who can shape change or make something/someone catch fire with a mere thought. Lone Star's Department of Paranormal Investigations, acting in conjunction with Star's Penal Department first developed **magecuffs** and **magemasks** (p. 215) to keep magicians dazed and confused while being detained or incarcerated for a short time. The effects of these are limited, particularly when it comes to unbalanced mages. This fact led to the creation of **Blackstone Prison** (p. 35) and **mystic cuffs/masks/jackets** (p. 214) by the Star's Penal Department. There is, of course, one more drastic step that may be taken: forced burnout of a magician through a combination of drugs and surgery. The death penalty might be more humane.

ASTRAL TOPOGRAPHY

When discussing the nature of magic, it's also important to consider the nature of the astral plane. The astral is a confusing place to the untrained. Life illuminates and emotions color a grey and shadowy mirror of the physical world. When astral projecting, you do not hear the din of the physical world, nor can you read written words. Technological displays and holographic images don't exist even as shadows on the astral plane. All the lifeless objects in the physical world appear as dull and intangible shadows to astral forms, allowing them to easily pass through. Details on these objects (color, texture, smell) are almost impossible to understand; a book's words are impossible to read, as is the context of the writing unless it's tied to some emotion that the character can perceive. All life has intangible auras that illuminate the astral world, while emotions can color them. Emotions can also color non-living objects if they have some significance to metahumanity (individually or as a whole). Within the silence, the magician can hear the crackle and hiss of mana being drawn into a spell or the subtle harmonies or cacophony of aspected mana as it flows through the astral plane.

At least, that is how it seems to me. Astral perception is a psychic sense, so where I see and hear light and sound, others may interact more through taste or texture. Your experience in the astral very much depends on who you are.

Regardless of the individual differences, the astral plane is a fascinating place, filled with phenomena quite worthy of note.

ASTRAL RIFTS

Astral rifts are spots where the barrier between the metaplanes have thinned, allowing a bridge between them. This rift allows Awakened and mundanes alike to astrally project and cross over to that particular metaplane. Uninitiated magicians can travel without being stopped by the Dweller on the Threshold. Not all of them are stable, so if the rift closes, an Awakened individual must find another way back. Note that Awakened individuals can stay on the metaplane without worry of ceasing to exist. Mundanes, however, are bound to the astral rift and must use it to get back to their body. If their body is removed from the rift area or it closes, the person risks fading off into oblivion in hours equal to their Essence stat.

ASTRAL SHALLOW

Astral shallows are places where the barrier between the astral and physical space has become thin, allowing even a mundane to use it like a window to perceive the astral plane. While within the astral shallow, Awakened people find astral perception to be easier, while mundane individuals may look at astral forms as if they had astral perception, though they cannot touch them. Communication visually and audibly can be easily done through an astral shallow. Astral shallows are normally temporary in nature, lasting a few hours or days.

GAME INFORMATION

Astral rifts: Mundane individuals lose their souls in astral rifts in a number of hours equal to their Essence stat.

Astral shallows: Awakened people who can normally astrally perceive can switch between astral and normal vision with a Free Action instead of a Simple Action.

Displacement alchera: Magical constructs placed upon the original terrain, such as anchored rituals and quickened spells, collapse when a displacement alchera appears. Any preparations on the displaced terrain have their potency reduced to 0.

Dweller on the Threshold: The Dweller on the Threshold is described on p. 317, *SR5*.

Materialized alchera: Characters in a materialized alchera must make an Intuition + Willpower (3) or suffer disorientation (–2 to all actions) for 10 minutes.

SAMPLE ASTRAL RIFTS

WATERGATE RIFT, WASHINGTON DC
(August 9, 2057 – July 18, 2073)

This was the most infamous of astral rifts, as it sat on the exact spot where the great dragon Dunkelzahn was assassinated on the inaugural night of his presidency. It appeared as a luminescent tear with nothing but blackness within the open space. In 2061 various new and unusual spirits, as well as the great dragon Ghostwalker, came through the rift. The rift closed after an increase in magical disturbances and activities involving four powerful magical artifacts.

NAZCA LINES, PERU

The various lines drawn are all mana lines (p. 35), and in 2061 they flared with magical activity and purpose. Each one created an astral rift allowing those that crossed to journey into one of the metaplanes. The Nazca lines have been stable enough for geomancers to study and attempt to copy.

ALCHERA

"Alchera" means "dreamtime" in the Aranda language of indigenous Australians. It's been adopted by the Awakened community to represent unusually complex astral terrain features that occasionally appear in the physical realm. Australian legend has it that there was a great spirit who created such sacred places in the co-existing past, present, and future in what we now call the astral plane. These aren't the astral images, auras, or shadowy impressions that one can see with astral perception of a place, but solid objects on the astral plane that can, for one reason or another, break through the barrier between the astral and physical worlds—or disappear from both places altogether.

Alchera have perplexed metaphysicists so much that well over a hundred papers have been published on them since they were first identified. Some scholars have attempted to construct their own alchera on the theory that this is how dragons could have preserved and concealed their corporeal bodies (naturally, no dragon has confirmed this). A competing theory is that the alchera form afters a significant emotional historical event. This has some plausibility with shapes found in Chicago or other spots with a connection to a world war. Another theory is that these phenomena manifest through interaction of other metaplanes as they intersect with the physical world. Why they take shape as they do is still a mystery. None of these theories totally explain all the alchera that have been found, though. What scholars have found to date is that there are three identifiable features that can be recognized in alchera.

MANIFEST ALCHERA

These appear on both the astral and physical plane, but are insubstantial on the physical plane and cannot be interacted with. In this way it is similar to the manifesting capabilities of a magician. They are ghostly images that can repeat events, but they don't affect or react to people or places on the physical plane.

MATERIALIZED ALCHERA

These unique alchera actually become dual natured and can be interacted with. Materialized alchera cannot replace existing terrain or objects and only appear in unoccupied space. They often have unnatural physical properties carried over from the astral plane. If the character is caught within a materialized alchera when it materializes or de-materializes, they may be disoriented, which can be dangerous. For the most part getting caught in a materialized alchera is rarely lethal (since the alchera will shove aside living beings when it materializes), but if the alchera de-materializes beneath the a disoriented, wandering person, it could cause problems—especially if they were high on an alchera slope when it vanishes.

SAMPLE ASTRAL SHALLOWS

ABERDEEN AND FUZHOU SKY TOWER, HONG KONG

The unique construction and placement of the Wuxing Sky Towers in Aberdeen and Fuzhou on intersecting mana lines have allowed a permanent astral shallow to form around both of them. Aberdeen's shallow has grown up to five kilometers in diameter, while Fuzhou Sky Tower's is at two kilometers in diameter.

TAJ MAHAL, INDIA

With the inhabitation of a great spirit at the Taj Mahal, the emotional domain also became an astral shallow, allowing many to believe they can see their deceased loved ones walking the halls.

PROFESSION: METAPHYSICIST

While the term "metaphysicist" used to refer to those who studied systems beyond the bounds of customarily measured reality, in the Sixth World it has a more concrete definition. It now comprises alchemists and artificers who like to tinker with magic and technology. Metaphysicists try to build manatech, a combination of technology with magical influences based on their understanding the properties of magic on the physical plane. Quite frankly the laws of physics sometimes get wonky when magic enters the equation. Metaphysicists try to find some sort of constant that can be used. They range from salesmen selling "patent pending" perpetual machines to corporate scientists working on rare exotic Awakened materials. Many metaphysicists get their ThD in Advanced Alchemy to get a better understanding of what alchemy can do, while others work toward understanding natural permanent and semi-permanent magical phenomenon in the attempt to replicate it.

SAMPLE MANIFEST ALCHERA

SEARS TOWER, CHICAGO, UCAS

Every Feb 10th, the anniversary of the fall of the Sears Tower, it manifests for twenty-four hours as it appeared before the loss. It has an ethereal glow to it, making it visible throughout the night.

NORTH MANITOU ISLAND, UCAS

Every year in August, Manitou Island lights up with hundreds of ethereal fires for a few hours. Legend has it that each fire represents a native who died in the Beaver Wars. Others reject that explanation, though they have no good counter-theory other than the fact than it's on an intersection of mana lines.

SAMPLE MATERIALIZED ALCHERA

VICTORIA FALLS

The water that flows over the falls is the alchera, even in drought conditions; it continues to flow over the falls, but after its descent, the water vanishes.

PHANTOM ISLANDS OF THE CARIBBEAN LEAGUE

There are various islands that may appear and disappear in the sea, causing navigational problems. These islands can be more than barren sandbars; they can have vegetation such as trees, freshwater, even wildlife. Legends abound of even more unusual islands, fully inhabited by strange creatures.

DISPLACEMENT ALCHERA

This kind of alchera works just like materialized alchera, but it replaces existing terrain and objects instead of simply sitting on top of it. These alchera tend to interfere with any magic in place, Wherever the previous terrain is sent to, living creatures do not go with it; they are instead moved and disoriented, similar to the effect of materialized alchera. Displacements are dual natured and can interac with physical beings.

SAMPLE DISPLACEMENT ALCHERA

DENVER

During a great storm, huge, floating mountains manifested for several hours above the hub, displacing the tops of various skyscrapers. No one was hurt, just dazed. DocWagon was on high alert throughout the occurrence, and in the end more than one hundred platinum members were "lost in the mountains".

DEEP LACUNA, CFS

In conjunction of the great twin quakes, many kilometers of tunnels appeared beneath the cities of San Diego and Los Angles. Some suggested that this is proof that G. Warren Shufelt a century and a half ago was right about inhabitants living underground to escape the apocalypse. Indeed, arcanoarchaeologists have found mundane artifacts and rumored remains of an indigenous people separate from the surface cultures.

BACKGROUND COUNT

Magicians are always talking about the background count affecting their mojo. Even in this document I talk about changes in the background count because of astral phenomenon. So to make this and further points more clear, we should clearly define background counts.

A background count is a measurement of a variance from normal of mana levels in the area. Arcane scholars have developed a scale to measure the strength of these areas, ranging from –24 to 24, with 0 considered normal mana levels. A negative value relates to lower-than-normal mana available to be used for magic (meaning mana ebbs and voids). A positive value relates to mana that has been aspected in some fashion, making it harder to control unless your aspect overlaps with it (domains and warps). Regardless if it's a positive or negative number, we use the absolute value in determining how it affects the Awakened's use of magic.

Background count affects the Awakened, by making drawing mana more difficult. Magic just feels sluggish, like slurping a milkshake through a, in more extreme cases, like slurping gelatin). That alone makes them troublesome for spellcasters and adepts, but then you have the additional danger of aspected domains, where magic might be harder for you to grab, but the person with the proper alignment can draw it faster. Facing opponent mages is hard enough; facing mages with a distinct home-court advantage is even more challenging.

Another combined challenge and opportunity that areas with background count provide is that astral entities can use high background counts to avoid being tracked or chased in astral space. The challenge areas with higher background counts present to assensing and astral perception means that spirits and other astral entities may duck into these areas to stay hidden. The advantage is they'll be tough to see; the disadvantage is if they're seen, they likely will have reduced magical abilities to draw upon in their defense.

ALIGNMENT

Acclimated individuals are able to ignore background counts, but aligned people take it one step further. They are able to completely mesh with the aspect of a domain, getting a boost from the mana in that area. Usually this occurs more through happenstance than through effort; that is, you are more likely to find a domain that lines up with a tradition than you are to change your thinking and practice to match a domain. Mages have switched traditions before, however, so aligning yourself to a certain domain is possible, but it is a long process.

EXAMPLES OF BACKGROUND COUNTS FROM DOMAINS AND WARPS

RATING 1-3

Significant, but brief emotional or magical impact or small but continuous spiritual or magical influence. Examples include an isolated violent crime or love affair, a bar frequented regularly by the Awakened (it would be aspected toward the regular patrons), a small-town church, or a series of days with higher-than-normal pollution. Natural rings created by the fungus Hag Bolette aspect mana toward Wiccan or druidic traditions.

RATING 4-6

Significant but brief emotional experience shared by a large group of people (more than fifty) or steady emotional or magical impact over several years. Examples include magical universities, sold-out rock concerts, high-security prisons, recycling centers, or alchemist or talisman shops. Cities that have heavy pollution or places with a dense population living in misery can also spawn this level of background count. For those domains connected to magic, the aspect is toward the traditions(s) taught or a certain magic skill set (such as Alchemy). Examples: Teotihuacan (Rating 4), The Great Cahokia Mound Web (Rating 6), UCLA and CalTech (Rating 5), MIT&T (Rating 4).

RATING 7-9

Significant events that continue to be repeated, generating emotional significance over years or decades. Most of the great mana lines and power sites fit this category. Examples: Gobekli Tepi nexus (Rating 8), Nazca Geoglyphs (Rating 9), Pyramids of Egypt (Rating 7).

RATING 10-12

Places that host significant events where the conditions that created them still exist; places that have generated emotional significance over centuries or powerful mana lines. Examples include Stonehenge (Rating 12), Sidney Song line (Rating 11), Arlington Cemetery, Sistine Chapel, Notre Dame (Rating 10).

RATING 13-15

The most powerful mana lines or events that have emotional or magical significance to most of humanity. Examples include the five sacred mountains in Chinese lore including T'ai Shan, where the great dragon Lung lives (Rating 15), The Great Cairn line in Tír na nÓg (Rating 14), The blast sites of Hiroshima and Nagasaki, Nazi death camps, or the Native American Re-Education Center at Abilene (Rating 13).

RATING 16-18

A positive background count of 16 or higher is considered a mana warp. Mana flows and surges chaotically in these areas. These levels of background counts are usually found in the upper atmosphere, but there are other odd places that have warped astral space. It is suggested that these places have a combination of a sudden, heart-wrenching, emotional event and a massive manipulation of mana. Examples include Auschwitz and Blackstone Prison (Rating 16), Aurora Borealis (Rating 18)

ACCLIMATED

Becoming acclimated to an area with a background count means that a domain doesn't affect an Awakened individual's use of magic, but they also do not benefit from it. For example, Teotihuacan magicians are used to the pollution, so it doesn't affect their spellcasting—or at least, it doesn't affect them the way it would affect a tourist. The same would go with Awakened patrons at a bar or an enchanter at his shop. It can take weeks or months of exposure to become acclimated to the background count before his skills aren't affected by it. Generally speaking, you should plan on one week of exposure per rating point of the background count. The trick, of course, is that background counts are variable, so sometimes they change before you have time to get acclimated to it.

HOW MANA ASPECTS

While magicians know that mana is sensitive, they still don't understand why it's psychoreactive. But not knowing why it works is not the same as not knowing how it works. Here are some of the ways mana has been seen to take on an aspect.

- **Positive and Negative Emotions:** Hate, love, or despair, are quick to aspect mana, especially when intense. They are also the least permanent of the aspects.
- **Specific Tradition:** When geomancers aspect a mana line, it aligns toward the geomancer's tradition. Magician lodges and circles, when active, are always aligned to the owner or owners' traditions. There are a few naturally recurring items and places that aspect the mana to a tradition without the interference of a geomancer.
- **Violence:** Sites of conflict, war, and death stir emotions in large groups of people, twisting the mana in the area.
- **Spiritual:** Many religious sites are also power sites with mana aspected toward the religion that holds away over the site.

- **Natural Alignment:** Some spots simply suit themselves to certain types of magic activities. There are forest groves that allow people of a certain tradition the calm needed to perform magic with greater strength, hot deserts that seem to almost spontaneously generate strong spirits of fire, and mountain caverns particularly suited to dark rituals. Finding the right spot for the way you practice magic can be quite a boon.
- **Pollution:** This of course is very common throughout the world, and fluctuates depending on factors such as weather or corporate policies. Heavily polluted areas can give rise to toxic domains, which are unpleasant for all concerned. Except for toxic mages, but they themselves are very unpleasant. The taint of a toxic domain is usually very difficult to cleanse without first performing a physical cleanup.

ASTRAL PHENOMENA

MANA EBBS

Mana ebbs are places where the flow of magical energies is reduced, though not as significantly as in voids. Astral forms and dual-natured creatures feel uncomfortable in mana ebbs, but they usually can endure them for a time—they don't flee them as they do voids. Mana ebbs generally are rated between -1 and -12.

MANA VOIDS

After several generations, the presence of mana is taken for granted. Many magicians don't have any conceptual idea of what a void is like unless they do something stupid like trying to practice magic on a suborbital flight

BACKGROUND COUNT RULES

A background count impose a negative dice pool penalty equal to its rating for all tests linked in any way to magic (such as spellcasting, summoning, and skill tests that use active adept powers such as Killing Hands or Improved Sense). The exception to this rule are background counts from domains, where a tradition, person, skill group, or skill may be exempt from the penalty as they are used to or aligned with the domain. Dual-natured creatures or purely astral creatures take a negative dice pool penalty to all actions equal to the background count. Again the exception of a domain can apply to specific types of creatures or spirit types.

Pre-existing active foci, sustained spells, quickened/anchored spells and rituals are reduced by the background count. If they are reduced to 0 or less, spells fizzle, wards and rituals collapse, foci deactivate. A foci cannot activate while under the influence of the background count. Anchored rituals and quickened spells if they have not expired revive themselves at 1 point of Force per hour, up to their preexisting Force. Preparations triggered while within a background count have their potency immediately reduced by the background count. Adepts may use a Simple Action to turn on or off a passive power in cases where penalties from background counts might exceed bonuses from their powers.

Background count makes Assensing, Astral Perception, and Astral Combat more difficult to do. Impose a negative dice pool penalty for tests associated with these skills. When attempting to track an astral entity through an area where the background count is higher than the target's Force or Magic Rating, the tracker loses the astral link at the point of the background count. Note that there is the capability to acclimate or alignment within domains regarding background counts. Some domains have no

specific aspected definition for the Awakened character to align to, so the Awakened can only get acclimated to it to avoid a negative effect on their magic.

ACCLIMATED

This is a benefit of the Home Ground quality (p. 74, *SR5*). The quality allows characters to ignore the customary background count of an area, and only count half of the background count tied to temporary events.

> James lives in on the edge of the Barrens (background count of 1) and has Home Ground. He's already acclimated to that background count. One day a riot occurs (no surprise in this area), causing an increase of the background count to 4 for that day. Because it's on his home ground, it's reduced by 2.

ALIGNMENT

The background count is applied as a positive modifier to the limit tied to the skill or skills for an Awakened character aligned to a domain. For example, a Wiccan shaman trying to conjure a Force 4 spirit within a Hag Bolette ring (Rating 3 aligned to the Wiccan tradition) will have a Conjuring limit of 7 (4 + 3).

A background count with an absolute Rating value of 12 or greater is dangerously powerful, regardless if it's from a domain or void. Anyone magically or astrally active in any way (dual natured, astrally perceiving, casting a spell, active adept power, etc.) takes background count – 12 Stun Damage each combat turn they are exposed to it. They can resist this damage with a Willpower Test.

(there's a whole trid warning Awakened on the dangers of that). Voids are so deprived of mana that even when it's introduced, it loses cohesion and quickly diffuses into the aether. Outer space is one large void, away from the biosphere and the emotional content of metahumanity, but because of pollution and crazy use of magic, voids have also occurred on Earth. SOX—the common name for the Saar-Lorraine-Luxemborg Special Administrative Zone—hosts perhaps the largest void on the planet, with about one percent of the area having no mana. Very little life survives or it does survive, but in misery because of the combination of pollution, magic, and radiation that created the situation in the first place. Voids are usually rated between –13 and –20. They can be as small as five hundred square meters (perhaps even smaller, though that makes them hard to detect) to areas four kilometers in diameter.

FOVEAE

Even more dangerous than a void is a void that moves. Foveae are invisible tornados ranging from a few meters to two kilometers in diameter. They are silent killers of dual-natured entities and astral beings, as their center entirely lacks mana energy. Astrally, foveae appear as a dark, swirling vortex that reduces the magical energies around it, while physically it can be noticed as a distortion of the air, similar to that caused by astral spirits, but larger. Foveae have been documented in Atzlan, UCAS near Chicago, and SOX. They are caused by high mana differentials from either heavy contamination or concerted mana manipulation. Foveae move like storms, though they are difficult to predict. Meteorologists have enough trouble forecasting physical tornadoes; disturbances on the astral, where wee don't understand the rules, are an even greater challenge. They are often temporary as the balance of magical energies is restored, though not before damage is done to both the physical and astral planes.

Foveae, insofar as they have been able to have been studied, have a negative background count between 7 and 12. Astrally they are tornado in shape, and its height is close to its rating in kilometers..

MANA WARPS

Mana warps are places where mana flares chaotically and behaves erratically. Mana warps cannot be aspected and therefore cannot be aligned or acclimated to. Mana warps can manifest mana storms (p. 36) into the surrounding astral plane. Normally mana warps exist at the cusp of the gaiasphere, ending violently in the void. There are two known places that hold lasting mana warps occurred on earth. Neither is completely understood as how the warps dame to be, though there are many theories. As with mana voids, the Awakened suffer damage from the uncontrollable power in the warp if they expose themselves to the astral plane. In addition,

SAMPLE MANA EBB

CRATER LAKE, TÌR TAIRNGIRE

While now off limits to the general public, this lake saw its ambient mana start dropping in the '50s. The drop continued until it became a mana ebb with a background count of –7. It appeared that the astral energies were being drawn toward an island on the lake known as Tesetelinsstea.

PROFESSION: ARCANOARCHAEOLOGIST

Since the discovery of magical items that existed before the start to the Sixth World, there has been a need for daring Awakened scholars who can find and analyze these unique artifacts. Many organizations such as the Atlantean Foundation and the Dunkelzahn Institute for Magical Research pay well for the services of arcanoarcheologists. Sometimes they are sent into the deepest wilds of the world, and sometimes they go to museums or private collections where artifacts may be stored, sometimes by individuals or organizations who do not realize the potential of the item.

SAMPLE VOID

CANTTENOM VOID, SOX

The largest and possibly oldest known void is that of Cattenom. It is assumed that the GAU disaster of '08 contributed the atmosphere, then the Awakening did the rest. Without any records or measurements we don't know if it grew to its size today or if other forces helped form the void. What we do know is that the Cattenom Void is roughly six kilometers in diameter (though it's border fluctuates, sometimes making it narrow but as long as ten kilometers), is centered over a nuclear facility, and has not moved nor changed size since its discovery. It's been rated at –20, which is pretty serious drek for something that is permanent and not in orbit. Foveae, caused by most likely the Crash warhead of '64, wander around the Cattenom void like small storms. These foveae do not wander far, so it is likely that some astral/special phenomenon attracts the storms to the void.

should you feel foolhardy enough to try to use magic within a mana warp, you'll suffer the effects of a mana surge (p. 34), which is a dangerous way to live. Mana warps have a rating between –16 and –20.

FOVEAE

Foveae have a negative impact on reagents. After passing through an area, treat the background count rating as the number of weeks it will take for the area to recover (p. 317, SR5). The absence of mana within the Foveae has an effect on preparations, hastening the loss of potency. While a preparation is in Foveae, the potency reduces by 1 every half hour instead of every hour (or if fixated, every 6 hours instead of every day).

Foveae do not last more than 24 hours. Every 2 hours, the force of the Foveae drops by 1. Once its force is below 4, it stops moving and dissipates into a mana ebb. This mana ebb is also temporary as the mana level returns to normal levels at the same rate.

MANA LINES

The rating of a mana line can serve as both sections of the dice pool for spell-like effects from the line (meaning spells may be cast with Rating x 2). Dragon lines can have fire or water elemental effects, ley lines can affect moods (similar to a Control Emotions spell), while song lines can do both as well as affecting movement, similar to the Movement critter power (p. 399, SR5).

Abbi Kadabra has found an old warehouse along a ley line (rating 2) connecting to a well-loved church. As she cleans up the space of trash, she finds that other squatters have been subconsciously compelled to do the same (as if affected by a Force 2 Mob Mood spell with a dice pool of 4).

MANA STORMS

The physical area affected by a mana storm is (Rating) square kilometers. This storm also disrupts a 100+ meter perimeter of natural weather phenomenon (rain, wind, hail, etc.), resulting from atmospheric disruptions caused by the mana storm's physical manifestations. A mana storm can move randomly up to its Rating in kilometers per hour. It dissipates at a rate of 1 point of Rating per hour as the mana levels disseminate through the gaiasphere. A mana storm can create a number of spell effects equal to its Rating every ten minutes. Treat the elemental and illusory effects as spells (chosen from the indirect combat or illusion spell) with a spellcasting test of Rating x 2 [Rating]. Any spell that needs sustaining can be sustained indefinitely for as long as the storm lasts, but the storm can only sustain a number of spells equal to its Rating. The Home Ground quality has no effect in mana storms.

After a storm passes, the background count of the storm is added as a positive modifier to tests related to hunting reagents (p. 317, SR5). These reagents only stable for two hours after the mana storm passes; after that the mana dissipates into the aether, and any unharvested reagents return to a mundane state.

When a magician casts a spell in a mana storm, roll on the mana surge table to determine the additional effects on the spell.

MANA SURGE TABLE

1D6	EFFECT
1	Drain becomes physical. No change in Force
2	Reduce Force by 1D6
3	No change
4	Reagents cannot be used with this spell/summoning (the magic smoke is released for any reagent used for this test and cannot be used again); no change in Force.
5	Increase Force by 1D6
6	Witch's Mark*

Witch's Mark: Spell or summoning does not occur. Instead, something totally unexpected happens. Water may catch fire with blue flames, a spirit from the Wild Hunt may appear, or frogs may fall from the sky. The gamemaster is encouraged to be creative. The player can spend a point of Edge so that the Witch's Mark does not negatively impact him (while not necessarily being beneficial).

MAYA CLOUD

The Rating of the cloud is applied as a dice pool modifier for Perception Tests within and through the cloud and is added as a noise modifier to signal ranges and devices.

MANA LINES

Heilige Linien, fairy paths, dragon lines, spirit lines, dream paths, ley and energy lines—all are different names for what we have universally defined as mana lines. Mana lines are concentrations of mana that flow across the astral landscape like rivers. Their appearance can be as diverse as a black crack through an urban environment to a prismatic beam of light or shimmering river. Enough study has gone into mana lines that procedures have been designed to control and aspect a line to a particular tradition through ritual magic (discussed on p. 122). Ratings of mana lines can range from 1 to 15. While all mana lines are considered equal, there are three subtypes that produce additional effects.

TYPE D: DRAGON LINES

These mana lines relate to geographic energies, including fault lines, volcanic hotspots, rivers, and lakes. Features that connect fire to water, like yin and yang, are more likely to host these lines. The flow of dragon lines influences the health of plants and animals; strong dragon lines can even clean polluted rivers. Dragon lines are the most abundant type of ley lines, and are also the most dangerous to manipulate. When disturbed, they can cause earthquakes and even change the path of rivers.

TYPE L: LEY LINES

These mana lines tend to be archaic tracks connecting man-made or non-human constructions. These mana lines cut more direct paths across the landscape than dragon lines do, and often they overlay trade routes. The flow of ley lines influence or are influenced by civilization and metahumanity. These lines are where people try to employ *feng shui* to bring them inspiration, luck, or health. These mana lines are also fought over by corporations trying to aspected the line toward their needs and give them an advantage over the completion. Traveling along a line that helps you move faster while slowing anyone else is an undisputed benefit. The problem is, the benefit is so clear that the corps tend to work hard to keep any of their opponents from realizing it.

TYPE S: SONG LINES

These mana lines are artificial, where someone has restricted or forced mana into a particular path. They are mostly found in the Australian continent and have traits related to both dragon or ley lines. What they are most notably known for is travel and navigation either across the physical plane or guidance to astral locations. People have performed tremendous feats of transportation in song lines, such as running a marathon in under two hours. Be wary, though—the opportunity to take advantage of their power comes with a risk Because of the nature of the construction of song lines, they don't hold mana very well and often generate mana storms (p. 36).

SHA AND SHENG EFFECTS

Mana flows regularly and smoothly along mana lines like rivers when there is balance, a well-maintained harmony of positive and negative energies. Mana lines are able to handle some imbalance by distributing energies along the length of the line. When the balance tips too far into negative energy, the mana line becomes blocked with what is known as a **sha effect**. A sha effect causes a mana ebb (p. 32) within a localized area, which can have a cascading effect along a mana line. Geomancers have learned to ritually replicate a sha effect (see p. 122 for more details on the ritual) as part of their efforts from making sure no competitors gain too great of a benefit from ley lines.

SAMPLE MANA WARP

BLACKSTONE PRISON, SIOUX

Constructed in 2035 on top of a particularly powerful mana warp, this prison is home to many dangerous Awakened.

The mana warp is just over one kilometer in diameter and is an ideal deterrent to escape. The prison contains circles of cleansing (p. 127) to keep the skeleton crew of workers safe. The workers are rotated regularly, as there are long-term psychological effects associated with the warp affecting even the mundane. Some archanoarcheologists believe that within the alluvium deposit is the remains of the entities that may have caused the warp, but so far nothing has been found.

SAMPLE MANA LINES BY TYPE

TYPE D

Harding Icefield (Force 4)
T'ai Shan Mountain (Force 15)
Yamuna (Jamuna) River (Force 6)

TYPE L

Great Cahokia Mound Web (Force 6)
Qhapaq Ñan (Force 10)
Great Cairn Line (Force 14)

TYPE S

Nazca Geoglyphs (Force 9)
Slighe Roads (Force 10)
Rainbow Serpent Path (Force 8)

On the other side of the ledger, a **sheng effect** is a localized increase in mana energy, also known as a mana surge. Mana surges can lead to mana storms as they escape the confines of the mana line. Sheng effects can occur when there is an uncontrolled or unnatural convergence of mana lines.

MANA STORMS

Mana storms are violent and unpredictable disturbances of magical energy. They move through the physical and astral plane in seemly random patterns, leaving magical destruction and chaos in their wake. They originate in places with higher-than-normal mana levels (meaning background counts of 4 or higher, or –4 or lower). They are triggered when mana surges from places of higher mana levels. Astrally, the storm appears as a shimmering swirling cloud, while physically the storm takes on the characteristics of the domain it grew from, meaning it can appear as storm clouds, sand storms, or tornadoes. The area covered by a mana storm varies from a kilometer to several kilometers wide. The most common characteristic of mana storms is the spontaneous manifestation of elemental energies. The storms surrounding mana storms can be ferocious and quite dangerous. The next, slightly less common trait, is illusory effects. The most famous of mana storms are the Maya Cloud, the frequent mana storms around Sydney, Australia, and Daoineann Draoidheil. Mana storms are normally quick and violent, lasting a few hours before they dissipate.

Mana storms appear both on the astral and physical plane. They can generate spell-like phenomenon in the form of spontaneous elemental and illusory effects. A mana storm's characteristics are based on the domain it was birthed from in both force and aspect. That means a domain aspected to anger from a riot could generate a mana storm that creates anger in anyone caught in it, while also generating the effect of phantom rioters within the storm.

A word of advice for anyone considering casting a spell in a mana storm: move. Spells or summonings performed in a mana storm are not only affected by the surging mana, but they might not go off at all, or the effect could be completely different than what was intended. Similarly, spirits summoned may also be stronger or weaker than intended, or even a different type. Preparations are safe from mana storms— until they are triggered, in which case they're affected just like spells.

There's very little you can do to make a mana storm work for you. You cannot be acclimated or aligned to the background count of a mana storm, as they are too unpredictable in nature.

Mana storms can have a positive influence on the availability of reagents, making them easier to find. Word of a mana storm travels fast through the magic community, and a decent supply of enchanters tends to descend on an area once a storm passes. The competition between them can get intense, so if you travel to such an area, be careful about getting caught in the middle of one of their spats.

SAMPLE MANA STORMS

DAOINEANN DRAOIDHEIL

Daoineann Draoidheil, or "Standing Storms," are intense storms that coincide with a mana storm around Tìr na nÓg. There are three of them permanently swirling off the coast. The first one exists around a ten-kilometer coastal area near the Giant's Causeway in County Antrim. The second runs along the northern shore of Dingle Bay, with the third sitting along the southern shoreline of Donegal Bay. The storms may move a few kilometers or change in size, but they never disappear. These storms were the first ones I studied many years ago. While they can be considered mana storms, they have some unique properties I have not seen elsewhere. First, as I've stated, they are permanent storms; a miniature manifestation of swirling clouds, rain, and lightning that can range from one to ten kilometers in size. The second unique feature is the magical domain is not as chaotic as a mana storm. This is more fractal in nature, which is more dangerous if you don't understand where the energy flows. A mundane example is shooting a laser at a disco ball made up of both mirrors and glass. You don't know where the laser light will end up. So imagine casting a fireball through a Daoineann Draoidheil; it may not hit the intended target, if it forms at all. And third, at the heart of each of the storms is a powerful web of energy.

Given the inherent dangers of sorcery in a mana storm, one would think that magicians would avoid affected locations. But there is one group, the Druidic Order of the Sun and Moon, that routinely sets up rituals to harness the mana storm into their endeavors. One such ritual is the formation of an astral gateway to the Northern Islands.

Daoineann Draoidheils are special versions of mana storms, permanent combinations of mana and physical storms aspected towards the Druidic tradition. The rating of these storms hovers between 8 and 12. They have all the qualities of a normal mana storm, but they don't dissipate lower than force 8, nor do they move from their relative physical position.

MAYA CLOUD

The Maya Cloud was one of the first, if not the first, of the great magical mysteries introduced into the Sixth World. It may have manifested before the Awakening, but magic was poorly understood at that point. Between March and October of 2011, there were the beginnings of unexplained disruptions of electronic equipment and communications, along with rumors of strange things appearing and disappearing like ghosts, and geological changes that formed over days instead of decades. With the Chinese military massing on Tibet in mid-October of 2011, things finally clicked astrally, and a massive wall of white rolled right over the Tibetan plateau, roughly to the border, right in front of the army. It was a dome between seventy-five to one hundred kilometers thick, more than five million square kilometers wide, and over three thousand kilometers high. Its name, Maya, comes from a Sanskrit word meaning "illusion." Maya is the nature of the world we can see, but enlightenment lies beyond maya.

The Maya Cloud has a rating between 14 and 16 and is aspected to magic unique to specific artifacts. The Maya Cloud perpetually generates elements of ice, lightning, and snow, making the area outside it hazardous for travel. The cloud covers entire mountains, making it a hazard to all but sub-orbital flights.

MAGICAL TRADITIONS

"Don't get out the book."

Quaha waved Lyran off and flipped open the red book. Another small piece of the cloth cover came off in her hand as she did so.

Lyran stomped toward plain wooden desk. "Close it! Close it now! We don't need it."

But Quaha was already leaning over the book, staring intently, flipping pages faster than she possibly could be reading them. She muttered as she scanned, the volume and speed of her utterances increasing with each turned page.

"It's happened before ... know it's happened before ... would've blamed it on vampires, back then ... not vampires, vampires don't work that way ... maybe not Infected at all?"

Lyran shook her head. "You know there's a window right by you? You know that it looks out on the whole world? It's out there, sitting there, ready for you to look at. It'll tell you the story a whole lot better than some falling-apart book."

"Mmm hmm ... yeah ... toxics, no, toxics don't work that way ..." Pages continued to flip by in a flurry.

Lyran rolled her eyes and then shifted her perception. The real world faded a touch, and around it appeared a glow of colors similar to when you face a bright light with your eyes closed.

She started nearby, at the bed in the crude one-room shack. The pain and the grief were obvious, almost overwhelming, even though the woman who had summoned them down to Aztlan was no longer there. The sadness threatened to coalesce, thickening and pooling in a puddle-like aura at her feet. But she couldn't get distracted by that, as overwhelming as it was. She had to look beyond it, past the general aura of the area, look for some other small difference ...

There. She saw it. It was a thin trail, a type of signature she'd never seen before. She had no idea what kind of creature left it, but as she stared she could recognize, barely some of the emotion. It was—satiation? Satisfaction?

In the room, the page flipping had stopped, and Quaha's muttering had briefly become more coherent.

"It's tempting to think it has to be a spirit because of the lack of signs of entry. But Palazzo's Study of Astral Menace suggests that spirits, left to their own devices, prefer astral attacks over physical because it fits better with the essence of what they are. That's not to say it's impossible, but we'd be better served looking for an alternate explanation."

The indoors were not talking to Lyran enough. She needed to be outside. She walked out the front door, put about ten meters between herself and the shack, then turned back to face it. She didn't stare at any one thing. She didn't examine her surroundings. She let her focus grow soft, and she waited for the surroundings to speak to her. The story was already in the land. She just needed to listen.

It was slow in coming, because she listened too much to Quaha. When she shut out her friend's voice, it got better. The auras became more vibrant, and she started to understand. There was a trail, a trail that started as need, left as fulfillment. A trail that never touched the ground. A trail that ...

"Don't stick to metahuman shapes," Quaha said. "Think of the whole range of sentient shapes. What are the ways in?"

Inside, Quaha's head snapped up. Outside, Lyran smiled and snapped her fingers. She trotted toward the house and came to the door just as Quaha was coming out.

"It was alive, corporeal, and flying ..." Quaha said.

"... and it came through the chimney," Lyran said, then smiled. "See? Told you we didn't need the book."

Quaha smiled back, though with a hard edge. "No one ever said we had to take the same routes to our destinations."

Lyran smiled broader. "You finally sound like a shaman."

THE BONES OF WHAT YOU BELIEVE

POSTED BY: JIMMY NO

There are, and always will be, stone-cold empiricists among us. They will tell you what is and is not, and they will tell you of it in clear terms. They bring this way of thinking to magic, believing it can be studied, measured, and given the same consistency as physics, biology, and other sciences. Magic was annoyingly chaotic when it returned, seemingly coming out of nowhere, erupting into the world and changing every corner of it, and doing things we could not explain. At least not at first. Then the empiricists stepped in, studied magic, and started being able to make predictions about how magic work, and to design formulae that made magic work in the way they said it would. They built models, and the models held. It seemed that once again, the empiricists reigned triumphant.

Or perhaps they reigned as the Newtonians did in the twentieth century, right before the quantum physicists started moving their way into the conversation and telling them that their predictions had their limit, and if they pushed hard enough, they quickly would find aspects of physics that did not work according to their models. Because that's what happened to magic. The models so many people have poured research into work—to a point. The formula a hermetic mage designs works well for other hermetics, as well as somewhat similar traditions such as Qabbalism, Wuxing, or Zoroastrianism. Transfer it to other traditions and things get shakier. And it's not that the magic doesn't work; it's that the mage sometimes needs a little extra time to get their head around it. A formula from a different tradition is sometimes like reading a foreign language. Sometimes it's worse—it's like trying to adjust your mind to some alien mode of thought, to some way of looking at the world that simply isn't yours. And then there's the problem of a magical lodge. If a lodge isn't attuned to your tradition, it simply will not work for you. It was shaped with the same mana you use to draw power out of the air, yet the design of the facility makes it inaccessible to you.

The question of why this is the case has occupied magic theorists for years. The basics of it are simple to understand. People regularly interpret the world through their own biases and pre-existing understandings. So if you grew up hearing, say, about religious clergy who had particular healing powers, or rumors of neighborhood people who used special, rare plants and other ingredients to cast fabulous spells, then it's only natural for your understanding of magic to fall into those outlines. And beliefs give people confidence. If you are acting within the confines of a system you understand, doing things you firmly believe will work, you feel better about what you're doing. You're more likely to act quickly and decisively and to not undermine yourself with doubt.

That's all fine and good, but the unresolved question is this: Why does magic care? We can have our varying perceptions, we can have a lack of confidence or be bold, but why would mana react differently? Science doesn't really work that way. You can believe that the Earth is flat if you want, but that doesn't mean if you're on a boat you're ever going to reach the edge of the world and fall right off. The Earth doesn't change its shape in response to your beliefs. So why does magic?

In the great tradition of university research, if you ask twenty different professors this question, you'll get twenty different answers. And at least ten of them will be so convoluted that you'll walk away before the academic is done explaining them. I'll quickly review the theories before telling you [spoiler alert] why none of them matter.

Here are some of the popular theories you'll find out there:

- **The unseen beings theory:** According to this one, mana is greatly influenced by unseen beings in the world. This could mean spirits, or it could include nature deities or other forces. It could even be the capital-G God. Whoever it may be, the being responds to your belief and grants you a boon of being able to shape magic. There are issues with this, including the fact that there are mages with no belief in a higher power and an adversarial relationship with pretty much all spirits who still manage to sling some serious mana, but we'll set that aside for now.

- The basic riposte to your concern is that there are different ways to access magic, but allegiance to the "true" way—that is, the one that involves your favorite deity or patron spirit—is a better and more pure way to do magic, and does not stain your soul the way the supposedly lesser forms do.
- Goat Foot

- **The mind-mana connection theory:** Neurologists know that belief—any belief, whether it's belief in deity, belief in science, or belief that Mr. Johnson is actually going to pay what he promised—lights up a certain section of the brain. We also know that mana is connected and responds to life. This theory says that when belief lights up your brain, it makes it more lively, and that there are certain strains of mana that respond to that activity, making it easier for you to do your magical work. It's a logical and elegant enough theory, though no one has ever confirmed the existence of different strains of mana.
- **The harmonic aura theory:** This one isn't too far from the previous theory, though it takes a slightly different tack. As anyone who has looked at a person's aura can tell you, emotions play a strong role in shaping your aura. When we have a certain belief, it tends to evoke a strong emotional response in us, which then plays a role in shaping our aura. According to this theory, the color and shape of your aura makes it easier to interact with different types of mana, and the intensity of your belief allows a channel of mana to flow to you. Again, it all sounds fine and good, but the actual evidence showing this in action does not really exist.
- **The placebo effect:** You knew this was coming, right? According to some, magical traditions work because people innately believe they should work. We think that's the way the universe should be, so we go out and act like it is. And lo and behold, we get a self-fulfilling prophecy. I don't think this one does an adequate job of explaining the true variety of magical manifestations I've seen out there, but then again the human mind is a remarkably powerful belief machine.

- There may be weaknesses to this last theory, but I think in broad strokes it's generally accurate. In particular, I've seen people switch traditions and greatly change the trappings of how they cast magic with little real difference in their results, even though they claim to feel entirely different. The mind tells you to feel different, or it wants to justify its own decisions, so it tells you that your beliefs are making a difference. Even when they are not.
- Winterhawk

- I understand the appeal of simple, elegant theories, but simplicity and elegance do not necessarily equal truth. Magic is huge, messy, and complicated. It is not any one simple thing. It is everything, nothing, and all points in between. We would do better to embrace its wondrous complexity than attempt to pare it into simplicity.
- Man-of-Many-Names

So those are the basic theories. Which one do I believe? I don't really care. Here's why.

I have a commlink, a Transys Avalon, and I love it. It brings my the info, the trids, and music, and calls, and the whatever else I want when I want it. It's highly customizable. I can arrange the parts I need to be easily accessible, and functions I don't care about to disappear. The borders on the AROs are a custom design by a friend of mine based on thirteenth-century versions of the Shangshu. When the thing has issues—a little lag in speed, or the occasional outright crash—I can usually get it up and functioning again by running the right utility and executing a few simple tricks I've learned over the years. Once I have it going again, it returns to being the powerful electronic beast I know and love.

The thing is, while I know how the commlink functions, I don't know how it *works*. I know some basic principles of optical devices and binary codes, but once you get past a certain elementary level, the description of how raw binary code is translated into programming and then translated into objects I see and interact with is a complete mystery to me. If the commlink broke down at a core level, I could do nothing to fix it. As long as that core level is working, though, I can do mighty things.

That's the way it is the magic, but more so. I may not know why mana works the way it does, how it decides to flow to one person and not another, or why some people are stronger than others and why beliefs play a role in shaping mana. All I need to know is that it works, and I can take advantage of it. As long as the core system of mana functions, I can access it and follow the rules I know to get it to keep me safe and smack down anyone who needs smacking. I don't need to be a technician. An end user is enough for me to make the earth shake.

- There is truth to that, but your analogy also shows the weakness. The true master of the digital domain is the one who fully understands the underpinnings. You may do great things with your current understanding, but how much more could someone who knows more than you accomplish? And what will happen when you come face to face with them?
- Icarus

- That assumes that the workings of magic are understandable in the same ways as the working of technology. I remain unconvinced.
- Man-of-Many-Names

TRADITIONS OF THE SIXTH WORLD

Common magic traditions of the Sixth World are presented below. The outlines of how to use traditions in *Shadowrun* are presented on p. 279, *SR5*. Each tradition presented below includes preferred spells and/or adept powers for that tradition. There are no benefits in game mechanics for choosing those spells; they are there so that players can give their characters the flavor of that tradition. The descriptions also include the type of spirits each tradition uses to perform particular functions, as well as the attributes they use for Drain. Mages of that particular tradition may only summon the spirits listed with the tradition, and they are restricted in the tasks they can assign them. Assigning tasks outside the general area of their tradition will not receive a response from the spirit (for example, a Buddhist mage telling an air spirit to heal him will get no response, as air is a Combat spirit in that tradition, while the Health spirit is earth). Descriptions also include notable teachers in each tradition who can be used in games to help characters advance in a particular tradition. Note that when a tradition is described as a "possession tradition," replace the spirit power of Materialization in any spirits summoned by conjurers of that tradition with Possession (p. 197).

AZTEC

Read the title again. It says "Aztec." Not "Blood." Blood Magic and Aztechnology are so closely intertwined in the minds of many in the shadows that they are viewed as one in the same (and both use the same term, nahualli, for their priests). But the magic as practiced by Aztechnology is not deeply tied to Aztec traditions—it's mainly connected to the way Aztechnology likes to function.

But enough about what the Aztec tradition is not. What it is, at the core, is the idea that every living being, even the gods, share a portion of their soul with an animal twin. Every nahualli must have a mentor spirit that represents their animal twin, and their relationship to that mentor is complex. They do not so much try to emulate the traits of their mentor as incorporate those traits in their magic, using the skills of their mentor to compliment their own abilities.

There are traditionalists following Aztec ways who insist that elaborate headdresses and flowery plumage are the only proper garb for one performing Aztec magic, but they are offset by others who believe the mana you wield does not much care how you look. To them, their relationship with their mentor and the spirits they can channel through them are what matters. If a weighty headdress helps you focus on your work, that's fine. But if you can do what you need with a baseball cap on while sparing yourself a headache, so much the better.

AZTEC TRADITION

Combat: Guardian
Detection: Fire
Health: Plant
Illusion: Water
Manipulation: Beasts
Drain: Willpower + Charisma

PREFERRED SPELLS

Calm Pack
Eyes of the Pack
Resist Pain

Compel Truth
Powerball

PREFERRED ADEPT POWERS

Animal Empathy
Natural Immunity

Enhanced Perception
Temperature Tolerance

In former times, ritual spellcasters were largely attracted to the Aztec tradition, but recent years have seen a number of individual spellcasters following this path as well. This is due, at least in part, to people separating Aztec from Aztechnology and deciding that following the one did not mean tying yourself in with the other. These spellcasters can often be found in more rural areas as they seek to better commune with their mentor in the wild. The rough life they sometimes lead has ended up being attractive to some adepts as well, who often enjoy a physical challenge.

Tlalli Ichtaca was on her way to becoming a nahualli in Tenochtitlan when she stumbled across a Matrix site explaining the differences between what she was learning and older Aztec traditions, and she decided the older ways were much more appealing. Aztechnology does not like to give up on its people easily, though, so she quickly understood that she'd be best serve leaving Aztlan. She managed to escape to the Pueblo section of Denver, where she figured she would be safe from Aztechnology's prying eyes. She set up shop teaching people her newfound ways, and became known for her patience and good humor. The recent return of Aztechnology to Denver has made her situation more precarious, though at least she now has a cadre of students to watch her back.

BLACK MAGIC

Interested in learning Black Magic? Start by taking your books by Crowley and LaVey, along with your fake Necronomicon, and throwing them out the window. Black Magic isn't messing around. It isn't dressing up "be yourself" platitudes in trappings of darkness. It's

not there to say "boo" and then go away so you can tuck yourself in at night and sleep soundly. It is mean, brutal, and focused. It has a bad reputation because it deserves it.

The key of Black Magic is to combine hedonism with sustainability. Any idiot can score some novacoke or drop a few nuyen on a prostitute, but that's bush-league stuff. Black Magic is not just about fulfilling a desire; it's about the satisfaction of having people line up to give you what you want, of bending them to your will so that they forsake everything they thought was important to them in order please you. If you cannot conceive of the satisfaction that can come from that, you have no place in Black Magic. Black Magic understands that evil is not about random, uncontrolled destruction—it is about the systematic breaking down of others to facilitate your own pleasure and enjoyment.

Perhaps the most dangerous thing about Black Magic is how appealing it can be. Sometimes practitioners will invoke the symbols from other religions or traditions—demonic horns, pentagrams, swastikas, the Masonic eye—mainly to get a rise out of people, or to convey the perception that they are doing something illicit, but don't be fooled. Black Magicians put little stock in the magical power of these symbols. They are primarily interested in how they can use those symbols to manipulate others—which is their real area of interest.

Black Magic can occasionally be in your face, but more often it relies on subtle insinuation, manipulation, and subversion so the practitioner can gently lead their targets where they want them to go. And then lower the spiked fist on them.

Black Magic takes all kinds of practitioners, as long as they are willing to dedicate themselves entirely to this way of doing business. Spellcasters can use magic to dominate the minds of others, conjurers can call forth spirits to do their bidding (predictably, Black Magic practitioners tend to be haughty toward their spirits), and adepts can use their social skills to talk people into giving what they want. And mystic adepts can do a little of everything.

While some Black Magicians work together when they find their interests overlap, they are not by and large a group that sees much virtue and benefit in collective action. They are more likely to work their way into the ranks of some other organization, make their way to the top, and then turn that whole organization into a Black Magic organization—or at least an organization that serves the needs and desires of a particular Black Magician.

The fact that a Manhattan mage named Juliette Burma put out a notice on the Matrix saying she was looking for "willing students of the dark arts" is reason enough for most people to steer clear of her. Black Magicians generally don't like teaching anyone anything, and if they are advertising it's because either they're lying about their abilities, they have some secret plan to take advantage of you, or both. But a few street mages who used to be good for nothing more than card tricks have popped up in The Pit demonstrating some startling new abilities and crediting their growth to Burma. So either she's legit, or she's working a very special, long-term operation.

BUDDHISM

The religion of Buddhism has spread across the Sixth World and is commonly practiced throughout Asia, with significant enclaves in North America as immigrants migrated to the continent, either forcibly by their own volition. The religion has developed into three major schools of thought, with only the Vajrayana, or Tantric, school accepting magic as a pathway to nirvana. The other schools largely believe the Awakening is another part of reality to be overcome along the road to enlightenment. While many practitioners of magic claim Buddhism as their religion, the majority of these casters practice a different tradition, normally Wuxing or Shinto. It is believed the majority of this tradition's followers are located in Tibet, although there are significant numbers in Imperial Japan and continental Asia.

The Vajrayana method of instruction is largely based on the relationship between the master and the pupil. Spells are taught, not studied from a formulae, and are usually part of a larger lesson for the pupil to understand. It is highly unusual for any member of this tradition to attempt to learn a spell from any source other than a teacher, although some practitioners claim Matrix instruction works in the same way.

Buddhist magical techniques include *mantras* for ritual techniques, with *yoga* as a method for meditation and physical exercise. Practitioners explain the metaplanes through the use of *mandalas* to serve as maps. Some Buddhist adepts have a mentor spirit which normally takes the form of *yidam*, an enlightened being that the yogi meditates on in an attempt to gain enlightenment. The majority of known followers of this tradition are mystic adepts, but that majority is a slim one with mages and physical adepts also well represented in their ranks.

Jeremy Blue Sky, a practitioner of this tradition, resides near Bellingham, Salish-Shidhe. It is considered unusual for a tribe member to practice what locals consider a foreign religion, but Jeremy was raised with Buddhism as the son of an MCT employee assigned to Tsimshian and a local resident. Shortly after reaching majority, Jeremy received Salish citizenship and established a shrine in Sedro-Woolley. He regularly teaches three pupils at the shrine, although only one is normally Awakened. He is also known to take on temporary students from the shadows, although he forbids outside distractions while teaching one of these individuals.

BLACK MAGIC TRADITION

Combat: Fire
Detection: Water
Health: Earth
Illusion: Air
Manipulation: Man
Drain: Willpower + Charisma

PREFERRED SPELLS

Chaotic World	Control Actions
Control Thoughts	Death Touch
Opium Den	

PREFERRED ADEPT POWERS

Commanding Voice	Cool Resolve
Killing Hands	Voice Control

BUDDHIST TRADITION

Combat: Air
Detection: Guidance
Health: Earth
Illusion: Fire
Manipulation: Water
Drain: Willpower + Intuition

PREFERRED SPELLS

Hibernate	Mask
Silence	Spatial Sense
Resist Pain	

PREFERRED ADEPT POWERS

Cool Resolve	Improved Physical Attribute
Improved Sense	Living Focus
Maintain Warmth	

CHAOS MAGIC

Degrees in Thaumaturgy. Lectures on how mana responds to different strains of plant life. Longitudinal studies on the effects of living adjacent to ley lines. All these things make Chaos Magicians cringe. They tend to view the academic view of magic as narrow and stultifying, spending so much time studying the individual notes that they completely miss the music. Magic, in their eyes, is not supposed to be confined and measured. It is to be experienced, felt, and enjoyed.

For some Chaos Magicians, performing magic is the path to fulfillment. For others, it's about power. Some Chaos Magicians believe they are more powerful when they do not limit themselves to the trappings of any one tradition. As they listen to and learn from others, and as they pay attention to their own experiences, they see what works and what doesn't. If it works, no matter what tradition it originates from, they use it. And if it doesn't, they throw it away. Their broad-mindedness makes them quite comfortable with technology. If tech—from electronic spellbooks to nanite-fabricated lodges—can make it easier for them to do their work, they'll embrace it.

In many ways Chaos Magic is a catch-all term rather than a dedicated school of magic. Two Chaos Magicians who encounter each other may spend months together and still not know they belong to the same tradition, because their ways of going about their business are so different. If you look hard enough, though, certain strains of similarity can be found. Chaos Magicians don't like large institutions, don't like structure, and don't like rigidity. If planning goes on too long they tend to get impatient, as they are more than willing to just go out and improvise something rather than think it to death. When situations heat up, they like taking actions that are wild and uncontrolled. Others may find themselves overwhelmed and confused in such situations, but that's where the Chaos Magician feels most at home.

Given its nature, Chaos Magic attracts all strains of Awakened. Mystic adepts, adepts, spellcasters, conjurers, enchanters, whatever—if you like magic and don't like order, if you think magic should be more felt than studied, then join the Chaos Magic tradition, get out there, and make it happen.

Reuben Patel came to Chicago as soon as he heard that Governor Presbitero wanted to resettle the Containment Zone. He figured things would be getting suitably weird there in short order and he'd find a lot of work to do. Unfortunately on his first run in, a lucky shot from a ganger ripped his kneecap off. He's going through an arduous healing process, and he decided to make money on the side by sharing some of the ideas of Chaos Magic with anyone who has a few nuyen and time. He's not easy to listen to—his train of thought takes the longest possible route to the station—but if you can somehow get on his wavelength, you might be in for some astonishing revelations about how magic could work.

CHAOS TRADITION

Combat: Fire
Detection: Air
Health: Earth
Illusion: Man
Manipulation: Water
Drain: Willpower + Intuition

PREFERRED SPELLS

Chaotic World (natch)   Flamethrower
Mana Static   Mass Animate
Shape [Material]

PREFERRED ADEPT POWERS

Adrenaline Boost   Improved Reflexes
Rapid Healing   Spell Resistance

CHRISTIAN THEURGY

Christianity made its transition to the Sixth World in fits and starts. For some people, it was easy. The supernatural had always played a role in their stories and beliefs, so they simply accepted magic as part of the belief framework they'd always held. Others, however, identified magic with the witchcraft and satanism they'd been warned about for years, so they put up walls (the Catholic Church in particular erecting some strong barriers). The *Imago Dei* encyclical helped break down those walls, but it also transitioned people away from the belief that magic was a manifestation of godly power. Christian Theurgists in general see magic as a tool they can use to perform God's work, rather than a direct channel to the divine. Spirits often make Christian Theurgists uncomfortable—they're not sure if they should treat them like the souls of the dead, angels, devils, or something else, so they're often more comfortable just leaving them alone.

Christian Theurgists are as organized as their particular branch of Christianity is. Members of the clergy, such as mages in the Order of St. Sylvester, have stricter controls on their behavior, while members of the laity of any denomination who happen to be Awakened may have some guidelines or principles to help them in their use of magic, but the degree to which the follow those guidelines is up to them.

In its ideal form, Christianity is about helping others and relieving their pain where possible, and there are Christian Theurgists who attempt to live up to this ideal. Throughout history, however, there have been all sorts of acts done in the name of Christianity, and that remains the case today. Depending on what part of Christian teachings they emphasize or how they choose to interpret them, Christian Theurgists may be involved in a wide variety of activities ranging from the charitable to the reprehensible. But whatever they do, it will have that certain tinge of a holy crusade.

Christian Theurgists of all stripes can be found throughout the Western Hemisphere, though they become less common in the Eastern (where they tend to be spellcasters). Their conjuring skills are often subpar, and their experience giving instructions to spirits is limited. If you want someone who can clearly word a task without leaving loopholes for the spirit, look elsewhere. They can be potent spellcasters and adepts, particularly when they feel they are advancing the cause of righteousness.

Nathaniel de Leon was led a small group of Sylvestrine monks during the Aztlan-Amazonia War, but his responsibilities essentially ended when all of his underlings were killed during the final purge of Amazonian elements from Bogotá. He is still considered a member of the Order, but his exact assignment is unclear. He has taken it upon himself to find new recruits to serve under him, and that means he is quite willing to pass on Christian Theurgist teachings and ideas to those willing to learn.

DRUID

The umbrella term "druid" encompasses a variety of beliefs, from the nature-centered perspective of Celtic druids to the heavily shamanic viewpoint of wild druids to the esoteric mumblings of English druids. The commonality between the beliefs is the invocation of spirits tied to particular locations and the desire of the druid to work with those spirits to gain a measure of control over what happens in that spot. The Celtic druid may believe in a spirit that predates the existence of humanity, while English druids believe the spirits were shaped by the places and by the humans living there, but in operative terms that is a minor distinction—both believe the spirit is important, and both want the spirit on their side.

There is a strong arcane side to druids as they attempt find the true spirit of the land. Anyone can summon a spirit (well, not *anyone*, but you know what we mean), but invoking the true spirit of a place is more difficult. Especially since spirits can be tricky beings and may claim to be the spirit of a place without being the real thing. So druids often delve into the history of a spot, looking for clues that may help them uncover the true spirit at the base of that location.

While druids have a great respect for the land, that attitude often is limited to their piece of land. They can be very territorial, working hard to protect their chosen lands while unleashing fury on spots they believe may be

CHRISTIAN THEURGY

Combat: Fire
Detection: Water
Health: Air
Illusion: Earth
Manipulation: Guidance
Drain: Willpower + Charisma

PREFERRED SPELLS

Detect Life	Heal
Increase Inherent Limits	Influence
Lightning Bolt	

PREFERRED ADEPT POWERS

Astral Perception	Danger Sense
Empathic Healing	Mystic Armor

DRUIDIC TRADITION

Combat: Beast
Detection: Water
Health: Plant
Illusion: Air
Manipulation: Earth
Drain: Willpower + Intuition

PREFERRED SPELLS

Camouflage	Control Pack
Invisibility	Resist Pain
Stunball	

PREFERRED ADEPT POWERS

Animal Empathy	Enhanced Perception
Plague Cloud	Traceless Walk

a threat to them. They are highly conscious background counts, mana ebbs, ley lines, and other astral phenomena, since they know how those elements can affect the defense of their territory. Many of them are quite proactive in aspecting the mana of their favored area toward their tradition, giving them a very useful advantage.

Conjurers are common among druids, as are practitioners of ritual magic. Druid rituals can be long, formal, and involved, but the results of this are often spells of sweeping, transformative power. Druid adepts are more rare, but they can still be found, ready to fiercely defend the area they have chosen—or that they believe has chosen them. Druids often avoid head-on fights, instead preferring to use their knowledge of the land and nature to hide them and give them the chance to strike out when they can do the most damage.

Ryanne Winter met a spirit she refers to as the guardian of the Bitterroot Forest of the Sioux Nation in 2064. She has communed with this spirit for over a decade, growing more eccentric as she resists the attempts of the Sioux government to drive her out. They are unhappy with her because she regularly defends the Forest agains neighboring territories, mainly by sniping at any hostile-looking creature that gets in her range, including Sioux law enforcement. Obtaining a private sit-down with her won't be easy, and she might not be entirely intelligible, but she'd certainly have a lot to say about building a relationship with the spirit of a particular place.

HINDUISM

The Hindu tradition is based on the Hindu religious system, and it is designed to provide a path for the enlightened to reach transcendence. The path is one of ritual devotion, asceticism, and karmic purity. While the exact strictures followed by each school vary, most accept the precepts from the *Vedas*, texts originally written in Ancient India. Those followers who are Awakened believe following the precepts of their faith assist them along the path.

The Hindu believes the soul is in a constant cycle of death and rebirth, governed by a relationship with karma. Those who follow their particular school of thought (*dasarnas*) and caste's rules are reincarnated into a higher caste, eventually reaching *moksha*, or transcendence. Those who refuse to follow their destined path are reincarnated as a lesser being.

The Awakened members of the Hindu faith who follow this tradition generally fall into two general categories. The *Brahmin*, members of the high caste, uses magic in a priestly manner and are usually magicians or aspected magicians. The *saddhu* practices the path of the ascetic, using yogic practices to reach their ultimate goal, primarily supported by adepts and mystic adepts. The summoning of spirits largely takes the form of calling on *devas*, roughly benevolent entities, while others call on the *asuras*, entities with less obvious motivations.

The practitioners of this tradition frequently use *bhajans* (devotional songs), mantras, and yoga in their spell casting or power usage. Magic and dance are normally major components of rituals, helping the caster focus their concentration and mana. Sanskrit is also frequently used, with the Vedic form largely used by the b*rahmin*, while the *saddhu* prefer the later, classic form of the language.

Adi Varma is a yoga instructor currently employed at Proteus' Fiji arkoblock. His primary role there is to assist physically regressing executives or their family members in returning to a healthy lifestyle, but Proteus is aware of his Awakened status and allows him to perform private instruction when his duties allow (provided the clients can pass their background checks and pay for their room and board at the arkoblock). On a professional note, nearly everyone who has reviewed his classes has commented on his apparent non-judgmental approach and his concern about their well-being.

ISLAM

Islam has a difficult relationship with magic. On the one hand, mainstream Islam is generally not fond of magic; on the other hand, Awakened individuals have been very useful in advancing the cause of Islam in some instances, so they cannot dismiss it entirely. More conservative factions forbid women from practicing magic (some extremists have been known to assense female babies and exile or kill them if they are Awakened), while progressive Muslims welcome female practitioners and use them to teach the next generation of Islamic spellcasters.

One common thread binding all Muslim Awakened together is the analysis they dedicate to their tradition. They are thorough and detailed, bringing a mathematical rigor to their study of magic. This results in some very advanced but elegant formulae and practitioners who are among the leading magic academics of our time.

Given the uncertainty over the nature of spirits, Muslim Awakened generally consider it better to steer clear of the whole area on the off chance that the immaterial beings are demonic. They don't take mentor spirits and

HINDU TRADITION

Combat: Beast
Detection: Water
Health: Plant
Illusion: Air
Manipulation: Earth
Drain: Willpower + Logic

PREFERRED SPELLS

Alter Temperature   Analyze Magic
Fast   Sense Removal

PREFERRED ADEPT POWERS

Attribute Boost   Flexibility
Improved Physical Attribute   Pain Resistance

often don't summon spirits at all. Some elite mages conjure *djinn* and *ifrit*, hoping they can control the fire and terror these beings tend to bring with them and harness their fierce abilities.

Islamic magic is disciplined. Practitioners believe there is a place for experimentation, and that place is most certainly not in the field. They do not like making things up on the fly. They generally do not need to, though, because they tend to be well-trained and well-prepared. They move forward knowing the spells and techniques they intend to put into play have been thoroughly tested, and they have a confidence that comes from reliability.

Muslim spellcasters and spell designers abound. Spell formulae from leading Muslim mages are usually sold for premium prices, since the confidence in their ability to work as expected is high. There are also a large amount of Muslim adepts, especially among the more conservative groups, as they channel their powers into acting as *mujahedin* (holy warriors) for their cause.

Ibrahim Addaya was a well-respected scholar at the Prince Sultan University until recently, when his unethical use of certain persuasive spells on his more attractive students was uncovered and he lost his job. He is currently unemployable, living off his savings and trying to develop an income by selling his own line of spells. Without the backing of the university, the market for his materials has dropped, but that has made him more willing to sell his services—and his services are now more affordable. The shadows of Riyadh have taken note of the opportunity to obtain top-notch formulae.

PATH OF THE WHEEL

Perhaps the most rigid of the major magical traditions of the Sixth World, the Path of the Wheel is rooted in the elven nation of Tír na nÓg. The tradition takes its name from the *Draesis ti Heron*, the Wheel of Life that describes five different paths souls take in their journey toward enlightenment and total understanding. These paths are: the Path of the Warrior, the Path of the Steward, the Path of the Bard, the Path of the Druid, and the Path of the Rígh. Travelers on the paths follow mentor spirits particular to their path, and the paths are also reflected in Tír na nÓg's social order. In fact, more than one observer has claimed that the Path of the Wheel is at least as much about social control as it is about advancing magic.

The use of magic in the paths is very formalized; several tomes outlining these practices exist. Or at least that's the claim, as very few people not part of the Paths have ever seen these volumes. The volumes describing the Path of the Rígh, which is reserved for the highest levels of Tír society, are said to contain rituals handed down from the Fourth World or earlier, which outstrip anything we think we know about magic.

The ostensible purpose for the Paths is to help individual souls develop, but most who are familiar with it

ISLAMIC TRADITION

Combat: Guardian
Detection: Earth
Health: Plant
Illusion: Air
Manipulation: Fire
Drain: Willpower + Logic

PREFERRED SPELLS

Detect Enemies	Fireball
Foreboding	Mass Agony
Spirit Zapper	

PREFERRED ADEPT POWERS

Combat Sense	Improved Reflexes
Killing Hands	Riposte

PATH OF THE WHEEL

Combat: Earth
Detection: Guidance
Health: Air
Illusion: Water
Manipulation: Fire
Drain: Willpower + Charisma

PREFERRED SPELLS

Ball Lightning	Detect Enemies
Disrupt [Focus]	Improved Invisibility
Influence	

PREFERRED ADEPT POWERS

Combat Sense	Critical Strike
Mystic Armor	Penetrating Strike

know the true purpose: to protect Tír na nÓg and advance its interests. Those following the Path of the Warrior make for fierce defenders, as anyone who has attempted anything illicit in the Tír can tell you. The rituals and general formalism exist to keep practices in line and to make sure the Awakened of Tír na nÓg color within the lines when they practice magic.

As might be expected of anything within the magic-soaked Tír, the Path of the Wheel encompasses all sorts of Awakened. Residents of the Tír are particularly comfortable with spirits, as they seem to spend most of their time with one foot in the spirit realm. They generally are neither commanding nor deferential to spirits; they simply treat them as just another member of the team on which they function. In general, Tír Awakened are extremely skilled with whatever talent they might have, though their rigidity can be used against them.

Practitioners of the Path of the Wheel are strictly forbidden from sharing their knowledge with outsiders. There have occasionally been members who have gone rogue, but they can generally measure their life expectancy in weeks once they do so. If you are skilled at disguise and infiltration, though, you might be able to visit Brigid Mullen, who lives south of Dublin. She is an expert on the Path of the Bard, and students demonstrating excellent potential are often sent to her for polishing. Her sight is failing her, but she has extremely sharp hearing—and perfect pitch. Getting in to see her would be an accomplishment. Getting her to sing for you would be a thrill.

QABBALISM

Perhaps the most ancient mystic tradition, Qabbalism is based on the teachings of the Torah and other works, including the *Zohar*, the *SeferYetzirah* and the *Bahar*. These works form the basis of the Hebrew mysticism and also a portion of hermetic lore. The tradition use a combination of esoteric philosophy and frequently refers to the mystical power of the Hebrew alphabet and true names to influence the universe.

Casters who follow Qabbalism tend to cast spells using ancient Hebrew, and their research features complex formulae and diagrams, with numerology and astrology forming a significant part of their theories regarding the flow of mana. This method of explaining the Awakened universe is also part of the hermetic paradigm, although the hermetics use other sources of information as well.

QABBALISTIC TRADITION

Combat: Air
Detection: Earth
Health: Fire
Illusion: Water
Manipulation: Task
Drain: Willpower + Logic
Note: Qabbalism is a possession tradition

PREFERRED SPELLS

Borrow Sense   Double Image
Nutrition   Slay

Qabbalist spirits are normally referred to as elohim. They do not manifest in the physical realm, but temporarily possess a living or inanimate vessel to influence the world directly. The classic example is a clay golem, which still has its proponents today amongst certain practitioners. Mentor spirits are typically related to the ten sephirot, the emanations through which the Ein Sof reveals itself.

There are two main schools of thought within the Qabbalstic tradition: those who have an almost secular method of belief, and ultra-orthodox Hebrews sects who follow what they believe to be undiluted texts from ages past. The former group is common and its members are often treated like a sub-branch of hermeticism, and there are many members in academic, entertainment, and business circles. The latter reside within Orthodox strongholds and Israel, with peaceful interactions with outsiders being rare.

Fredrick Rosen is a fairly new member of the University of Denver's faculty, with a known penchant for picking up strays. He appears frequently in public, with his near-unique accent and good looks making him a bit of a celebrity among the uninhibited wives of the CAS sector. He currently teaches a number of introductory magical theories classes and also holds an Awakening for Business class as part of the evening program. He has been known to sell spell formulae, and may barter for services instead of taking cash. He also advertises as a private tutor for promising students, most of whom are attractive females. While these traits may provide an enterprising runner with an opportunity, angering a mage and leaving them alive is rarely a good practice. Especially one with known connections to Mossad.

SHINTO

The official religion of Japan, Shinto has spread with the power of Imperial Japan and the corporations that originated there. Shinto features a number of public shrines devoted to the *kami*, or gods. Its tenets are largely based around harmony with *kami* spirits, with Awakened activities being considered a natural extension of this concept, and it lacks dogmatic approach to its worship. The religion currently has 115,000 shrines and over 25,000 priests in Japan, with more around the world. The Emperor has increased the influence of the religion in national politics by including practitioners part of the national rebuilding effort.

Shinto is one of the few shamanic traditions accepted into the ranks of the corporations, largely as many executives are immersed in aspects of the religious beliefs from a young age and do not find its practitioners too rebellious. Unlike Amerindian traditions, most *kannushi* do not have a single mentor but attempt to live harmoniously with all the *kami*. Key portions of this harmony are respect for nature and ensuring physical and spiritual cleanliness though proper ritual. Honoring the *kami* is important to the Awakened, as they regularly ask favors of the spirits, especially looking for assistance in the use of magic.

Shinto magic techniques are closely tied to the religion whose name they share. Protective charms, normally called *ofuda* are used to anchor wards within a building, normally placed within the home's *kamidana*, or household altar. Personal protection amulets, called *omamori*, are frequently used to ward off bad luck or to encourage success in different endeavors; for the Awakened they are commonly made into foci for Counterpelling or Banishing. Other protective charms are also used by believers to bring good fortune, fight against bad luck, or induce and bless child birth.

Shigetoshi Suzuki is a priest at the Atsuta shrine who frequently works as a tutor to promising young students. A former employee of Fuchi, he left as the corporation disintegrated and entered the private sector. His teaching methods are reportedly guided self-discovery, with the *kami* being the central focus of the lessons and sometimes guest instructors.

SIOUX

Perhaps the most important thing to understand about beliefs in the Sioux tradition is the term Wakan Tanka. By most interpretations it means "Great Spirit," meaning the power of life that animates everything in this world, from the sun to the earth to the plants and animals that live on it. Wakan Tanka has been described as a sheltering tree covering all the children of the one mother and one father.

But there is also an interpretation of Wakan Tanka that takes it to mean "Great Mystery." This serves as a reminder that the power that animates the world is not something mere humans understand, and that we should accept it in its mystery rather than trying to impose human understanding on it. Living with this incomprehensibility is part of life, and the sooner one can accommodate oneself to it, the sooner you can be more in harmony with the world and nature instead of living in conflict.

Don't let this goal of peace fool you into thinking that everything about the Sioux tradition is sweetness and light. Sioux mythology is full of a vast range of characters. Iktomi the spider and Coyote are always around to cause trouble, Unktehi the serpent makes trouble for the Thunderbird, and Double Face preys on humanity. The Great Spirit may be incomprehensible, but the trouble these other beings can cause is only too plain, and practitioners of the Sioux tradition are well aware of what they need to look out for. Or, if they are of a more mischievous frame of mind, who to emulate.

Rather than study formulae or ancient tomes, practitioners of the Sioux tradition try to take clues and hints from how to best do magic from the world around them. The world is full of information to those who take the time to observe it, and Sioux Awakened are usually willing to take that time. They observe carefully, letting the auras and beings around them speak, doing their best to hear the stories they are telling rather than impose their own meaning upon them. Once they have that information, though, they are swift and sure—and devastating, if they need to be.

There is a healthy tradition of Sioux adepts, practitioners who are well versed in the language of the land and use that knowledge to travel swiftly and silently and enter places thought to be secure. They often carry a bit of the spirit of Inktomi or Coyote with them, adding a twist of humor or mischievousness to their actions. There is also a strong population of Sioux enchanters and spellcasters, channeling their knowledge of the life

SHINTO TRADITION

Combat: Air
Detection: Water
Health: Plant
Illusion: Beasts
Manipulation: Man
Drain: Willpower + Charisma

PREFERRED SPELLS

Astral Window	Control Emotions
Stun Bolt	Thought Recognition

SIOUX TRADITION

Combat: Beast
Detection: Plant
Health: Fire
Illusion: Air
Manipulation: Guardian
Drain: Willpower + Intuition

PREFERRED SPELLS

Clout	Control Thoughts
Forced Defense	Invisibility
Silence	

PREFERRED ADEPT POWERS

Critical Strike	Freefall
Increase Reflexes	Missile Mastery

given by Wakan Tanka into strong protections for creation—or into devastating strikes against the flaws they perceive.

Snana Cansasa meditates in her lodge and spends a part of each day contemplating her place in her surroundings, but don't go looking for her on a mountainside or on the plains. She is an analyst with Eagle Security in Cheyenne, and her understanding of designing defenses against Awakened threats is perhaps unparalleled. She will not, of course, willingly pass any of her knowledge with shadowrunners, but a team that can generate the right cover story may be able to get an appointment to see her in her lofty office.

VODOU

Perhaps no tradition besides Blood Magic has been as maligned as Vodou, though in Blood Magic's case the defamation is usually warranted. Vodou has years of baggage connecting it to frenetic, out-of-control practitioners and dolls crafted with an intent to do harm at a remote distance. While these images perhaps touch on some aspects of Vodou, they miss the larger picture.

The centerpiece of Vodou is the concept of *les invisibles*, the unseen beings that populate the spirit world. The spirits are referred to as *loa*, and they are what the Vodou Awakened serve. There are degrees of loa, both major and minor. The general goal in Vodou is to gain the favor of a major loa, either by interacting directly with that spirit or by gaining influence within that spirit's court. One good way to get on a loa's good side is to give them some time to play around on the material plane, which in the Vodou tradition is accomplished by allowing them to possess the body of the summoner or of one of their servants (or perhaps the body of some lunkhead the Vodou conjurer brought along for just that purpose). The loa like to live it up during their possession time, which partially explains some of the wilder and more exuberant aspects of Vodou rituals.

Vodou practitioners are not just respectful to the spirits they summon—they are deferential. In their view, their magical abilities hinge on keeping the loa happy, so they will do everything in their power to please these beings, including engaging in flattery or obsequiousness. A Vodou conjurer would never refer to a spirit owing her "services." Instead, she would say that the spirit has granted her gifts, or some other phrasing that makes her subservient relationship to the spirit clear.

Conjurers are by far the most common type of Vodou practitioner, though their focus on material objects to use in their rituals means that enchanters have a place in their ranks as well. Spellcasters play an important role in the rituals of the tradition, though this role is often filled by strong conjurers who have also built up a bit of spellcasting prowess. Adepts are rare in Vodou; they work so hard to get the utmost control over their bodies that they often don't like the idea of turning that control over to *les invisibles*.

Benoit Delatour of Port-au-Prince is not going to be the one to quash any stereotypes about Vodou theatrics. Fond of brightly colored, beaded robes and often accompanied by snakes, Delatour is only too happy to court the attention of onlookers. He practically carries an "Ask me about Vodou" sign; if you do so, he will regale you with lectures about the evils of greed, the importance of unity, and the right loa to beseech for any favor you may need. As it turns out, his knowledge of loa is more than encyclopedic, and anyone wanting to increase their knowledge of the denizens of other planes would do well to talk to him.

WICCA

The Wiccan tradition is the Awakened manifestation of one of the Sixth World's largest recognizable neo-pagan movements. Wicca is collection of beliefs, tenets gathered from nineteenth century sources and New Age reasoning merged with earlier, pre-Christian concepts. The central tenets of the religion are harmony with nature and the *Wiccan Rede* or a similar code.

Wiccans generally venerate two deity-like figures, the Horned God and the Great Mother, although some believe they are aspects of a single being. Mentor spirits for the tradition are generally the Wise Warrior for adherents of the Horned God or the Peacemaker for the Great Mother. All Wiccan magicians who summon a spirit show deference and normally make a small payment of some kind, as the *Law of Threefold Return* is a constant theme in the tradition's teachings.

VODOU TRADITION

Combat: Guardian
Detection: Water
Health: Man
Illusion: Guidance
Manipulation: Task
Drain: Willpower + Charisma
Note: Vodou is a possession tradition.

PREFERRED SPELLS

Clairvoyance — Entertainment
Mind Probe — Mob Mind
Stunbolt

PREFERRED ADEPT POWERS

Astral Perception — Commanding Voice
Improved Sense — Rapid Healing

Wiccan followers are not part of a monolithic entity but are composed of several different sects or lineages, frequently called *traditions*. The largest tradition, known as Gardnerian or British Traditional Wicca, follows a hierarchal model of leadership within their covens, with witches and wizards attaining higher levels of initiation within the religion through mandated rituals, whether or not they are Awakened. This tradition is nearly hermetic in their approach and largely follows *The Book of Shadow*. The other traditions are frequently referred to as the Eclectic or Goddess Wicca and are a collection of less-structured organizations.

Katherine Stubbard maintains a talismonger shop in Ontario with a large inventory of ceremonial bowls and candles for sale. The middle-aged dwarf rarely shows her talent, although she has stopped three different burglary attempts since she opened her shop. A member of the local Gardnerian coven, she frequently helps young Awakened find places to help their understanding of the changes affecting them. While the other members of her coven are unknown, it is unlikely Katherine is alone in the city. They also seem to have no problem accepting any strays she decides to keep on rather than pass off to other magicians, although they are rarely seen in the area after initiation. One of her first jobs is to remind newcomers that initiation into a coven is not standard magic initiation—you do not gain any powers as a result of the action. You do, she'll continue, get started on the right path.

WUXING

The central concept of the Wuxing tradition is the idea of *qi*, the force that connects and binds all life. *Qi* manifests itself in many ways and is often connected to the five basic elements of the tradition: fire, water, earth, wood, and metal. It also acts in connection with the two poles known as yin and yang, which are sometimes compared to order and chaos, or peace and tumult.

Much of the efforts of a wujen (which is what practitioners of Wuxing are called) are focused on getting various elements of *qi* to line up properly. As such, wujen often focus on ritual magic, particularly when those rituals can help them adjust background counts or ley lines to their liking.

The Wuxing tradition tends to be orderly, and it has found a home in many corporations (such as Wuxing, of all things). Wujen often thrive in orderly corporate environments and are skilled at working their way through hierarchies. This translates to their view of spirits, as they tend to have a hierarchical, almost bureaucratic view of the spirit world. This means that they are generally respectful to spirits, if a little stiff.

Wuxing is not tied to any larger religion, so there are no connections between wujen and any larger organizations (besides the corporations that often hire them). Within a corporation or similar organization, wujen tend

WICCAN TRADITION

Combat: Fire
Detection: Water
Health: Plant
Illusion: Air
Manipulation: Earth
Drain: Willpower + Intuition (Goddess Wicca)/Willpower + Logic (Gardnerian Wicca)

PREFERRED SPELLS

Analyze Magic	Confusion
Control Emotions	Prophylaxis

WUXING TRADITION

Combat: Fire
Detection: Earth
Health: Plant
Illusion: Water
Manipulation: Guidance
Drain: Willpower + Logic

PREFERRED SPELLS

Control Actions	Mana Barrier
[Sense] Removal	Silence

PREFERRED ADEPT POWERS

Astral Perception	Attribute Boost
Cool Resolve	Kinesics

to be friendly and collaborative with each other, especially when it comes to *feng shui*-related rituals seeking to make mana in an area flow as they would like. They do not, however, tend to cross organizational boundaries well, and often wujen from one corporation or equivalent organization will view others with a degree of suspicion, as if they were not truly pure in their practice of the tradition.

The orderly nature of Wuxing thought translates into the ways wujen often use magic. They like to be in control of any situation; if an encounter seems to be going off the rails, their first actions are generally aimed at getting everything calmed back down so they can deal with things the way they would like. Often this involves conjuring spirits to restrain those that need to be calmed

down and impose order on an unruly spot. Wujen tend to have significant conjuring power, though pure spell-casters can also be found in the tradition. Adepts are somewhat less common, as their particular fly-in-the-ointment-style exploits do not always lend themselves well to Wuxing thought.

If you want the best teachers of Wuxing, go to Hong Kong. But not everyone can get there, and the teachers over there charge an arm and a leg for their services. For a better bargain, visit Charlie Sun in Vancouver. Recently retired from a Evo subsidiary, Sun has been finding fulfillment in his downtime by sharing his work experiences with whoever might be willing to listen. He can be rambling, but he is getting a growing body of friends because they say that as long as you pay attention, you'll find out the old man had a depth of knowledge that far surpassed the middle management position he obtained.

ZOROASTRIANISM

The forerunner of most modern monotheistic religions, Zoroastrianism is not a tradition for those who just want to sit an contemplate things. It is an active faith, one that sets a stark difference between good and evil, order and chaos, and tells the devout in no uncertain terms that they need to be working on behalf of good.

The central deity of Zoroastrianism is Ahura Mazda, the creator, who works in opposition to Angra Mainyu, the destructive force of chaos. Followers are implored to actively work on the side of goodness and creation, as that is the only way to defeat chaos. Adherents often use rituals involving the life-giving forces of water and especially fire to purify themselves if necessary. Frequent prayer, meditation, or mental focusing is important to the tradition.

Zoroastrianism often focuses on dualities: good and evil, order and chaos, mind and body. The dualities are not perfectly aligned—for example, neither mind nor body is judged to be good or evil—but practitioners are aware of the separation and desire to have mind and body working in harmony with each other. All types of Awakened individuals can be found in the Zoroastrian tradition, but mystic adepts often find it particularly appealing as they feel the focus if the tradition allows them to put the two sides of their magical talent into greater alignment.

There are no governing bodies of the Zoroastrian religion beyond the leaders of particular communities. These religious communities are often not welcoming to outsiders, but the magical communities are more open. They often see themselves as warriors involved in a great fight, and they are willing to have others join them in the fight, as they are well aware the struggle will not be easy.

Zoroastrian mages tend to be blunt and direct. They certainly understand the value of stealth in a fight, but they also tend to like to let their enemies know just who they're up against. They like to hit fast, hit hard, but leave their enemies intact. They also want to be sure they can heal up damage as necessary when the dust settles, and are generally willing to provide care to their opponents to keep them alive. They often have a poise and bearing to them that others find unsettling.

Hester Khorasani had a career for a time as a special effects wizard for Horizon's Pathfinder Multimedia, but as her talents developed she decided she needed to do bigger things. Rather than drop out of the Hollywood scene, though, she used the connections she had built to open her own small studio that focused on trids with messages subtly supportive of Zoroastrian beliefs (though to a casual observer, they often seem like flicks about powerful mages kicking ass and taking names). Profits from her studio are funneled into a teaching center that is open to all who want to know more about her philosophy, whether they are Awakened or not. By most accounts, the lessons presented to people who drop by are simple and cursory, but rumors persist that Khorasani keeps her eye out for particularly powerful visitors, and then invites them to attend special advanced classes she leads herself.

ZOROASTRIAN TRADITION

Combat: Man
Detection: Water
Health: Fire
Illusion: Air
Manipulation: Plant
Drain: Willpower + Logic

PREFERRED SPELLS

Analyze Truth	Armor
Detect Enemies	Heal
Stunball	

PREFERRED ADEPT POWERS

Commanding Voice	Danger Sense
Metabolic Control	Pain Resistance

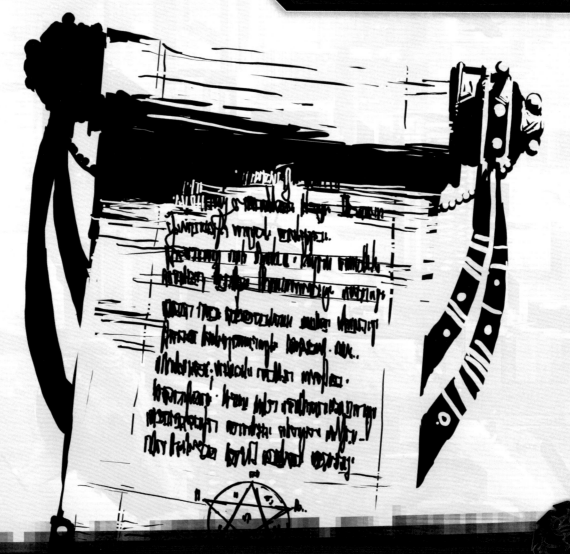

MAGICAL SOCIETIES

The soft thrum of the guitar from Aginor and rhythmic beat of the synthbass pumping in through the small but powerful speakers set the mood for the ritual. Grant stood proudly near the podium, the focal point at the center of their form. He was the leader of the Soft Seven.

Aginor was at the sky peak, the upper point of the six-pointed star, connected by the lines of power to Chase and Madeleine at the anchors, the Seven's title for the three and five points of the star. Tycho controlled the synthbass from the point of tombs, opposite the sky peak, connected to Kelly and Micah at the doorways, points two and six, by the link lines.

The Seven had chosen the six-pointed star, often called the Star, or Shield, of David, not because they were in any way followers of Judaism, but because it had six points and a center. A total of seven spots in which they could perform rituals. The Soft Seven didn't have a standard tradition. They grew up together behind the high walls and tight security of an Evo arcology, devoid of religious or arcane tradition in their bland corporate education. When the Talent awoke in each of them, the corporation shifted them to a nice quiet camp where they were taught the bland principles of Universal Magic. But those lessons only took them so far, and eventually the Seven developed their own tradition to investigate the true depths of the arcane.

Kelly and Micah joined the harmony next with their pan flute and triangle, respectively. Micah was a virtuoso on a violin but claimed the triangle was a simple and truer expression of the soul for him. As the gentle singing ring and melodic lilt filled the air, a glow began to emanate along the line between the doorway points—the gate line. The glowing pulsed with the beat of the synthbass, holding a little more of the light after each beat until the glow was steady and bright.

Chase poured a fine grey powder from his pouch and began the forms. The patterns they had chosen were from a wide array of cultures, but each shape symbolized the same thing, grounding. The glow of the gate line began to slither down toward Tycho, expanding with the pulsing bass. With the first touch of light on the terra line, the grey powder flashed, burning the symbols around the anchor point into the concrete floors with a white-hot fire.

The blinding flash cast an eerily dark silhouette on the wall, portraying the next stage of the ritual in a dark dance.

Madeleine's shadow arms extended out, one ending in the slim shadow of a knife, the other a lively flapping form that matched its raven-black body. The ends of shadowy arms crossed, bringing the flapping to a stop and exchanging the lively flutter for the steady flow of a thin line reaching to the floor. Crimson lines traced patterns, more pieces of their mosaic magical style, that brought the glow down the other link line in pulsing steps from gateway to anchor.

As the second glowing strip touched the terra line, it sparked to life. The light shot along the terra line to each anchor point, reflected at the corner, and flew toward the sky peak. The glowing lines crossed where the two triangles met. As they touched the triangle, the tomb began to glow a soft red. The pulsing lines met at Aginor's feet, the sky peak, turning a bright blue as they crossed the threshold of the gateway line.

Their six-pointed star was fully alight.

Grant's sextuplet of shadows deepened despite the growing light. He responded by casting lines of light that strengthened gradually and sent the shadows into retreat. They seemed to shrink toward Grant's feet, as if the ritual leader were absorbing them. As the shadows disappeared, the melody stopped, with all the players in perfect sync.

Grant extended a single arm outward and tossed the podium away with an inhuman strength his fifty kilos should not have possessed. The podium smashed on the distant wall, splintering despite its sturdy construction. No one flinched. Grant slowly lowered himself to his knees then reached out and touched each point on the inner hexagon. A small flame flared to life with each tap of his fingers. As the sixth flame arose Grant stood and took a long step out and over Aginor. As he passed the plane of the hexagon, a shadowy form peeled from his body and coalesced into a wispy humanoid shape.

Grant turned back to the shadowman and bowed.

"Soul of Shadow, we of the Soft Seven wish your patronage in our quest for arcane enlightenment. We have brought you here and ask that you guide us. Are we worthy?" Grant kept his tone steady, hiding his surprise that all this was actually working.

"We shall see," the shadowy spirit spoke in a gravelly whisper.

The Soft Seven smiled in unison.

So did the Soul of Shadow.

POSTED BY: LOTHAN THE WISE

I have never found it necessary to link myself to any single group. I hold fellowship memberships in many organizations just to stay up on the latest news in theoretical thaumaturgy but none have ever been intriguing enough to fully pique my interest. That does not mean I haven't run across my share of interesting collections of arcanists. For that I've been asked by the three amigos to share my wisdom on those groups. Business in Chicago happens to be going well so I agreed and have prepared this fine document.

I'll begin by briefly covering the various reasonings behind why those with the Talent choose to gather together. The majority of my work here will be focused on giving my unbiased opinions and viewpoints on several magical organizations with which I am familiar. I'll start with the public groups, followed by corporate organizations, move into some of the historical and religious groups, then open the curtain on some of the more secretive societies, follow that up with what I call the "hysterical" societies, and wrap up with some smaller local groups. I'll add in a little at the end discussing what those without the Talent can bring to an arcane association, as I understand not all those who will read this are gifted.

WHY WE GATHER

There are a multitude of reasons why those with the Talent gather, but there are only a few which a large majority share. I have summed up the reasons for gathering in five basic areas: Social, Informational, Causal, Conspiratorial, and Initiatory. Most organizations will have a combination of reasons behind their existence, but there is usually one at the core, a desire that is fundamental to the existence of the group.

Socially motivated organizations cover the widest spectrum of arcane associations. These range from small community, collegiate, or even familial-based groups with no more than four or five magicians gathering together to simply "shoot the drek," all the way up to the world-spanning MagicNet, which marked its one millionth member on December 11, 2074. Members join these groups for the social and networking benefits, especially groups like MagicNet that allow for at least

a small amount of social interaction between megacorporations that are normally very controlling of the range and scope of interactions their citizens are allowed to have. With primarily social groups, there is very little exchange of actual arcane information such as formulae or theories on metaplanar physics. In fact the members often speak very little on actual topics of arcana and spend more time focused on sharing stories of life as one of the Talented and spending time with others who face the same world full of discrimination and fear.

With socialization often comes stratification. The larger a social group is, the more of this occurs. Then the standard feelings of envy or pity come along and cause the demise or splintering of these social groups. Those that do not fall apart are those that allow upward mobility within their social ranks. Providing a way to climb the tiers, or at least supplying the illusion that the tiers are ascendable, is a key to long-term success. The most important part of groups like this for many of the Talented who join is the prestige of being among the elite of that social circle. They often wear their ranking like a badge of honor, sometimes literally, to laud over those who are beneath them.

- ❂ The ego of some people.
- ❂ Kane

- ❂ Despite the power they have, most Awakened people are still only metahuman and still suffer the same weaknesses as everyone else. Self-doubt, self-loathing, and a penchant and desire to make themselves feel better at the expense of others are a part of most metahuman personalities.
- ❂ Arete

Social groups are, by far, the largest category of magical organizations, but they are not the most widely valued. That title belongs to Informational groups. Informational groups are those where members gather to exchange information on various magical phenomena. Arcanists exchange information on magical formulae, new meta-planar explorations, rare spirits, and, in general, any information not considered proprietary corporate material. Most would think this should be the largest and definitely most popular type of organization, but megacorporate control tends to limit how often they want their wagemages exchanging information with wagemages from other corporations or those who work for independent organizations. MagicNet is a popular gathering place for the magically gifted and has faced numerous corporate injunctions through the Corporate Court to prevent precious information from being disseminated to unauthorized sources.

> * Which is interesting since MagicNet is wholly owned by MCT. Independence is an illusion.
> * Slamm-0!

Arcane informational societies come in two main varieties—simply put, legal and illegal. The legal exchanges are those hosted by reputable groups where sanctioned information can be exchanged between the Awakened. There aren't many of these out there that are specifically about exchanging information. Information simply isn't free in this day and age. All the megacorporations have a few of these groups that act as gateways for information between the various divisions and subsidiaries of the parent megacorporation, but information does not flow out easily.

Smaller informational societies exist as well, but those that choose to abide by the law are heavily monitored by the megacorporations to insure they aren't trading on any corporate secrets. The monitoring also keeps tabs on the more intellectually astute members so that the corps can identify potential recruits or promising ideas. I myself was once approached due to a particularly interesting hypothesis I was developing on foci identification. I have been told I should have avoided the conversation, but it served its purpose and got me the meet I wanted. Which means that when the corps come looking after their own interests, you shouldn't forget that you can always twist things to your own ends.

As for the informational exchanges that do not abide by the law—well, those are far more valuable and far more dangerous groups with which you may associate. These societies hold a wealth of arcane data and training, especially in fields that are highly restricted or outlawed in various jurisdictions. Membership in these societies requires an introduction by a current member, since they are always on the lookout for infiltrators. A humorous point on that security measure is that every one of these black magic societies have infiltrators, or at least members who answer to higher masters, already present. These moles share just enough to avoid suspicion but never more than their corporate masters allow.

> * No different than us. We vet the newbs, know the dirt on the lifers, and we still expect that info's gonna leak. It's all part of the game. A great way to get things done is disinformation. Direct through misdirection.
> * Thorn

Causal groups are some of my favorite to speak about. They gather together because they have some similar drive, goal, or cause they wish to achieve. Be it religious, political, explorational, monetary, or something more unorthodox, every member of a group shares this belief. Groups vary in size from a few members to hundreds but rarely break the four-digit mark. Many of these groups have a large number of non-Awakened periphery members who also believe but are not part of the arcane aspect.

Causal societies, like their informational counterparts, can fall on both sides of the law. Their legality is usually based on their end goal, but sometimes based on the means which they are willing to employ to gain those goals. The Mystic Crusaders are fully sanctioned and granted rights by their patron corporation, the Atlantean Foundation, and therefore function within the law (albeit AF's laws in most cases). On the other side, the Brotherhood of Darkness functions outside the law in their battle against evil and must maintain their secrecy to help protect their members.

The best thing about causal societies is the fervor and passion with which they seek their prize. They are often single-minded and frequently blind to any truth that is not their own. There have been instances in the past where societies were formed to oppose already existing societies; both groups spawned from the same tree of nuts, but each possessed their own view of reality. These groups are known to employ individuals of the SINless variety in order to bolster their numbers or even to blindly fight their battles for them. Many a victory has been won by the faithless and claimed by the faithful.

> * These groups run the gamut for payrates. You might end up working for peanuts for one group and get buku bucks on the next gig for another. The real zealots are the ones to watch out for though. They'll have little problem running a double-cross on a non-believer. First bad sign is if a member hires you direct instead of using a professional Mr. Johnson.
> * Fianchetto

Conspiratorial societies are similar to causal societies in their desire for a particular outcome, but these groups are always large, secretive, and veil their activities behind mundane—meaning plain, not un-Awakened—means and methods. These arcane societies are rare, or at least rarely revealed, but I know of many from my years of digging and turning over rocks that likely were best left undisturbed.

My experience with societies of this nature has taught me two things: Never judge a book by its cover, and never accept coincidence when it comes to the arcane. Conspiratorial groups thrive on manipulating others using those two concepts, using people's misconception and willingness to accept coincidences. Strings are pulled, minds are bent, and events unfold to benefit the conspirators while no one understands who is really behind the scenes, either because they're just too mild-mannered or they're not nearly powerful enough.

These societies operate around, behind, and between the law. They act in ways undefined by the current laws or even change laws to better fit what they desire. All the while getting outsiders to believe the ideas behind their legal maneuverings were theirs, and the conspirators had nothing to do with it. And when they can't manage either of those things, they make sure to have the right people in the right places to bend the right will or manipulate the right minds. These are the groups that Plan 9 and his ilk talk about. But still get wrong.

- The views may be skewed but at least we dare to view them. These groups don't play nice, ever. If you think you're winning, good; at least you'll die happy.
- Plan 9

Initiatory societies are one of the most important but usually the smallest of magical groups, and they often fit inside other societies. I think they are important enough, and often independent enough, that they should be talked about on their own, if for no other reason than they are also the most likely magical organization for a runner to join.

These societies provide assistance and guidance along the paths to the deeper mysteries. Some are bathed in the traditions and trappings of their parent society or their founders, but many are simply small groups of the Awakened getting together to help each other out based on nothing more than friendship or even a simple desire for arcane power.

- Initiatory groups are widely varied, but Lothan's categories are pretty solid. I'd disagree that runners are most likely to join an initiatory group, though. Most runners are too paranoid, egotistical, or whacked in the head to join one. They tend to form their own societies instead of joining others.
- Lyran

- Initiatory societies are different than a group. They tend to have more social rules and a hierarchy in place. Most limit progression based on rank, which is a social distinction.
- Winterhawk

PUBLIC GROUPS

As stated earlier, as we move forward I will break down the groups into something different than the reasons they gather. The first class of magical societies I'll discuss are those with a very public face. These groups operate completely in the open, are often all over the Matrix with information on their beliefs, teachings, or goals, and have the least to offer when looking into the shadows. They are, though, a wealth of information when stepping out into the light.

These operations are a great place to have a friend, or seven, who aren't opposed to chatting about some of the details of their work, or spreading rumors about some of the other members who "just don't belong." Getting credentials from one of these groups can be a good way to add realism to a fake SIN, since membership isn't that expensive and adds that touch of detail that quick scans often find persuasive. Word from the Wise.

ASTRAL SPACE PRESERVATION SOCIETY (ASPS)

Members (est.): 150
Dues: 100¥/year
Areas of expertise: Aspected domains, astral space, mana ebbs and warps

The ASPS was started back in 2058 as one of the many decrees of the Great Dragon Dunkelzahn's Will. Its purpose, as the name somewhat implies, is the protection and preservation of astral space and its residents. In the early years the group, formed under the patronage of the Dunkelzahn Institute for Magical Research (DIMR), was given every opportunity to fail. It had a Board of Directors with no interest in their positions, a massive funding shortage, and no shortage of difficult and expensive projects it was expected to pursue. After the organization stumbled for a few years, Ibu Air, a free spirit member of the board from the beginning, stepped up, took the reins, and made a big decision that shifted the course of the society. Ibu Air opened the ASPS to funding outside the DIMR and Draco Foundation. The group traded the leash of one dead draconic master for another much more lively, Hestaby. Since, the society has felt the wedge driven deep between itself and its founders, to the point of shadow enmity between them, but has found plenty of other friends in the magical community.

With Hestaby as a benefactor, the ASPS developed strong connections to the Shasta Shamans, to the point of once having four of them on the board. Now there are none. With the events of recent years and the stripping of Mt. Shasta from Hestaby by her dragon kin, the fate of that relationship is now a matter of intense speculation. Even with the move against their largest single patron, the ASPS has made enough friends to keep aloft and moving forward. The UCAS still values the ASPS for their help with the study of alchera; the investigation of astral rifts, in particular the now-closed DeeCee Rift; their work in Chicago helping to understand the relationship between the Cermak Blast and astral space as well as the nature and potential threat of insect spirits and their shamans; and the hunt for shedim all over, including the support provided in the elections to clear the candidates in Fredericton. The society is likely to bolster their presence in Seattle if gubernatorial candidate Eliza Bloom becomes the next governor of Seattle, as she was a former member of the board and is still a registered member of the ASPS.

To those of us in the shadows, the ASPS also has value thanks to three major facets of the society's operations. For those runners who like to operate in that twilight area between the shadows and the light, the ASPS posts bounties on insect shamans that can be collected with a decent fake SIN and bounty hunting licensure. If those runners are a little light in the licensure department they can use that fake SIN (decent quality, remember) to sign on to work for one of the ASPS's field research teams. Expect to be employed at least six months, usually over a year, and sometimes more. For those who lack any of those fancy faux accouterments, the ASPS hires the occasional shadowrunner team to help acquire items or secure locations that do not, strictly speaking, belong to them.

Membership in the ASPS offers access to the groups various facilities all over the world, though the greatest concentration is in North America. The current state of affairs with Hestaby has lead many members to become less vocal of their membership, and participation at group meetings and functions has dropped in the past few months.

- ◉ Operations with ties to the ASPS have increased, with members acting as Johnsons and fixers for Hestaby while she endures her exile. If you're getting a job with ASPS fingerprints on it, odds are you're playing a part in one of Hestaby's elaborate schemes. It may seem like a mundane run, but you are a single ripple adding to the waves. Be wary of possible tsunamis.
- ◉ Lyran

- ◉ Don't give Ibu Air a pass just because Hestaby is out there. That spirit is wily and uses shadow assets all the time, especially on dangerous expeditions to study alchera or astral rifts. The group is public, but they've had to have their fair share of cover-ups. They've lost three registered members in the past six months, which means they've probably lost at least triple that in shadow mages.
- ◉ Pistons

- ◉ When I have a moment, I need to brief you all on some bizarre astral stuff in Antarctica I encountered. ASPS would definitely be interested, but I don't really want them—or anyone who's not us—to know what's going on.
- ◉ Elijah

UNITED TALISMONGERS ASSOCIATION (UTA)

Members (est.): 250
Dues: 500¥/year
Areas of expertise: Enchanting, foci, reagents, telesma

The UTA started up in the California Free State as a loose association of talismongers and enchanters looking to survive in a world dominated by the megacorporations. They grew quickly and now help small independent talisman and lore shops to stay independent of the megacorporations without having to go the organized crime route. They've been very successful in the CFS and exist as the largest network of independent yet interconnected arcana suppliers in that country, and they stand as the second largest arcana suppliers in the country behind only Mitsuhama. The group has managed to expand their influence north and bring several Seattle shops into the fold, but the move has met its share of difficulties.

Seattle is a very corporate city. Independence in the city is often a well-spun and artfully crafted illusion. Efforts to reach out have met with varying degrees of megacorporate reciprocity. From simple denial to acceptance and infiltration, the megacorporations haven't taken kindly to this organization's desire to "unite and empower the little guy."

While in its original form, the UTA was actually a terrible enterprise for runners, since it kept the field of talismongering very much on the up and up. With its latest troubles and its strong desire to stay independent, the UTA has become much more shadow friendly. Well hidden behind layers of frontmen and Johnsons, even the UTA President Tamara Nimbus has dipped her toes into the shadowy side of life in order to help maintain the group's independence from corporate control. The UTA has also found itself in competition with the Illuminates of the New Dawn, who are well acquainted with the world of shadowrunners and thus have the advantage of experience.

Recent scuttlebutt about these two organizations focus on rumors of negotiations. Some have said that the IOND is looking to more fully intermesh the UTA with their existing network. This would definitely be a boon for the IOND but would cost the UTA its prized independence. Many of the UTA members aren't too keen on the idea of standing under the umbrella of the IOND and their magocratic politics.

- ◉ The UTA has never been that militant, but a small group of shop owners in NorCal have been actively opposing IOND activity in the area and are becoming more strident by the day.
- ◉ Slamm-0!

- ◉ The Seattle shops that have signed on have been receiving trouble from the IOND. Much of it veiled behind the politics of the New Century.
- ◉ Sounder

Signing up as a member of the UTA requires a valid SIN and an operational business dealing in the production or retail sales of arcane objects, reagents, or lore. That leaves out many of us in the shadows (although

I actually qualify), but for those who have managed to maintain or build themselves a nice little slice of a non-shadowy existence, this group can provide business advice, networking, discounts with suppliers and manufacturers, legal assistance, and, of late, contacts within the shadow community willing to work on a barter system. Whether they sound immediately appealing to you or not, their members are a good lot to have stored in the contacts folder.

- Their barter system is usually only of value to a team's mage or adept, but if you can make it work you can get hard-to-find items for perhaps less blood, sweat, and tears than you'd expect.
- Picador

ILLUMINATES OF THE NEW DAWN (IOND)

Members (est.): 750
Dues: 200¥/month
Areas of expertise: Laws and magic, magic artifacts

The Illuminates of the New Dawn (IOND) is the world's largest public magical group, promoting members' development while lobbying for a progressive and magocratic political and social ideal. If you want the party line, pick up the book "Legacy of the American Dream" by Dr. Rozilyn Hernandez. It delivers all the magocratic and pro-Awakened rhetoric you'd expect while at the same time subtly stating that the "American Dream" can be returned through magocratic progressivism. That philosophy was one of the primary platforms that Hernandez ran on when she made a bid for the White House back in '57, heavily backed by the IOND. She is still the High Magus, the highest-ranking member of the society, and rumors abound about the various political positions she may be seeking so she can improve her chances at making another run at the UCAS presidency.

Hernandez runs everything from the Grand Lodge in DeeCee. Below her is the Magus Council, formed from Magi members of the Inner Order. Each Magus of the Inner Order leads their own Lodge in major cities around the world, with a primary focus in North America and the UCAS. These Magi are usually individuals with economic or social clout in their region. Lodges are populated by and oversee local chapters of mages that make up the Outer Order. Local chapters never have more than a dozen Awakened members but may include any number of mundane supporters in their membership. The number of mundane supporters has seen a steady increase since '57, with spikes around election times, as people join for the politics, seeking a brighter future through magic, hoping a magocracy could challenge the might of the megacorporations. The arcane ranks of the IOND only accepts mages, though followers of other traditions occasionally join as part of the Outer Order. The IOND is a magicker network second to none. As long as you're

able to tolerate egotistical mages, being a member has plenty of value.

- Obviously we can.
- Slamm-0!

Though a public—and perfectly legal—organization, the IOND has had plenty of interactions with the shadows. Assistance in recovering, or acquiring, items of value for the Illuminates has been the most common activity in the past few years, but they have also contracted assets for some of their covert research projects and expeditions. Even if the group was to suddenly cease all of that, their need for runners would not end anytime soon as the IOND and Black Lodge continue their shadow war.

If membership, rather than employment, is what one is seeking, you simply need a valid SIN and a willingness to pay some healthy dues each month. The benefits of membership come in the standard variety—discounts, training, networking, etc., and even if you don't need discounts on arcane items or help figuring out the intricacies of summoning, having a network of mages to do small, legal jobs, for you or provide a little insider info on some arcane doings is valuable to all.

- I have friends in the IOND who put together preparations for me. Handy, and often pricey, little tricks to get me out of trouble.
- Kane

- Ha. Kane said he had friends. A lot of IOND members are New Century, so political jobs pop up a lot around election time. Be wary, though—politics is a dangerous game, and allegiances change quickly.
- Kay St. Irregular

THE GATE OF ISHTAR

Members (est.): 20
Dues: 500¥/year
Areas of expertise: Laws and magic, magical security, metaplanes

Public, but also extremely private, this small group spends most of their time with their collective noses in a book. When they do get out, most of the time it is sans their body, as they go off exploring some remote section of astral space or undertaking a metaplanar quest seeking answers to the mysteries of magic. The group is open to arcanists of all traditions, but the present majority is held by hermetics, with only a single shaman (that I know of) among their ranks.

The group is headquartered in Seattle, but they have properties in several other cities. These places are usually simple apartments converted for meetings or short-term stays. They tend to have excellent astral and physical security measures. Members can use any of these locations in their studies and have, on occasion, allowed their benefits to be borrowed by less-scrupulous individuals. They won't rent out the space as a safehouse to hold someone or to hide from law enforcement, but they have no problem with those who need an astrally secure place to rest their meat while busy in the astral.

Speaking of law enforcement, one of the reasons why the members won't go so far as to aid and abet an active criminal is because they like to keep the consulting contracts they have with smaller security corp offices. The members contract out their arcane investigative services to security corps that don't have enough nuyen in their contracts for permanent magical support staff and small corporations that can't afford their own magical division. This lucrative side business is the reason the group can operate with such extensive assets, despite their small size.

Membership for runners is not likely, but sometimes the only way the group can keep its lucrative contracts is to subcontract with the mage on the street. These business arrangements occasionally lead to an offer to join the society, though not often. The members tend to be very selective of new blood and usually only allow a new member if they think it can help out their own situation within the group. Internal politicking is the second most common activity within the group, the first being book reading.

Those without the Talent but with a passion for the arcane have a place within their ranks as a researcher or data archivist. The group draws many of these individuals with their special rewards program. Mundane members earn coins for their hours of service that they can turn in once each year for the opportunity to participate in a field research expedition. These expeditions travel all over the world to investigate astral phenomena that mundane members get a chance to experience via Astral Window spells.

- The expeditions are never quiet. Extractions, pissed-off spirits, and unexpected arcane outbursts occur almost every year. They have been contracting plainclothes security the last few years. So if you can resist strapping on full-body armor, you could get a tagalong gig.
- Hard Exit

VIGILANT IRON SCHOOLING HOUSE

Members (est.): 200
Dues: 50¥/month
Areas of expertise: Adept combat, adept powers

This "society" started as a small and simple training house that grew thanks to the ork that started it and the membership it attracted. The founder, Jekkik, an ork adept with a heart of gold and fists of iron, set up the school in an abandoned gym on the edge of Redmond. He invited people to train there not based on their Talent, or talent, but instead based on their need to protect themselves in the harsh world of the Barrens. He treated members with respect and taught them in turn to respect the art and the power it gave, and then to pass on their knowledge in the traditions he had given to them. Today the Vigilant Iron principle is taught in more than thirty schools around the world, most with an initiatory group of adepts at their core.

The schools have far more mundanes studying there than adepts, but all who train there are expected to give back. All members are expected to spend some time training others, whether it be helping them practice with sparring, working out, learning new techniques, supplying their fellow members with a cup of soykaf, or supporting community interventions when the trouble a student faces is greater than they can handle alone.

The schools are a fine place for a runner with a conscience to learn and give back at the same time. An adept can advance even further by initiating within the Vigilant Iron, especially since the group does not have much in the way of structure or burdensome requirements beyond continuing to teach at the schools. A member can be expelled if they fail to give back or violate the traditions of the school. Returning to good graces usually requires some act of contrition on the part of the violator. I have participated in a number of these, assigning members to tasks for me, with no compensation for them besides the ability to train at the school.

- Depending on the severity of the transgression, the acts of contrition can get wild. Dace Nu, a member in Boston, killed a student while teaching techniques beyond his skill. The contrition was an astral quest to seek the true name of a spirit of air on their native plane. The true contrition was returning, over a year later, to admit it was a task beyond his skill.
- Lyran

CORPORATE SOCIETIES

Magic is a valuable commodity. Corporations love controlling valuable commodities. Corporations love controlling magic. Simple associative logic. Every megacorporation has a magical society accessible only to citizens of the corporation, some have more than one. Many smaller corporations, be they subsidiaries of megacorporations or independent, also have their own magical societies. These groups are loyal to their corporations, well-funded, and usually full of corporate greed and backstabbing. They're a great place to look for intel on rival corps, the latest R&D that might need a little field testing, or even membership if you happen to have a good enough fake SIN. They're a terrible group to piss off. Those born with the Talent know they are a rare lot, and most have the ego to match. The problem with those egos is that when they get hurt, whether you thought it was business or not, they take it personally. I've known my fair share of runners who've ended up on the wrong side of a ritual because they took a job, ran afoul of a corp wagemage, and had the audacity to shoot at them, or even just violate their lab. Be careful.

⦿ On a similar note, I'd like to add something for the "geek the mage first" crowd. Don't make it something you are known for. It's a common enough saying on the street, but runners who make this part of their street cred are going to hit a plasteel ceiling. Corporations don't like having their really valuable toys broken, and many of them have an unspoken understanding. They know the Talent is hard to come by, and they have no desire to keep losing those with that particular gift. If they have a file on you—and they will if you're in the shadows long enough—be assured that it mentions how you handle arcane opponents. If your body count gets too high, expect that one of them will eventually unleash the hounds on you.
⦿ Winterhawk

MITSUHAMA RESEARCH UNIT 13

Members (est.): 12
Dues: None (members are Mitsuhama employees)
Areas of expertise: Combat spells, magical security

Legendary. I could leave it at that one word and many out there would understand. The name is whispered like the bogeyman, though the members walk among us. "MRU 13" appears subtly in their PAN, on a patch on their uniform, and even tattooed on their flesh. To step into their ranks is to know you've made it—and to find out you're nothing compared to those there before you.

Scared yet? If you just said "no," you're either a dragon or a fool. Which is it?

Others have said it before me and said it well, so allow me to use their words. These men and women are an elite group of fiercely loyal magical specialists and troubleshooters that also doubles as an initiatory group for its members and a research tank for magical countermeasures to threats to Mitsuhama. It has long been rumored that the earliest members of this group were the minds behind the MCT "zero-zone" policy, and the mentality remains firmly in their minds.

MCT uses this unit for testing internal security in all its aspects through the use of some very unpleasant spells—the same spells they use interrogating potentially harmful assets and vetting the loyalty of the megacorporation's most valuable staff. The group provides training to MCT's security forces to deal with arcane threats, and it acts as Special Responders when magic is used against the company. The total number of members doesn't exceed a dozen to my knowledge and though that may sound small, a single member of Unit 13 stepped into the Zen-Marsh Chemicals facility that was taken over by twenty TerraFirst! guerrillas last year, including three shamans, and walked back out unscathed.

⦿ Heal spell. Mend Spell. Good as new. Used the same trick myself with a little help from a friend.
⦿ Kane

⦿ That's twice you've said friends. /dev/, are you jacking Kane's posts?
⦿ Slamm-0!

⦿ Nope, just improving his social skills.
⦿ /dev/grrl

The biggest reason for Unit 13's continued success is their complete and utter rejection of failure. Members of Unit 13 who fail have three options; flight, death, or dishonor. Those that run are hunted. Usually by other members, but if their failure was particularly deserving of punishment, they will contract runners to shame them in death. The job is high risk, high reward, and never to be spoken of to anyone. I only learned of the tradition from a friend lost to FAB. Those who choose death are allowed to take their own life in a traditional ceremony of seppuku. This method clears their name and leaves their family with honor as well as the member's death benefits. Those that choose dishonor are stripped of their name and corporate citizenship, transferred to one of the divisional headquarters, and left to serve the corporate officers of the division in whatever capacity they desire, except one. Commonly referred to as ronin, they often operate within the shadows on orders from one of their corporate masters. The one thing they cannot do is talk of their operations for any of the corporate officers to anyone, including the other officers. The ronin will sometimes end up working both sides of a run when internal politics are at play. Be wary of this happening, as the assets on all sides seem to be exceptionally expendable during these rare events.

⦿ A member of Unit 13 was working in Amazonia a few years back. He botched the job and decided to take the flight option Lothan mentioned. During his time on the lam he worked to fix his frag-up. The Azt-Am war finally gave him the chance he needed to make it right. After he succeeded he walked straight into the MCT Latin America HQ and into an officers meeting where he set down his ceremonial mat, pulled out his tanto, and offered himself as ronin to that division. The officers voted "no" unanimously, and the mage tried committing seppuku in their meeting room but was instead shot by the CEO's bodyguard.
⦿ Mihoshi Oni

⦿ Waste of a perfectly good asset.
⦿ Thorn

- Not in their eyes. They weren't willing to give him back the honor he had lost. Traditions make MCT strong.
- Mihoshi Oni

DUNKELZAHN INSTITUTE OF MAGICAL RESEARCH (DIMR)

Members (est.): 375
Dues: 350¥/month
Areas of expertise: Laws and magic, magic artifacts

If the ASPS is the unwanted step-child of the Draco Foundation family, the DIMR is their golden-boy. Also formed from the bequests of the late Dunkelzahn's Will, this group got the funding, the flash, and the personnel, including a sitting prince of Tír Tairngire at the time, Ehran, on their Board of Directors. The DIMR is not some small magical society. They are a corporate entity that just happens to be focused solely on the study of the secrets and mysteries of magic in the Sixth World.

Joining this group means corporate employment, and for most of those reading this that is not in their future. But fear not, runners of the shadows they are not completely on the up and up. You won't gain access to any of their magical resources until you have proven yourself valuable, but they have been known to offer membership, a.k.a. "employment," to promising arcanists with the right mentality and set of skills. And yes, it requires both. Since they are a small organization (at least, relative to some of their corporate siblings) and lack that magical extraterritoriality that the megas have, they can't afford loose cannons, no matter how much mana you can sling.

Enrollment in their ranks grants you access to their libraries and lodges as well as discounts on foci and re-agents that the company buys in bulk for their research. For an arcanist with a team, they offer something else of great value: employment. As long as a team's magical talent will vouch for his mates, the company can find work for them. The work isn't always local and doesn't pay top scale, but what they lack in straight nuyen they'll make up for in access to equipment and incidentals.

- Just remember that they are still a corp. I know the whole world turns all ooey-gooey over anything with the big D's name on it, but no matter how philanthropic the dead wyrm was, he doesn't pull the strings anymore. They're a business.
- Clockwork

Since interactions with the DIMR can occur outside of membership, I'll mention that many runner teams find themselves involved with this organization when looking for some big money and trying to collect the bounties they issue on toxic shamans and blood mages. Never forget that the reasons the bounties are so large is that this is not easy money. These bounties aren't placed on the heads of the local Rat shaman who happens to be a little twitchy because of all the chems that have been dumped at his favorite trash yard. The monsters the DIMR seeks are the stuff of nightmares.

- The bounties are also only paid on the living, making it that much harder to earn. On the other hand there are less scrupulous corps, like Renraku and MCT, that offer comparable, sometimes even larger, bounties on the dead.
- Hard Exit

- A friendly reminder that those bounties can only be collected by citizens of the corporation. There are a few fixers I know who are brokering for some industrious corporate citizens trying to use the bounty offerings to pad their retirement funds. You don't get the full listed bounty, but you get a piece.
- Fianchetto

MYSTIC CRUSADERS

Members (est.): 33
Dues: None
Areas of expertise: Arcane history, Awakened threats

I have in the past had a reason to do a lot of digging into the history, culture, membership, and operations of the Mystic Crusaders for reasons I will not reveal here. They are far more than the Atlantean Foundation's magical special forces, as many think of them, and are in fact allied with the AF by a choice of their own. The relationship is far more beneficial to the Crusaders than it is to the Atlanteans. Those who look at them so shallowly never gain a full understanding of what the Crusaders are doing for the Sixth World.

When I speak of the Mystic Crusaders here, know that I am talking about the Inner Circle, the initiatory magical society that exists at the core of the overall group. The familiar uniform is worn by mundanes and Awakened alike, but only the true Mystic Crusaders bear the mark of their order, a tattoo of the crescent moon over the crossed sword and banner. Each banner is unique to one of the thirty-three members of the Inner Circle. If a Crusader dies, their banner is passed down to the next in line. Anyone caught wearing a tattoo of the order who is not a member has it flayed from their body. If the offender was part of the company, they are immediately expelled. If they are an outsider, their fate is determined by their intent. Those who are glorifying the Crusaders are flayed and left to live with the warning. Those who bear the mark but bring shame to themselves through dishonorable acts are flayed and then executed.

The Crusaders' system of honor and justice is based on a chivalric code deciphered from an ancient mystic codex. The same codex sets out their purpose in the world, and that purpose has aligned with the work of the Atlantean Foundation for years. Both groups seek to understand magic in the Sixth World, acquire artifacts of previous eras, and to keep those artifacts from being used or controlled by those they deem unworthy. Which is pretty much everyone but them. The Crusaders' efforts also fall heavily into hunting Awakened threats. Infected, toxics, blood mages, insect shamans and spirits, shedim, shadow spirits, and more are all targets for the Crusaders. Anything that harms the manasphere or is brought over into our metaplane with harmful magic can fall into the crosshairs of the Crusaders. My investigations revealed four cybermancy subjects who were permanently terminated by the Crusaders due to their unnatural taint.

Recently, the handling of events by the AF involving a few particular artifacts has created a small rift between the organizations. The AF has been apologetic, but the Crusaders are a stern lot. They do not forgive and are expecting the AF to repent and atone for their actions. In the meantime the Inner Circle of initiates has been refusing to aid in the AF's operations. Other mundane and Awakened members of the group are still working for the Atlanteans, but the heavy hitters are currently focusing on their own agenda.

The Crusaders are not a group any runner I know has ever managed to join up with. The Crusaders actually look very poorly on most runners, and you really need to prove you aren't a scumbag before they'll treat you with even a modicum of respect. The flip side of that coin is that they work in the shadows a lot and often have to call upon runner teams as backup or distractions for their operations. They can be trusted to pay what they promise, but don't expect them to treat you with the respect you think you deserve. If they feel like putting you in your place because they believe you have been disrespectful, let them. You may not like it, but it's better than turning it into a big issue, since that well may mean losing the job and being put on their drek-list. If it makes any of you ego-filled muscleheads feel better, no one looks down on you for getting shut down by one of these guys. They really are that good.

- ⦿ Runs for the MC are currently heavily calling on deckers, riggers, and technomancers, as the AF holds the leashes on most of the tech guys in the organization and are leaving the Crusaders in short supply
- ⦿ Netcat

MALAKIM

Members (est.): 11
Dues: Unknown, but possibly includes a piece of member's soul
Areas of expertise: Ares operations, insect spirits

I've only recently caught more than just whispers of this group. In the wake of some of Ares' recent troubles, the Malakim have become more emboldened in their personal vendetta against Ares and in particular Damien

Knight. Most assume by the group's name that they are an off-shoot of the Seraphim, former special operatives for Cross Applied Technologies (CATCo), and though I have no problem letting others believe rumors, I do not like to be so casual with my connective accusations. The entire group consists of eleven members. Six are former Seraphim, three are former CATCo security personnel, and the final two are independents with a strong dislike for Ares. I list them here among the corporate groups because of this former association and the fact—yes, *fact*—that they are receiving funding from former CATCo firms.

- ❂ "Strong dislike"? Raziel and Remiel HATE Ares. This pair lost their entire runner team to an op against UnlimiTech where the Johnson, an Ares boy all the way, sent them in as a test for the security team. Ares guys chewed them up but didn't kill them. Raz and Rem ran into their mates a few months later, complete with their new multifaceted eyes and chitinous skin. They're out to burn Ares to the ground for that and so much more.
- ❂ Sticks

As you can see by the presence of a pair of independents, I don't mention these fellows as simply a warning. If you have a strong enough distaste for Ares, Damien Knight, or both, they might give you a chance to enter their mystical society. They accept all practitioners and particularly favor mystic adepts. They've got some excellent training techniques for mixing the powers of spellcasting and adept abilities, and they teach their members some interesting martial magic maneuvers. The whole society tends to operate out of the same city, but they send three-man teams ahead when they move as well as leaving three-man teams behind after they've wrapped up an operation.

- ❂ The Malakim and the Fallen, both groups of former Seraphim agents, do not get along as one would expect. Though they both despise Ares, the members of the Malakim have a much more mystical outlook on things and feel the taint of cyber is the taint of Ares. They don't actively oppose the Fallen, but they won't work with them. The opposite is a bit worse. The Fallen think the Malakim have become tainted during their operations against Ares, and specifically UnlimiTech. The Fallen think the Malakim are bugs.
- ❂ Sticks

BROTHERHOOD OF THE IRON CRESCENT

Members (est.): 60
Dues: 200¥/year
Areas of expertise: Adept combat, combat spells
The Brotherhood is the initiatory corps of the 10,000 Daggers mercenary company. The group has been around since the '50s, formed by Awakened mercs looking for an edge. All Awakened contractors on long-term contracts are offered membership into this elite combat mage society, and very few turn down the offer. Members work their standard tour, assigned as part of various units in cadres of three or four members each, and they get discounts on supplies as well as access to the group's facilities. Though spread across the world and traversing many traditions of magic, the group remains tight-knit. After their tour, members are given the offer to stay part of the initiatory corps as long as they do not work for any competing mercenary agency or work against the 10,000 Daggers as an independent operator.

The Brotherhood has its base of operations and training in Istanbul. They have access to their patron company's facilities on the outskirts of the central Tokapi palace district. That means they have nice facilities, but in order to train and climb the initiatory ranks you have to go to Istanbul.

GLADIO

Members (est.): 32
Dues: 500¥/year
Areas of expertise: Adept combat
Adepts around the world know this group. Initially formed by adepts facing discrimination in professional sports leagues, they used their mystical talents and the Matrix to showcase the value of adepts in a wide range of sports through amazing live demonstrations. The success of the campaign emboldened the small group of adepts who, knowing they couldn't gather enough members to form a team sports league, pooled resources and purchased the franchise rights to the Ultimate Fighting Championship. They pulled in fighters from across the globe—adept, mundane, and cybered alike—and turned the franchise into a premiere combat sport, with fans all over the world.

Their success made the five founding members of Gladio rich beyond their imaginings back in '59 when they started, but this past year likely made them feel they'd earned every nuyen. The rekindled excitement and success of the UFC caught the attention of Aztechnology. Though the founders of Gladio were not keen on taking an offer from the megacorp to purchase Gladio Enterprises, they had little choice once the Azzies started putting the pressure on. The founding five are now a founding four, and Gladio Enterprises is now a wholly owned subsidiary of Aztechnology. The Gladio magical society and initiatory group is still intact, however, and now benefits from a reduction in dues thanks to the support of a megacorp that knows the true value of bloodsports.

- ❂ Royce, one of the founding five, was dead set against selling to AZT, but the Azzies know how to prey on the weaknesses of others. They offered the five founders a deal: a private fighting tournament between the ten best of AZT and the ten best of Gladio. The Azzies win, the five take their offer and sell the company. Gladio wins and AZT walks away from the table and has to match one percent of Gladio's profits in the upcoming year. Thanks to a whole lot of hubris, Royce and the others took the bet and chose their fighters, including Benito "The Cannon" Gomez, one of the founders. The only results that are known to anyone but the fighters involved are that AZT won and Benito Gomez, along with three other Gladio fighters, did not survive.

- ◉ Picador

- ◉ Footage of the fights supposedly exists and would be worth a small fortune to the right buyer.
- ◉ Netcat

- ◉ Azzies cheated somehow.
- ◉ Slamm-0!

- ◉ And the sky remains blue.
- ◉ /dev/grrl

PATHFINDERS

Members (est.): 21
Dues: None (members are PCC employees)
Areas of expertise: Astral phenomena, magical security

Very similar to MCT's Unit 13, the Pathfinders are the Pueblo Corporate Council's version of a magical investigation and protection service. They are fully funded by the PCC and coordinated under the Pueblo Security Force to research magical phenomena and problem-solve all arcane issues in the nation. What makes them unique is the depth to which they will investigate before they decide on a course of action. They are slow to action and believe the best course of action is always the informed, enlightened one. They believe no magical phenomena occur without a reason and that reason is best known before a solution can be considered in order to maintain the delicate balance of the magical universe.

As a part of the PSF, the Pathfinders might be expected to always be on the other side of the sights when it comes to runners, but as most corporations understand, the denizens of the shadows have their value and their place. The Pathfinders hire runners, mundane and arcane, to provide support on operations that threaten the PCC for two primary reasons. The first is operations that need to be kept at arms length from government involvement due to tribal, spiritual, or political reasons. The second involves arcane issues that do not necessarily fall within their national boundaries but still put PCC citizens at risk. The reasons for a runner to end up trading high-velocity arguments with members of the Pathfinders usually involve another megacorporation, either to keep them from discovering their involvement or to control whatever phenomena the Pathfinders seek to understand.

SECRET SOCIETIES

Do not confuse secret with evil. There are those among this list that have dark and nefarious goals, but there are also those that hide because they do not wish to be a target for the darkness they fight. Now don't get me wrong, not every group that keeps themselves hidden is either good or evil. Some of these groups simply choose anonymity to avoid the attention of authorities, not due to illicit activity but because they want to function in peace. The modern world is full of controlling powers, and control is not maintained by handing out freedoms, it's maintained by creating the illusion of freedoms. Staying in secrecy means avoiding the confining illusions.

ORDO MAXIMUS

Members (est.): 3,200
Dues: 700¥/year
Areas of expertise: Arcane history, arcane research, the Infected

As a whole, this magical society is not a true secret. Membership is a status symbol, and status symbols only work if others know of them. The reason I include them here is for the secrecy of their leadership and the rumors that always abound about the society and their dark doings. The truth is, Ordo Maximus is not some demon-worshipping cult of evil monsters trying to take over Europe and eventually the world. They are an elitist social network for the rich and powerful in Europe who want to increase their arcane power and then flaunt that power over their peers. Those members have, at times, utilized their position, and the positions of their peers, for some less-than-pleasant projects.

That's the overview. Remember it when you meet those minor nobles who are hiring you and flaunting their membership in your face. But when your hacker comes back and tells you after some serious digging they found connections between your Johnson and Ordo Maximus, remember the following.

If Ordo Maximus were an apple, it would have a rotten core. Their is an initiatory group of very powerful HMHVV-positive members who have used their power and access to the membership of the Ordo to unearth secrets and powers that should not be trifled with. And they trifle with them. This group hides within the society and is the reason they started as a secret society back in the '50s. The additional layers have hidden them further among other power-mad, egotistical megalomaniacs. But remember, when dealing with people tied to Ordo Maximus, this is the exception rather than the rule. The society numbers over three thousand, while the vampiric cabal likely numbers less than a score.

Knowing that this dark heart exists may make some think twice about joining, but membership has its privileges. First off, membership is not something you seek. It is something that seeks you. If you have a noble title, even a simple knighthood, you have the basic, but most limiting factor of membership. Next, you need money, or at least the image of money. Finally, you must have connections. Members are joining a magical social network when they first enter the fold, and if you don't have strong connections to bring to the group, what good are you?

Once you're in, they'll introduce you to a few other members near and just above your ranking and offer you a few guilds to join. The guilds are the Ordo's initiatory groups. Members can wait to select one, but they have only three moons to do so. If they haven't selected by then, they're expelled from the society. I'm not quite sure why the time limit is in place. Mundanes likely assume it has some mystical meaning behind it, but I've found nothing. It may be a mystical-seeming trial period to keep people from joining just to abuse the connections, or from trying to infiltrate the group while they still have outside connections.

VIGOR SANGUIS

Members (est.): 20
Dues: Unknown
Areas of expertise: Laws and magic, magic artifacts

There are very few paths to power as fast, or as morally despicable, as sacrifice magic. Though as I say that I must also say that this society does not present as some cloister of murderers and psychopaths looking for the fastest route to power. While operating in secret, they seek to bring enlightenment to others on the cultural and historical significance of sacrifice magic. The members of this society do not completely hide in the shadows. Most only hide their ability or at least the expressions of their ability in the shadows; the rest of their lives they live in the light, with those around them no more aware of their magical habits then they are of the weather on Venus.

This is the face the Vigor have presented to myself and the members of the magical community who are aware of their existence. My problem is I don't trust this image when it comes to those who tread such a steep slope, slick with blood. Whatever dark secrets they are hiding, they hide them well.

- I've seen signs of their darker side in both Seattle and Dallas. Suspicious deaths with links to suspected members. The local law enforcement doesn't have enough to even question them, but there are always others who might want answers beyond the law.
- Fianchetto

THE BLACK LODGE

Members (est.): 10,000
Dues: Unknown
Areas of expertise: Arcane research, dark magic, magic and politics, magic secrets

No matter how secret your secret society is, rumors of it will eventually find their way out into the world. If your organization is powerful enough, they can silence the rumors or label the rumormongers as crazies and extremists. If you are one of the most powerful arcane secret societies in the world, you can seem to disappear and reappear at will throughout history, and though the rumors keep coming back, they never stick around long enough for any fingers to be pointed at specific targets, and even when they are, you have the power to rewrite the records of those accusations.

This is the Black Lodge.

The Black Lodge has existed for longer than the current age of magic, and rumors persist that they were able to use magic in the down-cycle through elaborate and powerful rituals. Now, with magic abundant, these rituals are easier and far more powerful. There are about ten thousand members of the Black Lodge arranged in seven-person lodges over five expanding tiers (Merlin, Mordred, Morgana, Rasputin, and Nostradamus). They are spread all over the world. Every member is Awakened, and most are in positions of power. They have mundane and Awakened associates as well, and their reach is extensive. They have members in almost every major government and megacorporation in the world.

The purpose of this organization is not world domination so much as world control (a fine distinction, I grant you). They do not want to crush the world beneath their alligator-skin shoes, but instead bend the leaders of the world to their will and lead them from behind the curtain. They do not wish to be the king, only the trusted advisor. That way if things don't work out they simply let the king take the blame and disappear, only to find a new power to bring to the throne.

They have the resources and ability to get anything they want or feel they need, but their desires are curbed by centuries of knowing what it takes to stay in the shadows. They rarely bring brute force against an enemy. When they feel that force is the best or only option, it comes in one of two forms: like a whisper in the night or a crack of thunder beside your head.

The majority of the Black Lodge doesn't know what other members of the Lodge are doing as they are organized in independent cells, much like a terrorist group. It's one of the ways they maintain their anonymity and secrecy while being so large. The organization's size and power tend to make a lot of enemies, and the Lodge has two particularly powerful enemies that have kept them in check and, in recent years, given them quite a beating. The Lodge has an adversarial relationship with elves, in particular, the so-called immortal elves as well as the dragons. Over the past few years the dragons have been using their disagreements and war to bring the fight to the Lodge. Though the open war against metahumanity has been settled, the shadow war will continue. The dragons have been busy contracting runners and making sure those runners aren't working blind.

- With Hestaby in exile, the Black Lodge may be in more trouble than they realize. There are even those who are speculating that her exile is just part of a plot to put her in the shadows to break the Black Lodge and other dark societies.
- Plan 9

- Dragons do not need to be in the shadows to manipulate them.
- Frosty

THE BROTHERHOOD OF DARKNESS

Members (est.): 300
Dues: 800¥/year
Areas of expertise: Dark magic, magic artifacts

The Dark Brotherhood, as they are sometimes referred, focuses on unearthing and obtaining ancient magical artifacts and using them in their ongoing battle against evil. Founded by a group of Romanian academics after Dunklezhan's rift released shedim and other dark spirits into the world, the Brotherhood has grown more martial over the years. Their members dedicate themselves to the principles of self-denial and overwhelming force, sacrificing material wealth and raining down the Furst Wrath on the darkness in the world. Rivel Furst was the founder of the order, a mystic adept of considerable power. He died in the intervening years, sacrificing his life in the battle against dark arcane forces, but the legend of Furst has drawn a high percentage of mysads to the Brotherhood. The group is headquartered in Eastern Europe but has attracted members from all over the world. Evil knows no borders, as members say.

The group provides funding and arcane support for archaeological digs in Europe, Africa, and Asia. The Brotherhood has safehouses, which they use as meeting halls, in the UCAS, CAS, Eastern Europe, Japan, and Cape Town. Their endeavors bring them into conflict with a number of other arcane groups, in particular the Atlantean Foundation, Dunkelzahn Institute of Magical Research, and Black Lodge, all of whom also seek artifacts as well as the vampiric cabal within the Ordo Maximus.

Joining the Brotherhood provides access to the group's assets, which includes a small collection of artifacts as well as a large selection of foci that have been turned over to the society as spoils. While most people think of assets as physical, this society started in the halls of academia, and members can reach out to their fellow members for a wide range of information.

- These guys are creepy. They're cold and passionate at the same time. Working for them, with them, or against them are all almost equally unpleasant.
- Thorn

BENANDANTI XXV

Members (est.): 25
Dues: None
Areas of expertise: Arcane history, astral phenomena, draconic magic, theoretical magic

The goal of this society is to explore and fathom the mystical enigmas of the Sixth World and its Awakened inhabitants to better understand the underpinnings of magic. I read that somewhere once. If there were any magical society I would choose to elevate with my membership, this would be the one for three very important reasons.

First, the group's base of operations, the converted Clementium monastery in Prague. This place has lodging, ritual buildings, enchanting shops, and magical lodges for most magical traditions. All this sits inside a beautiful historical building. Second, they are dedicated to exploring the great mysteries of the Awakening, searching for new paths to enlightenment and magical power. Third, the great dragon Schwartzkopf. I've been around long enough to know and understand the "Never Deal with a Dragon" tenet, but as a professor of thaumaturgy at Charles University in Prague, Schwartkopf always struck me as a different sort. He's the patron of the organization and has been recruiting the best and brightest from the university for years. Along with magical instruction and initiatory support, members have access to one of the largest archives of arcane information in the world in the personal collection of Schwartzkopf.

In return, members operate as the dragon's eyes and ears in the Awakened community, while others investigate and catalogue magical phenomena, critters, and spirits for the great dragon. Schwartzkopf also uses the group for specific missions, but prefers if the members seek their own wisdom, as long as that wisdom eventually finds a home in his libraries. Society members spend the majority of their time working in the field, seeking out sites of unexplained magic events, strange spirit manifestations, and other types of magical weirdness, and reporting their findings back to their draconic master.

- Ops are frequent for Benandanti. They often involve a lot of internal doublecrossing and backstabbing as the members seek to gain the eye and favor of Schwartzkopf.
- Fianchetto

- Schwartzkopf is not a fan of his members working in that way. Or maybe he is, and is just being a typically inscrutable dragon.
- Frosty

HYSTERICAL SOCIETIES

Perception is reality to the perceiver. Skew your view far enough and you end up here. I won't say these groups do not have power, but their belief system, op-

erations, or even their very existence, gives me enough pause to place them here. It's a personal point of view. Remember, *my* perception is *my* reality.

CHILDREN OF THE DRAGON

Members (est.): 1,350
Dues: 600¥/year
Areas of expertise: Draconic magic

I would be less inclined to consider them crazy if the preliminary tale of their fairly new religion did not have so much similarity to the Christian mythos of Jesus and his sacrifice for our sins. Replace Jesus with Dunkelzahn, and sins with a lesson in hope and harmony, and you get the same sacrifice for the betterment of mankind. The group was founded by David Dragonson, and they have quite the headquarters on Prince Edward Island, with everything a dragon-spirit-worshipping cult could need. That includes arcane assistance and a strong initiatory group as well as extensive resources and a plethora of mundane followers to do a wide variety of things for them. In fact, the Children have far more mundane than

Awakened members, but the Awakened members have the vast majority of the power.

They are currently at odds with a number of other magical societies and groups, including the IOND, DIMR, and what remains of the Shasta Shamans. The Illuminates are not happy that the Children have stepped into the UCAS political arena by looking to represent the district of Prince Edward Island in the House of Representatives. The two have been digging and tossing dirt at each other since the Children first put a candidate in the race. There are some cooler minds who think the two should join magical forces, but their fundamental beliefs are so different it's hard to see them working together. Stranger things have happened, though.

The DIMR is not happy with the group's view on their mutual benefactor and hasn't been since Dragonson first started preaching his special brand of crazy. The two are also often on opposite sides of shadow operations, looking to gain control of some of the Big D's more elusive items. This includes items from his will that the Children believe belong to them based on their worship of the dead president, as well as items from his hidden hoards. Even the rumor of a Dunkelzahn relic will get some investigation by someone in this group. Faith goes a long way.

As for the remaining Shasta Shamans, things were good until Hestaby got exiled. Since then, there has been tension between the two. I don't know the exact reason, but the tension's there. Work has been finding its way into the shadows working the angles between these two dragon-connected societies.

- It's sad. Dunkelzahn is assassinated, Hestaby exiled. Seems any dragon who cares for metahumankind gets the short end of the stick.
- /dev/grrl

- Dunkelzahn is gone. Hestaby is simply working from a place closer to ours. She has accepted the punishment handed to her without question. The Orange Queen must have a plan.
- Frosty

THE TECHNOMAGICIANS

Members (est.): 300
Dues: 50¥/month
Areas of expertise: Technology and magic

This group is dangerous and feared by most average citizens as well as the corps. The society is socially open, and they aren't terribly strict on who can and can't join, or the limitations on beliefs of their members. The group includes both Awakened and Emerged individuals. I'll admit my knowledge of technomancers is limited, but I am not biased by popular opinion. Evil is in the man, not the power. Having a closely-knit group with individuals who can manipulate all the planes—astral, physical, and Matrix—is the thing of nightmares for the powerless corporate wageslave, and even for his masters.

I haven't gotten very close, but the information I have says this society accepts Awakened from all walks of life as well as technomancers. They have groups for both initiatory and submersion rites for their members. I have heard the rumors of technomages but have seen no proof of their existence in the real world.

- I scour the freak nodes often, and the closest I've seen is rumors of a runner named Zero Cool. Nothing ever claimed by him, but others have mentioned he has adept and techno abilities. He disappeared in Africa awhile back.
- Plan 9

- There are gifts of Submersion that can reflect and appear as the gifts of the adepts, and the two can be easily mistaken. That is likely the source of the rumors.
- Netcat

THE PAINTED HORSE LODGE

Members (est.): 150
Dues: 200¥/year
Areas of expertise: Mentor spirits, shamanic magic

I will not lie, I have many friends within the Painted Horse Lodge. I also have a number of acquaintances, and I am not without enemies within the society. They are a rich and diverse lot. They accept all who follow the shamanic tradition and hold themselves accountable to a mentor spirit, a spiritual guide for their magic, and that creates a nearly unmatched diversity just on its own. From the secretive snake to the psychotic shark, the spectrum is wide.

The society is based, to some degree, out of Dallas, Texas, CAS. That was the home of the original lodge, and that lodge still holds a hint of additional authority in this anti-authoritarian community of non-conformists. Lodges all over the North American continent, including down in Aztlan, are actually independent sects of the whole. Each has their own goals, fundamental drives, and even rules for joining. The only universal points are the shamanic tradition and mentor spirit. This means shamans of non-Native American traditions can join as long as their sect allows it. Currently the largest number of Lodges are in Tír Tairngire and the Pueblo Corporate Council, specifically the section that was once the Ute Nation, but Seattle recently took the lead as the largest single lodge.

The overall society espouses inclusion of the shaman in regular society. From the promotion of classic shamanic traditions, such as Bear shamans in the healing community or Wolf shamans in small specialized combat units, they work to fill in a role for shamans in every aspect of life. To see just how successful they have been, think about how comfortable you would be if a man came into your operating room post-surgery wearing a big dirty grizzly bear fur, holding a bag of supposedly mystic powders, and putting you back together.

If you're a runner, that's normal, if you're Average Joe on the street, that's off-puttingly strange. But they're working on it.

Individually, I know there are Lodges studying the various metaplanes related to Mentor spirits, metaplanes related to elements, alternate uses for alchemy, and aggressive spirit types, especially shadow spirits and shedim. I'm sure other Lodges are studying things other than these, but that is the maximum breadth of my confirmed knowledge. And as I've said before, I am a talismonger, not a rumormonger.

That said I will state with near certainty that at least two Lodges that I know of contain shamans with Toxic Mentors. These Lodges are located in Seattle and Chicago, both cities with their fair share of toxic domains. What I do not know is if the ranking members of the Painted Horse know this or not. Members that I am allied with will not bring such harmful accusations against their brethren without ironclad proof, something I do not have. Be wary.

For shamans who work in the shadows, the Painted Horse is one of the few publicly known groups that will accept you. As such an anti-authoritarian lot, they put little stake in SINs and other such "shackles of an oppressive civilization." Their words, not mine. Joining the Lodge can get you contacts in other cities, access to premium shamanic reagents, and connections to some rather extreme nature groups such as TerraFirst!.

SHASTA SHAMANS

Members (est.): 18
Dues: 1,000¥/year
Areas of expertise: Astral phenomena, draconic magic, shamanic magic

If you had asked me to speak of this society only a year or two ago, I would be telling a much different tale. With the change in their patron's status among her dragon kin and the attack on Mt. Shasta to claim her hoard, the Shasta Shamans are a magical society in ruin. The remaining shamans, less than two dozen after all the attacks, have slipped into the shadows.

Their numbers have dwindled further over the past year as the remains of the once peaceful and proud organization waged a vengeful war against the other dragons, the runners they hired, the corps they backed, and anyone who even spoke a positive word for their enemies or a negative word against Hestaby. As one would expect, they haven't been able to do all of this on their own. Despite the public absence of Hestaby, her influence has still been felt all around the world through the anger of her former followers.

- ⊘ The eyes of the Orange Queen would weep if they fell upon the remains of her children. There is a darkness among them.
- ⊘ Man-of-Many-Names

- ⊘ Toxics, one and all.
- ⊘ Lyran

MANA

Members (est.): 50
Dues: None
Areas of expertise: Combat magic, wizzer gangs

This is the fundamental definition of a street mage society. Originally formed by a ganger and stocked with Awakened recruits from other gangs or those with the Talent living in the Redmond Barrens, or other desolate strips where Mana has spread, the gang is short on resources but long on attitude. And they take care of the essentials—they don't check for SINs when you sign up, and they'll come to your aid if you make the call.

But don't think things in this group are all brotherly love. Many members are still gangers from rival gangs, and though Mana meetings at their HQ in Redmond are neutral ground no one ever accused gangers of knowing how to follow the rules. The group started in Seattle, out in the Redmond Barrens, when Argus, a former Halloweener, made a desperate call for help while his chapter of the Halloweeners was getting downsized. The response from other Awakened gangers was surprising, and to help each other out on the road to power they set their colors aside and focused on their commonality, the Talent.

The group has spread to two other cities with a considerable barrens area. The MDC and FRFZ Mana dosses are not as large as the Seattle group's, which currently has over two dozen members, but they are both approaching a dozen each. The dosses in the other cities were founded by members originally from Seattle who weren't exactly happy when they left but not to the "don't show your face around here ever again" level. Since then, they've drifted further apart, almost to the point of zero cooperation between the groups.

The Mana group in the FRFZ is having trouble with the Alley Catz, a local wizzer gang in the Aurora Warrens. Neither force is the gang-war-in-the-park type but they are definitely more apt to throw in some arcane assistance for anyone looking to hinder the efforts of their nemesis. Good to know if you're working in Denver and happen to end up in opposition of either of these arcane groups.

If you need some arcane assistance in any of those cities, Mana is the group to call. They're spellslingers for rent and they're street gangers, so they don't charge the arm-and-a-leg rates that the corporate wagemages do. I don't recommend them for important or quiet work as they aren't bought for long, and they tend to be very overt in their casting.

Don't think that any assistance or affiliation you develop with Mana comes without a price. The group has a rather poor reputation with the astral community due to their unbecoming treatment of spirits. Expect some blowback from any spirits you may summon who know of your affiliation or association with Mana, and be ready for some creative interpretations of your commands.

- ⊘ The unfettered of the mountains have begun seeking retribution from the abusers of their kin. Mana's time in the mountains will not likely be long.
- ⊘ Man-of-Many-Names

SOCIETY OF THE PHOENIX ARISEN

Members (est.): 18
Dues: 200¥/year
Areas of expertise: Magical burnout, technology and magic

In the Seattle news extensively around the New Year when their annual party in Bellevue went up in flames, the Society of the Phoenix Arisen has yet to rise from those ashes. The group took a massive hit to their core membership, and the remaining members have scattered to the wind in fear that the events were an attack and not just a freak arcane accident. I would not have included them at all if not for the whispers in the shadows of the cause of this group's explosive implosion.

For those who do not check the screamsheets, the Society of the Phoenix Arisen is a small collection of arcanists who have, for one reason or another, felt the need to mettle with the purity of their bodies by installing artificial augmentations. It is common knowledge that augmentations interfere with the channeling of mana, and that extensive augmentation can lead to burnout—the complete loss of magical potential. The Phoenix believed there was a way to mend the broken soul and help those who had lost or lessened their abilities through genetic treatments, removal or replacements of the augmentations with higher quality parts, and ritual magics to mend the spiritual connection. I cannot speak to the success of those efforts; I am simply relaying what they believed.

As for their untimely decimation, the whispers relate to a certain unnatural virus that has been making many people nervous over the past year. The Cognitive Fragmentation Disorder, or CFD, virus is a growing urban legend with terrifying stories of people's minds being taken over by the viral mind. The Phoenix believe the virus is somewhat technological in nature and their members were infected. Whether the New Year's event was an attack aimed at eliminating the infected or an attack by the infected to try to eliminate their brethren, no one seems to know, but the remaining members are now out in the shadows and potentially of interest to the rest of us.

- Really? CFD, Lothan? You're pushing the limits of your title of "the Wise." As much as all of us here are believers in CFD after 'Jack and me, thinking this can snag and use the Awakened is a stretch at best.
- Plan 9

- Don't forget the other arcane society that has a beef with these guys, the Aleph Society. Another group making the "we can heal burnouts" claim, the Aleph aren't too keen on another society horning in on their action. They could have been behind the New Year's attack. In fact, that's far more likely than some head case mage flipout.
- Lyran

ALEPH SOCIETY

Members (est.): 80
Dues: 500¥/year
Areas of expertise: Free spirits, magical burnout

So much has changed with them since Nickson called out to "the shattered souls" back in '56. He had a tome in his possession known as the Book of Gaf, that, according to him, held rituals for healing the wounds of the souls of those who had lost their connection with magic, the burnouts. He had success that most think was the result of a pact with the free spirit Gaf. Despite the crazy ideas, they were successful and popular until the mid-'60s when the group stopped taking new members and fell out of the spotlight.

Flash-forward to '69. Nickson disappears mysteriously, his trusted chief lieutenant, Sylvia LaGuardia, takes the reins and seeks to honor her mentor's memory by expanding once more. They've grown since that time, but their reputation has taken a number of serious hits over the past few years. Quite a few of the new members are some seriously violent fraggers, and they're not just normal runner violent—they're closer to psychotic. Some blame the change on the influence of Tak, a second free spirit associated with the club after they acquired the Book of Tak following its discovery in the PCC. There is supposedly a third book that the group still seeks.

- There are quite a few groups that are actively opposed to letting the Aleph's discover their third book for fear the trio, once brought together, will unleash something terrible.
- Arete

RELIGIOUS ORGANIZATIONS

Religion and magic have been tied together since man first witnessed something they could not explain and could not tell the difference between magic and the acts of the gods. Throughout history men have used religions to bring others to their cause, and if that cause happens to have someone who can heal the sick, transmute water to wine, call lightning from the sky, or control flames, then they lend that much more credence to the existence of the higher power they describe.

Now I'm not here to debate the existence of a higher power—shamans, druids, and all others who summon gifts from their mentors are proof enough of that, though the nature of the power can be (and has been) debated endlessly. What I want to talk about is the societies that have formed around religions since the Awakening and the changes that have occurred in those that existed long before magic returned to the world.

ORDER OF ST. SYLVESTER

Members (est.): 200
Dues: Tithing expected, but amount set by members
Areas of expertise: Arcane history, astral phenomena, Catholic Church, magical theory

I'll make the history lesson brief. The Catholic Church was vehemently opposed to magic when it first returned to the world. They eventually changed their thinking and accepted magic, considering it neither good nor evil; they instead said that good and evil was within the person not the power. To any who lived in the faith during the tumultuous era of the '10s and '20s I apologize for the brevity when discussing such a trying time.

The Order of Saint Sylvester, also known as the Sylvestrines, is a Catholic Church-sanctioned society of the Awakened who work to promote an understanding of magic within the context of church's teaching. The Awakened priests and monks of the order, all theurgists, are dedicated to the use of beneficial magic and investigating magical phenomena for the church's Vatican Library. They are especially interested in those events that demonstrate a connection, even if only a loose one, to places or gatherings of the Catholic Church. Their investigations can be guided by their own interest, an order from the Vatican, or at the request of a local bishop. The initiatory members of the Sylvestrines are also tasked with hunting down arcane enemies of the Church, in particular Infernalists, those that seek their power through the worship of dark forces.

Obviously this is not the arcane society for shadowrunners, so when looking at them we should look at the value a devout religious group could have to low-life runners. Their ubiquitous presence, their extensive knowledge and understanding of things Awakened, and their need for distance from actions that may tarnish the reputation of the Church all could be of possible use to shadowrunners.

The Catholic Church has a presence in every nation in the world, and has often been in place for longer than the nation itself has existed. Though nations no longer run the world, they are the borders that determine legality, the governments that monitor the masses that the megacorporations do not employ but seek to exploit, and the power structure most easily influenced through the religious devotion of their population. This means a group like the Sylvestrines can be found anywhere and move anywhere in the world. Moving in some places that are not fond of the Catholic religion or across borders with artifacts or information that would normally be controlled by the government for the betterment of its citizens is not easy. The Catholic Church, and especially the Sylvestrines in their work of seeking artifacts, are experts at using their worldwide network to move objects or people. Smuggling for the Vatican is full-time employment for several runner teams I know, many of whom are contracted through, or run by, a Sylvestrine monk.

> ● The Sylvestrines operate frequently in Aztlan thanks to the government's anti-Catholic policies. The Catholic Church there is an interesting mix of conservatives and liberals who argue over how they should act within the borders of Aztlan. The conservatives seek to obey the Aztlan government and avoid confrontation. The liberals are where you find the Sylvestrines, and they are outspoken

and active in opposing some of the less-mentionable rituals of the national Neo-Aztec religion.
> ● Picador

Being connected to or having friends within the Sylvestrines can help you get access to a vast library of arcane knowledge. The Sylvestrines are the keepers of the largest Theurgist library in the world, which also includes a library of hermeticism that was begun in the 12th century, well before the full return of magic to the world. As the Vatican's primary seekers of all things Awakened, the Sylvestrines have also consolidated the church's doctrines on parazoological creatures. The Sylvestrines have written well-evidenced papers on the appearances of Awakened species before 2011. Their research points to complex rituals or natural events that concentrated the thin mana into spikes great enough to activate the metagene in certain species. The papers are all quite interesting. More interesting to runners, though, is the vast library of information on paracritters to which the Sylvestrines have access. And possibly the greatest part of their arcane library is the concentration of data on magical phenomena. Gathered by the Sylvestrines themselves as well as the runner teams they have hired, these data cover everything from spontaneous spirit summoning to fovae and alchera, as well as everything in between.

> ● The records are not completely digitized yet, but getting a skilled decker into their system could get a team a nice chunk of paydata.
> ● Lyran

The work done by the Sylvestrines is often not entirely legitimate in the eyes of all people. That means that in order to maintain the proper image of the church and the Order, the Sylvestrines must rely on the denizens of the shadows. The work is often low-paying, but having favors owed by the Sylvestrines can be far more valuable than nuyen. Churches make great bolt holes, often with decent wards and security, especially if Sylvestrines or other church-sanctioned arcanists are present. Escorting smuggled products or people, assisting in studying magical events in hostile areas, providing Matrix and physical security for Sylvestrine operations, and a plethora of other opportunities are available if you have a Sylvestrine who will pick up when you call.

The Order of St. Sylvester is not one single initiatory group. It is too large for that. All members who initiate within the Order follow the same patron spirit, the Archangel Michael. This is the same patron as another smaller Order within the church that is housed under the Order of St. Sylvester in order or to provide concealment for this conspiratorial sect. The Order of the Temple, or Knights Templar, are a sub-sect of the Sylvestrines hidden within the ranks of the greater group. The Templars are a far more militant and martial sect that not only seek to discover and study magical phenomena but also work to undermine those organizations, religions, corporations, and governments that promote, study, participate, or even dabble in magics deemed unacceptable by the Catholic Church. This includes blood and sacrifice magic, toxic magic, summoning of insect spirits, necromancy, inhabitation or possession magic, and any magic that damages or shifts the aspect of mana in opposition of the Catholic Church. They are zealots, and one would be wise to be wary of employment from a zealot.

- ⦿ The Knights rarely work directly with runner teams. If a job points to the Order of St. Sylvester but stinks of sacrificial diversion, you are likely working for a Templar and not a standard Sylvestrine. That said, make sure you just plan well and make it through while completing the job, because having your name on a Templar's dreklist is bad news.
- ⦿ Bull

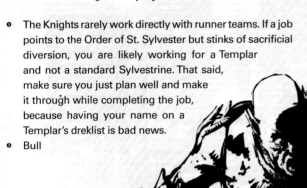

JAMIL ISLAMYAH

Members (est.): 250
Dues: None
Areas of expertise: Covert magic, fundamentalist Islam, magical theory

This Islamic brotherhood of Awakened is looked upon as a cursed abomination against the Muslim faith. Fundamentalist Muslims do not believe magic has a place in their religion. The Jamil Islamyah commit their lives to their own redemption as they devote their Talent and their lives to an existence as mujahideen in service to Allah and their brothers in faith.

The leaders of this sect believe the best way to fight the enemies of Islam is using their own dark tools against them, but those tools must be controlled. Members of Jamil Islamyah work together and initiate in a "darasa" (class) of three to nine members lead by an "ulema" (scholar). They operate as a team at all times, traveling the world on missions to advance the teachings of Islam. The position of ulema is filled by any remaining members of a darasa once its numbers drop below three. Due to the kinship members foster in their years together, there is never an overabundance of ulema.

The members operate in secret and though they are often assigned to protect important members of the Islamic faith, those faithful are kept unaware of the guardianship of their cursed brethren. Currently the society has close ties with the Arabian Caliphate and has acted as special operations units for the government under the same veil of secrecy, while also supplementing some of their units in a more overt fashion.

- Though Lothan is nice enough to mention the mujahedin sect of Jamil, he leaves out the assassins that play an important role in this group. These members are all loners, often former ulema or members who just couldn't play nicey-nice with others. They're killers one and all who make every killing in Allah's name. No innocent casualties allowed. Precision always.
- Thorn

CRACKING THE BONES

Members (est.): 300
Dues: 200¥/year
Areas of expertise: Astral phenomena, conjuring, vodou magic

A society in the loosest of terms, this coordination of voodoo practitioners is more of a religious alliance. They gather in small groups (none I know of has more than seven members) throughout the CAS, UCAS, and Caribbean League. Not to anyone's surprise, the greatest concentration of members is located in New Orleans, Louisiana, CAS. The city has several different sects of the Bones, each with their own agenda and rules. The society as a whole is very loose, with sects answering to the larger group based on their own desires or the requests of other groups. If a member wants to visit another group's meeting, they're more than welcome, but no group has the ability to order other members to attend their planned, or unplanned, sessions.

- If you want to roll in on a meeting with this group this is a great way, especially since they have very little issue with mundanes and frequently have a lot of voodoo groupies at their meetings, which often closely resemble parties.
- Kane

The society's openness can be very useful for traveling around the continent or to the islands of the Caribbean League. With little effort a member can usually get contact information for another member near where they wish to travel, and all members of Cracking the Bones welcome their brethren. The visits also often come with a trade-off between the members as the traveler can be asked to help in rituals, summonings, or watching over the body of an astral traveler while they are around. Impromptu meetings and gatherings also occur when a visitor is in from out of town to share information, whether that means stories, formulae, spirit names, or metaplanar news. I don't know of any sects within any of the Native American Nations, but there are groups in Seattle, Denver, and Caracas, as well as one in CalFree, a few major cities and several rural areas of the CAS and UCAS, and all the major islands of the Caribbean League.

The group's members are a great source for intel on any spiritual or astral happenings in their vicinity or major events around the continent. They also commune with spirits so often they have a finger on the pulse of many of the metaplanes. Getting a straight answer from any houngan (a practitioner of voodoo) is not the norm. Expect answers from them to come in the form of riddles, vagaries, and symbolistic stories. Fun for them, frustrating for someone on the clock or lacking the patience of a saint. Be prepared if you seek answers from them.

- And don't try threatening them. Life and death are trivial concepts to a houngan, and they see death as gaining free rein over the spirit realm, which is not something they particularly fear.
- Arete

LOCAL GROUPS

I made a few calls to my people in sprawls all over the world and asked a few poignant questions about the arcane societies in their strip of the sprawl. Some of them were good enough to connect me straight to the source, but I made sure to get a little unbiased information before I called to get it straight from the horse's, or in many cases jackass's, mouth. I'm gonna try and keep these tight but I invite anyone else who may have experience with these groups to post. I'll drop the sprawl in with the names so you can skip over any city you don't need to know about.

PLANESTRIDERS (DEECEE)

Members (est.): 22
Dues: None official, though members are expected to contribute to the society's well being.
Areas of expertise: Astral phenomena, metaplanes

Led by a shaman who answers to Amber, their focus is on astral exploration via projection. They believe understanding the metaplanes to be a way of enhancing one's consciousness. Amber also believes the planes may contain other versions of our own. She has dedicated her group to explore the planes thoroughly. She speaks with the tone and lilt of a vapid debutante, but her words are full of wisdom and knowledge. All of the Planestriders make great guides when heading out to a known metaplane, and they will frequently seek out teams of other trustworthy magi to accompany them on journeys to volatile, dangerous, or unknown metaplanes.

- There are those in the Striders who claim knowledge of paths for mundanes onto the metaplanes. I'll believe it more when I talk to a mundane who has been there.
- Kay St. Irregular

SOCIETY OF HAWKS (MANHATTAN)

Members (est.): 95
Dues: 1,000¥/month
Areas of expertise: Famous mages and shamans, magic artifacts, magic theory

Members of this arcane society, full of Manhattan's richest mages, make the pages of the MDC's screamsheets almost daily with their lavish personal lives. Naturally, they rarely cross paths with the likes of us. The group has both money and magic, but as one can expect that means the members are always trying to one-up their rivals or working to keep up with the most upper of the upper crust.

The society demonstrated their monetary power with the purchase and renovation of Belvedere Castle in Central Park, Manhattan from the MDC early on in the corporate consortium's existence. They allow certain areas of the building to be rented for private events and host many of their own galas on the premises as well. The members use the bulk of the castle for holding private meetings and housing the collections of artifacts and antiquities that the members want to show off. The castle does not hold every piece owned by the Hawks and only rarely holds their most prized pieces,

but it's still quite valuable and is often targeted by other organizations and even other members of the society.

- Security is above average most of the time and gets upgraded during major events. Expect all three aspects—magical, mundane, and Matrix—to be covered, and plan accordingly.
- Ma'Fan

- Heard you had some trouble there a few years ago. The security that good?
- Mika

- I would have had no problem. The team I was working with lacked the level of subtlety I am used to.
- Ma'Fan

DEAD WARLOCKS (MERSEYSPRAWL)

Members (est.): 13
Dues: 250¥/year
Areas of expertise: Combat magic, wizzer gangs

There are those who would call them a wizkid gang, but there is nothing childlike about this gang. The members of this gang are vicious and unrelenting in their search for personal power and the advancement of the gang's place in the hierarchy of the Merseysprawl underworld. When they started cutting out their slice of the underworld, Johnny Dee, their current leader, honed the gang to a razor's edge. With a combination of brutality and precision, the gang worked their way to the top of the heap in Merseysprawl and now act as a council of kings over the underworld of this UK sprawl. Their numbers have grown over the years, but they maintain the same limit on the society's official initiatory group and the official council. Other members wait in the wings and jockey for any position that happens to become vacant.

- The newest member is one of the many SURGEd in the Merseysprawl. A fox-like changeling with an affinity for manipulating the minds of others. There are rumors among the lower ranks that he got his spot using his best tricks. Proof of that could lead to a major play in the Warlock's ranks.
- Chainbreaker

- The lower ranks of the gang have lost three members in the past few months. The orks of Liverpool are really putting some pressure on them. It's more of a shaking-the-tree move than a try at chopping it down, but the Warlocks are going to have to answer the call. I wouldn't want to have tusks in Liverpool in the near future.
- Thorn

HERMITIC ORDER OF THE AURIC AURORA (DOWNTOWN, SEATTLE METROPLEX)

Members (est.): 25
Dues: 200¥/month
Areas of expertise: Defensive magic, hermetic magic, wizzer gangs

Magical scholars one and all, the HOAA seeks to advance the study of magic as a positive force in the universe. Obedient to a higher moral code (as they believe all hermetics should be), the Order actively opposes the harmful or abusive use of magic. They are a limited order with a maximum of twenty-five initiatory members at any one time. The members occupy three rankings, called Circles. The Triumvirate, a Circle of three, leads the Order. The Ennead, a Circle of nine, has members that represent the four elements, the fifth element of man, and the four cardinal directions. The final Circle of thirteen has no title.

The HOAA often interacts with runners when assistance is needed in one of their scholarly endeavors, especially their efforts to prevent the formation of wizzer gangs, as they see them to be a path to magical abuse as the members use their skills to fight or oppress others. While the members believe magic should not be used to harm they still understand the world can be a dangerous place. They are not a rich organization and will offer favors, often in the form of defensive spells and preparations, or counterspelling assistance for runners who help them out. Remember their belief system when you have casters on your team. They've been known to freely counter violent spells no matter who is casting them.

The Order is based out of Blue Moon, a lore store near Pacific University. The store is also the home of Dylan Pike, the current leader of the Order. The HOAA lodge is in the basement with a meeting hall and ritual area. Members often locate potential recruits and offer training and membership when it is available, guiding those who could become lost to the power of abusing magic. Pike always has two apprentices that he personally trains. The pairing is a test. He watches for rivalry between the two and casts out any student who abuses his gifts to get ahead. The plan has built him quite a cadre of unhappy former students.

- The Aurics have a lot of bad blood with the Order of Merlyn, a wizzer gang in Seattle. The Merlyns have recruited most of Pike's cast-offs. Word on the street is a coming strike by the cast-offs with Pike as the target.
- Sounder

- That's been the word for half a decade now. If the Merlyns go after the HOAA, expect it to be hits all over the place. They know hitting other members of the Order will hurt Pike far more than going after him.
- Lyran

THE RAT PACK (MANHATTAN)

Members (est.): 14
Dues: None, though members are expected to make contributions from proceeds earned through societal activities
Areas of expertise: Covert magic, healing magic, shamanic magic

This coven of urban shamans believes they embody the last remaining wilderness and powers of the natural world amidst the glass-and-steel canyons of the rebuilt corp enclave of the Manhattan Development Consortium. Where once they were exclusively followers of Rat, now the group contains members who are not Rat shamans. All are still devoted to Rat as a patron, and they seek to help the squatter community that has grown around their base, located in an old buried Broadway theatre. The group provides extensive aid to the local community, especially in the form of curative magic. To support the people in their area of the underground, they sell their services to others in need. They also make the most of their support funds with smuggling, black-market sales, and guide services through the underground tunnels, sewers, and abandoned subways. They are an excellent resource for any runner working in, under, or around the MDC.

- But don't get on their bad side or dare insult them and ask for help. They've been known to instruct their spirits to guide those folks right into trouble or get them lost in the maze of tunnels beneath the MDC.
- Fianchetto

SISTERHOOD OF ARIADNE (SNOHOMISH, SEATTLE METROPLEX)

Members (est.): 13
Dues: 450¥/month
Areas of expertise: Divination, healing magic, shamanic magic

They could be qualified as a religious group as well since they only allow true followers of Wicca into their ranks but they are a group limited only to Seattle. The Sisterhood has thirteen members, a standard coven. They follow the traditions of Wicca and devote themselves to the protection of the Earth, upholding the rights of women, and the beneficial use of magic. They allow no harmful use of magic unless in defense of self, sister, or Mother Earth and even then you will not see a Sister throw lightning or fire.

For those on the street the Sisters are a source of healing, divination, and female empowerment. Men will always pay for any services by the Sisters but women receive them free or at a discount depending on how the Sisters feel about them. Potential young witches are almost always treated for free and invited to stay with a

Sister if they need a home. This occasionally brings the Sisters into contact with runners in search of an executive's daughter or when a Sister feels the need for a little more support in protecting a budding young witch.

- They aren't keen on helping men at all. Definite feminists, some more than others. Make sure you know which witch is which.
- Glitch

THE PERIPHERY

When you do not have the Talent, being a part of any gathering of those who do can leave you feeling uncomfortable, to say the least. They can see another world, they speak to beings unseen, and they can draw upon energies to do amazing things. Those things, combined with the holier-than-thou attitude that almost all of the Awakened have, tends to leave everyone else feeling ostracized for one reason or another. That discomfort does not prevent the need for those with experience beyond the realms of the arcane or the desire for those with that experience to look to magic for an advantage.

Like any organization, most magic societies have the basic tasks that need to be taken care of by people with a range of skills. Deckers take care of the Matrix, mundane muscle keeps an eye on the physical plane, augmented muscle intimidates people in peacefulness, and a few people with the right skills work the reception desk or keep the books. So right there, you have some possible openings for non-Awakened people. Beyond that, the jobs they hire shadowrunners for may have arcane goals, such as retrieving artifacts or extracting talented mages, but the arcane slant of the goal doesn't mean the basic skills of a good runner team are not needed. Punching critters in the face, hacking security cameras and locks, and sneaking in somewhere you're not supposed to be all remain very much part of the job, meaning the non-Awakened members of the team still have their roles to play.

Those who lack the Talent are often allowed as periphery members of most societies. Public groups almost always have these positions. Magical groupies usually fill the spots and pay just to be around the Awakened, but runners who join their teammates in a society can gain access to meetings and be present as security. They may also get jobs from the society that they normally wouldn't give to a runner team unless they trust them, be hired on as security for other members who don't have such rough and tumble associates, or even act a volunteers to practice new spells, rituals, or preparations on.

- Magic causes enough problems when it goes right. There's no way I'd ever let myself be a test subject. Can't they just buy a whole bunch of bunnies or something?
- Cayman

- That's mean!
- Chainmaker

- Better them than me.
- Cayman

As a member, they are still expected to pay dues and attend meetings when asked. When a meeting is about rituals or arcane work, the mundanes usually get the night off, but runners are a different story. These activities usually require a little extra security, and that's when they bring in members of the society who are runners (if they have any). One exception is runners who are part of another society. Sometimes teammates do not have the same belief structures and thus join different societies. There aren't many societies, even public ones, that allow members of other societies to attend their less-than-public meetings.

DARK MAGIC

He rode the tube home that night. There was no need to take a more private form of transportation. The meager possessions he was carrying home would not arouse suspicion, unlike what he had carried home on so many other nights over the last few months. He held the small packages of soy and other essentials on his lap, trying to contain his excitement. His anticipation. While he was annoyed at having to go out to gather such a mundane thing as food when he was so close to achieving his goal, it was a necessity that couldn't be avoided. It would do him, and his beloved, no good if he were to die of thirst or hunger before his triumph. He thought back on everything that had led up to this point, all of the work.

No one sat near him. Not another person sat in the same rail car as the mag-lev train sped through the city. That was fine; he had become quite used to solitude. At least, solitude from other people. His home was much the same. There was no one around anymore. At one time, when he was just beginning, there were many people. Vagrants, homeless, SIN-less, the dregs of society. That had been a boon in those early days—it was why he had selected the location he had for his home. None of those wretched souls were around anymore. A good many of them were not around because of his actions, but the rest had left of their own volition. He supposed that the drifters protected their own. When word got around of the disappearances, the rest had fled. That was when things had gotten more difficult for him. The work had to continue, to be sure, but it had been slow and difficult. He had ventured far and wide to take people back to his home. Transportation was the largest issue. He could not be caught with them; that would ruin everything. He also took no joy in the act, despite what some people might think. It was something that needed to be done—it was for his beloved after all—but he did not have to enjoy it. He hated it most when they screamed, when they struggled. Silence. How he learned to enjoy silence.

Getting off at his stop, he started his walk back home, picking up as much pace as he dared. He yearned to get back home as soon as he could, but he did not want to arouse suspicion. There were still eyes here. People could be watching. As he moved to areas of greater desolation, his pace quickened. Not far now. He would be reunited with his beloved.

With shaking hands he opened the door to his home and descended the stairs. The warmth, the silence wrapped him like a comforting blanket. He felt at ease. With confident strides he headed for the inner chamber. Soft moans came from the sticky sacks that lined the hallway and filled the offshoot chambers. He paid them no mind. Soon enough they would be finished. Soon enough they would join his family. All his thoughts were focused on his beloved.

There she was. Hanging in that sticky, gooey sack at the other side of the room. Sweaty, matted hair covered her face. He walked over to her and brushed the hair away to reveal the bulging, distended features underneath. His hand on her abdomen felt the pulsing and writhing changes happening underneath. It was almost time. He absolutely quivered in anticipation. Soon it would be done. Soon they would be united, and he would feel complete. Soon he would see in the flesh the one he had so yearned to see since that first day she had spoken to him so long ago.

His beloved. Mother.

POSTED BY: WINTERHAWK

I love magic dearly but not unreservedly. I've always held that true love means acknowledging your beloved's flaws instead of ignoring them. So it's time to explore the darker side of magic, the things that make up many of our nightmares. You're not likely to run into this stuff every day, or maybe not even anytime soon, but this stuff is out there, somewhere, waiting in the darkest corners. Should it find you, the information I'm about to give you could save your life.

THE DARK ARTS

I know most of you probably think that all magicians are the same—mysterious, crazy, power-hungry, and/or evil. That may be how the sims tend to portray it, but it is not reality. Real magicians are normal people with their own individual sets of morals and values. Most of them have lines of ethics and morality that they absolutely will not cross. But there are some—a very few, thankfully—that choose to leave those morals and reservations behind and pursue a path of power that disregards the costs. Heed my warning, though—these types aren't anything like those sims, either. They're *much* worse.

There are areas of knowledge and sources of power in the world that magicians of any tradition—from the tribal shamans living in the wilderness to the Ph.Ds at MIT&T—can agree are extremely dangerous or downright evil. These can come from within humanity, where magicians draw power from the most awful and debased emotions and acts that metahumanity can produce. Or possibly even worse, they can emerge from a source of power outside of metahumanity altogether—entities from beyond the physical realm. Entities with their own entirely alien, and all too often malevolent, intentions.

What makes these individuals so dangerous is that they have left some—and in many cases *most*—of their metahumanity behind in the pursuit of their agenda. The sources of power and magical practices they employ are universally derided because they provide no collective benefit to metahumanity. They are inherently destructive. To these individuals, though, they are a means to their ends, and they do not see or care that they risk bringing ruin to us all.

- Laying the doom and gloom on a little thick, aren't you?
- Sticks

- You may think the language dramatic, but I can say from personal experience that you cannot underestimate the danger that these kinds of magicians pose.
- Ecotope

FALLING INTO DARKNESS

So why does someone begin practicing one of these repulsive forms of magic? Does the motive matter? Perhaps. By examining the most common situations and motivations that lead a magician to take up these dark arts, we may allow you to better anticipate their actions and counter them. Below I've listed some of the most common reasons for Awakened people to turn to some form of forbidden magic.

INSANITY

Plainly put, some of them are simply crazy. For any number of causes, the person has lost their grip on reality. When asked, a mad magician may give any number of reasons for why they practice a dark art, but in the end the root cause is their madness. For some forms of magic, insanity seems to be a prerequisite. I do not see how anyone but a madman would practice something such as Insect magic.

- I can add that one of the most dangerous aspects of a crazy mage is their unpredictability. Because their mind is off the chain, you can never know for certain what they're going to do. I did a job once to uncover the source of some hits against corp property. I tracked it down to this crazy toxic mage who was making some homemade explosives. When my team moved in to take him out, he just turned around and chucked a fireball into the whole lot and blew himself—and four of my team—to kingdom come.
- DangerSensei

VENGEANCE

Many of those who practice dark magic are doing so to right what they see as a wrong or some great injustice in the world. While it is often the result of something traumatic that happened to them or a close family member, others may be driven to vengeance just by observing (perceived) injustice being done to others.

- This is also the case of a villain being the hero of their own story. These guys *think* that they are the good guy, and that any questionable actions they take are justified or necessary to achieve the greater good that they are working toward—"good" being a relative term here.
- Jimmy No

- If they believe they are working for some cause, they can sometimes be reasoned with. If you can convince them that what they are doing really isn't going to help in the long run, you can talk them down. It doesn't work very often, though. Most dark mages motivated by revenge are so obsessed that they won't listen to anything that doesn't get them closer to their goal. They only hear what conforms to their conception of reality and ignore the rest.
- Lei Kung

POWER

Though it is a sad reflection on metahumanity as a whole, some individuals will do anything—sacrifice any person, leave behind any morality—if it means gaining power for themselves. These individuals don't care where their power comes from or how it is achieved. They have only their selfish goals and desires in mind.

- Sounds normal to me.
- Kane

THE DARK TWIN

Many magicians believe they are guided by a mentor spirit—a perfect embodiment or personification of some personality aspect or animal. Some even believe that their magical abilities were bestowed on them by their mentor for the express purpose of carrying out its will.

- You speak as if you doubt this truth. There are those of us who know this to be true.
- Lyran

- Let's not turn this into a religious or philosophical discussion. What cannot be denied is that magic in the Sixth World is intimately tied to what a person believes to be true. What they believe becomes reality in their magic, so it is true in pretty much all the ways that matter.
- Ethernaut

In some cases, when an Awakened person embraces their new path of magic, they lose contact with their mentor spirit—either it leaves them or they leave it. In many other (fascinating) cases, the mentor remains but is changed, just as the metahuman performing the magic has changed. In the same way that the magician practicing these dark arts reflects all the worst, undesirable qualities that we wish were not part of us, the patron spirit of the fallen one begins to exhibit the darker side of its nature. It's not that the patron spirit has fundamentally altered its nature, just that different qualities come to the fore. If the spirit was a light-hearted trickster before, it may become a spiteful and vindictive prankster who delights in others' misery. A spirit that embodied fierce independence may become aloof and paranoid. Which corruption came first, the mentor or the protégé, is a chicken-and-egg question—unimportant in light of the plain fact of their existence.

TAINTED SPIRITS

In the same way, the common types of spirits known to all magicians—earth, air, fire, water, beasts, man—take on a form to reflect their summoner. The appearance of a spirit when manifested becomes more fierce, violent, feral, or corrupted when called forth by a dark conjurer. Oddly enough, the tendencies and actions of the spirit also reflect the more aggressive posture of the summoner.

- Is he talking about the *personality* of the spirit? I thought they just carried out the will of the wiz giving them orders.
- /dev/grrl

- Only partially true, but not so simple. A spirit reflects the will of its summoner, and they are given commands that they must obey. But the way in which they carry out those actions involves some "personality" (which may not be the exactly right term, but is close enough for our purposes) of the spirit itself. Two summoners may order a spirit to defend them, and one spirit will do so passively, but another will do so aggressively, with deadly force. Spirits are not drones, and it is dangerous to think and treat them as such.
- Axis Mundi

PATHS OF DAMNATION

I've used the term "dark magic" as an umbrella term, but let's take a closer look at the various and distinct forms of forbidden magic that have significant followers in the Sixth World today.

TOXIC MAGIC

The imprudence and carelessness of today's corporations continues to cost the natural world around us.

Undeniably, magic is linked very strongly to the natural world, and when the natural world—through technological impropriety—is damaged, magic is damaged along with it. While most magicians find this change vile, there are those who embrace it and find strength in it. Toxic mages have learned to harness the twisted magic in the polluted places of the world. They seek to spread that corruption, or even strike back at those who would cure it. Be most cautious of encountering them in wasteland areas. Their ability to draw magical sustenance from the area, while your magic may well be limited, puts them at an extreme advantage.

BLOOD MAGIC

Although brought to the notice of the wider world by the mages of Aztlan, the ability and practice of drawing magical power from violent actions is not exclusive to their traditions. Many others have their own forms, and unfortunately the knowledge and practice of this method of power continues to draw followers. Not just followers who seek short-term gain, but those who make it their life's work to perfect the techniques involved in this barbaric ritual. Blood mages and adepts require the mana energy "burst" of a violent sacrifice in order to draw their additional power, so preventing this activity will critically weaken them. Beware a foe that has drawn on this wellspring of power, though; they can wield a level of magical potency that you will not see anywhere else.

INSECT MAGIC

Possibly the most bizarre of all those who operate in the dark are the ones who choose to collude with the extraplanar entities called insect spirits. Anyone need simply search for Universal Brotherhood or Chicago Containment Zone on the Matrix to see the kind of destruction this brings. Despite this, there are still those that for any of the reasons I previously mentioned—and others, including a deep and twisted curiosity—choose to practice this form of magic and ultimately do the bidding of these alien entities. Insect spirits require a metahuman host in order to remain anchored on our plane, and the process of inhabiting the metahuman vessel takes many hours. Thus, the insect shaman will find a secure location to form the "hive," where victims are taken for implantation of the insect spirits. Hives must be found and destroyed at all costs, though beware, as the shaman and any spirits summoned thus far will defend it with fanatical abandon.

MALEVOLENT SPIRITS

The final category of threat comes from free spirits—those who have broken the bonds of their summoner, or never had one—who have remained on this plane to do harm. To be clear, many free spirits are either be-

nevolent or at least not overtly aggressive; only a few are out-and-out dangerous. Those that are dangerous, though, are very much to be avoided. The methods and abilities of these entities vary greatly, depending on their needs. Shadow spirits seek to manipulate from afar so they can feast on the negative emotional energy caused by their machinations. Shedim inhabit the bodies of the deceased and seem to seek nothing less than the destruction of all life.

This is only a brief summary of what you may encounter. Be watchful, study up, and when it comes to facing any of these dark threats, remember that discretion is the better part of valor.

THE UNKNOWN

- Opening up this section for a discussion on anything magical or mystical in nature that you've seen or have some information on that has no current explanation. Let's see if we can shed some light on it.
- Glitch

- I've got a good one. I took a job in Malaysia a few months back where I saw the strangest thing in the Awakened world, I swear to ghost. I was working for a fairly wealthy and prominent person in the country (I won't say who, of course), doing an investigation and counter-hit job. It seems this prominent (married) man had a mistress (no surprise) who was also pregnant (oops). Shortly before I took the job, something very strange happened to this mistress. She was out in the jungle at some out-of-the-way resort (perfect place to stash a mistress you don't want found), and one morning woke up to find that her unborn baby was dead. What was most unusual was the way the baby died. It looked like something sucked the little bugger's heart right out of the womb. Right out of the body. There was a small puncture mark on her belly (she was sleeping at the time) unlike anything I had ever seen. Of course this was considered suspicious, but my employer couldn't go to any legit authorities, otherwise he'd have to explain who this woman was and how that baby got there in the first place. So I get called to look into the matter and find out if it was a hit by a rival, blackmailer, or what.
- Pistons

- That's odd on a couple different levels. First, the method of death is highly unusual, that's a given. But second, the fact that the child was *killed* before any sort of communication or notification doesn't make any sense. If someone found out about this guy's bastard child and wanted to use it against him, the last thing they'd do is kill it.
- Haze

- Maybe it was a mistake? They were trying to extract a blood or DNA sample and screwed up?
- Mihoshi Oni

- That would be the fuck-up of a lifetime.
- Haze

- No, there was no mistake. The doctors were very clear that the removal of the heart was very intentional. A lot of blood was pulled out as well.
- Pistons

- Something to do with ritual sorcery?
- Ethernaut

- The mages I paid to look into it said there was a strange magical signature they couldn't identify, so I started thinking about magic. I'll skip all the dead ends I looked into and get right to the good stuff. I finally got a lead when I described the case to this old-school witch doctor woman. She had the idea to check some of the other little villages out in the jungle to see if any other women had their babies eaten. Turns out she was right—they had.
- Pistons

- Wait, there was more than one case of babies being eaten right out of their mother's womb?
- Nephrine

- Sadly, yes. So we're staking out this village that has a pregnant woman who hasn't had her baby eaten yet. We watch the place for three days, but the night of the fourth something finally happens. I'm dozing, almost asleep, when my AR flashes a warning from a perimeter sensor I'd set up. I send over a surveillance drone to the location and bring the visual feed up in my AR. I was not expecting to see what I saw. There, striding in the dim moonlight, is a naked, butt-ugly old woman. Just as I'm wondering what the hell is going on she sprouts bat wings from her back and—I shit you not—her torso fucking rips off of her legs and flies off. Well, I'm still in shock from what I saw when another sensor alarm goes off in my AR—this one for the inner-most motion sensor in the bedroom of the pregnant woman. So I grab my guns and haul ass into the house.
- Pistons

- That's unlike any spirit or critter I've ever heard of, and I know quite a few.
- Axis Mundi

- Once inside I get a better look at the top half of the thing. Like I said, it had bat wings, wicked claws, and a long, thin snake tongue. I didn't wait around to engage this thing in conversation or anything, I just flipped to full auto started

putting bullets into it. Thing is, I didn't really seem to be *hurting* it, and I had to roll away from a couple nasty swipes from those claws. Once the witch doctor showed up and starting slinging mojo, the thing buggered off. Right away she asks me if I've seen its legs. Good thing my drone was still tracking them back where it left them, so we hoofed it over there as quick as we could.
- Pistons

- Its legs were still walking around and shit? Freaky.
- /dev/grrl

- Yeah, so we track down the legs. Witch woman tells me to keep its top half away while she tackles its legs and starts grinding some special magic powder or some shit into the "open" top end of them. That's when the top half comes at us like a bat out of hell, literally. I'll shorten things up to say that was one hell of a fight, and I've been in more than a few in my life. Both me and the doc got raked and were bleeding something fierce when she suddenly said she was done and ran for the hills. I didn't stop to ask questions until later, while she was dressing our wounds. She said the special salt she rubbed on the legs would prevent the thing from reattaching and it would be dead by morning. She went to go check the next day, but I had an answer for my employer, and enough of that hellhole, so I left.
- Pistons

- I have heard scattered legends of such a thing, a manananggal. I had cautiously hoped they were not real. Pity.
- Lei Kung

- I've got another strange one. I have this chummer who was always a down-on-his-luck kind of guy, a real "lovable loser." Great guy, but just never seemed to catch a break, you know?
- Turbo Bunny

- That sounds just like my brother-in-law, only without the lovable part.
- Rigger X

- Anyway, about six months ago things suddenly turn around for him. Drek that normally always seemed to go wrong for him, just turned around and things started magically working out. At first it seemed like just dumb luck, random happy chance. Like he was finally catching a few breaks.
- Turbo Bunny

- What's weird about that?
- Rigger X

- Nothing, and I didn't think anything of it at the time. I was happy for him. But it wasn't just a temporary run of good luck. Things **kept** going good for him, on and on and on. He was making deals bigger than ever before, pulling jobs like a pro, and scoring chicks like a player.
- Turbo Bunny

- Sounds like his luck just turned around. Karma of the world just rebalancing itself, I guess.
- Jimmy No

- As I said, I didn't think much of it at the time. It's only after what happened to him in the end that I'm starting to question things now. A few months into his run of good luck, he took me out for dinner. I suspect he was trying to get me into bed, but whatever. Anyway, while we're chatting and he's more than a little drunk, I make some comment about his luck finally turning around, universe giving him a break or something like that. Anyway, in response he says the strangest fucking thing I've ever heard him say, "Fuck the universe, I made a deal for my luck."
- Turbo Bunny

- What kind of deal?
- Ethernaut

- That was my question too, so I asked him. He goes on to tell me this story about how he was out hiking in the back woods one night on one of his excursions for a big score of reagents. While he's out he comes to a place that seems like it's busting at the seams with magic. Wandering around in this place are some creatures that he's never seen before, and I've never heard of. He could never really tell me what they looked like, just that they were very small, look vaguely metahuman shaped, but appeared "hazy," almost like they weren't really there. Any smart person would walk away from some strange thing in the woods they've never seen before, but my friend being the dumb screw-up that he is, walks right up and starts talking to the things. I guess he was still looking to make a nuyen from them or some shit.
- Turbo Bunny

- There are still a great many things we do not know about this Awakened world. It is always best to be cautious.
- Axis Mundi

- Yeah, well, my friend wasn't exactly known for his good decision-making. Anyway, he tells me that he talked with the "little glowing things" (as he called them) and they offered him a deal. He does some stuff for them, and they turn his life around—make things better for him. Again, my chummer not being the sharpest blade on a

street sam, he agrees to the deal. He does what they ask: plant some special seed in a different part of the forest, he said. No big deal. That's when things started to turn around for him.

• Turbo Bunny

• I've heard of such Faustian deals before—they always start small. Simple. They never end that way.

• Ethernaut

• So, life starts looking up for him. He just goes into the forest and does whatever they say. He figured he'd hit the jackpot of a lifetime. By this time in the evening he was way past piss drunk and could see he wasn't going to get a lay out of me, so he headed home. He called me (royally hung over) the next day, and he sounded like his was pissing his pants. He just kept saying over and over that he should never have told me about "them," that I should forget I heard anything he said. Made me swear not to tell anyone. Null sweat. Then I didn't hear from him for a couple of weeks.

• Turbo Bunny

• I think I can see where this one's going. One day fortune stopped being his bitch?

• Clockwork

• One night he shows up at my door in the middle of the night and he looks like hell and smells worse, drunk again. Through his tears he tells me that what "they" have been asking for has gotten harder, worse. It's not simple anymore, it's big stuff. Tough stuff. Now he's had enough. Last night they told him to set fire to a house full of kids. He wouldn't do it, he wanted out of the deal. They told him he couldn't get out of the deal, and if he didn't do what they wanted there'd be consequences.

• Turbo Bunny

• The other shoe drops. No such thing as a free lunch!

• Clockwork

• Try not to be so cavalier—this is a good friend we're talking about. True to his word, he tried to stop, but that's when things started going bad. *Real* bad. I thought he had bad luck before, but that was nothing compared to this. All kinds of crazy, random bad shit started happening to him. He suddenly can't stop popping chips when he's never touched them before, he can't sleep at night, contacts won't talk to him, he gets panic attacks just being out in public, and he goes into anaphylactic shock from something that he's eaten a million times before. Few days ago he's walking out of the hospital and gets pasted by a runaway autocab. "Autopilot malfunction" the company says. Tragic accident. Accident my ass, I know who was

behind it. If I ever find those "little glowing things" they'll have a score to settle with me.

• Turbo Bunny

• The day metahumanity outgrows its temptation to engage in deals with the devil, whatever shape that devil may take, will be a remarkable one indeed.

• Ethernaut

TOXIC MAGIC

When magic first returned to the Sixth World, it was readily apparent that it was tied to nature and the natural world. Wherever nature was allowed to thrive, untouched by man, magic was more potent, thriving in tandem. Conversely, wherever nature was plowed, bulldozed, and overridden by the machinations of man, magic waned and fizzled. What no one anticipated was what would happen to magic when nature was not removed and replaced, but instead tainted into something foul. While the fires of industry churned on, fueling the insatiable appetites of consumers, the by-products of those factories were dumped in forgotten places, away from prying eyes. In these places, where unnatural chemicals seeped and fouled like a sickness, nature turned into a dark and twisted parody of itself. So too did the magic that pooled there.

Mana flows from the metaplanes and other unknown sources into the physical world. As it collides with the emotions and circumstances of the physical world, it acquires something like a taste or flavor of the people and past events in particular locations. When it eventually crashes into the shores of astral space, it has absorbed the essence or character of the location where it co-exists. Thus, in a place where careless dumping has turned nature from inviting and life-giving to cruel and harsh, so too will the magic—and especially spirits—of that place be spiteful, twisted forms of what they once were. This is toxic magic.

THE TWISTED WAY

In areas where pollution has corrupted nature, mana is also corrupted. Just as a mundane would find the polluted physical space sickly and detestable, the Awakened find corrupted astral space abhorrent. Simply being in the area is often too much for most Awakened, but should they try to use the mana there, they find it saturated with a sick and bitter taste. Most Awakened, metahuman and otherwise, avoid areas of toxic magic. There are a few magicians, however, that embrace, or perhaps have been driven mad by, the mutated magic of the area. Instead of being revolted by the toxic magic, they revel in it.

Those magicians who follow the toxic path almost always live a solitary life. To become a toxic magician is to give up everything, leaving behind family, friends, and even their mentor spirit (if they had one). In their new life the toxic magician follows an agenda of hatred, destruction, and revenge. Cut off from the rest of society, their lifestyle, habits, and motivations grow more and more alien, diverging from the world they were once a part of.

When a magician becomes toxic, they abandon their previous view of magic and the world for a completely new one; in this way they take on a completely new tradition, following all the basic rules (see **Traditions**, p. 279, *SR5*). However, the views vary widely from one toxic to another, and the degree to which an individual's outlook changes is entirely dependent on their own flavor of insanity. A magician following a Toxic Tradition may select which five toxic spirits they are able to summon, as well as which Mental Attribute they use for Drain (in addition to Willpower).

AVENGERS

Some toxic magicians are driven by a deep desire for revenge. They are the emotional aspects of the land personified. They feel angry and deeply hurt by what has been done to the land (and themselves), and in some cases seek to vent this anger on those whom they perceive as responsible. They are often over-broad in how they define their opponents. In the eyes of the toxic, nearly anyone can be seen as linked to, or responsible for, the poisoning of the land: by creating pollutants, aiding those who create them, working or associating with polluters, purchasing products that cause pollution, those who knowingly do not act to prevent pollution, and even those that know nothing about it (ignorance is no excuse). Any person may be declared guilty at the whim of the avenger, in order to further their insatiable desire to exact some punishment on the world that created them, and the polluted land. Given what they, and the land, have become, toxic mages driven by revenge will often loathe themselves just as much as those they deem responsible. This self-loathing, however, only drives them to perform further acts of violence and depravity.

POISONERS

Poisoners are toxic magicians who view what they have found as a new source of power. These insane individuals believe that they have discovered a new elemental power in the world, and only they have the skill and talent to wield it. Unlike avengers, who are bitter, self-loathing, and out for revenge, poisoners fully embrace and enjoy what they have become. These individuals are often arrogant in the extreme, espousing and believing that they are the heralds or avatars of the very power, the essence, of pollution itself. As mankind continues to grow and industry expands, they believe that the inevitable end of all nature is to be consumed by the byproducts of industry, that all the world will be taken over by the detritus of society. With this belief they carry out an agenda that seeks to spread toxic areas, intensify those that exist, and stop those who would seek to clean the land. They are selfish and power-hungry individuals, driven to further their agenda through any means necessary. While sometimes completely mad and erratic, many poisoners possess a devious genius and a malicious cunning. They are capable of taking the long view, believing that their victory is inevitable, and may bide their time, or slowly build their power, until everything is right for their strike.

TOXIC ADEPTS

Turning to the toxic path is not exclusive to magicians, though they are the most likely to do so. Adepts can also turn to, or be corrupted into, the path of the toxic. They are driven by the same kinds of motivations as magicians, but draw and manifest their toxic powers in ways more in keeping with their abilities. Due to their magical abilities being so closely tied to their physical bodies, toxic adepts are universally loathsome in appearance. Drawing the raw essence of the polluted magic into their bodies, the physical form of the toxic adept warps and mutates to match the nature of the corrupted mana flowing through them.

Some toxic adepts will become covered in boils, warts, and sores as their skin takes on a sick and diseased look. Others seep puss, bile, or filthy chemicals from their very pores. Drawing the toxic magic may give some a greatly enhanced physique, with their bones and muscles swollen and distended to enormous proportions, pulsing with malicious power. Others gain a sickly and emaciated appearance, mirroring the sick and shriveled aspects of the poisoned land. Their skin is pallid and drawn; their eyes sunken and discolored. Yet this appearance belies the fact that they still possess the same supernatural quickness and strength as they did before (if not more).

Toxic adepts have the same motivations and goals as toxic magicians, but they often favor more direct and aggressive means that suit their abilities. As a result, they are equally dangerous or frightening to encounter. Toxic adepts follow all the normal rules for adepts, with access to the additional powers and abilities for toxic adepts (see **Twisted Arts**, p. 87).

TOXIC MENTOR SPIRITS

While no sane magician has encountered a toxic mentor spirit, many of those who have turned to the toxic path claim they are guided and taught by a patron spirit. Like all aspects of toxic magic, the thoughts and motivations of a toxic Awakened embody the worst and darkest possibilities of mankind. The thought of a powerful metaplanar force that embodies the purest form of these motivations is truly chilling.

Toxic mentor spirits follow all the same rules for standard mentor spirits (p. 320, *SR5*). A toxic magician or toxic adept may, but is not required to, follow a mentor spirit.

DOOM

Doom embodies the desire of toxics to bring an end to all life on the planet. They seek to hasten the inevitable (as they see it) apocalypse and turn the world into a barren, polluted landscape. Followers of Doom see humanity as too tragically flawed to be allowed to survive, and thus carry out an agenda of total destruction. As a result of their nihilistic outlook, followers of Doom are isolationist and anti-social.

ADVANTAGES
- **All:** +2 to Demolitions or a single Combat Skill of the character's choice
- **Magician:** +2 dice for spells, preparations, and spell rituals of the Combat category
- **Adept:** Free Killing Hands power

DISADVANTAGES
Followers of Doom must succeed in a Willpower + Charisma (3) Test to avoid a fight once it has begun, or to not enact a plan to do violence. If they fail, they must engage in combat until all opponents are defeated or flee.
- **Similar Archetypes:** Destroyer, Reaper

DISEASE

Disease embodies the infection and virulence that is rampant in many areas of toxicity. It is the ultimate parasite of the world, subsisting off of the waste of others, growing and gaining strength in hidden or forgotten places. Followers of disease seek to spread its influence throughout the world, in a slow but steady infection of all things. Contrary to the norm, followers of Disease collaborate with each other and work in groups to achieve their goal. They find strength in numbers and avoid direct confrontation whenever possible, preferring to spread their infection and sap their enemies' strength in subtle ways.

ADVANTAGES
- **All:** +2 to resist all pathogens and toxins
- **Magician:** +2 dice for summoning or binding plague spirits (toxic spirits of man)
- **Adept:** Free Plague Cloud power (see p. 173)

DISADVANTAGES
Followers of Disease must make a Charisma + Willpower (3) Test to not flee or seek cover whenever in a combat situation, unless they outnumber their opponents. If they begin a fight with greater numbers but then their side is reduced so that they no longer outnumber their opponents, they must make a test to avoid fleeing.
- **Similar Archetypes:** Pestilent Rat, Contagion

MUTATION

Mutation is the ultimate changer of ways. It seeks to alter every living thing into a new form, a new creation in its image. Mutation doesn't hate life, but wants all life to be remade into whatever new forms it chooses. Followers of mutation conspire to control, manipulate, and change all living things. To that end, they spread pollution and corruption in subtle ways to make the change of mutation happen. Mutation also believes in improving living things through experiment and change. Its followers are obsessed with self-improvement, always looking for ways to make themselves better.

ADVANTAGES
- **All:** +2 dice to a Physical skill of the character's choice
- **Magician:** +2 dice for spells, preparations, and spell rituals of the Health category
- **Adept:** Free Attribute Boost (level 2) power for a Physical Attribute of the character's choice

DISADVANTAGES
If a follower of Mutation finds themselves inferior to an opponent, they suffer a –1 penalty on all actions until they defeat their rival in that area, or overcome or compensate for the weakness in another way (such as acquiring a new power, spell, or augmentation).
- **Similar Archetypes:** Mutant Beast, Dark Darwinist

POLLUTION

Pollution embodies the defilement of the natural world and its destruction. Followers of pollution celebrate in the rape of the natural world and believe that pollution is the ultimate primal force in the Sixth World. Followers of Pollution believe they grow stronger as the industries of mankind grow and produce more of the irresistible power of corrupting chemicals.

ADVANTAGES
- **All:** +2 dice for Chemistry Tests when dealing with pollutants in any way; may default even if they do not have the Chemistry skill
- **Magician:** +2 dice to summon or bind toxic toxic spirits of air, earth, or water (choose one)
- **Adept:** Free Toxic Strike (see p. 176) power

DISADVANTAGES
If they are in an area cleaner than their normal habitation, followers of Pollution must make a Willpower + Charisma (3) Test every day. If they fail, they must spend at least eight hours that day actively despoiling the land, regardless of any other plans they had for that time.

SITES OF CORRUPTION

Followers of toxic magic are, more than almost any other magic practitioner, tied to specific physical areas as the focal point for their magic. Many Awakened turn to the toxic path as a result of the despoiling of a particular piece of land. The chief aim of many toxic followers is to enhance the power of their chosen area, or to spread and create new sites of corruption throughout the world.

A toxic will invariably make their home at a location that has seen considerable environmental damage due to pollution of some kind. This can be an urban environment that has been the site of (legal or not) dumping of industrial byproducts, a rural area that was the site of some environmental disaster, or other such area. Magicians will look to set up their magical lodge in such a location (see **Magical Lodges**, p. 280, SR5) to further their studies in the toxic arts. When they have found a site that is suitable for their needs, a toxic will often look to strengthen the toxic magic there and will encourage or aid further pollution of the area.

Encountering a toxic follower in any normal location is worthy of concern, but facing one in a toxic domain is a truly frightening experience. Sites of toxic magic have a background count of between 1 and 6, usually. They are always Domains of toxic magic, and a toxic magician or adept will always be at least acclimated to the Domain, and will usually be aligned. This gives the magician a considerable advantage, as the Rating of the background count increases the limit for all tests linked to Magic while in the Domain. See **Background Count** (p. 30) for full details.

TWISTED ARTS

In addition to their altered outlook, toxic magicians and adepts employ an array of unique powers and abilities that they use to further their ends. Toxic magicians, exclusively, may learn the spells Pollutant Stream, Pollutant Wave (p. 106), Radiation Beam, and Radiation Burst (p. 105). They may also learn the toxic metamagics of Corruption and Taint (p. 87) and can learn and perform the ritual of Leeching (p. 133).

Toxic adepts, exclusively, may learn the Toxic Strike power (p. 176) and the Plague Cloud power (p. 173).

CORRUPTION

Corruption is a metamagic technique that allows a magician to twist a spirit into a toxic version of itself. This is done by making a standard Banishing Test (p. 301, SR5). The toxic magician may add his initiate grade as a dice pool bonus to the test. If the toxic magician succeeds in a Summoning Test after reducing the spirit's services to 0, the spirit immediately turns into a toxic version of itself (see **Toxic Spirits**, p. 87).

TAINT

Taint is a metamagic technique that increases the background count of an area. It uses all the same rules as Cleansing metamagic (see **Cleansing**, p. 122), with the sole exception of increasing the background count instead of decreasing it. In all other ways it follows the rules for Cleansing.

TOXIC SPIRITS

Spirits, by their very nature, are tied to the conditions of the area from which they are summoned, and they are affected by the personality of their summoner. Toxic magicians are warped and twisted people, so they summon warped and twisted versions of the spirits familiar to other magicians. Any spirit powers listed that are not in SR5 can be found under **New Spirit Powers**, p. 193.

NOXIOUS

(TOXIC SPIRIT OF AIR)

Noxious spirits are the essence of choking, smothering fumes that permeate the polluted areas of the world. Whereas spirits of air are fluid, flowing, and light, noxious spirits are heavy, stagnant, and oppressive. Noxious spirits appear as clouds of concentrated, discolored fumes. While they are often formless, they may also form into a serpentine or cyclonic shape.

B	A	R	S	W	L	I	C	M	ESS	EDG
F–2	F+3	F+4	F–3	F	F	F	F	F	F	F/2

Physical Init.	(F x 2) + 4 + 2D6
Astral Init.	(F x 2) + 3D6
Skills	Assensing, Astral Combat, Exotic Ranged Weapon, Perception, Running, Unarmed Combat
Powers	Accident, Astral Form, Concealment, Confusion, Engulf (Air), Materialization, Movement, Sapience, Search
Optional Powers	Fear, Guard, Noxious Breath, Psychokinesis, Weather Control

ABOMINATION

(TOXIC SPIRIT OF BEASTS)

Abomination spirits are the mana representation of beasts and creatures twisted and mutated by toxic domains. They may appear similar to a particular creature or as an unnatural conglomeration of several beasts. They always appear sick, distended, or mutated in some way, and they are always aggressive.

B	A	R	S	W	L	I	C	M	ESS	EDG
F+2	F+1	F	F+2	F	F	F	F	F	F	F/2

Physical Init.	(F x 2) + 2D6
Astral Init.	(F x 2) + 3D6
Skills	Assensing, Astral Combat, Exotic Ranged Weapon, Gymnastics, Perception, Running, Unarmed Combat
Powers	Animal Control (Toxic Critters), Astral Form, Enhanced Senses (Hearing, Low-Light Vision, Smell), Materialization, Movement, Mutagen, Natural Weapon (DV = (Force) Physical damage, AP —), Pestilence, Sapience
Optional Powers	Concealment, Corrosive Spit, Fear, Guard, Mimicry, Search, Venom

BARREN

(TOXIC SPIRIT OF EARTH)

Barren spirits are the avatars of ground that is bereft of all of its former life-giving properties. Where once the earth cradled and nurtured life, feeding plants and holding water, barren spirits seek to kill all life in its grasp. Like soil that holds poisons for hundreds of years, some toxic magicians claim that barren spirits have a "memory" of all that has transpired in their domain. Barren spirits appear as vaguely humanoid mounds of earth, or a gestalt form of objects littered around the grounds of an area.

B	A	R	S	W	L	I	C	M	ESS	EDG
F+4	F−2	F−1	F+4	F	F−1	F	F	F	F	F/2

Physical Init.	((F x 2) − 1) + 2D6
Astral Init.	(F x 2) + 3D6
Skills	Assensing, Astral Combat, Exotic Ranged Weapon, Perception, Unarmed Combat
Powers	Astral Form, Binding, Elemental Attack (Pollutant), Engulf (Earth), Materialization, Movement, Sapience, Search
Optional Powers	Accident, Concealment, Confusion, Fear, Guard
Weaknesses	Allergy (Clean Earth, Severe)

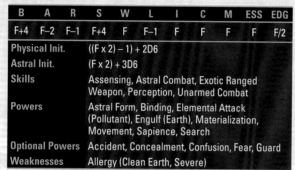

NUCLEAR

(TOXIC SPIRIT OF FIRE)

Nuclear spirits represent the all-consuming fire of lethal radioactivity. They reflect a desire to burn away everything with an unnatural, perpetual heat. Spirits of the atom appear as clouds of isotopes or fallout, often burning so bright that it is difficult to look at them.

B	A	R	S	W	L	I	C	M	ESS	EDG
F+1	F+2	F+3	F−2	F	F	F+1	F	F	F	F/2

Physical Init.	((F x 2) + 3) + 2D6
Astral Init.	(F x 2) + 3D6
Skills	Assensing, Astral Combat, Exotic Ranged Weapon, Flight, Perception, Unarmed Combat
Powers	Astral Form, Elemental Attack (Radiation), Energy Aura (Radiation), Engulf (Fire), Materialization, Sapience
Optional Powers	Confusion, Fear, Guard, Search

PLAGUE

(TOXIC SPIRIT OF MAN)

Plague spirits are the avatars of the disease carriers of mankind. They appear metahuman, but always with obvious, hideous maladies covering their bodies: boils, seeping lesions, sores, and mutations. In character they exhibit the worst qualities of metahumans—they are violent, hateful, and care nothing for other living things.

B	A	R	S	W	L	I	C	M	ESS	EDG
F	F	F+2	F−2	F	F	F+1	F	F	F	F/2

Physical Init.	((F x 2) + 2) + 2D6
Astral Init.	(F x 2) + 3D6
Skills	Assensing, Astral Combat, Perception, Spellcasting, Unarmed Combat
Powers	Accident, Astral Form, Desire Reflection, Enhanced Senses (Low-Light, Thermographic Vision), Fear, Materialization, Mutagen, Pestilence, Sapience, Search
Optional Powers	Concealment, Confusion, Guard, Innate Spell (any one spell known by the summoner), Movement, Psychokinesis

SLUDGE

(TOXIC SPIRIT OF WATER)

Sludge spirits are the mana manifestation of liquid pollutants. They sometimes appear humanoid, but other times they have an indiscernible shape. These spirits have a cloying, smothering, and consuming tendency, seeming to revel in a steady and inevitable encroachment over all.

B	A	R	S	W	L	I	C	M	ESS	EDG
F+1	F+1	F+2	F	F	F	F	F	F	F	F/2

Physical Init.	((F x 2) + 2) + 2D6
Astral Init.	(F x 2) + 3D6
Skills	Assensing, Astral Combat, Exotic Ranged Weapon, Perception, Unarmed Combat
Powers	Astral Form, Binding, Elemental Attack (Pollutant), Engulf (Water), Materialization, Movement, Mutagen, Sapience, Search
Optional Powers	Accident, Concealment, Confusion, Fear, Guard
Weaknesses	Allergy (Clean Water, Severe)

BLOOD MAGIC

Blood magic is a catch-all term used to refer to any form of practicing magic where power is drawn from harm done to living beings. Blood magic is most well known in traditions of Aztec magic, but they are far from the only practitioners. A magician from *any* tradition of magic may become a blood mage if they engage in the practice of drawing power from pain. Being an inherently violent act, blood magic is illegal is nearly all nations, with the notable exception of Aztlan, where the practice is as much religious as it is magical.

In game terms, a magician is considered a blood mage if they have turned their studies to the learning of a select few metamagic techniques and rituals. Generally, a magician is considered a blood mage once they have learned the metamagic technique of Sacrifice.

THE PATH OF BLOOD

The reasons and motivations of a magician turning to the study of blood magic are as varied as the individuals who practice them. No one, save the truly mad, who practices blood magic can be blind to the inherently harmful nature of its practice, so the motivations for beginning to practice it must be strong enough to override any moral objections the individual may have. They may have experienced some trauma (mental or physical) that pushes them to make compromises for the sake of abilities. The individual may have been reared in a social setting where the practice is considered normal, and the acts honored rather than abhorrent. More commonly, though, individuals are lured in with the promise of power. Since blood magic can never be learned through self-study, a magician is always drawn onto the path of blood through a third party: a beguiling spirit or powerful individual or group. Through the temptations and promises offered, the magician is taught the forbidden arts and experiences the power they can harness as a result. Once they have tapped into the wellspring of raw mana produced by blood magic, few can ever turn away. They become addicted, or hopelessly dependent on it, driving them to further levels of debauchery until they are unrecognizable as the person they once were.

Gamemasters should be cautious about allowing player characters to learn blood magic techniques and should be very clear on the costs—social, moral, and in game terms—about choosing this path. The use of blood magic will show up in their aura, which has a strongly negative effect on any who assense them (excepting other blood mages).

METAMAGIC

SACRIFICE

Sacrifice is the metamagic technique that defines a magician as following the path of Blood. In essence, it is the ability to draw magical power from the act of inflicting harm on another living being, with sentient beings generating the most amount of power. Blood magic in all its forms is universally derided by other practitioners of magic. Sacrifice is an exclusive metamagic technique that can only be learned from another magician of the same tradition who already knows it, or from a spirit that knows it. It can never be self-taught.

In order to use Sacrifice, the magician must inflict Physical damage on another living thing, using a melee weapon that draws blood. The drawing of living blood is the powerful symbol that generates raw magical power referred to as Blood Magic Points. To do this the magician makes a standard melee attack using the weapon. If the target is able to defend themselves they may do so, but if they cannot resist (due to being restrained, for example) then the attack is unopposed. Additionally, if the victim is restrained and unable to defend themselves, the magician receives a +4 dice pool bonus on their attack.

While any living creature can be used, the magic is more powerful when harm is inflicted on sapient creatures, especially the unwilling. If damage is inflicted on a living creature without the Sapience power or the victim is willing (such as the magician themselves), then every 3 boxes of Physical damage inflicted generates one Blood Magic Point. If damage is inflicted on a Sapient critter or unwilling metahuman victim, then every 1 box of Physical damage generates one Blood Magic Point. Spirits can never be used as victims, even if they possess a living body.

If not used, Blood Magic Points are lost after the following Combat Turn. Blood Magic Points generated by the act of Sacrifice can then be used in any of the following ways, in any combination:

- Increase the Force of a spell being cast by one per Point; this can exceed twice the caster's Magic Rating.
- Increase the caster's Magic Rating for the purposes of determining if the spell's drain is Physical or Stun, by one per Point.
- Reduce the amount of Drain the spell inflicts by one per Point, to a minimum of 0.
- Store any number of Points in an athame focus (see **Athame**, p. 90).
- Summon a Blood Spirit (see **Blood Spirits**, p. 91).

CANNIBALIZE (ADEPTS ONLY)

Adepts and mystic adepts who follow the path of blood may learn a unique metamagic technique related to Sacrifice. When using Cannibalize, the adept draws blood from a victim and then consumes it to gain a measure of power. In game terms, the adept inflicts physical damage on a willing or unwilling victim exactly as per the Sacrifice metamagic to generate Blood Magic Points. The adept can then increase a physical attribute by 1 for every 3 Blood Magic Points they spend, up to the individual's augmented maximum in that attribute. The same or different attributes may be increased in any combination with one Simple Action. This increase lasts (Magic x initiate grade) Combat Turns, but if the adept immediately spends Karma equal to the total number of attribute points increased, the duration is increased to (Magic x initiate grade) days.

POWER BLEED (ADEPTS ONLY)

Prerequisite: Cannibalize

Power Bleed is an advanced metamagic technique that builds upon the Cannibalize power. Power Bleed functions the same as Cannibalize, except that instead of generating 3 Blood Magic Points, the adept can siphon one critter or adept power possessed by the victim (if they have one), and may then use this power as if it were their own. The effect lasts for (Magic x initiate grade) Combat Turns, but the adept may immediately spend 3 Karma to extend the duration to (Magic x initiate grade) days.

FOCI

Magicians following the path of Blood are classically power-hungry and will often use foci to enhance their abilities. They can use any of the foci available to any other magician, and one additional type exclusive to blood magicians: the athame.

ATHAME

Athame is the name given to a new kind of focus used exclusively by blood mages. Named after an object that traditionally takes the form of a dagger or small knife, the first athames did in fact take this traditional form. Aztec blood mages were among the first to be seen using them, in the form of sharpened daggers made from obsidian. Lately, blood mages of other traditions have been making athames in forms more keeping with their own traditions, such as the razor-edged flint axes of the Native American blood shamans or a sickle used by some blood mages in India. A magician must know the metamagic of Sacrifice in order to bond an athame.

Athames have a unique function as a focus—they can store the magical power generated by a Blood Rite ritual (see p. 125) to be used at a later time. Blood Magic Points stored in an athame can be used with a Free Action at the time a spell is cast for any of the uses listed for Blood Magic Points in the Sacrifice metamagic (see p. 90). The number of Blood Magic Points that can be stored in the athame is limited to its Force.

The magical energy generated from a Blood ritual is tied to the spike in emotions that coexist with the violent act. As time passes and the emotional imprint of the event fades, so too does the magical energy associated with it. As such, half the amount of current, unused Blood Magic Points stored in an athame are lost after the following time intervals from the initial Blood Rite ritual: 1 week, 1 month, and 3 months.

BLOOD SPIRITS

A magician who knows the Sacrifice metamagic may summon blood spirits. Summoning a blood spirit follows all the normal rules for summoning except that the magician must use the Sacrifice metamagic as part of the summoning. The amount of Blood Magic Points generated sets the maximum Force of blood spirit that can be summoned. All other rules for summoning and commanding spirits apply normally. Blood spirits can be bound in the same manner as other spirits, if the magician is brave enough.

BLOOD SPIRIT

Blood spirits always take a twisted, painful appearance. They can be an unsettling cloud of red mist from which tortured and dying faces seem to swim and shift, or a kind of hideous animal amalgamation with claws and a bird-like beak dripping with gore. Most frightening of all is when they take a form very much like a metahuman, with gaping, bleeding mortal wounds on their neck, wrists, head, or abdomen. A blood spirit is a transient thing that slowly degrades after the magical energies of its initial violent summoning begin to fade. As a result, blood spirits need to use their Essence Drain power to replenish themselves in order to stay on this plane. A blood spirit whose Essence reaches 0 immediately departs for its native metaplane—generally howling with an inhuman hunger as it does so.

B	A	R	S	W	L	I	C	M	ESS	EDG
F+2	F+2	F	F+2	F	F–1	F	F	F	F	F/2

Physical Init.	(F x 2) + 2D6
Astral Init.	(F x 2) + 3D6
Skills	Assensing, Astral Combat, Perception, Running, Unarmed Combat
Powers	Astral Form, Binding, Energy Drain (Essence, Touch, Physical Damage), Fear, Materialization
Optional Powers	Concealment, Confusion, Guard, Movement, Natural Weapon (DV = (Force) Physical Damage, AP —), Noxious Breath
Weaknesses	Essence Loss (1 point per day)

BLOOD RITUALS

If the leader of a spell being cast with ritual spellcasting (see p. 295, SR5) knows the Sacrifice metamagic, they may use it during the ritual to generate Blood Magic Points (see **Sacrifice**, p. 90), and expend Blood Magic Points generated in place of drams of reagents (see **Give the Offering**, p. 296, SR5) on a one-for-one basis.

If a group of magicians all know the Sacrifice metamagic, they can perform the Blood Rite ritual to collectively generate and store power in their athames (see p. 90), distributing Blood Magic Points around their foci as they see fit.

BLOOD SPIRIT INVOCATION

A magician who knows the metamagic techniques of Sacrifice and Invocation may create a truly frightening entity—a great form blood spirit. This is done with a Summon Great Form Spirit ritual (see p. 136) as per normal, with one exception. During the ritual, a metahuman victim must be killed; this is required to fuel the ascension of the blood spirit. If the summoning granted a Greater Power, the blood spirit gains the unique power of Hemorrhage.

HEMORRHAGE

Type: P **Action:** Complex
Range: [Magic] meters **Duration:** Instant

With this frightening power, the spirit is able to burst blood vessels and rupture veins inside any living beings in close proximity. Make a Magic + Willpower [Force] vs. Strength (unaugmented) + Willpower Opposed Test for every living thing within range of the effect. Each net hit the spirit achieves causes one box of unresisted Physical damage. Additionally, all targets that took at least one box of damage are wracked with extreme pain. Treat the damage as if it had the Nausea effect (p. 409, SR5). Targets are incapacitated by this effect only if the number of boxes inflicted exceeds their Willpower.

SHADOW SPIRITS

Shadow spirits are the classic "evil spirits" that frequent the stories and legends of so many cultures around the world. Although known by many different names, in the end they are all the same kind of spirit. Shadow spirits are drawn to metahumanity to feed off of a particular set of emotions. When they are in close proximity to an expression of their preferred emotion, they draw sustenance from it at the expense of the person expressing it. Their desire to indulge in this feeding is such that they will use any means necessary to provoke their desired emotion. Being entirely selfish creatures, they have no boundaries of morality to inhibit them, and are heedless of any repercussions (short-term or otherwise) that their deceptions cause.

All shadow spirits use the rules for free spirits (p. 202). Regardless of type, all shadow spirits are driven to extract emotional energy in the form of Karma from their victims. They do this by coercing their victims into performing a specific action or set of actions that produces the emotion that the specific type of shadow spirit desires. The shadow spirit simply needs to see the victim when the emotion is expressed to drain Karma. While exhausting, this process is not fatal to the victim, causing Stun damage. All of this follows the rules described for Energy Drain on p. 195. A shadow spirit is free to spend Karma drained from victims in any way that a Free Spirit can.

TYPES OF SHADOW SPIRITS

While all shadow spirits share a base similarity in goals and methods, this is only in broad strokes. Those in the Sixth World who study them have so far identified five different types of shadow spirits, classified by their preferred emotional "diet."

MUSE

A muse feeds off of the emotions of highly creative and expressive people, primarily artists. In an almost symbiotic relationship, the muse can inspire an artist to levels of expression and creativity they may never have achieved alone. This is the dangerous temptation that a muse spirit offers, often finding its prey among those who were once highly successful, or those who struggle and have the desire but not the raw talent to succeed. While the draining of the victim's Karma by a muse is not inherently fatal, victims will often become enraptured by the experience of creative expression, to the point where they neglect their own basic needs such as sleep, food, or water. A muse will often take the form of a fey or sinuous humanoid, though it will adjust to whatever may be most appealing to its potential victims.

NIGHTMARE

A nightmare is a spiritual bully that feeds off of the terror it causes in its victims. Being both greedy and cowardly, the nightmare seeks victims in which it can induce the most terror, while being the least threatening to it. Most commonly it preys on the elderly or children, striking when they are alone and feel the most vulnerable. Since a nightmare feeds off of the fear of its victims, it does not intentionally seek to harm them, since a dead person can feel no more fear. Thus, nightmares shape their form into that which the victim dreads the most. They are the quintessential bogeyman or thing that goes bump in the night.

SHADE

A shade feeds on misery, depression, and despondency, of which there is a great supply in the Sixth World. When a shade chooses a victim, it takes great delight in deepening and prolonging the suffering, using its abili-

ties to manipulate their emotional state. This causes the poor soul to make more bad decisions, deepening their sorrow, loss, or loneliness. As their self-esteem reaches its lowest point, the victim of a shade frequently attempts suicide, which the shade works to ensure is done poorly, thus creating a new emotional low. Shades appear roughly metahuman, though drab, grey, and downtrodden.

SUCCUBUS

Succubi thrive on sexual energy. Unlike many of its shadow spirit kin, the succubus is not content to watch and manipulate mortals, but instead takes a much more direct approach. The succubus uses its powers to take on an attractive metahuman form in order to seduce one (or often several) others. At the height of the sexual act, the succubus feeds off of the victim's raw lust and passion. However, a succubus does not have to participate; it can merely be present during a sexual act in order to feed. Being the very essence of a sexual predator, the succubus embodies only the worst aspects of sexuality. It cares nothing for meaningful bonds, caring, or relationships, only for the emotions of destructive lust and guilty pleasure. It will use, abuse, and discard people at it sees fit to draw energy from more victims. A succubus has the ability to take on an almost infinite variety of highly realistic human forms.

WRAITH

Wraiths feed off of pure and simple violence. The most highly destructive type of shadow spirit, the wraith delights in causing as much death and carnage as possible. They are creatures of opportunity that enjoy gorging themselves on highly concentrated outbursts of emotion over a short period. To this end, the wraith will find a suitable skilled or armed individual, then wait until they are in close proximity to a high number of vulnerable targets, then use its powers to induce an uncontrollable rage. Wraiths materialize as dark, vaguely humanoid shapes that appear to be wearing dark robes or a cloak.

SHADOW SPIRIT

B	A	R	S	W	L	I	C	M	ESS	EDG
F	F+3	F+2	F	F+1	F	F+1	F+2	F	F	F/2

Physical Init.	((F x 2) + 3) + 2D6
Astral Init.	((F x 2) + 1) + 3D6
Skills	Assensing, Astral Combat, Con, Gymnastics, Intimidation, Perception, Unarmed Combat
Powers	Astral Form, Banishing Resistance, Energy Drain (Karma, LOS, Stun damage), Influence, Magical Guard, Materialization, Sapience, Spirit Pact
Muse	Compulsion (Creation), Mind Link, Realistic Form
Nightmare	Fear, Mind Link, Shadow Cloak
Shade	Compulsion (Sorrow), Shadow Cloak, Silence
Succubus	Compulsion (Lust), Desire Reflection, Mutable Form, Realistic Form
Wraith	Compulsion (Homicidal Rage), Confusion, Fear

SHEDIM

One of the strangest and most alien kinds of spirits that has ever been seen in the Sixth World is the she-dim. Shedim are spirits that occupy the bodies of the deceased in order to anchor themselves in the physical world from whatever deep and distant metaplane serves as their home. Their very nature seems to defy identification, or any known expectations of spirit behavior. Prior to the arrival of shedim, all other spirits have viewed the physical plane as a place to escape, or as a breeding/feeding ground. Shedim have shown a desire to travel to the physical plane, though it is extremely difficult for them to stay there, but have also shown nothing but utter hatred for mortals. They come to where life exists so that they may extinguish it.

First observed during the Year of the Comet in 2061 during a magical surge of the now sealed Watergate Rift, their nature and abilities were unknown until they began to take possession of the bodies of the deceased. Just when the rest of the world had taken stock and developed some protections against this, a new type of shed-im emerged: the master shedim. Whereas previous she-dim appeared to be intellectually primitive entities filled with hate and violence, the master shedim exhibited a deep and malicious intelligence. Master shedim take possession of the recently deceased, just as all shedim, but the master shedim are able to access all of the memories and knowledge of the person whose body they now possess. This, combined with the fact that all master shedim are magicians and are able to summon other shedim via their Astral Gateway power, made them incredibly dangerous.

The scope of their plans was not fully realized until a key leader in the militant New Islamic Jihad was revealed to be a master shedim. Conflicts started by the NIJ cost thousands of lives, all under the direction of this malevolent entity. Clearly, the shedim orchestrated the conflict merely to instigate widespread death, and many fear what other carnage these beings might be planning.

Reported shedim activity has declined since the closing of the Watergate Rift. This, however, does not mean that the shedim have become any less dangerous. Indeed, there are worries that the lack of a link to their home plane is increasing the desperation of the shedim to find a new connection and bring more spirits over. And "desperate shedim" is a phrase to send a chill into the heart of any Sixth World resident. Many worry that the current relative silence is merely the eye of a storm set to grow more ferocious.

SHEDIM

B	A	R	S	W	L	I	C	M	ESS	EDG
F	F	F+2	F+1	F	F	F	F	F	F	F/2

Physical Init.	((F x 2) + 2) + 1D6
Astral Init.	(F x 2) + 3D6
Skills	Assensing, Astral Combat, Perception, Unarmed Combat
Powers	Astral Form, Deathly Aura, Energy Drain (Karma, Touch range, Physical damage), Fear, Immunity (Age, Pathogens, Toxins), Paralyzing Touch, Possession (Dead or Abandoned Vessels), Sapience
Optional Powers	Accident, Aura Masking, Compulsion, Regeneration, Search, Shadow Cloak, Silence
Weaknesses	Allergy (Sunlight, Mild), Evanescence

MASTER SHEDIM

B	A	R	S	W	L	I	C	M	ESS	EDG
F	F	F+2	F+1	F+1	F+1	F+1	F	F	F	F/2

Physical Init.	((F x 2) + 3) + 1D6
Astral Init.	(F x 2) + 3D6
Skills	Assensing, Astral Combat, Counterspelling, Gymnastics, Perception, Spellcasting, Unarmed Combat
Powers	Astral Form, Astral Gateway, Aura Masking, Banishing Resistance, Compulsion, Deathly Aura, Energy Drain (Karma, Touch range, Physical damage), Fear, Immunity (Age, Pathogens, Toxins), Possession (Dead or Abandoned Vessels), Regeneration, Sapience, Shadow Cloak, Spirit Pact
Optional Powers	Accident, Noxious Breath, Search, Silence
Weaknesses	Allergy (Sunlight, Mild), Evanescence
Notes	Master shedim are aspected magicians (Sorcery). The gamemaster determines what spells the master shedim knows.

INSECT SPIRITS

Ever since magic returned to the Sixth World, metahu-manity has encountered different kinds of spirits from the "Deep" (or Outer) metaplanes. To the average citizen, these creatures are mostly unknown. The most notable exception to this has been insect spirits. These creatures still present a significant threat to the world at large, and any mention of an insect hive has the danger of causing immediate panic.

SUMMONING INSECT SPIRITS

Insect spirits cannot enter into the world without the aid (at least initially) of a metahuman magician. These magicians act as the insect's terrestrial agents, finding the host bodies that the insect spirits need. For even with the aid of a metahuman agent, insect spirits have difficulty staying manifest in our world without some sort of anchor. Indeed, without some sort of body to invest, an insect spirit summoned would last on the material plane for mere hours, getting weaker by the minute, before being forced to return to its home metaplane. For this reason, metahuman bodies serve as sheaths for the insect spirits. When summoned into these bodies, they undergo a slow metamorphosis into something new, taking a brand-new form. Some continue to appear metahuman, others become a metahuman-sized insect, and many others a bizarre amalgamation between the two. Regardless of the final form, the person that serves as the host for such a process is utterly destroyed in the entirely unpleasant ordeal.

Summoning insect spirits follows all the normal rules for summoning a spirit, but such spirits quickly fade due to Evanescence. The shaman prepares a host body for the spirit, according to the usual rules for preparing a vessel for Inhabitation (p. 195). The host vessels are prepared by putting them in some kind of cocoon constructed by the Queen or Mother spirit (if present) or by the shaman or one of his spirit allies. Placing the spirit in the host immediately halts the effects of Evanescence. A shaman can affect the results of the Inhabitation roll by adding their Binding skill to either dice pool. If the Queen/Mother is present, it may add its Force to the spirit or the vessel's dice pool (as desired).

INSECT SHAMANS

The metahuman agents who carry out the gruesome task of finding human vessels and preparing them for insect inhabitation are insect shamans. Why any person that has a scrap of sanity would do such a thing is not known. Many have theorized why some magic practitioners begin to follow the insect way, but no insect shaman has survived with their mind intact enough to tell a coherent tale. Some may be mad, others driven by promises or dreams of power, and some (tragically enough) may simply be seeking a place of belonging that they have never found among their own species. Whatever the reasons or events that led up to it, at some point in the life of an insect shaman, they make contact with a frightening entity best described as an insect mentor spirit.

Once contact is made, the magician leaves behind whatever tradition or framework of magic they previously practiced and embraces this completely alien form of magic. An insect mentor is always of a particular type of insect (see below), and from that moment on the shaman only summons spirits of that sort. There is no known case of a shaman ever changing their patron insect.

Guided by a new set of goals and instructions, the shaman works to summon spirits of their patron insect. This involves finding a secure location where hosts can be brought and put through the delicate process of inhabitation. The summoned insects will protect and obey the shaman as they work together to enlarge and protect the hive that is being built. Shamans following the mentor of a hive insect will also be obsessively driven to work on summoning a Queen spirit.

QUEEN AND MOTHER SPIRITS

The ultimate goal of every insect shaman is to summon a Queen or Mother spirit. They see this as the physical avatar of the mentor spirit that has been guiding them. Summoning a Queen or Mother uses a specialized ritual taught exclusively to insect shamans for the express purpose of summoning the Queen/Mother. First the shaman must create a spirit formula in the same manner as for an ally (p. 200). The ritual must be done in a magical lodge with a Force equal to or greater than the desired force of the spirit. The shaman must also know the metamagic of Invocation. Next, an already present (and highly honored) nymph spirit is selected to be transformed into the Queen/Mother. This process follows all the normal rules for Summoning (p. 300, SR5), and when completed, the nymph completely transforms into a Queen or Mother spirit of her type.

INSECT SPIRIT TRADITION

The following rules can be used as the tradition followed by the insect shaman. Although this rules framework is provided for consistency, in game terms the methodology followed by insect shamans is wholly alien to any other magic practitioners in the Sixth World. Insect shamans always adopt a mentor spirit of one of the insect orders listed below, though the mentor spirit provides no specific bonuses or penalties. Insect shaman spellcasting and summoning appear to be a series of bizarre gestures and incomprehensible clicking and clacking. Insect shamans often manifest a (rather frightening) shamanic mask.

Insect shamans have a lodge that is often the "breeding ground" where they perform the bulk of their summoning, in the hive or nest of the insect spirits. They may even use fetishes, foci, or reagents, which take the form of bones or scraps of insect organic material or detritus.

Combat: Soldier
Detection: Scout
Health: Caretaker
Illusion: Nymph
Manipulation: Worker
Drain: Willpower + Intuition

A Queen/Mother will always be a larger-than-human-sized version of the insect she represents, often four to six meters long. Once the summoning is complete, the Queen/Mother automatically becomes a free spirit (p. 202).

Once the Queen/Mother emerges, she immediately becomes the focal point of power and control for the nest (or hive). Depending on the motivations and degree of devotion the shaman has for the patron mentor spirit, they may vie for control of the hive with the new Queen/Mother spirit. This usually results in the expulsion or death of the insect shaman, but if the Queen/Mother sees mutual benefit, she can enter into a spirit pact (p. 205) with the shaman. A shaman can only ever summon a single Queen or Mother spirit.

All Queen/Mother spirits have the Astral Gateway power (p. 194) and thus no longer need the shaman to summon new insect spirits from their home plane; they can do this themselves. If the Queen/Mother spirit is ever disrupted, she returns to her home metaplane and must be brought back using the exact same process as the initial summoning. If the Queen/Mother spirit is ever destroyed, the insect shaman immediately loses their magical abilities; their Magic attribute is set to zero and cannot be increased with Karma or through other means. Additionally the shaman becomes a mental and emotional wreck. Any true-form spirits that are part of the hive are also destroyed, while any flesh or hybrid forms lose all cohesive intelligence and wander aimlessly or act randomly.

HIVE INSECT SPIRITS

Hive insects are highly social creatures, working together as a group to build a collective society. Although all insect spirit types are noticeably different in appearance and abilities, all hive insect spirits exhibit similar tendencies in how they gather, organize, and construct their hive. Even the hives themselves have similarities in structure and form. The chief aim of all hive insect spirits is to prepare for and summon a Queen of their kind. Hive insect spirits have a highly ordered society, and the Queen forms the fundamental pillar of that society. Prior to the arrival of the Queen, the entire hive society works toward preparing and protecting the hive for the arrival of the Queen. Once the Queen has arrived, all members of the hive selflessly carry out her will.

Queens are utterly merciless in their dominance of all aspects of the hive and suffer no rivals to their totalitarian control. To this end, mature nymphs may sometimes be destroyed if they are perceived to be rivals, and even the shaman that previously summoned the Queen may be exiled or killed if the Queen believes he or she no longer fulfills her needs.

ANT

The most highly social and cooperative of all hive spirits, ants form a very efficient and populous hive. These hives comprise numerous members of all insect spirit types: caretakers, workers, and nymphs. As exceptional and prolific builders, ant hives quickly expand and are often the largest hives encountered. These hives follow a logic and pattern that only these alien beings can understand, leaving any metahumans that attempt to navigate them utterly confused and easily lost. Ants work to accomplish any goal in groups of at least two or three, never alone. Small groups are only employed by the shaman or queen when subtlety is necessary. In all other cases, ants solve their problems by dedicating a large number (often more than is necessary) of members to the task. Ant spirits are also highly territorial and respond swiftly and with overwhelming force to anything that threatens their territory, be it metahuman or another hive of insect spirits.

Unique Qualities: All physical damage done by ant spirits is also considered acid damage (see **Acid Damage**, p. 170, *SR5*). Ant spirits are highly dependent on their hive mentality and on its controlling force in particular. If a single ant spirit is ever isolated from all others of its hive (e.g., through physical distance or due to a mana barrier), or if the shaman or Queen of the hive is killed, the ant(s) suffer a –2 penalty on all tests.

LOCUST

While classified as a hive species due to their social organization, locusts do not create a physical hive in a single location. Instead they form into a migratory swarm that moves from place to place. Locusts are the prototypical "destroyer" insect. They travel to wherever a food source is abundant, consume everything in a hyperactive flurry, and then move on, leaving nothing but a barren wasteland behind. The only other time a locust swarm will halt its movement is to replenish its numbers. Locust swarms have a singularity of purpose that functions like a force of nature. When the Queen of the swarm sets a direction to travel, the swarm goes, destroying anything that is in the way and consuming everything in their path. Locusts are legendary for their insatiable hunger and their ability to digest nearly anything as food.

Unique Qualities: All locust spirits can fly and have the Flight skill, as well as the Devouring power (p. 194). Locust spirits are single-minded to the point of being oblivious to their surroundings. When fighting a foe or feeding, all locust spirits (except the Queen) have a –3 penalty to Perception Tests.

TERMITE

Termites, like ants, are highly social hive spirits. Though instead of the totalitarian leader system of the ants, termites exhibit a complex caste system, where more mature members of the hive exhibit authority over junior members. Termites build large, highly ordered hives, but whereas ants build them underground, termites build them above ground. Typically they construct them in abandoned buildings in barrens, ghettos, or other isolated urban areas. The most unique aspect of termite hives is the material that makes up their construction. The walls of a termite hive are made of a concrete hard material that is made from mixing sand (or another ballast-type material) and their saliva.

Unique Qualities: All termite spirits have the Reinforcement power (p. 198).

WASP

While described as "wasp," the term refers to several families of the hymenoptera order, including wasps, bees, and hornets. Wasp insects form a highly ordered society, entirely matriarchal in nature. Most members of the hive, especially the worker and soldier types, are not overly intelligent, but the nymphs and Queen exhibit an above-average to exceptional intelligence, with a high level of malevolence and deviousness. Under the direction of such females, wasp spirits have been observed employing spies, using decoys, feigning retreats, and laying traps. Wasp hives are physically smaller than those of other insect spirits but are more densely populated, so they will have as many or more members. Wasp hives are always built in high places in the open air, such as the upper stories of buildings and other such structures.

Unique Qualities: All wasp spirits can fly and have the Flight skill (p. 394, *SR5*) and the Venom power (p. 401, *SR5*).

SOLITARY INSECT SPIRITS

Solitary insect spirits do not form large hives or colonies, but instead sometimes form small family groups. All solitary insects are far more independent, intelligent, and adaptable as individuals. Any particular spirit in a group would feel comfortable leaving to achieve some individual goal. Although there is no singular totalitarian leader like a Queen spirit, a shaman following the totem of a solitary insect spirit will eventually summon a Mother spirit. In a distinct contrast to hive insects, there can be multiple Mother spirits in a group, as each Mother can summon others. This allows the solitary spirits to spread far more widely and rapidly than their hive brethren.

BEETLE

Like the Earthly insects they resemble, beetle spirits come in many different varieties, but all exhibit the same basic characteristics and tendencies. Oddly, summoned beetle spirits will take on the appearance of different kinds of sub-types (stag beetles, dung beetles, etc), despite all coming from the same group. Beetle spirits make their lairs underground, in moist areas,

but range far to find sources of food wherever they are available. Beetle hives, when they gather in significant numbers, are overseen by one or more mother spirits. Beetles are among the more territorially aggressive insects and attack any perceived intruder with little provocation or warning. Beetles are known for their exceptionally tough, chitinous hides.

Unique Qualities: When calculating the Hardened Armor value for a beetle's Immunity to Normal Weapons, add +4 to the value. All beetle spirits also have the Mystic Armor power (p. 399, *SR5*).

CICADA

Cicadas are grasshopper-like, flying insects. They have wide prominent eyes, and wings made of a thin membrane that is almost transparent. Being extremely migratory, cicadas travel in small packs searching for food sources wherever they can be found, and they have exhibited a preference for plants and other organics. The most prominent feature of cicadas is the noise they produce using their internal membranes. Using this ability as a weapon, a cicada spirit can amplify the sound to over 100 decibels (approximately the noise level of a power tool).

Unique Qualities: All cicada spirits can fly, have the Flight skill (p. 394, *SR5*), and have the power of Sonic Projection (p. 199).

FIREFLY

Firefly spirits are soft-bodied fliers that are most well known for the intermittent glow they produce from their abdomens. Fireflies only glow for specific reasons: when agitated, for communication, or when in close proximity to a Mother spirit. When being invested into a new host as a larva, the firefly emits a fainter, but constant, glow. Mother spirits appear to know the vulnerability this causes, and they make attempts to hide their young, moving to different locations to reproduce. Fireflies are the least aggressive of all insect spirits, preferring to evade foes. For this reason scouts and nymphs are by far the most common type of firefly spirits.

Unique Qualities: All firefly spirits can fly, have the Flight skill (p. 394, *SR5*), and have the Confusion power (p. 395, *SR5*).

FLY

Fly spirits, in all their various varieties, subsist as scavengers off of metahuman waste. Thriving in unclean areas where refuse is abundant, fly spirits propagate to match the supply available. They prefer dark, moist environments where disease and pestilence run rampant, inevitably becoming disease carriers themselves. Fly spirits are mostly self-sufficient, but they gather to mate or feed where food supplies are particularly abundant. When they gather and make a nest, the area becomes a noisy, chaotic cesspool, with an overpowering odor that most metahumans find unbearable.

Unique Qualities: All Fly spirits have the Flight skill (p. 394, *SR5*), the Pestilence power (p. 197), and Immunity to Disease.

MANTID

Mantid spirits are the most unusual of all insect spirits. They appear as large, bipedal insects, with a pair of large scything talons as upper arms, and two large mandibles around their mouth. The most remarkable aspect of the mantid spirit, however, is their means of reproduction. Mantid spirits are the apex predators of the insect spirit world: they reproduce by "eating" other insect spirits. Mantid spirits are extremely strict about gender roles among their kind, with the females always being the leaders and soldiers, and the males being caretakers and workers. These gender roles are enforced through the sex of the vessels they choose to invest with their spirits. Mantid spirits never have a Queen or Mother and only rarely produce a nymph. In the rare cases that this happens, the other mantid spirits treat the nymph with a high amount of respect and deference, as if she were a sort of tribal elder.

Female mantid spirits reproduce by "eating" other insect spirits. In actuality, the mantid consumes the spirit energy within the host vessel. When a sufficient amount of energy has been accumulated, the female can incubate a new mantid into an empty host vessel (as described under **Inhabitation**, p. 195). This energy can also be used to enhance the spirit's own abilities instead.

Mantid spirits are notoriously difficult to summon and dangerous to control. Because of their ability to reproduce without the aid of a shaman, they rarely see the need to continue to cooperate with one. Gender roles and the matriarchal nature of mantid culture is so strong that all known mantid shamans have been female. Flesh-form mantid spirits have been known to hide and integrate into metahuman society in order to aid in their hunting, reproduction, and survival.

Unique Qualities: All female mantid spirits have the Energy Drain (Insect Spirit Force, Touch, Physical Damage) power (p. 195). Force drained in this manner can be spent as Karma to improve the skills and attributes of the spirit as per the rules for free spirits (p. 202). When a female mantid has gathered Force equal to its own, it can spend it to "give birth" to a new mantid spirit that inhabits a living vessel (see p. 135).

MOSQUITO

Mosquitoes are a unique type of spirit that subsists off the life force of living beings. They appear as small, hairy, flying insects, with a prominent proboscis in the center of their face. While all spirits appear the same, only the females actually attack to consume blood. They appear

to need to draw the life force of other living creatures in order to power the infestation of a new spirit into a host. The males (typically soldiers and workers) act as scouts and protectors of the females so they can focus on propagation. Some have been known to become carriers of virulent diseases. They are among the most hated and actively hunted of all insect spirits.

Unique Qualities: All mosquito spirits have the Flight skill, "females" (as determined by the gamemaster) have the Essence Drain power (p. 396, *SR5*); some spirits may also have the Pestilence power (at the gamemaster's discretion; see p. 197).

ROACH

Cockroaches are omnivores, gathering food primarily as scavengers. Unusually for insect spirits, they form what appear to be "family" units, centered around the Mother spirit or shaman that "birthed" them. They also build nests, though not nearly as large as the hive spirits, that can have one or more family units living in them. Roach spirits, like their terrestrial counterparts, are famously hardy and resistant to damage. Roaches can withstand extreme temperatures, radiation, go without food for extended periods of time, and even hibernate when necessary.

Unique Qualities: All Roach spirits have +2 to Damage Resistance tests, and all have Allergy (Light, Mild) in addition to the normal insecticides Allergy.

INSECT SPIRIT TYPES

While not all insect spirits have the same social organization, every group can include individuals of these five spirit types. Some types are more or less common, depending on the variety. All insect spirits with wings can fly, and every kind can walk on walls and other flat surfaces.

CARETAKER

Caretaker spirits are summoned to take care of the nest or hive along with the spirits undergoing inhabitation. They are less common, but not unheard of, among solitary insect spirits. Caretakers often create protective wards to defend the hive from intruders or predators.

B	A	R	S	W	L	I	C	M	ESS	EDG
F	F+1	F+1	F	F	F	F	F	F	F	F/2

Physical Init.	((F x 2) + 1) + 2D6
Astral Init.	(F x 2) + 3D6
Skills	Assensing, Astral Combat, Leadership, Perception, Spellcasting, Unarmed Combat
Powers	Animal Control (Insect Type), Astral Form, Guard, Hive Mind, Inhabitation (Living Vessels), Innate Spell (Physical Barrier), Sapience
Optional Powers	Binding, Confusion, Enhanced Senses (Smell, Thermographic Vision, or Ultrasound)
Weaknesses	Allergy (Insecticides, Severe), Evanescence

NYMPH

Nymph spirits are juvenile queens or mothers and resemble immature (smaller and underdeveloped) versions of their parent. Lacking the raw size or magical power of a true Queen or Mother, nymphs still make use of their spell-like or pheromone abilities to assist the hive. Insect shamans tend to prefer female vessels for nymphs, as the inhabitations tend to produce better results.

B	A	R	S	W	L	I	C	M	ESS	EDG
F–1	F	F+3	F–1	F	F	F	F	F	F	F/2

Physical Init.	((F x 2) + 3) + 2D6
Astral Init.	(F x 2) + 3D6
Skills	Assensing, Astral Combat, Perception, Gymnastics, Spellcasting, Unarmed Combat
Powers	Animal Control (Insect Type), Astral Form, Enhanced Senses (Smell, Thermographic Vision, or Ultrasound), Hive Mind, Inhabitation (Living Vessels), Innate Spell (any one Illusion Spell known to the summoner), Sapience
Optional Powers	Compulsion, Fear
Weaknesses	Allergy (Insecticides, Severe), Evanescence

SCOUT

Scout spirits often operate outside the boundaries of the hive, seeking to uncover threats before they arrive or discovering new opportunities to expand. They are the most subtle of insect spirits, using subterfuge and guile to achieve their goals. Whenever possible a shaman or Queen/Mother will attempt to make a flesh-form scout (see **Inhabitation**, p. 195).

B	A	R	S	W	L	I	C	M	ESS	EDG
F	F+2	F+2	F	F	F	F	F	F	F	F/2

Physical Init.	((F x 2) + 2) + 3D6
Astral Init.	(F x 2) + 3D6
Skills	Assensing, Astral Combat, Gymnastics, Perception, Sneaking, Unarmed Combat
Powers	Animal Control (Insect Type), Astral Form, Concealment, Enhanced Senses (Smell, Thermographic Vision, or Ultrasound), Hive Mind, Inhabitation (Living Vessels), Movement, Sapience, Search
Optional Powers	Confusion, Guard, Natural Weapon (DV = (Force) Physical damage, AP 0), Noxious Breath
Weaknesses	Allergy (Insecticides, Severe), Evanescence

SOLDIER

Soldiers are second only to the Queen as the most feared kind of insect spirit. They are the militant arm of the hive, protecting its members and eliminating any threats. In solitary species, the soldiers hunt as lone predators, while more collective hives have their soldiers fight with lethal coordination. They are even hardier than the average bug spirit, being highly resistant to physical attacks and even more resistant to insecticides than the other bugs.

B	A	R	S	W	L	I	C	M	ESS	EDG
F+3	F+1	F+1	F+3	F	F	F	F	F	F	F/2

Physical Init.	((F x 2) + 1) + 2D6
Astral Init.	(F x 2) + 3D6
Skills	Assensing, Astral Combat, Counterspelling, Exotic Ranged Weapon, Gymnastics, Perception, Unarmed Combat
Powers	Animal Control (Insect Type), Astral Form, Fear, Hive Mind, Inhabitation (Living Vessels), Natural Weapon (DV = (Force + 2) Physical damage, AP –1), Sapience
Optional Powers	Concealment, Binding, Magical Guard, Noxious Breath, Skill (a soldier spirit may be given an additional Combat skill instead of an optional power), Venom
Weaknesses	Allergy (Insecticides, Light), Evanescence

WORKER

Workers are by far the most common type of insect spirit and form the backbone of the hive. They do the work of constructing and expanding the physical space of the hive and acquiring the resources it needs to survive.

B	A	R	S	W	L	I	C	M	ESS	EDG
F	F	F	F+1	F	F	F	F	F	F	F/2

Physical Init.	(Fx2) + 2D6
Astral Init.	(Fx2) + 3D6
Skills	Assensing, Astral Combat, Perception, Unarmed Combat
Powers	Animal Control (Insect Type), Astral Form, Enhanced Senses (Smell, Thermographic Vision), Hive Mind, Inhabitation (Living Vessels), Movement, Sapience, Search
Optional Powers	Concealment, Enhanced Senses (Ultrasound), Venom, Skill (a worker spirit may be given additional Technical or Physical skill instead of an optional power)
Weaknesses	Allergy (Insecticides, Severe), Evanescence

QUEEN/MOTHER

The Queen or Mother spirit is the central figure in the Hive or group to which she is summoned. Her ability to use the Astral Gateway power to summon more of her kind makes her the single greatest threat of any kind of bug spirit to metahumanity.

B	A	R	S	W	L	I	C	M	ESS	EDG
F+5	F+3	F+4	F+5	F+1	F+1	F+1	F	F	F	F/2

Physical Init.	((Fx2) + 5) + 2D6
Astral Init.	(Fx2) + 3D6
Skills	Assensing, Astral Combat, Con, Counterspelling, Gymnastics, Leadership, Negotiation, Perception, Spellcasting, Unarmed Combat
Powers	Animal Control (Insect Type), Astral Gateway, Banishing Resistance, Compulsion, Enhanced Senses (Smell, Thermographic Vision or Ultrasound), Fear, Hive Mind, Sapience, Search, Spirit Pact, Wealth
Optional Powers	Concealment, Guard, Natural Weapon (DV = (Force + 3) Physical damage, AP –1), Noxious Breath, Venom
Weaknesses	Allergy (Insecticides, Severe)
Note	All Queen/Mother spirits are free spirits (p. 202)

CREATURES OF THE UNKNOWN

MANANANGGAL

The manananggal is a highly unusual type of vampiric creature. Like traditional vampires, it subsists on a diet of metahuman essence, but that is where the similarities end. Manananggals prefer, but are not required, to consume essence from the unborn children of pregnant women. It also possesses the ability to detach its torso from its legs, gaining the ability to fly when it does so. It must do this in order to feed. While detached it is the most vulnerable. If salt is applied to the area between the torso and legs while the creature is detached, it is unable to reattach as long as the salt remains. Without the legs, the winged half weakens and dies within twenty-four hours.

MANANANGGAL (WHOLE)

B	A	R	S	W	L	I	C	M	ESS	EDG
4	3	4	4	4	3	4	3	4	2D6	3

Condition Monitor (P/S)	10/10
Limits	Physical 6, Mental 5, Social (variable)
Physical Init.	8 + 2D6
Skills	Assensing 4, Astral Combat 3, Gymnastics 4, Perception 4, Running 4, Sneaking 5, Unarmed Combat 5
Powers	Dual Natured, Immunity (Age, Pathogens, Toxins), Regeneration, Sapience
Weaknesses	Allergy (Sunlight, Mild), Dietary Requirement (Metahuman Blood), Essence Loss

TORSO (WHILE DETACHED)

B	A	R	S	W	L	I	C	M	ESS	EDG
4	3	4	4	4	3	4	3	4	2D6	3

Condition Monitor (P/S)	10/10
Limits	Physical 6, Mental 5, Social (variable)
Physical Init.	10 + 2D6
Skills	Assesnsing 4, Astral Combat 3, Flight 5, Gymnastics 4, Perception 4, Unarmed Combat 5
Powers	Dual Natured, Essence Drain, Immunity (Age, Pathogens, Toxins), Natural Weapon (Claws, DV 5P, AP—1, Reach 0), Regeneration, Sapience
Weaknesses	Allergy (Salt, Severe), Allery (Sunlight, Moderate), Dietary Requirement (Metahuman Blood), Essence Loss

LEGS (WHILE DETACHED)

B	A	R	S	W	L	I	C	M	ESS	EDG
2	2	2	3	4	3	5	3	4	2D6	3

Condition Monitor (P/S)	9/9
Limits	Physical 4, Mental 5, Social (variable)
Physical Init.	7 + 2D6
Skills	Gymnastics 4, Running 4, Sneaking 5, Unarmed Combat 2
Powers	Dual Natured, Immunity (Age, Pathogens, Toxins), Regeneration
Weaknesses	Allergy (Salt, Severe), Allergy (Sunlight, Moderate), Dietary Requirement (Metahuman Blood), Essence Loss

ENGKANTO

Engkanto are a type of spirit from a deep and previously unknown metaplane. Their link to the physical plane is weak, and they can only manifest in an area with a background count of 5 or more. Even then, their forms cannot leave the physical boundaries of such a domain. They appear as small shapes, less than half a meter tall, and vaguely metahuman, though they are mostly insubstantial. Always seen in groups, they have a form of hybrid or collective intelligence and communicate with metahumans as a group, though they refer to themselves as a single being.

Their motivations are entirely alien and unknown, but they always attempt to entice a mortal into a unique kind of spirit pact (p. 205). This pact involves the mortal performing a series of seemingly random actions, which generally start small and simple, but increase in complexity as time goes on. As long as the mortal performs the task, the engkanto continue to provide the benefits of the Karmic Boon (see p. 101). Should the mortal ever refuse the tasks given them, the engkanto revoke the benefits and punish the mortal with their Karmic Curse (see p. 101).

The exact nature of the tasks, and how to get out of the spirit pact (if at all possible), are entirely up to the gamemaster. Engkanto use the rules for free spirits (p. 202).

ENGKANTO

B	A	R	S	W	L	I	C	M	ESS	EDG
2	4	4	1	5	8	8	9	6	6	6

Condition Monitor (P/S)	9/11
Limits	Physical 3, Mental 10, Social 10
Physical Init.	12 + 2D6
Skills	Astral Combat 4, Con 10, Etiquette 8, Instruction 6, Intimidation 8, Leadership 6, Negotiation 10, Perception 10, Spellcasting 6
Powers	Accident, Concealment, Confusion, Immunity (Age, Pathogens, Toxins, Normal Weapons), Influence, Sapience, Spirit Pact (Karmic Boon/Curse)

KARMIC BOON/CURSE

This is a type of spirit pact unique to the engkanto spirit. A metahuman enters into the spirit pact as per the rules on p. 204. As long as the metahuman is in good favor with the engkanto, they can use the Karmic Boon aspect of the pact to give (at no cost to the mortal) one or more Positive Qualities (though from a story perspective some will make more sense than others). Should the metahuman fall out of favor, the engkanto can revoke the Positive Qualities granted via Karmic Boon, and impose one or more Negative Qualities that cannot be removed through any means, except by the will of the engkanto or the ending of the spirit pact.

EVANESCENCE (WEAKNESS)

Extraplanar beings want a physical anchor, and staying in full spirit form is hard on them. Evanescence reflects the difficulty some of these creatures have in staying in our midst. For every twenty-four hours that a spirit with Evanescence remains in full astral form, their Force is permanently reduced by one. If the spirit's Force reaches 0, it dissipates, either destroyed or returned to its home plane (for purposes of us on the prime material, the two results are pretty much the same).

The benefit of Evanescence is that any spirits who have lost at least one point of Force due to this weakness are hard to make out, and a –3 dice pool penalty is imposed on any Assensing Tests that might spot them. The spirits also get +3 dice pool bonus when attempting to pass through mana barriers.

All effects of Evanescence are negated as soon as the spirit inhabits or possesses a vessel, but they start up again if it is driven out of the vessel.

EXPANDED GRIMOIRE

INTRODUCTION

The old adage knowledge is power is literally true for a spellcaster. A single spell can turn the tide on a dangerous run. The spells found in the core book (p. 283, SR5) represent the body of common-knowledge workhorse spells that are most widely accessible to any spellcaster for the right price. The spells here, by contrast, dive into more esoteric and rare collections of knowledge. These formulae may be tough to come by, as spellcasters are notoriously jealous of their secret weapons and many will not share them—at least, not without a costly price tag attached. After all, when running the shadows, everything's for sale.

At the gamemaster's discretion, the spells in this chapter may be available to magicians and mystic adepts at character creation or may be learned later in game. These spells follow all the same rules for spellcasting as detailed on p. 281, SR5.

THE RIGHT SPELL AT THE RIGHT TIME

Want to be an ace spellslinger instead of just some guy doing card tricks on the street? Then you need to know when to cast a spell for maximum effect. Casting Camouflage can be a great strategy in the jungle; casting it in an office setting is less effective. Similarly, if you cast Opium Den on the denizens of a no-tell motel, most of the denizens will be only too happy to sink into a bleary haze of pleasure. Cast the same spell in an executive boardroom, and there's a better chance that someone will see through the sensation they're feeling and know that something suspicious is going on.

Gamemasters should note when players cast spells in a particularly incongruous way and provide extra dice to targets to resist those spells, or at least to notice that they are under the effects of magic. Conversely, if a spellcaster uses a spell in a perfectly appropriate way, such as employing a Stench spell downwind from an abattoir, the gamemaster may want to make it a little tougher for the targets to resist.

COMBAT SPELLS

Spellcasters leverage mana to cast combat spells to directly or indirectly harm their enemies. The complete rules for casting and utilizing combat spells may be found on p. 283, SR5.

CORRODE [OBJECT]

(INDIRECT, TOUCH, ELEMENTAL)

Type: P	**Range:** T	**Damage:** P
Duration: I	**Drain:** F – 3	

MELT [OBJECT]

(INDIRECT, ELEMENTAL)

Type: P	**Range:** LOS	**Damage:** P
Duration: I	**Drain:** F – 2	

SLUDGE [OBJECT]

(INDIRECT, AREA, ELEMENTAL)

Type: P	**Range:** LOS (A)	**Damage:** P
Duration: I	**Drain:** F – 1	

These spells conjure a sizzling blast of corrosive spray that inflicts Acid damage (p. 170, SR5) upon their targets similar to Acid Stream and Toxic Wave (p. 283, SR5). The corrosive nature of these blasts only affects the specified object for which the spell was created to harm. All other objects remain unharmed. Different objects require separate spells, such as Corrode Wall, Melt Electronics, Sludge Armor, and so on.

DISRUPT [FOCUS]

(DIRECT)

Type: M	**Range:** LOS	**Damage:** Special
Duration: I	**Drain:** F – 2	

Disrupt [Focus] channels and then diverts mana into disrupting a specific active magical focus dealing temporary damage to its astral form. A focus that receives damage equal to its Force from this spell is disrupted and becomes inactive. The magician bonded to the focus can't gain dice bonuses or any other benefit from the focus until it's reactivated. A number of boxes

of temporary damage equal to the Force of the focus are "healed" at the beginning of the next Combat Turn. The owner may spend a Simple Action to reactivate the focus when all damage is healed. Disrupting a sustaining focus also disrupts the spell it is sustaining. Astrally projecting magicians whose foci become disrupted cannot reactivate them until their astral form gets back into their physical body.

DESTROY [FREE SPIRIT]

(DIRECT)

Type: M   **Range:** LOS   **Damage:** P
Duration: I   **Drain:** F – 3

Destroy [Free Spirit] is a very specialized variant of Slay (p. 104) designed to take out a specific free spirit. Each unique spirit requires a different version of this spell, which must incorporate the target's spirit formula. This spell doesn't affect other spirits, even one of same type as the free spirit. The spell formula counts as a copy of the spirit formula for all purposes.

DESTROY [VEHICLE]

(DIRECT)

Type: M   **Range:** LOS   **Damage:** P
Duration: I   **Drain:** F – 3

Want to rule the waves, roads, or skies? This one's for you. Destroy [Vehicle] is a variant of Slay (p. 104) designed to target a type of vehicle (or drone). Each type of vehicle (e.g., aircraft, watercraft, groundcraft) requires a different version of this spell, such as Destroy Aircraft. This spell has no effect on other vehicles.

FIREWATER

(INDIRECT, ELEMENTAL)

Type: P   **Range:** LOS   **Damage:** P
Duration: I   **Drain:** F – 2

NAPALM

(INDIRECT, AREA, ELEMENTAL)

Type: P   **Range:** LOS (A)   **Damage:** P
Duration: I   **Drain:** F

These spells do a hell of a lot more than defoliate. They combine two elements, fire and water, to create a terrifying and devastating effect. Flaming Water causes Physical damage that is considered to be both Fire damage (p.171, *SR5*) and Water damage (see **Elemental Damage** sidebar, p. 105). Armor with specific modifications, such as Fire resistance, Chemical Seal, and Chemical protection) may protect target from the damage (see p.437, *SR5*).

Firewater is a single-target spell, while Napalm is an area spell.

INSECTICIDE [INSECT SPIRIT]

(DIRECT, AREA)

Type: P   **Range:** LOS   **Damage:** P
Duration: I   **Drain:** F + 1

Insect spirits are exceptionally dangerous to magicians. After the fall of Chicago, this spell started to become quite popular as the "Bug Menace" grew in importance. Insecticide is a specialized variant of Slay (p.104) designed to target a specific type of insect spirit. Each unique type of insect spirit requires different version of this spell, such as Insecticide Ant Spirits or Insecticide Roach Spirits.

ICE SPEAR

(INDIRECT, ELEMENTAL)

Type: P   **Range:** LOS   **Damage:** P
Duration: I   **Drain:** F – 3

ICE STORM

(INDIRECT, ELEMENTAL, AREA)

Type: P   **Range:** LOS (A)   **Damage:** P
Duration: I   **Drain:** F + 1

Spellcasters that weld this set of spells can attack their enemies with shards of ice of frightening potency that cause Cold Damage (p.170, *SR5*). This may cause unusual damage to certain critters and damage armor or gear. Armor with specific modifications, such as Insulation, Chemical Seal, and Chemical protection) may protect target from the damage (see p. 437, *SR5*).

Ice Spear is a single-target spell, while Ice Storm is an area spell. Ice Storm also acts as an Ice Sheet (p. 293, *SR5*) spell over the affected area

ONE LESS [METATYPE/SPECIES]

(DIRECT, TOUCH)

Type: M **Range:** T **Damage:** P
Duration: I **Drain:** F – 6

SLAY [METATYPE/SPECIES]

(DIRECT)

Type: M **Range:** LOS **Damage:** P
Duration: I **Drain:** F – 4

SLAUGHTER [METATYPE/SPECIES]

(DIRECT, AREA)

Type: M **Range:** LOS (A) **Damage:** P
Duration: I **Drain:** F – 1

These are variations of the Death Touch, Manabolt, and Manaball spells (p. 284, *SR5*). They're specialized, designed to target a particular species or meta**Type:** One Less Naga, Slay Ork, Slaughter Dwarfs, and so on. The target of each spell is designated by the spell formula. These spells only discriminate based on biological species, not social status or any other quality.

One Less requires the caster to touch the target. Slay affects a single target. Slaughter is an area effect spell.

RAM [OBJECT]

(DIRECT, TOUCH)

Type: P **Range:** T **Damage:** P
Duration: I **Drain:** F – 5

ELEMENTAL DAMAGE

POLLUTANT

Pollutant attacks deliver a concentrated burst of chemicals and other invasive elements that cause a severe reaction. Effects depend on the strength of the attack and the target's ability to resist, but can range from mild discomfort to complete and debilitating shutdown of the target's body. Treat any Pollutant attack as a toxin with the following characteristics:

Vector: Inhalation
Speed: Immediate
Penetration: 0
Power: (DV of attack)
Effect: Physical damage, anaphylactic shock (see below)

Armor provides no dice to resist a Pollutant attack. Armor upgraded with a Chemical seal (p. 437, *SR5*) provides immunity to the damage and toxic effects.

Anaphylactic Shock: If the damage from the attack with this effect is not completely resisted, the victim enters anaphylactic shock, resulting in muscle spasms and autonomic system failure if left untreated. The victim continues to take 1 box of unresisted Physical damage each Combat Turn until death, or until the victim is treated as per Stabilization (see **Stabilization**, p. 209, *SR5*).

RADIATION

Radiation powers and spells used by toxic spirits, magicians, and adepts cause highly concentrated bursts of radiation to be inflicted upon the target(s). Immediate effects are burns similar to being exposed to extreme heat. The ongoing effects, however, are much more damaging, causing the body to begin to break down at the cellular level.

Radiation attacks cause Physical damage. Armor provides no dice to resist Radiation damage, unless it has an upgrade to provide Radiation resistance, which provides dice equal to its rating for the Damage Resistance Test and the following Toxin Resistance Test. Treat every Radiation attack that hits as a toxin causing Nausea (see **Toxins**, p. 408, *SR5*) with a DV equal to net hits of the attack (before the Damage Resistance roll).

WATER

Water damage comes into play when water is delivered with sufficient force and pressure to cause injury. Water damage does not directly affect any Condition Monitors; instead, it has a chance to knock characters down. The base Water damage for knockdown purposes is the Force of the spell. The targeted character rolls Agility, reducing the Water damage by the number of hits. If the remaining damage is higher than the character's Physical limit, the Water damage knocks them down, as if they had been forcibly taken a free Drop Prone action. Additionally, the area around the target with a radius of (Force / 2) meters is slippery for the next ten minutes. Any action involving movement in this area, including Defense Tests, take a –2 dice pool penalty. Active fires in that same area have their DV reduced by the spell's Force. Also, any exposed and unsealed electronics may be damaged. For any such devices, make a Device Rating (3) Test; failure means water hit the sensitive innards of the device and bricked it (see **Bricking**, p. 228, *SR5*).

WRECK [OBJECT]

(DIRECT)

Type: P	**Range:** LOS	**Damage:** P
Duration: I	**Drain:** F – 3	

DEMOLISH [OBJECT]

(DIRECT, AREA)

Type: P	**Range:** LOS (A)	**Damage:** P
Duration: I	**Drain:** F – 1	

This set of spells is a variant of Shatter/Powerbolt/ Powerball (p. 284, *SR5*) that only affect a specific type of inanimate object. Different types of objects require a separate spell such as Ram Door, Wreck Furniture, Demolish Gun, and so on. This spell cannot be used against vehicles. Objects resist this spell with their Barrier Rating (in the case of doors and walls); other items resist with their object resistance (p. 295, *SR5*). Partial damage reduces the effectiveness of the item similar to the way damage affects a metahumans. For every three points of damage the item suffers, there is a –1 modifier to any tests using the item. Body Wreck affects only a single target while Demolish is an area spell. Ram requires the caster to touch the target.

RADIATION BEAM

(DIRECT, AREA)

Type: P	**Range:** LOS	**Damage:** P
Duration: I	**Drain:** F – 3	

RADIATION BURST

(INDIRECT, ELEMENTAL)

Type: P	**Range:** LOS (A)	**Damage:** P
Duration: I	**Drain:** F – 1	

These spells channel and unleash the vicious and invisible power of radiation on their target, causing Radiation damage (see **Elemental Damage** sidebar, p. 105).

Radiation Beam is a single target spell. Radiation Burst is an area spell. These spells can only be learned by a magician with a lodge made for the Toxic tradition.

POLLUTANT STREAM

(INDIRECT, ELEMENTAL)
Type: P   **Range:** LOS   **Damage:** P
Duration: I   **Drain:** F – 3

POLLUTANT WAVE

(INDIRECT, ELEMENTAL)
Type: P   **Range:** LOS (A)   **Damage:** P
Duration: I   **Drain:** F – 1

Oozing green chemicals, sulfurous brown smoke, and more—these spells release a pure form of nature-abhorring chemicals, causing Pollutant damage to their target (see **Elemental Damage** sidebar, p. 105). Pollutant Stream is a single target spell. Pollutant Wave is an area spell. These spells can only be learned by a magician with a lodge made for the Toxic tradition.

SHATTERSHIELD

(DIRECT, TOUCH)
Type: M   **Range:** T   **Damage:** P
Duration: I   **Drain:** F – 3

Shattershield is a variant of Death Touch (p. 284, *SR5*) designed to splinter manna barriers (see p. 315, *SR5*) in a very satisfying way. The caster must touch the mana barrier's physical component or astral form. The barrier resists with Force (its Structure rating) + Counterspelling (if anyone happens to be protecting it).

DETECTION SPELLS

Spellcasters know that five senses are far too few, and even a sixth sense is somewhat limiting. They like to have as many senses at their disposal as possible—that's where Detection spells come in. They grant the subject a new sense or improve a sense the subject already has, for as long as they are sustained. For complete rules on handling Detection spells, see p. 285, *SR5*.

ASTRAL MESSAGE

(PASSIVE, DIRECTIONAL)
Type: M   **Range:** T
Duration: I   **Drain:** F – 3

Astral Message is a variant of the Astral Projection spell (p. 313, *SR5*) designed to send short verbal messages (one hundred words or less) through the astral plane without summoning a watcher. The spellcaster must have personal experience with the target's astral form or possess a material link (p. 296, *SR5*). The message will seek out the target and be delivered to her the next time she is present in the astral plane or if she summons a watcher (p. 313, *SR5*).

The message only lasts for a limited time. The minimum duration is twenty-four hours; this is extended by an extra twenty-four hours for each hit on the Spellcasting Test.

ASTRAL CLAIRVOYANCE

(PASSIVE, DIRECTIONAL)
Type: M   **Range:** T
Duration: S   **Drain:** F – 3

Astral Clairvoyance is a variant of the Clairvoyance spell (p. 286, *SR5*) designed to work in the astral plane. The subject may project her assensing ability as though she were astrally present at a chosen point within the sensory range of the spell. This "visual point" may be moved to any other location within the sensory range of the spell at will. During the spell, the subject's normal assensing is overlaid with the insight gained from this spell. This has the unfortunate side effect of blocking out her natural physical senses.

Magicians cannot use Astral Clairvoyance to target others with spells.

BORROW SENSE

(ACTIVE, DIRECTIONAL)
Type: M   **Range:** T
Duration: S   **Drain:** F – 3

ANIMAL SENSE

(ACTIVE, DIRECTIONAL)
Type: M   **Range:** T
Duration: S   **Drain:** F – 5

EYES OF THE PACK

(ACTIVE, DIRECTIONAL)
Type: M   **Range:** T
Duration: S   **Drain:** F – 1

This collection of spells allows the spellcaster to tap into the senses of her target.

Borrow Sense enables the subject to borrow a single sense from a chosen target within range of the spell. If the target fails to resist the spell, the subject perceives with the target's sense as if it were his own. Any Perception Tests made by the subject using the target's sense use the caster's net hits on the Spellcasting Test as the limit. Note that anything sensed by the target does not make a Spell Resistance Test. The caster must touch the subject while casting the spell. The target of Borrow Sense remains in control of his own actions and senses; the subject is merely along for the ride. The subject cannot communicate with the target or direct her to focus on anything specific. Nor may the subject leverage his own augmented senses (including astral sight) through the target's senses. The subject cannot target spells through the target's senses. As long as the caster sustains the spell, the subject can switch from one of the target's senses to another with a Simple Action. Senses that the subject does not normally have can be borrowed (such as bat sonar). Note that a target's astral sight is considered a separate sense for purposes of this spell (i.e., the subject can borrow sight or astral sight, but not both at the same time).

Animal Sense is a restricted version of Borrow Sense that can only be used to borrow a sense from a non-sapient, non-paranormal animal.

Eyes of the Pack is a variant of Borrow Sense that only works with voluntary targets and only allows the sense of sight to be borrowed. Switching from the sight of one member of the pack (pack size limited to Force x 2) to another requires a Simple Action.

CATALOG

(ACTIVE, AREA)

Type: P **Range:** T
Duration: S **Drain:** F – 3

By casting Catalog, the spellcaster mystically empowers the subject to compile a comprehensive, itemized list of all the non-living items within the area of the spell. The gamemaster makes a roll to beat the Object Resistance of the highest category of objects in range (p. 295, *SR5*), and the subject can write or dictate a list of the items falling under a successful Object Resistance test. Alternately, the gamemaster may choose to make independent rolls for specific objects. Net hits obtained in the spellcasting indicate the level of detail and description the list provides.

Items in the area that the subject would not recognize by sight are listed as "unknown." The caster must touch the area targeted by the spell.

DIAGNOSE

(ACTIVE, DIRECTIONAL)

Type: M **Range:** T
Duration: I **Drain:** F – 3

Diagnose grants the subject information on the target's general health and any illnesses, injuries, or other mundane medical problems the target might possesses. The net hits determine the detailed level of the information provided, as noted on the Detection Spell Results table (p. 286, *SR5*). It provide more details than Assensing would at comparable hit levels. The caster must touch the subject to trigger the spell.

DRAGON ASTRAL SIGNATURE

(ACTIVE, PSYCHIC, AREA)

Type: M **Range:** LOS (A)
Duration: S **Drain:** F + 5

Rumors suggest that this spell was developed by an S-K Prime operation monitoring dragon-hunter groups operating in Europe and Asia, and it has been leaked into the underground to test how the dragons will respond to this new threat. The caster gains the ability to assense the astral signatures of her local astral environment to determine if a dragon is present or if there is a touch of dragon magic on anything in the area (assuming the aura has not yet faded due to the passage of time).

ENHANCE AIM

(PASSIVE, DIRECTIONAL)

Type: P **Range:** T
Duration: S **Drain:** F – 1

Enhance Aim magically improves a voluntary target's natural ability to aim by reducing range modifiers against targets (similar to using image magnification; see p. 178, *SR5*). Each hit scored by the caster reduces the effective range for the shooter for the purpose of calculating Range modifiers by 10 meters. Unlike image magnification, the target does not need a Take Aim action to lock onto a target, as the spell does that auto-magically. The effect of Enhance Aim is cumulative with other targeting devices, implants, and abilities (laser sights, scopes, smartlinks, Improved Ability adept power, etc.). The caster must touch the subject to trigger the spell.

HAWKEYE

(PASSIVE, DIRECTIONAL)

Type: P **Range:** T
Duration: S **Drain:** F – 1

Hawkeye improves a voluntary subject's visual acuity. Each hit scored by the caster provides a +1 dice pool modifier for visual Perception Tests. This effect is cumulative with other perception aids, implants, and abilities (vision enhancement, adept powers, etc.). The caster must touch the subject to trigger the spell.

MANA WINDOW

(ACTIVE, DIRECTIONAL)

Type: M **Range:** T
Duration: S **Drain:** F – 3

ASTRAL WINDOW

(ACTIVE, DIRECTIONAL)

Type: M **Range:** T
Duration: S **Drain:** F – 3

These spells are advanced versions of Clairvoyance (p. 286, *SR5*) and Astral Clairvoyance (p. 106) that allow the caster to grant a subject the ability to see or assense through mana barriers (which normally stop Clairvoyance and are opaque on the astral). If the barrier does not resist the spell with its Force, the subject can see/assense distant scenes through the barrier as if physically or astrally present within the sensory range of the spell. Magicians cannot cast spells at targets they see using these spells. Casting these spells does not alert the creator of the mana barrier.

Mana Window bypasses mana barriers on the physical plane with its clairvoyant physical sight. Astral Window bypasses astral mana barriers with its clairvoyant assensing. The caster must touch the subject of the spell, and for Astral Window the subject must be astrally active.

MINDNET

(ACTIVE, PSYCHIC, AREA)

Type: M   **Range:** T (A)
Duration: S   **Drain:** F

MINDNET EXTENDED

(ACTIVE, PSYCHIC, EXTENDED AREA)

Type: M   **Range:** T (A)
Duration: S   **Drain:** F + 1

Mindnet is a variation of the Mindlink spell (p. 287, *SR5*) designed to allow telepathic communication between a group of voluntary people. Everyone in the group can freely talk, exchange images, and emote as long as they remain within range of the target of the spell (the person touched when the spell is cast). The number of people participating in the group (excluding the target) serves as the threshold for the Spellcasting Test. Once any participants have left the range of the spell, it must be recast for them to once again to gain the benefits of Mindnet, though the other participants may continue to participate in the link as long as they remain in range and the spell is sustained.

Mindnet is an area spell, while Mindlink Extended is an extended area spell.

NIGHT VISION

(PASSIVE, DIRECTIONAL)

Type: P   **Range:** T
Duration: S   **Drain:** F – 3

Night Vision grants a voluntary subject low-light vision like that provided by the low-light vision cybernetic eyeware enhancement (p. 444, *SR5*).

[SENSE] CRYPTESTHESIA

(PASSIVE, DIRECTIONAL)

Type: M   **Range:** T
Duration: S   **Drain:** F – 3

Sense Cryptesthesia ("paranormal perception") is an advanced form of Clairvoyance (p. 286, *SR5*) and Clairaudience (p. 286, *SR5*). Each Cryptesthesia spell allows the subject to utilize a different augmented sense such as low-light vision, thermographic vision, enhanced smell, or ultrasound at a chosen point within the spell's range. These senses mimic the effects of headware cybernetic enhancements (p.451, *SR5*). The subject need not possess the sense to utilize it while the spell is

powered. However, each sense requires a different spell (for example, Sonar Cryptesthesia or Enhanced Vision Cryptesthesia).

Magicians cannot use senses granted by Cryptesthesia to target others with spells. The caster must touch the subject to trigger the spell.

SPATIAL SENSE

(PASSIVE, AREA)

Type: P   **Range:** T
Duration: S   **Drain:** F – 3

SPATIAL SENSE, EXTENDED

(PASSIVE, EXTENDED AREA)

Type: P   **Range:** T
Duration: S   **Drain:** F – 1

Spatial Sense grants the subject an innate awareness and knowledge of his physical surroundings within range of the spell in terms of landscape, geography, and architecture. The layout knowledge lasts as only long as the spell is sustained and is not retained when the spell ends (though the subject can make a map or recite directions before ending the spell). The net hits scored on the Detection Spell Results table (p. 286, *SR5*) determine how much detail the spell provides, progressing from a general idea of what's where, to a rough map of the area, to knowing each exit and how secure they are. The spell works in all directions (three-dimensional) and may uncover hidden layout features such as ventilation shafts, secret rooms, and sewer tunnels. It will not detect security features or living things. Areas that are protected by a mana barrier are experienced as "blank spots."

THOUGHT RECOGNITION

(ACTIVE, PSYCHIC, DIRECTIONAL)

Type: M   **Range:** T
Duration: S   **Drain:** F

AREA THOUGHT RECOGNITION

(ACTIVE, PSYCHIC, AREA)

Type: M   **Range:** LOS(A)
Duration: S   **Drain:** F + 2

This set of spells is a less intrusive form of Mind Probe (p. 287, *SR5*). The caster grants the subject the ability to scan the target's surface thoughts for a particular word, phrase, sound, or image chosen when the spell is cast. This spell does not dig through the target's brain for information; it merely verifies if a target is actively thinking about a particular person, place, event, or thing. Investigators use this spell to determine if a target has knowledge of something (such as a murder weapon) that they otherwise wouldn't to determine if they are involved with a crime. Spies use this spell to determine if someone is tailing or looking for them.

Thought Recognition is used on one particular target, while Area Thought Recognition scans the minds of everyone within the area.

TRANSLATE
(ACTIVE, PSYCHIC/DIRECTIONAL)
Type: M **Range:** T
Duration: S **Drain:** F – 4

Translate creates a low-level telepathic connection between the subject and a specific target within range of the sense (chosen when the spell is cast). This allows the subject and target to understand each other's speech as if the subject spoke the target's native language. The spell translates general intent rather than exact phrasing. This is useful for simple conversations, but not delicate diplomacy where the tact of a skilled translator is needed. This spell is often used for international corporate and government conversations. Translate may be used to communicate with any sapient species that uses language (such as sasquatch or merrow), but may not be used to communicate with non-sapient animals. The hits from the Spellcasting Test determine the quality of the translation. The caster must touch the subject to trigger the spell.

HEALTH SPELLS

Health spells enable a spellcaster to lay hands upon a subject to mystically heal physical injuries, cure diseases (or inflict symptoms), detoxify poisons or drugs (or mimic their effects), and modify attributes. *All Health spells require the caster to touch the target to activate the spell.* No techniques currently known to magic can erase Stun damage or cure psychological conditions. All health spells require the magician to physically touch the subject of the spell.

The complete rules for handling Health spells can be found on p. 287, *SR5*.

AMBIDEXTERITY
(ESSENCE)
Type: P **Range:** T
Duration: S **Drain:** F – 3

Ambidexterity allows the spellcaster to temporarily grant the Ambidextrous quality (p. 172, *SR5*) onto a willing subject. Every hit scored by the caster increases the duration of this spell by 1 Combat Turn for a minimum of 2 Combat Turns. The spellcaster must touch the subject to activate the spell.

ALLEVIATE ADDICTION
(ESSENCE)
Type: M **Range:** T
Duration: S **Drain:** F – 6

Alleviate Addiction temporarily reduces the effects of addiction on the subject's body and mind (p. 77, *SR5*). Every net hit reduces the addiction level by one (from Severe to Moderate, for example). This spell does not remove the addiction; it only alleviates its effects, and it can only address the effects of one addiction at a time. This cure only last while the spell is powered and then the Addiction returns at full force. Note that this spell does not work against the effects of Focus Addiction (p. 319, *SR5*).

ALLEVIATE [ALLERGY]
(ESSENCE)
Type: M **Range:** T
Duration: S **Drain:** F – 6

Alleviate *Allergy* temporarily blocks or reduces the effects of an allergy on the target's body and mind (p. 78, *SR5*). Every net hit reduces the allergy level by one (from Moderate to Mild, for example). This spell does not remove the allergy, only alleviates its effects, and it only alleviates the effects of one allergy at a time. The Allergy returns at full force once the spell ends.

AWAKEN
(ESSENCE)
Type: M **Range:** T
Duration: S **Drain:** F – 3

Awaken allows the spellcaster to immediately wake an unconscious target and instantly bring them to full alertness, temporarily alleviating the effects of Stun, including modifiers from damage. This spells works on a subject that is unconscious due to an external cause such as injury, medication, or chemicals.

The caster must achieve a threshold equal to the Stun modifiers (or 1 for targets simply asleep) the subject currently experiences. The subject remains conscious as long as the spell is sustained. At the end of that period, the character relapses into unconsciousness. Afterwards, the subject must endure all the Stun damage (this includes any new Stun damage accumulated while awake) at twice the typical duration. This effect lasts until all Stun damage is healed. Sadly, the caster may not cast this spell on herself.

CRANK
(ESSENCE)
Type: P **Range:** T
Duration: S **Drain:** F – 3

Crank alleviates a voluntary subject's physical need for sleep. Every hit scored approximates one hour of sleep for purposes of resisting Fatigue (p. 172, SR5). Popular among student magicians, Crank has a significant downside. At the gamemaster's discretion, a character who abuses Crank to avoid actual sleep for long periods may find themselves addicted to magically aided sleep deprivation (p. 172, SR5).

DECREASE REFLEXES

(NEGATIVE)

Type: P   **Range:** T
Duration: S   **Drain:** F – 2

Decrease Reflexes allows the spellcaster to decrease the reflexes (as represented by Initiative Score) of a target. The target resists with Reaction + Counterspelling. The Force of the spell must equal or exceed the target's Reaction. Every net hit achieved reduces the target's Initiative Score by 1.

ENABLER

(NEGATIVE)

Type: M   **Range:** T
Duration: S   **Drain:** F – 3

Enabler is the opposite of the spell Antidote (p. 288, SR5). This spell increases the target's susceptibility to drugs or toxins. Naturally, Enabler is popular with wiz-gangers to help themselves and other druggies get a better high. The target resists with Body + Counterspelling. Each net hit scored reduces the target's dice pool by 1 for the Toxin Resistance Test. Enabler must be sustained until the toxin effect kicks in, otherwise it does not affect the Resistance Test.

FAST

(ESSENCE)

Type: M   **Range:** T
Duration: S   **Drain:** F – 3

Fast grants a voluntary subject the ability to supplant feelings of hunger or thirst for as long as the spell is sustained. Each hit allows the target to ignore the symptoms of one skipped meal. Fast does not alleviate the biological need for food or water. Once the spell ends, the subject immediately suffers any effects of from dehydration or starvation. The wealthy sometimes use Fast as a painless "diet spell." Hunger pangs and the effects of not eating and drinking immediately return to the subject.

Subjects under the effects of this spell for more than seventy-two hours risk permanent damage. The gamemaster should apply Fatigue damage and the Disorientation effect (p. 409, SR5) as appropriate to any subject that uses Fast excessively.

FORCED DEFENSE

(ESSENCE)

Type: M   **Range:** T
Duration: I   **Drain:** F – 1

A trained runner learns to control and master her survival instincts to take calculated risks. Forced Defense triggers these primal urges to survive at all costs. The spellcaster must succeed in a Magic + Spellcasting Test opposed by the target's Body (+ Counterspelling). The target of this spell is forced to interrupt her current action to go on Full Defense (p. 191, SR5). The number of hits scored by the caster determines the number of Combat Turns that the target is forced to remain at Full Defense. This spell does not force the target to remain in the area or the combat. For more information on Active Defenses, see p. 190, SR5.

INCREASE INHERENT LIMITS

(ESSENCE)

Type: P   **Range:** T
Duration: S   **Drain:** F – 1

DECREASE INHERENT LIMITS

(NEGATIVE)

Type: P   **Range:** T
Duration: S   **Drain:** F – 1

Every character has three inherent limits (Physical, Mental, and Social) that determine how many of the hits from your initial roll you can actually use to determine the result of the test (p. 47, SR5). This set of spells allows a spellcaster to temporarily help a subject overcome these limits for the duration of the spell.

The spellcaster must touch the subject to activate the spell and then select a single inherent limit to affect with this spell. Only one inherent limit may be altered at a time. Recasting the spell on a subject wipes away the previous alteration. Each net hit achieved increases or reduces the target's selected inherent limit by 1, to a minimum of 1. The target resists Decrease Physical Limit with Strength + Willpower, Decrease Mental Limit with Logic + Willpower, and Decrease Social Limit with Charisma + Willpower.

Just so we're clear: Increase Inherent Limits increases the limit of a subject while Decrease Inherent Limits decreases the limits of a target.

ILLUSION SPELLS

The subtle art of Illusion spells allows spellcasters to deceive, disorientate, and confuse the senses. The complete rules for casting and utilizing Illusion spells can be found on p. 289, *SR5*.

CAMOUFLAGE CHECK

(REALISTIC, SINGLE-SENSE)

Type: M	**Range:** LOS
Duration: S	**Drain:** F - 2

PHYSICAL CAMOUFLAGE

(REALISTIC, SINGLE-SENSE)

Type: M	**Range:** LOS
Duration: S	**Drain:** F

This set of spells colors the subject in a camouflage pattern that matches her surroundings and provides 1 die per hit to resist attempts to spot their physical body. Camouflage works only against living viewers, while Physical Camouflage works against living viewers and technological sensors.

DECOY

(REALISTIC, MULTI-SENSE)

Type: P	**Range:** LOS
Duration: S	**Drain:** F - 3

CHAFF

(REALISTIC, MULTI-SENSE, AREA)

Type: P	**Range:** LOS
Duration: S	**Drain:** F - 1

Decoy is a variant of the spell Chaos (p. 290, *SR5*) that only affects non-living sensor devices. The sensor is bombarded with a storm of input that confuses its targeting program. For each hit scored over the Object Resistance threshold, the sensor's rating is reduced by 1. Decoy affects a single target; Chaff is an area spell.

DOUBLE IMAGE

(REALISTIC, MULTI-SENSE)

Type: P	**Range:** T
Duration: S	**Drain:** F - 1

Double Image allows the spellcaster to create an illusionary doppelganger of the subject that is an identical image of the subject and mimics everything he does. The spellcaster has limited control of the duplicate and can adjust its movement (to keep it from walking through walls and so forth), though in tight quarters this may be difficult. Making the duplicate take a distinct action requires a Simple Action by the caster. The spellcaster must touch the subject to activate the spell, and the duplicate exists as long as the spell is sustained. Casters may only have one duplicate of a single individual at a time, though they may cast the spell multiple times to duplicate multiple people.

Targets who fail to resist the spell cannot tell the original and double image apart as the double sounds, smells, and looks like the original. The double is insubstantial; bullets and melee attacks go right through it. It can neither make attacks nor cast spells. Double Image affects both physical beings and technological sensors.

DREAM

(REALISTIC, MULTI-SENSE)

Type: M	**Range:** LOS
Duration: S	**Drain:** F - 3

Dream allows a spellcaster to craft a dream sequence (including visuals, sounds, emotions, etc.) and transmit it to a sleeping target. Manufactured dreams cannot cause actual harm to the target. However, if the spellcaster is wily, the manufactured dreams may soothe or frighten the target and alter his actions in the waking world.

The spellcaster's net hits determine the dream's vividness and complexity. Targets who have severe nightmares (requires at least 5 net hits) do not recover Stun damage while they persist, and any rest during that time is lost. The target will vividly remember the dream when they wake up but will not necessarily know that the dream was mystically altered. The Dream spell is often cast using ritual spellcasting (p. 295, *SR5*) as a means of sending warnings, threats, or torment to an enemy. It is also used in modern psychological and therapeutic counseling involving directed dreaming.

EUPHORIA

(REALISTIC, SINGLE-SENSE)

Type: M	**Range:** LOS
Duration: S	**Drain:** F - 3

OPIUM DEN

(REALISTIC, SINGLE-SENSE, AREA)

Type: M	**Range:** LOS (A)
Duration: S	**Drain:** F - 1

This set of spells provides the spellcaster with an unusual set of non-lethal tools to distract his enemies by forcing great pleasure upon them. Euphoria envelops the target in the stimulating throes of a great high comparable to an empathogenic drug high or sexual climax. Many magicians utilize this spell in their private lives, granting willing targets a thrilling ecstasy. However, using this spell on unwilling subjects is considered a criminal act by law enforcement officers in many jurisdiction. Spellcasters known to excessively cast this set of spells may gain an unsavory reputation.

Each net hit scored by the spellcaster applies a -1 dice pool modifier to all of the targets' actions as they are

BRYAN SYME

distracted by the sensation. At the gamemaster's discretion, a character who suffers a dice pool modifier higher than his Willpower is completely incapacitated and preoccupied. Euphoria affects a single target; Opium Den is an area spell, affecting enemies and allies alike.

FOREBODING

(REALISTIC, MULTI-SENSE)

Type: M   **Range:** LOS (A)
Duration: S   **Drain:** F – 3

Foreboding is an area spell that mystically broadcasts feelings of imminent danger, fear, and unease to any living being who enters the spell's range. Targets simultaneously feel chilled and nervous. Their hackles rise, and they feel slightly panicked. Characters that fail to resist the spell suffer a –1 dice pool modifier to all actions for each net hit scored by the spellcaster, representing their shaking, fear, and nervousness for as long as they remain in the area of effect. At the gamemaster's discretion, characters who suffer a dice pool modifier greater than their Willpower may be compelled to flee the area, or they may simply curl up into a gibbering ball. The drawback to this spell is that the spellcaster can not limit or control who is targeted by this spell, and it effects enemies and allies alike.

HOT POTATO

(REALISTIC, SINGLE-SENSE)

Type: M   **Range:** LOS (A)
Duration: S   **Drain:** F – 3

Hot Potato is an area-effect spell that allows the spellcaster to create the illusion that all metal within the range is extremely hot to the touch. Characters who fail to resist feel as though any metal they are in contact with (weapons, armor, implants, piercings, etc.) is burning them. If the character does not drop, remove, or otherwise disengage contact from the metal, they will a dice pool modifier equal to the caster's net hits to all actions as they are distracted by the burning sensation. Once they lose contact with any metal, the distraction is over. The drawback to this spell is that the spellcaster cannot limit or control who is targeted by this spell, as it effects enemies and allies alike.

[SENSE] REMOVAL

(REALISTIC, SINGLE-SENSE)

Type: P   **Range:** LOS
Duration: S   **Drain:** F – 3

MASS [SENSE] REMOVAL

(REALISTIC, SINGLE-SENSE, AREA)

Type: P   **Range:** LOS
Duration: S   **Drain:** F – 1

This set of spells allow the spellcaster to mystically strip the target of a specified sense (sight, hearing, taste, etc.) Each sense requires a separate spell. The target suffers a -1 dice pool modifier to all Perception Tests involving that sense for every net hit scored by the caster. Implants and other technological sensors that use that sense are also affected. The drawback to this spell is that the spellcaster cannot limit or control who is targeted by this spell—it affects enemies and allies alike.

[Sense] Removal affects a single target, while Mass [Sense] Removal is an area spell.

STINK

(REALISTIC, SINGLE-SENSE)
Type: M **Range:** LOS
Duration: S **Drain:** F - 3

STENCH

(REALISTIC, SINGLE-SENSE, AREA)
Type: M **Range:** LOS
Duration: S **Drain:** F - 1

This set of spells provides the spellcaster an obnoxious tool to distract her enemies by creating an illusion of a sickening, gut-wrenching stench. Every net hit scored by the caster applies a -1 dice pool modifier to all of the target's actions as they gag and retch. At the gamemaster's discretion, a character who suffers a dice pool modifier higher than his Willpower is completely incapacitated and pre-occupied with throwing up. Thankfully, the spellcaster is immune to the effects of this spell.

Stink affects a single target, Stench is an area spell, affecting enemies and allies alike.

SOUND BARRIER

(REALISTIC, SINGLE-SENSE, AREA)
Type: P **Range:** LOS (A)
Duration: S **Drain:** F - 3

Sound Barrier is a variant of the Silence spell (p. 291, SR5) that allows the spellcaster to create a perimeter of silence around the area of effect (rather than creating a mass area of silence). Those inside the sound barrier cannot hear outside noises but can hear sounds within the globe and vice versa. Only sounds crossing the border are affected, in the same manners as the Silence spell. Sound Barrier also affects technological devices, infrasound, and ultrasound.

SWITCH VEHICLE SIGNATURE

(REALISTIC, MULTI-SENSE)
Type: P **Range:** T
Duration: Special **Drain:** F + 1

Switch Vehicle Signature is a variant of Physical Mask (p. 291, SR5) designed to switch the electronic signal unique to a vehicle (or a drone) with another vehicle of roughly the same size for a limited time. Electronic sensors (such as those from other vehicles or drones) will read the vehicle signature of one of the affected vehicles as though it were the other targeted vehicle. This spell does not grant additional verification codes that paranoid security systems might require to grant access to secure areas, but it will help a vehicle sneak past casual security monitoring. This deception is only effective as long as the two targeted vehicles are within a five kilometers of each other. Once the targeted vehicles exceed the range, the vehicle signatures snap back to normal. This sudden switch will trigger an alert by most security systems looking for abnormalities. In addition, should one of the vehicles be destroyed, the effects of this spell are automatically canceled.

The spell's duration is ten minutes plus an additional ten minutes for each net hit scored by the caster.

VEHICLE MASK

(REALISTIC, MULTI-SENSE)
Type: P **Range:** T
Duration: S **Drain:** F - 3

Vehicle Mask is a variant of Physical Mask (p. 291, SR5) designed to mask the identities of vehicles and drones. By touching the targeted vehicle, the spellcaster creates an illusion that masks it to appear to be a completely different vehicle of roughly the same size. In addition to the visual mask, this spell affects the vehicle's sound, smell, and other identifiable characteristics. Vehicle Mask can also modify a vehicle's Signature (p. 184, SR5); each net hit scored by the caster can be used to raise or lower the vehicle's Signature modifier by 1. The caster must be actively touching the vehicle being masked to sustain the spell.

MANIPULATION SPELLS

Spellcasters often dream of shaping the world to suit them, and Manipulaiton spells are how they pull this off. Manipulation spells involve controlling or transforming matter and energy according to the whims of the spellcaster. The complete rules for casting and utilizing Manipulation spells can be found on p. 292, SR5.

BIND

(PHYSICAL)
Type: P **Range:** LOS
Duration: S **Drain:** F - 2

NET

(PHYSICAL)
Type: P **Range:** LOS (A)
Duration: S **Drain:** F - 1

MANA BIND

(MANA)

Type: M	**Range:** LOS
Duration: S	**Drain:** F – 2

MANA NET

(MANA, AREA)

Type: M	**Range:** LOS (A)
Duration: S	**Drain:** F – 1

This set of spells is used by the spellcaster to bind a target with invisible bands of magical energy that impede movement. Every net hit reduces the target's Agility by 1. If Agility is reduced to 0, the target is bound and unable to move his limbs. While bound by the spell, the target may attempt to crawl or hop short distances (at one-quarter their normal movement rate). Bound targets may still defend and dodge against attacks, but they suffer a dice-pool modifier equal to the caster's net hits. A bound target may attempt to break free of the bindings by making an Opposed Test, pitting Strength + Body against the spell's Force x 2.

Bind works on single targets, while Net is an area spell. These spells may be used against inanimate objects such as drones to restrict moving or rotating parts, though this may not stop some drones and vehicles, depending on their method of propulsion.

Mana Bind and Mana Net work against astral or dual-natured entities, and the Opposed Test to break free is Willpower + Charisma vs. spell's Force x 2. Mana Bind only works on a single living or magical target, while Mana Net is an area spell that works against living/magical targets.

BUG ZAPPER

(ENVIRONMENTAL, AREA)

Type: M	**Range:** LOS (A)
Duration: S	**Drain:** F + 1

Bug Zapper is a modified version of the Mana Barrier spell (p. 294, SR5) designed to work against insect spirits and insect spirit powers. After the fall of Chicago, this spell started to become quite popular as the "Bug Menace" grew in importance. When cast on the physical plane, Spirit Zapper impedes materialized spirits, creating a mana-based object that "zaps" any insect spirits that come into contact with it. The barrier inflicts Physical damage equal to its Force. Otherwise, Bug Zapper functions the same as Mana Barrier. Note that this spell does not damage any other types of spirits or astral forms.

CALM ANIMAL

(MENTAL)

Type: M	**Range:** LOS
Duration: S	**Drain:** F – 3

CALM PACK

(MENTAL, AREA)

Type: M	**Range:** LOS (A)
Duration: S	**Drain:** F – 1

Calm Animal allows a spellcaster to calm any non-sapient creature (normal or paranormal), making it non-aggressive while the spell is sustained. Calm Animal affects a single creature, while Calm Pack is an area spell. Affected animals still defend themselves if attacked.

CATFALL

(PHYSICAL)

Type: P	**Range:** LOS
Duration: S	**Drain:** F – 3

A spellcaster may utilize Catfall to slow a target's fall to help him land safely without suffering falling damage (p. 172, SR5). Gamemasters can determine the maximum distance (in meters) the target may fall without danger of injury by multiplying the spellcaster's hits by the spell's Force. If the target falls a greater distance, subtract the maximum distance of the spell before calculating damage.

CLEAN [ELEMENT]

(ENVIRONMENTAL, AREA)

Type: P	**Range:** LOS (A)
Duration: P	**Drain:** F – 3

Clean [Element] is an area spell that clears all impurities out of the volume of a particular element within range. Each element requires a different spell (Clean Air, Clean Water, etc.). For example, Clean Air could be used to cleanse a room of toxic fumes, or Clean Water could purify a drinking supply. The caster's hits determine how thoroughly the element is cleaned; slightly muddy water would require only 1 hit to clean, while contaminated runoff water could require four hits to make it drinkable. The amount of an element cleaned equals the caster's Magic Rating x 10 in cubic meters.

COMPEL TRUTH

(MENTAL)

Type: M	**Range:** LOS
Duration: Special	**Drain:** F – 1

Compel Truth is a spell that forces the target to speak only the truth as she knows it. The target can say something he or she believes to be true, even if it is not. The subject may choose not to speak or to withhold information but cannot directly lie. Some jurisdictions (like the UCAS) consider the use of this spell by law enforcement authorities to be a violation of a suspect's right against self-incrimination. Others have been known to use this spell (among others) to get to the truth in legal cases. The spell lasts for a number of minutes equal to the net hits on the Spellcasting Test.

CONTROL ANIMAL

(MENTAL)

Type: M	**Range:** LOS
Duration: S	**Drain:** F - 3

CONTROL PACK

(MENTAL, AREA)

Type: M	**Range:** LOS
Duration: S	**Drain:** F - 1

This set of spells is a variant of Control Thoughts and Mob Mind (p. 293, SR5) designed to work on non-sapient animals (both normal and paranormal). The spellcaster first seizes control of the animals' minds and actions and then may issue verbal commands that must be obeyed with a Simple Action. Gamemasters should consider the intelligence of the targeted animal and the complexity of the command when determining how effectively the targeted animal obeys.

Control Animal affects a single creature; Control Pack is an area spell.

DEFLECTION

(PHYSICAL)

Type: P	**Range:** LOS
Duration: S	**Drain:** F - 1

Deflection grants the spellcaster the ability to cast a spell of protection over a willing target. Every hit scored grants the target a +1 dice pool modifier for defending against ranged physical attacks. The effects of this spell are subtle enough to be discounted as a missed shot or poor aim (at least at first).

[ELEMENT] AURA

(ENVIRONMENTAL)

Type: P	**Range:** LOS
Duration: S	**Drain:** F + 1

[Element] Aura creates a rippling aura of elemental energies around a willing subject's body, granting her some of the properties of said element. Each element requires a different spell such as Flame Aura, Electrical Aura, Cold Aura, and so on. Said auras increase the Damage Value of any melee attacks by the caster's hits depending upon the nature of the element. Attacks are also treated as Cold, Electricity, Fire, or some other elemental damage (p. 105 and p. 170, SR5), and have the armor penetration appropriate to each attack. Any successful physical melee attack against the subject also means that the attacker must resist similar damage from the aura.

[ELEMENT] WALL

(ENVIRONMENTAL, AREA)

Type: P	**Range:** LOS (A)
Duration: S	**Drain:** F + 2

[Element] Wall allows the spellcaster to create a wall composed of the specified element named in the spell. Each element requires a different spell, such as Fire Wall, Ice Wall, Smoke Wall, and so on. The elemental wall may have a height and length up to the spell's Force in meters. Alternatively, the caster may craft a dome with a radius and height equal to half the Force in meters. The width of the wall can be up to one meter. In addition, the caster may adjust this size as he would adjust any area effect radius (see p. 282, SR5).

Anyone coming into contact with the wall faces damage, AP, and effects as appropriate to the element (p. 170, SR5), with a Drain equal to the spell's Force. Note that some elemental walls (fire, smoke, etc.) are not solid and do not block attacks, though they may inflict Visibility modifiers as determined by the gamemaster. Solid walls (earth, ice, etc.) have an Armor and Structure rating equal to the caster's Spellcasting hits.

FASHION

(ENVIRONMENTAL, AREA)

Type: P	**Range:** T
Duration: P	**Drain:** F - 1

This spell instantly tailors clothing, transforming garments into any fashion the caster wishes. The net hits over the clothing's object resistance (defense pool for the clothing can be between 6 and 9, depending on the complexity of the material and whether it interweaves electronics into the threads) measure the degree of style in the tailoring. The spell cannot change clothing's protective value, only its cut, color, pattern, and fit. The weight of the clothing does not change, and it must cover approximately the same amount of area (for example, a jumpsuit can't be converted into a bikini). The caster must touch the clothing.

FASHION HITS TABLE

NET HITS	RESULT
1	The tint of the color can change (e.g., dark blue to light blue, but not blue to green); minor adjustments such as mending bullet holes can also be performed
2	Adjustments to the fit of the clothing can be made, but nothing drastic about the nature of the clothes (for example, pants are still pants). Color can change slightly (e.g., blue to green or purple, but not red).
3	Full spectrum of color can be manipulated. Simple geometric patterns and designs can be added, but nothing as elaborate as corporate logos or name tags. Modifications such as the addition or removal of pockets or pants to a skirt can be done. Repairs and cleaning of the clothing can also be performed.
4+	Clothing can be changed with enough specificity to mimic a uniform, provided enough material is available. Color changes can help mimic missing accessories such as buttons, labels, badges, ribbons, etc. These changes, however, are only convincing at a distance if the physical accessories are not present. The closer a target gets to the subject, the more likely they will notice the actual accessories are missing (a gamemaster would call for a Perception Test to see if the person notices). Patterns and designs on clothing can be as intricate as the magician desires.

FIX

(PHYSICAL)

Type: P   **Range:** T
Duration: P   **Drain:** F

Most spellcasters have devoted their efforts towards learning spells rather than mechanics. This can leave a magician in a bad situation when there is a need for an emergency repair during a run. Fix allows the spellcaster to repair damage to non-living materials, including drones and vehicles. The caster must first touch the object and then achieve enough hits to beat the item's Object Resistance threshold (p. 295, SR5).

Fix can repair any item with a weight equal to the Force x the spellcaster's hits in kilograms or less. This spell can only repair broken items when all the pieces are present. The weight limit applies to the damaged part, not necessarily the entire vehicle. For example, if you have a busted wheel, you would count that weight not the weight of the entire vehicle. Each hit scored repairs 1 point of Structure rating or 1 box of damage. An object may only be affected by Fix once and thereafter may not be repaired again by this spell.

GECKO CRAWL

(PHYSICAL)

Type: P   **Range:** T
Duration: S   **Drain:** F - 3

Gecko Crawl spell allows the caster to grant a willing subject the ability to walk along vertical or overhead surfaces at a movement rate equal to Force x hits in meters per turn. Although the subject has amazing climbing abilities for the duration of the spell, he is still affected by gravity and will fall if his hands or feet are physically separated from the surface. The gamemaster may elect to require Climbing Tests in order for the subject to climb especially slick surfaces.

GLUE

(PHYSICAL)

Type: P   **Range:** LOS
Duration: P   **Drain:** F - 3

GLUE STRIP

(PHYSICAL, AREA)

Type: P   **Range:** LOS (A)
Duration: P   **Drain:** F - 1

Glue allows the spellcaster to bond a target to any one surface to which it is currently in contact. The target must be touching the surface at the time of the spellcasting. The caster must beat the surface's Object Resistance threshold (p. 295, SR5) in order to create the mystical bond. Pulling the two surfaces apart requires an Opposed Test between the spell's Force x 2 and the separator's Strength + Body. If a target or surface has a Body

or Structure rating lower than the spell's Force, the skin/surface will be torn apart in the process of being separated (suffering Physial damage equal to the difference). Glue affects a single target, Glue Strip is an area spell.

INCREASE NOISE

(PHYSICAL)

Type: P   **Range:** LOS
Duration: S   **Drain:** F - 3

DECREASE NOISE

(PHYSICAL)

Type: P   **Range:** LOS
Duration: S   **Drain:** F - 1

Noise is the static on the wireless Matrix that saps your signal and slows down your access (p. 230, SR5). Spellcasters can leverage this set of spells to artificially increase or decrease the noise within the range of the spell. The spellcaster is not immune to her alternations of the noise and may indeed be hoisted on her own petard should she attempt to use the Matrix after she has increased the noise.

The spellcaster must achieve enough hits to beat the item's Object Resistance threshold (p. 295, SR5). Each net hit achieved increases or reduces the noise of the Matrix by 1 within the boundaries of the spell. For more information about the effects of noise and the Matrix, refer to the chart on p. 231, SR5.

Unusual changes in the noise of a specific area may attract undue attention and increase the Overwatch Score (p. 231, SR5). Every point of Force of this spell above 3 adds one to a hacker's Overwatch Score each minute.

INCREASE GEAR LIMITS

(PHYSICAL)

Type: P   **Range:** T
Duration: S   **Drain:** F - 1

DECREASE GEAR LIMITS

(PHYSICAL)

Type: P   **Range:** T
Duration: S   **Drain:** F - 1

Quality gear isn't always easy to come by in a tight spot. Sometimes a runner has to make do with what she can scrounge. This set of spells allows a spellcaster to temporarily upgrade or downgrade targeted gear by increasing a single limitation category, such as Accuracy (p. 417, SR5). Wily spellcasters secretly use Decrease Gear Limits to sabotage rivals and enemies without them ever suspecting the true the instrument of their downfall.

The caster must first touch the object, select a single limit to affect, and then achieve enough hits to beat the item's Object Resistance threshold (p. 295, SR5). Only one limit may be altered at a time for any particular piece of gear. Each net hit achieved increases or reduces the target's selected inherent limit by 1, to a minimum of 1.

Increase Gear Limits increases the limit of a subject while Decrease Gear Limits decreases the limits of a target.

INTERFERENCE

(ENVIRONMENTAL, AREA)
Type: P   **Range:** LOS (A)
Duration: S   **Drain:** F - 1

Interference creates a barrage of static in the electromagnetic spectrum jamming radio and wireless signals. This spell jams all signals in the area of effect with a Signal rating less than the hits scored by the spellcaster, just like a jammer (p. 248, *SR5*). Sadly, the spellcaster's personal equipment is not immune to this spell.

LOCK

(PHYSICAL)
Type: P   **Range:** LOS
Duration: S   **Drain:** F - 1

Lock allows the spellcaster to telekinetically hold a door (or portal, hatch, closure, or similar blockage) closed with a Strength equal to the Force. The caster must beat the item's Object Resistance threshold (p. 295, *SR5*) to hold the blockade into place. Opening the portal requires an Opposed Test between Strength and the spell's Force.

MANA STATIC

(ENVIRONMENTAL, AREA)
Type: M   **Range:** LOS (A)
Duration: P   **Drain:** F - 1

Mana Static allows the spellcaster to create a background count that impedes magical activities. For every hit scored by the caster, the background count is increased by 1. Once the spell is made permanent, the background count from this spell recedes at a rate of 1 point per hour. Mana Static affects everyone in the affected area, including the caster.

MAKEOVER

(PHYSICAL)
Type: P   **Range:** T
Duration: P   **Drain:** F - 3

Makeover allows the spellcaster to grant a "makeover" to voluntary subject that mystically alters cosmetics, hair color and style, and nails. These changes are magical in nature and do not depend upon the caster's knowledge of grooming or fashion. The effects of the makeover are as permanent as those made physically in a beauty salon. Each hit scored by the caster measures the degree of style and skill in the makeover.

MIST

(ENVIRONMENTAL, AREA)
Type: P   **Range:** LOS (A)
Duration: I   **Drain:** F - 3

Mist creates a thick fog that blankets the entire area of effect. The mist is dense and difficult to see through, imposing a visibility modifier equal to the hits scored by the caster. The mist dissipates quickly based on the surrounding temperature and winds. Generally speaking, this means the vision modifier is reduced by 1 per Combat Turn, though gamemasters may make this reduction slower in cool, damp areas and faster in hot, dry areas.

OFFENSIVE MANA BARRIER

(ENVIRONMENTAL, AREA)
Type: M   **Range:** LOS (A)
Duration: S   **Drain:** F + 3

Offensive Mana Barrier is an amped-up version of the Mana Barrier spell (p. 294, *SR5*). It allows the spellcaster create a mana barrier that "zaps" any spirits, dual beings, or astral forms that come into contact with it. The barrier inflicts Physical damage equal to its Force. Otherwise, Offensive Mana Barrier functions the same as Mana Barrier.

PRESERVE

(PHYSICAL)
Type: P   **Range:** T
Duration: I   **Drain:** F - 3

Preserve allows the spellcaster to keep inert organic matter from drying out, decaying, or putrefying. It can be used on such mundane things as food and drink, but it is most often used by forensic spellcasters to protect cadavers from decay before autopsy, or to preserve small organic samples (hair, skin) taken from a crime scene for use as a material link (p. 296, *SR5*). The amount of time the material stays fresh and preserved is determined by the Spellcasting hits; multiply the number of hits + 1 by the time matter would normally stay fresh to determine how long it lasts. For example, 4 hits would preserve a substance for 5 times as long as it would normally last.

PROTECT VEHICLE

(PHYSICAL, AREA)
Type: P   Range T
Duration: S   **Drain:** F - 1

A wily magician knows how to protect her getaway vehicle from rival spellcasters. Protect Vehicle casts a protective barrier over a targeted vehicle. The caster must beat the surface's Object Resistance threshold (p. 295, *SR5*) in order to create the mystical bond between the caster and the vehicle. Each net hit scored by the caster then increases the vehicle's Object Resistance threshold by 1. In addition, for the duration of the spell, the caster may share her Spell Defense with the entire vehicle and its occupants (even if the number protected by Spell Defense exceeds the caster's Magic rating). Note that only one target within the vehicle, or the vehicle itself, may utilize said Spell Defense during a single Combat Turn.

PULSE

(ENVIRONMENTAL, AREA)

Type: P	**Range:** LOS (A)
Duration: I	**Drain:** F + 1

Pulse sends out a brief, highly charged burst of electromagnetic energy, emanating from the spellcaster, that plays havoc with electrical systems. This spell erases standard RFID tags and may affect other non-optical and non-hardened electronic circuit systems within the range of the spell. Most modern electronics are optical-based, but they still have some electronic components that this spell can effect. It also can affect some archaic devices and power systems. All such devices within the spell's range, no matter who owns them, are affected.

The caster must beat the item's Object Resistance threshold (p. 295, SR5) to affect it with Pulse. Affected systems may suffer data loss, power outages, or burn out entirely at the gamemaster's discretion. The number of hits scored by the caster determines the level of disruption of the systems within the range of the Pulse. In addition, Pulse also disrupts wireless reception and radio communication for a brief instant.

REINFORCE

(PHYSICAL)

Type: P	**Range:** LOS
Duration: S	**Drain:** F - 1

Reinforce allows the spellcaster to increase the structural integrity of an object no larger than caster's Magic in square meters. Each hit scored by the caster increases both the Armor and Structure rating by 1 as long as the spell is sustained.

SLOW VEHICLE

(PHYSICAL)

Type: P	**Range:** LOS
Duration: S	**Drain:** F + 4

Slow Vehicle is a dangerous spell that magicians use as a last report when an enemy is getting away and there isn't any way to stop them. Should the caster achieve enough hits to beat the vehicle's Object Resistance threshold (p. 295, SR5), she may physically absorb excess kinetic energy causing a decrease in relative speed. This causes a good deal of extra Drain, but for every hit scored, the caster may decrease the Speed Attribute by one for the targeted vehicle. This spell can be quite effective in slowing a target down during a chase. If the driver is unfamiliar with the

effects of this spell, the gamemaster may require a Stunt action to keep the vehicle steady (p. 204, SR5).

SHAPE [MATERIAL]

(ENVIRONMENTAL, AREA)

Type: P	**Range:** LOS (A)
Duration: S	**Drain:** F - 2

Shape [Material] allows the spellcaster to move and shape a volume of a specified inorganic element or material (air, earth, water, fire, mud, lava, plasteel, concrete, tar, etc.) within range of the spell. First, the caster must beat the material's Object Resistance threshold (p. 295, SR5) and then mentally command it to his whims. The material can be moved and reshaped in any way the caster desires at a maximum Movement Rate of (net hits) meters per turn. Loose material can be moved and re-shaped easily, but material that is connected or reinforced (such as walls or other material part of a structure) must be broken apart by reducing its Structure Rating by the caster's net hits per Combat Turn. This spell allows the caster to rapidly dig holes, redirect streams, fill balloons, create a path through a fire, construct a barricade, or create a doorway where one didn't exist before.

Each element/material requires a separate spell such as Shape Sand, Shape Ice, Shape Wood, Shape Concrete, and so on. Elements or materials reshaped by the caster remain frozen in that form when the spell ends. If that form cannot be supported by the material, it will collapse into rumble. The material/element can also be spread out, extinguished, or evaporated. For example, a fire could be extinguished by reducing the Power by the caster's Spellcasting net hits each turn.

SHAPECHANGE

(PHYSICAL)

Type: P	**Range:** LOS
Duration: S	**Drain:** F - 3

(CRITTER) FORM

(PHYSICAL)

Type: P	**Range:** LOS
Duration: S	**Drain:** F - 2

Shapechange transforms a voluntary subject into a normal (non-paranormal) critter, though the subject retains human consciousness. The subject can only assume the form of a critter whose base Body Rating is 2 points greater or less than her own. Consult the Critters section, (p. 392, SR5) for the subject's Physical attributes while in critter form. Add 1 to the critter's Base attribute Ratings for every hit the caster generates. Her Mental attributes remain unchanged.

This spell does not transform clothing and equipment. Magicians in critter form can still cast spells but cannot perform tasks requiring speech. The subject may not turn into a swarm.

Critter form works like the Shapechange spell but only allows the subject to change into a specific non-paranormal animal. Each critter form is a different spell (Hellhound Form, Devil Rat Form, and so on).

SPIRIT BARRIER

(ENVIRONMENTAL, AREA)

Type: M	**Range:** LOS (A)
Duration: S	**Drain:** F – 1

SPIRIT ZAPPER

(ENVIRONMENTAL, AREA)

Type: M	**Range:** LOS (A)
Duration: S	**Drain:** F + 1

This is modified version of the Mana Barrier spell (p. 294, *SR5*) designed to work again spirits and spirit powers. When cast on the physical plane, Spirit Zapper impedes materialized spirits. It has no effect on spells, foci, or non-spirit dual beings and astral forms.

STERILIZE

(PHYSICAL, AREA)

Type: P	**Range:** LOS (A)
Duration: I	**Drain:** F – 3

This spell allows a spellcaster to kill all bacteria (and other microorganisms) and destroy organic material such as skin flakes, stray hairs, and spilled blood. Material affected by this spell cannot be used as a material link. Because the spell does not affect biomaterial attached to a living being, it does not kill the various helpful and harmful microorganisms living inside a creature. Each hit scored by the caster inflicts a –1 dice pool modifier to any skill tests made to collect and use sterilized biomaterial for forensics or material link purposes. Shadowrunners often employ this spell to eliminate incriminating trace evidence, especially if blood has been spilled. The area sterilized equals the caster's Magic Rating in cubic meters.

TURN TO GOO

(PHYSICAL)

Type: P	**Range:** LOS
Duration: S	**Drain:** F + 1

Turn to Goo allows a spellcaster to transform living tissue into a sticky, glue-like substance. The caster must win an Opposed Test pitting her Magic + Spellcasting against the target's Body (+ Counterspelling). Additionally, the spell's Force must equal or exceed the target's Body. Non-living material—including clothing, gear, and cyberware—are not affected.

The target is not conscious while under the effects of this spell, and any damage suffered by the gooey form affects the target normally. The goo has a barrier Armor Rating equal to the Body + net hits (see **Barriers**, p. 364, *SR5*). Cyberware remains still, as though frozen in amber. If removed, the target may suffer significant physical damage (depending on what is removed) as determined by the gamemaster.

SHADOW RITUALS

The Esteemed Leading Knight Rasmusen sat lost in thought, his back to his desk as he gazed unseeingly into the evening beyond his office window. It was easy to imagine false portents in the subdued play of lights and shadows that troubled the diffuse glow of dimly lit streets and houses emanating upward from the subterranean suburbs of Butte Below. But it was only imagination. Bringing his mind back to the task at hand, he swiveled his chair to face his desk and the array of dossiers—each representing a candidate for Montana Tech's Hermetic Order of Geomancers.

"Scott Peters," he said, pulling up an AR image to hover above his desk. "GPA 3.1. Low, but his instructors are unanimous in their high opinion of his potential."

"Taken," a grumbly voice responded. A dense fog formed in the far corner of his office and quickly coalesced into the deceptively average form of a domestic feline. The Cat crossed the room and leaped to the top of Rasmusen's desk, casually strolling through Scott Peter's holographic image on its way to a stool beside his high-backed chair.

"Who? The Tau Mu Tau?" he guessed, going with the most likely match to Peters' strengths. "Those frat boys haven't recovered enough from giving Astral Hazing a whole new meaning to begin recruiting."

"No, Lord Rasmusen," the Cat smiled an uncatlike smile. "There are other forces working to gain this boy's attention."

"Who? Pentacles? MageWerks? Damn it, Blix, don't just sit there practicing that infernal cryptic smile of yours. Peters is the best in only a handful of sophomores that would fit in our order." He frowned ominously. "If I am to lose a potential member to a corporation there'd best be some compensation."

Blix's smile became a grin at Rasmusen's threat, revealing rows of glowing galaxies where an honest cat had teeth.

"I would not be me if I were any more specific," he said in reasonable tones. "But I will tell you that try as you might, any attempt to recruit Scott Peters will be futile."

With a growl of frustration, Rasmusen waved his hand and the holographic images of dossiers and candidates disappeared. When he pushed himself to his feet, Blix flowed with moon-gravity grace to the floor and followed the human out of the office and across the hall.

Galaxies still glittered from his smile, but there was a tension in the way shifting shades of blue pursued each other down his feline length.

Rasmusen pushed the heavy wooden doors to the room across the broad hall from his office just wide enough to allow himself and Blix to slip inside. Candlelight seemed to give the polished darkwood floor and the intricately carved bureau against one wall subtle highlights. 'Seemed' because there were no candles; an indirect, sourceless light filled every corner with a warm glow not unlike a cozy fire. In the center of the room was a mage circle, burned into the floor and filled with a silvery liquid that seemed to tremble with energy.

Hugging the wall, Blix sauntered to a high stool tucked in the corner farthest from the bureau and made a show of stretching before leaping easily to the seat. His pose of patient amusement was spoiled somewhat by the bands and blots of muted colors wandering across his fur.

Rasmusen took a deck of tarot cards from one of the bureau's many drawers and stood for a moment shuffling them without obvious intention.

"I'm curious. Who that I do not know—or know of—is poaching my students?"

Blix did not answer.

Stepping over the shimmering boundary of the mage circle, Rasmusen settled himself comfortably on the floor and took a moment to center himself. Focusing intently on every motion, he shuffled the tarot cards thoroughly, then set the deck carefully on the floor.

Rasmusen's lips twitched at the sight of the first card, the questioner's card; he'd always considered the King of Cups to be *his* card. Shaking his head against the distraction, he narrowed his focus to the ritual as he placed the opposition card. Death. Which meant change—catastrophic, unexpected, complete, or merely uncomfortable—not necessarily and end of life. He lay the card across the King of Cups before reaching to draw the foundation card from the top of the deck.

Rasmusen grunted. He turned the card in his hand over, comparing its back to the deck on the floor, then picked the opposition card back up and compared it to the one in his hand.

"What is it?" Blix asked.

"A second Death card," Rasmusen answered. "Identical to the original."

"From another deck?"

"This deck. The cards are unique."

"Then place it."

Rasmusen looked at Blix, unsurprised that the cat's face revealed nothing. He replaced the opposition card, then paused—recapturing the serene focus of the reading took effort. At last he placed the foundation card below and to the left of the others.

The cards burst into flames. A glaring silver-white light rose from the mage circle, enclosing him in a column of cold fire.

As quickly as it had begun, it ended. Rasmusen sat in the center of the ring of grey sludge that had been the silvery mage circle, smudges of black ash marking where the tarot cards had lain, and stared directly ahead.

Blix flowed from his stool and crossed the now inert circle to stand in front of the human.

"And now, my lord, you know as much as I do."

Rasmusen turned his face toward the sound of the cat's voice.

"Fear not, the blindness is temporary," Blix assured him. "If you will grasp my tail, I'll lead you out of this chamber."

Reaching the doors exhausted Rasmusen; he collapsed against the wall in the corridor, gasping as though he had run a race.

"I saw nothing," he said at last. "Or something. What did I see?"

"You saw someone—two someones—who do not wish to be known, my lord," Blix said. "You saw two powers, each powerful enough to ruin the foundation of the ritual, clash. You saw what they let you see as a warning to you not to delve farther. Two Death cards; they were both telling you the penalty for persistence would be death."

The Esteemed Leading Knight Rasmusen slumped against the wall, waiting for his breathing and his heart rate to slow down. Against the darkness of his blindness darker forms moved. He did not understand how he could see the black-on-black images nor what they meant, but one was unmistakably the silhouette of a wolf.

INTRODUCTION

Modern society's addiction to too-easy technology and instant gratification has all but snuffed out the patience and discipline needed to master ritual magic. Even in the trid *Odd Coven*, which purports to center on ritual magic, shortens or even eliminates the "boring" rituals for fear of losing the audience's attention. What people tend to overlook is that while spellcasters may look cool and powerful slinging fireballs and lightning bolts, ritual magic every bit as powerful and has a depth and subtlety flash-bang spectacle can't match. In the Great Ghost Dance, Daniel Howling Coyote and his shamans erupted four—four!—major volcanoes simultaneously and brought the United States to its knees with ritual magic. Puts those pretty pyrotechnics in perspective.

The fundamentals of ritual magic are defined (p. 295, *SR5*), but the gamemaster and players are encouraged to tailor a ritual's actual performance and requirements toward each player's background or tradition. A shamanic adept, for example, might need to best a wild animal in combat to become the alpha for the Attunement ritual. A druid may have to anoint every stone with the Aspect Mana Line ritual before placing them along the mana line.

By its nature ritual magic takes time, preparation and discipline. This chapter contains information to help practitioners of ritual magic explore the possibilities of their craft. Effective use of some rituals may require initiation into an art; some rituals incorporate keywords and/or are subject to special rules.

ADEPTS AND RITUALS

There are various rituals available to the adept, where the adept's relevant skill or attribute fulfills the role of ritual spellcasting (steps 4 and 5). Examples: Animal Handling for Attune Animal and Imbue; Armorer, Artisan, or Automotive Mechanic for Imbue Item. The gamemaster has final say on what skill the adept can use in substitution of Ritual Spellcasting.

RITUAL KEYWORDS

Anchored (p. 296, *SR5*)

Adept: These rituals are specific to the nature of an adept's internal magic and can only be learned/performed by an adept or mystic adept. These rituals do not allow group assistance unless otherwise stated.

Blood: These rituals require the death of a sapient subject. These rituals normally are not available to any sane player character.

Contractual: These rituals require two or more willing participants to complete. The ritual forms a bond between the parties involved.

Mana: Practice of rituals with this keyword must be performed on a mana line or domain (p. 30)

Material Link (p. 296, *SR5*)

Minion (p. 297, *SR5*)

Organic Link: Necromancy requires whole or partial physical remains of a once-living subject as a material link for the ritual. This may be specific material link needed in the ritual (blood, eyes, etc). This material link cannot be substituted for a sympathetic or symbolic link.

Spell (p. 297, *SR5*)

Spotter (p. 297, *SR5*)

RITUALS
ASPECT MANA LINE (MANA)

This ritual enables the geomancer to aspect a portion of the mana line towards his tradition (p. 41). The number of meters along the mana line that can be aspected in this manner is determined by multiplying the leader's Magic Rating by 20. In accordance with geomantic lore, a permanent magic lodge must be constructed during step 4 of the ritual. The Force of the ritual is equal to twice the mana line's Force rating.

If the mana line is aspected by another organization/geomancer, add the leader/geomancer's Magic Rating in dice to the Opposed Test in sealing the ritual (step 7).

For the aspect to become permanent, this ritual must be successfully completed each month for a number of

LINE OF INFLUENCE (LOI)

The line of influence is a cylindrical region that surrounds the mana line. The radius of this cylinder is equal to ten meters times twice the Force of the mana line.

consecutive months equal to the Force of the mana line. An offering must be made (step 5) every month at various points within the aspected line to alter the flow of mana energies. Failing the ritual in one month does not undo what has been done, but adds a month to the process. Other geomancers may compete for the same territory; when this happens only the geomancer with the most net hits during a given month has control for that month. The controlling leader, organization, or tradition can use the force of the mana line as a dice pool modifier when performing magic on this "home turf."

Aligning the magical flow of an aspected mana line increases the probability of the controlling magician finding valuable or necessary reagents. Add the Force of the mana line in dice to the magician's Search Test.

This ritual takes (Force) hours to complete. **Requires Geomancy.**

ALARM WARD (ANCHORED)

Alarm Wards alert their creator when a spell or astral form has entered or crossed any area they are set to observe. Alarm Wards are tenuous, designed to be as unobtrusive as possible so as to blend into the local astral space and allow any intruder to pass through, (hopefully) unaware she has been detected. Astral entities must make an Assensing + Intuition [Astral] (3) Test to notice the ward before passing through it. Those on the physical realm or using spells like Clairvoyance would only notice the ritual marking and anchor of the ward with a perception test and a threshold of 5. This is to notice the "magical markings" but not understand their intent. That is a standard Arcane Knowledge check. It is possible for a person to recognize the sensation of passing through the astral form of the ward and realize she has tripped an alarm. Use the same Perception Test as noted in astral detection (p. 314, *SR5*). Alarm wards send the same notification whether someone or something passes through it, or it is attacked. Intruders aware of the ward can trip the alarm to distract its creator from an incursion elsewhere. This ritual takes (Force) hours to complete.

ALLY CONJURATION (MINION)

See **Ally Spirits,** p. 200

ASTRAL DOPPELGANGER (SPOTTER, MATERIAL LINK)

The Astral Doppelganger ritual allows the leader to alter the astral signature of one or all ritual participants so that it appears identical to that of an individual the leader/spotter has assensed.

If the subject whose astral signature is being duplicated is consciously cooperating with the ritual, the minimum Force of the spell required is equal to the number of participants whose astral signatures are being changed. If the subject is unwilling or is unaware she is the subject of the ritual—such as a person selected by a spotter— add +2 to the minimum force required. If the ritual is successful, the doppelgangers' auras are indistinguishable from the original. This change is temporary for up to net successes of the ritual in hours. This ritual can make astral tracking (p. 315, *SR5*) more difficult with an increased threshold equal to the number of participants with the new astral signature. It also can be used to allow the participants to fool wards (p. 135).

The Material link is optional to the Spotter portion of the ritual. This allows for the use of a Material link to determine the astral signature of the subject, if the subject cannot be found through observation. **Requires Flexible Signature.**

ATONEMENT (CONTRACTUAL)

To cleanse herself of spiritual crimes—whether accrued over a period of years or as the result of a single mission—the magician must perform a ritual similar to that of a Metaplanar Quest (p. 140). The magician must face the Dweller on the Threshold and submit to the punishment laid out for her (gamemaster's discretion). Force of the ritual is equal to twice the astral reputation. Any reagents used must be of refined quality. If the magician successfully completes the ritual, she may spend Karma up to 1 plus the net hits achieved with the ritual. Each point of Karma spent this way reduces her Astral Reputation by 1. The magician can only reduce her Astral Reputation to 0.

ATTUNE ANIMAL (ADEPT)

With this ritual adepts can bond with a mundane, non-sapient animal. This will not work if the animal is coerced, so the adept must first befriend the critter. This requires an Animal Handling + Charisma [Social] (12, 1 week) Extended Test. It is not possible to attune an animal vessel because the magical aura of a prepared vessel interferes with attunement.

Once a rapport is established, the adept must perform this bonding ritual (with Animal Handling) with a minimum Force equal to the willpower of the creature. If the ritual is successful, the adept then spends karma equal to the animal's essence to make the bond permanent. The ritual takes (Force) hours to complete. A bonded animal gains the power of Sense Link (p. 198).

This ritual must be learned for every type of animal (e.g., Attune Animal (Lynx), Attune Animal (Crow)) to which the adept wants to attune. A character may only attune a number of individual animals equal to her initiate grade. The minimum Force of the bonding ritual increases by 1 for each existing bonded animal. The adept may not receive the benefit from more than one attuned animal in a single action. The attunement bond may be voluntarily severed as a free action or if the animal (or character) dies. Karma spent on the bond is lost when the bond is severed. Attuned animals may be used as a material link (p. 297, *SR5*) to the adept. Attuned animals can be further enhanced through the Empowering ritual (p. 128).

ATTUNE ITEM (ADEPT)

When performing this ritual, the adept must first familiarize himself with the object to be attuned. The familiarization process involves a thorough acquaintance with the item's function, specifications, construction, and limitations. This involves an appropriate Logic + Technical skill [Mental] (12, 1 week) Extended Test. Example Technical skills used in this test would be Armorer for a katana or gun, Automotive Mechanic for a bike, or Performance for a musical instrument. Alternatively, the adept may elect to build the item for himself from scratch following the normal rules for building/repairing items; the building process becomes part of the bonding process (p. 318, *SR5*).

Once the adept has familiarized himself with the object, he must perform a bonding ritual (with appropriate technical skill) with a minimum Force equal to the hits rolled using the appropriate dice pool on the Object Resistance Table (p. 295, *SR5*). Ritual takes (Force) hours to complete. When the adept has succeeded he must then spend Karma as stipulated in the Item Attunement Table to make the bond permanent. Gamemasters are advised to use this Item Attunement Table as a guideline. Increase the relevant limit of the item by the initiate grade of the adept using it. The skill used with the item must be an active skill relating to a physical attribute. The attuned item's limit increase can stack with the adept's Enhanced Accuracy power.

Attunement provides no bonus when the item is controlled through an electronic interface (digital, VR, AR, or DNI), nor does it work on the complex magical auras of foci, prepared vessels, or enchanted items. Attunement provides no bonus to Active Magical skills. This ritual applies only to one specific type of object (e.g., Attunement (Bike)). If an adept wants to attune a different item, he must learn a new ritual. The adept may only attune a number of individual items equal to his initiate grade, and he may not receive benefits from more than one attuned item in a single action. The minimum Force of the bonding ritual increases by 1 for each existing bonded item. Attunement may be voluntarily severed at any moment (invested Karma is lost) and is automatically severed if the item is destroyed. Attuned items may be used as a material link (p. 297, *SR5*) to the adept.

Attuned items can be further enhanced through the Imbue Item ritual (p. 133)

AUGURY AND SORTILEGE (MATERIAL LINK)

Augury is the ritual of divination. To use this ritual, the magician must assense the subject (person, place, or object) or have a viable material link (p. 297, *SR5*). Within the ritual circle, the initiate enters a mild trance and interprets the symbolism and metaphors presented to him through the aether. Sortilege is the use of specific reagents (casting bones, reading tea leaves, etc.) or fetishes (tarot cards) as part of the divination ritual.

In gameplay there are two parts to divination. The first part is the successful completion of the ritual. The leader may ask one question about an event in the subject's future. The question is answered through portent appropriate to the tradition and/or the divination technique. The second part is the leader's interpretation of the answer. Using Arcana with a threshold based on the question asked, the leader rolls Arcana + Logic with a limit based on the net successes of the ritual. Subsequent divinations on the same subject matter increase the threshold by 1. This ritual takes (Force) hours to complete. **Requires Divination.**

Failure to meet the threshold results in a useless answer; the leader might as well have used a Magic 8 Ball. Net successes from the Arcana Test above the threshold determines how helpful or understandable the answer was to the leader. One net hit means a cryptic reply containing an underlying truth. Two net hits, the answer is mildly helpful. Three or more net hits achieve corresponding levels of detail.

In some cases it may be advisable for the gamemaster to roll the Divining Test for the character secretly so as not to give away undesired information based on the number of hits. Regardless of the number of hits achieved, the

ITEM ATTUNEMENT TABLE

GEAR	KARMA COST
Simple non-mechanical or handcrafted items (Handmade implements, traditional musical instruments)	5
Modern crafted or mechanical items (Machine-forged blades, mechanical lockpick kit, mechanic's toolkit)	6
Basic mechanical production line products (Basic firearm, simple combustion engine vehicles (pre-1990s))	8
Tech-intensive products and electronics (Smartgun, electronic supported vehicles (post-1990s))	9
High-tech items and advanced electronics (Mono filament whip, thunderbird, commlink)	10

DIVINATION TABLE

The gamemaster must consider both the subject of the question and the time frame to determine a question's level of specificity and use the higher value to determine threshold.

DIVINATION QUESTION	THRESHOLD
Vague (Are my enemies catching up to me? Will I make any friends this month?)	2
General (Will I get hurt shadowrunning? Will my enemies catch up to me this week?)	3
Specific (Will Mr. Johnson take a bribe? Will I get hurt on this Run (in the next few days)?)	4
Very Specific (Will Mr. Johnson take an offer from the Yakuza? Will Mr. Johnson be willing to take a bribe today?)	5

gamemaster should adjust the answer to be as specific or vague as suits the story and to maintain drama.

A glitch in the ritual or Arcana Test means the vision is misinterpreted and misleading information conveyed.

BLOOD BOND (MATERIAL LINK)

This dark ritual uses blood magic to bond the magician to a genetically related subject. As life energy is related to mana, the connection between kin relates to both. Blood magic exploits this in the Blood Bond ritual. The minimum Force of the ritual is equal to the subject's Willpower. Once the ritual is complete, the leader may spend Karma equal to 2 + Willpower of the subject to make the bond permanent. This bond creates a low-level telepathic link between the leader and the subject (they know each other's emotional state and general whereabouts). The magician may use a form of Empathic healing (p. 171) to transfer physical damage from himself to the subject, if the subject is within (100 x Magic Rating) meters from the magician. The leader can bond up to his Charisma in subjects. This ritual takes (Force) days to complete. **Requires Sacrifice.**

BLOOD RITE (BLOOD, ORGANIC LINK)

Blood Rite is a specialized ritual that can only be performed if all magicians know the Sacrifice metamagic (p. 90). Performing the ritual works exactly like performing the Sacrifice, except that multiple victims can be used to generate Blood Magic Points, up to net successes of the ritual. The minimum Force of the ritual is equal to the victim's willpower. Blood Magic Points generated during this ritual may be stored in an athame (p. 90) that is bonded to the magician using the Sacrifice metamagic. Multiple magicians may take turns using the Sacrifice to "charge" their athame. This ritual takes (Force) hours to complete. **Requires Sacrifice**

BLOOD SIGHT (ORGANIC LINK)

The Blood Sight ritual allows the magician to discern details of the person who left blood behind. The ritu-

al offering must contain a sample of blood; if circumstances warrant, the ritual circle can be drawn around the blood rather than collecting a sample to be used elsewhere. Magical cleansing, environmental contaminants, and other factors can hinder a Blood Sight reading; add each hindering factor to the Force Resistance of the ritual. This ritual takes (Force) minutes to complete and cannot be performed on blood more than twenty-four hours old. This ritual takes (Force) minutes to complete. **Requires Necromancy**

BLOOD SIGHT RESISTANCE FACTORS

ADDITIONAL RESISTANCE FACTORS IN COMPLETING THE RITUAL

+ Force Cleanse Spell

+ Force Smudging Ritual

+1 Per 6 hours of exposure to the environment and/or contaminants

BLOOD SIGHT TEST TABLE

NET HITS	SUCCESS DESCRIPTION
1	Blood type/If the person uses nanites/If the person uses drugs/If the blood is human
2	Gender of the person, type of drugs in the blood, type of animal (if not human)
3	Ethnic and metagenic race
4	Is Awakened, has had gene therapy, or is infected by HMHVV
5+	Can get brief impressions of the person

CALLING [SPIRIT TYPE] (CONTRACTUAL)

The Calling ritual is the occult way to call forth spirits that the magician would not normally conjure for their tradition. This is not the same as conjuring, as the spirit owes no services to the magician and may be hostile when/if it arrives. Some thaumaturgists would say that the calling ritual is the fundamental root for the Conjuring skill, before knowledge of the existence of metaplanes. They say that just to pick a fight with other thaumaturgians. Each calling ritual is unique to a spirit type, but not to a specific spirit or classification. So the Calling Fae ritual would be used in calling the Wild Hunt, while Calling Phantoms would be used in calling ghosts. For the actual class of spirit, the magician must create paraphernalia.

Paraphernalia is the magical link that will call the said spirit to the ritual area. Paraphernalia are unique kinds of conjuring materials (specific reagents), such as Ouija boards, or saucers of milk that are needed for the ritual. It can also include certain places that the ritual has to be practiced at or specific astronomical events have to occur at the time of the ritual. The exact nature is ultimately up to the gamemaster. Crafting paraphernalia requires a successful Alchemy + Magic [Force] (Force of the target spirit, 1 day) Extended Test.

At the gamemaster's discretion specific refined or radical Reagents (p. 210) may be needed to manufacture certain materials. All reagents are consumed or incorporated into the finished product. Paraphernalia can be crafted by the magician himself or purchased from a capable talismonger (i.e., a contact with the necessary skills and resources to create the paraphernalia) as long as the magician understands the composition of the requested paraphernalia. The magician must understand the composition of the paraphernalia before the talismonger begins work.

The ritual Force required to call a spirit is equal to the Force of the spirit being called. In establishing the ritual's foundation, a circle similar to a basic ward is prepared. This circle is the only thing separating the spirit from the magician while they barter. The ward may be broken by the magician or anyone else participating in the ritual by physically breaking the circle. The ward may also be broken by the spirit if the spirit's Force is greater than the Force of the circle and the spirit wins an Opposed Test against it (Force of the spirit vs. Force of the foundation).

The paraphernalia are expended as part of Give the Offering, step 5 of the ritual (p. 307, *SR5*). Once the ritual has been completed, the spirit that was called appears in the center of the circle. If the ritual fails, the spirit doesn't appear, and the paraphernalia and reagents are lost. The magician who wants to see another day can only hope there is no glitch when he calls a spirit.

For every two successes (not net successes) the spirit has, the gamemaster may raise the Force of the next spirit called. (for example, the magician wants a Force 5 apparition and instead calls a Force 6). If the spirit gets four or more successes, the gamemaster may also choose a different spirit class of the same type to have been summoned (praying mantis instead of a cockroach in calling an insect spirit). This uncertainty and escalating risk make the calling ritual dangerous and unreliable to dabblers in magic.

The spirit stays within the circle used in the ritual for a number of hours equal to the Force of the ritual before returning to wherever it originated by way of astral space. While in the circle, the spirit is temporarily immune to any inherit weakness and protected from any attacks by the magician. Reduce successes of any attacks by the force of the circle. All bets are off if either side breaches the circle.

The spirit called is obligated to materialize and negotiate with the magician. Note that although the spirit who answered the call is inclined to negotiate and not necessarily hostile, it may lose patience or become angry if not shown the respect it believes is due. This would be done through the usual story play and negotiation skills. Be wary of bargaining with spirits that have been called, as they may trick the caller into entering a spirit pact (p. 137).

The Calling ritual is conceptually a very old ritual. Awakened and mundane occultists are able, with the proper paraphernalia, to call a spirit. It is believed that the paraphernalia, not the magician, powers the ritual. When a mundane is performing this ritual, substitute Arcana for Ritual Spellcasting.

OCCULT KNOWLEDGE

The composition of paraphernalia is always specific to the class of spirit (e.g., shedim, leprechaun, etc.). Identifying the necessary paraphernalia to call a specific spirit type requires a Logic + Arcana [Mental] (20, 1 day) Extended Test, though gamemasters may opt to require that characters earn such knowledge through game play. This kind of occult lore is often hidden, inherited, or found only in ancient tomes or folios that must be found and understood.

ARCANA AND THE MUNDANE

Arcana is the only magic skill not tied to the Magic attribute. As such, the gamemaster can optionally allow a mundane to acquire this skill to represent their limited understanding of the arcane documentation available to anyone. This knowledge then can be used by the mundane to recognize rituals, preparations, traditions, etc. The gamemaster can set a difficulty threshold to use the skill in determining details such as a preparation's trigger, magician's tradition, or type of spirit.

CHARGED WARD (ANCHORED)

Charged wards behave like an electric fence; they strike back against intruders or astral attackers. Charged wards respond to astral attacks by discharging mana energy, much like a successful direct combat spell. It deals stun damage with a Damage Value equal to the force of the ward. If the ward is attacked with spells, the Charged Ward can reflect the spell back onto the caster at half the original spell force (round up) if it successfully resists the attack (Force 1 spells are not reflected). Net hits from the resistance becomes the hits in the reflected spell's Spellcasting Test, limited by the Force of the spell. A Charged Ward may be "pressed through" like a standard ward (see p. 297, SR5), but if the ward wins the Opposed Test, the intruder must resist the ward's Force + net hits in Stun damage as if attacked by a direct combat spell. A Charged Ward is difficult to distinguish from a basic ward. It takes a Assensing + Intuition [Astral](3) Test to spot the difference. **Requires Reflection (p. 151)**

CIRCLE OF HEALING (ANCHORED, SPELL)

This ritual uses Health Spells and is described on p. 297, SR5.

CIRCLE OF CLEANSING (ANCHORED, MANA)

This ritual allows the magician to weave a construct of mana energies that would counteract the effects of positive background count (and only the background count) surrounding him. Even though it's called a circle, it creates a sphere around the anchor that has a radius in meters equal to the leader's Magic rating. Mana ebbs and voids (negative background counts) are not affected by this ritual. The Force of the ritual must be equal to the background count level. Net success from the ritual reduce the background count by 1 within the sphere. Those within the circle can perform magical activities based on the reduced background count. The base duration of the effect is one hour, plus one additional hour for each net success. If there is a change in background count such as from a mana storm, surge, or warp, reduce its effects by the Force of the circle against those within the circle. This ritual takes (Force) hours to complete. **Requires Cleansing**

CIRCLE OF PROTECTION (ANCHORED)

This ritual is described on p. 297, SR5.

CREATE ALLY SPIRIT (MINION)

This ritual is described in **The Immaterial Touch**, p. 200.

CURSE (MATERIAL LINK, SPELL)

This ritual is described on p. 297, SR5.

DEATH MARK (ORGANIC LINK, SPOTTER)

Every death, violent or not, leaves an impression on the astral plane. When a corpse is moved, it leaves a faint trail that contains traces of the person's death and the decay of their body. The Death Mark ritual makes it possible to follow this trail from the body back to the point of death through astral tracking (p. 315, SR5). Net Successes from the ritual adds dice to the spotter's test to follow the track to its point of origin. This astral mark is temporary, lasting the person's essence in days. While it may not influence the background count, it can be cleansed (p. 154), treating the mark with a force equal to the essence of the person. This ritual takes (Force) hours to complete. **Requires Necromancy**

ASTRAL TRACKING MODIFIERS FOR DEATH MARK

CONDITION	THRESHOLD MODIFIER
Every 2 hours that have elapsed since time of death	+1
Body has been dismembered (only a portion of the body is available to use with the ritual)	+4
Path crosses a river or mana line	+2 or +Force of the mana line
Body was of someone Awakened	–2

DISPERSION CIRCLE (ANCHORED)

Dispersion Circle is actually a sphere centered on an anchor and with a radius equal to the magician's Magic Rating in meters. The magician can diffuse the power alchemical preparation uniformly throughout the sphere. When a preparation enters the sphere, roll an Opposed Test of the Force of the ritual vs. the Force of the preparation. Each net success quickens the time decay of a preparation by 10 minutes (e.g., If the decay of potency is 1 hour, then with 3 net successes, it now reduces by 1 every 30 minutes). This ritual takes (Force) hours to complete. The Circle lasts for (Force) hours.

DOOR WARDS (ANCHORED)

Door Wards are mystical enchantments that specifically cover the entrance to rooms or buildings. The myth in the

Practitioners of magic often consult reference books to learn formulas, study ways to tweak techniques, or identify unknowns they may have encountered. There is no shortage of books about all things magical in nature. This is not to say that Magiknet isn't helpful, but a shelf of authoritative tomes is not only traditional, but it also looks a lot cooler than a terminal screen. Books vary in price depending on age, condition, etc. Unless the book is really old (more than two hundred years), the gamemaster should estimate the price to less than five hundred nuyen.

Book of Shadows: Contemporary book from the 1950s, revised in 2029. It contains the fragments of purported Wiccan rituals. Later editions contain variations ritual formulas based on the author's background (Gardnerian, Alexandrian, Valiente, etc.) and speculation as to the original purpose of those rituals.

Corpus Hermeticum: A core book for hermetics in learning basic formulas. The original was written in the second or third century, but it has been added to over time. The current edition includes Prof. Schwartzkopf's seminal lecture on Unified Magic Theory, though wealthy wizards are likely to prominently display a copy of the ornate sixteenth century first printing.

Visions of Zosimos: Third century book of alchemy and rituals. Zosimos' formulae for creating men of lead and brass provided the basis for the first ritual to successfully create a homunculus.

Papyrus of Ani: The Egyptian Book of the Dead. A classic set of spells for the Egyptian tradition and the authentic alchemists of the early Hellenistic period.

The Grimoire, The Manual of Practical Thaumaturgy: Also known as the Digital Grimoire because so many carry digital copies with them for quick reference. It is the most authoritative and widely used book for thaumaturgical studies of any tradition. First published in 2036 the book has been through thirty-nine editions and been the standard of universities and serious practitioners for over a quarter of a century. The Grimoire presents almost all traditions neutrally and fairly, giving each equal attention and space.

De Forma Absolutionis: Thomas Aquinas' examination of mysticism in the Christian tradition. More of a practical and ethical guide for Awakened Christians than a book on rituals, but it contains some sample rituals.

Walking the Light: Published in 2018 by James Michael Killearn, it is more a religious meditation on the ideals of the Path of the Wheel than a book of magic. It is now known that James Killearn never existed; one more mystery tied to the elvish tradition. While not a book of practical magic, it has spiritual significance to the followers of the elvish tradition.

Emerald Tablets: Published by Hermes Trismegistus (Hermes Thrice Great). Traditional lore has it he original tablets are irrecoverably lost, but there are translations available—the latest dating from the thirteenth century. Isaac Newton referenced the emerald tablets in his treatise on physics. The formulas reportedly etched on the emerald tablets allude to—and give tantalizing hints about—higher levels of magic.

good luck horseshoe over the door, the carved Gorgonian, or the painted Nazar that wards off evil spirits or magic were the starting points for the research and experimentation that ultimately perfected this ritual. Door Wards are anchored to a lynchpin that absorb sustained magic crossing the threshold. For each sustained spell that crosses through, reduce the net successes of the sustained spell by 1. Active foci that are less than the Force of the ward are deactivated when crossing the ward. This ritual takes (Force) hours to complete. Door Wards last (Force) days.

EMPOWER (ADEPT)

With this ritual, the adept can temporarily lend one of his own adept powers to an attuned animal (**Temporary Transfer**) or permanently qi-mark the beast for its own adept power (**Qi Marked**). The minimum force of the ritual must equal to four times the power point cost of the power that will empower the animal. If the ritual is successful (with Animal Handling), the adept must then spend Karma equal to four times the power point cost of the power.

If the animal does not possess an appropriate skill required to use the power, it instinctively taps the adept's own natural (unmodified) skill rating for any relevant test, but with a –2 dice pool modifier. This ritual takes (Force) hours to complete. Requires **Attune Animal.**

TEMPORARY TRANSFER

The adept can empower his animal companion by transferring one of his own power to it. After the ritual is sealed, the adept needs only to make a Complex Action any time she wants to transfer that specific power to her animal companion. Only one power may be transferred at a time; this power is unavailable to the adept during the time it is transferred. Though an adept may empower more than one animal companion, the same power cannot be transferred to more than one animal at a time. If the adept power was increased after the Empowering ritual, only the level of the power that was used in the ritual will be transferred until the Empower ritual is performed again at the new power level (Karmic cost is only the delta increase). It takes a complex action to return the power back to the adept. The adept can never transfer more than his initiate grade in power points.

QI MARKED

The adept can empower his animal companion with qi marks (qi foci given to animal companions), which give the animal its own adept abilities, not just a transfer from their own list. Once the ritual is sealed, the adept needs only make a Simple Action any time she wants to activate the animal's qi mark. The adept must be within the Sense Link power range of the animal companion to activate the adept powers. If there are multiple qi marks on an animal companion, only one can be activated in any action. It takes a Free Action to turn off the power. The Force and number of the qi marks given to animal companions must be factored into the adept's foci limit (p. 318, SR5). The total maximum levels available for any given power (adding up levels in qi marks and the adept's own levels in the power) is still the adept's Magic Rating. Qi marks can be disenchanted in the same way as other foci, but cannot be deactivated (p. 305, SR5).

GRAVE BINDING
(ANCHORED, ORGANIC LINK)

This ritual centers warding magic on the deceased to protect the corpse against inhabitation or manipulation. Many traditions have revised their burial practices to incorporate Old World spiritual protection. Forensic thaumaturgists use the ritual to prevent evidence walking away. Any spirit less than twice the force of the ritual cannot use the possession or inhabitation power on the corpse. This ritual can be used on a prepared vessel to thwart the use of the vessel in such a ritual, adding the force of the ward to the opposed test. For spells the ward adds the force in dice to counterspelling the effects of spells on the body. Once warded, the body cannot be moved more than one meter or the ward will be broken. The ward will last (Force) weeks unless Karma equal to the Force is spent to make it permanent. Grave Binding makes the body the anchor for the spell, so physical damage other than natural decay, such as an autopsy, breaks the ward. This ritual takes (Force) minutes to complete.

GROUP BOND (CONTRACTUAL)

A group bond, allows several magicians to work together to further advance their knowledge of magic. A group bond enables a magician to rely on his fellow magicians in initiation (and thus be cheaper in Karma).

To form a mage group, you first must have more than two magicians; it's just not a party with only two. Second

as part of offering step to ritual magic, the magicians must agree on strictures for each individual and group as a whole. Each group must answer a few strictures from which the bonds will be founded and modify the force of the ritual.

When the Group bond is first formed, the group may opt to entreat the patronage of a specific mentor spirit that is in sync with and symbolic of the group's beliefs and purpose. For example, the Bear Doctor Society reveres the Bear totem, while a group of Shinto practitioners might worship the powerful kami whom they believe resides at a particular temple. While it provides no positive or negative modifiers to members, the mentor spirit takes an active role in the group as a guide and counselor—as long as the group remains faithful to the group's purpose. The Force of the ritual equals 12 - stricture modifiers, with a minimum Force of 5. As an addition to sealing the ritual, each new member must spend 5 Karma in its completion. This expenditure is also required in the initial creation of the group bond. This ritual takes (Force) hours to complete.

GROUP STRICTURES

STRICTURE	MODIFIER
Courting a mentor spirit avatar for the group	+4
Each additional tradition admitted	+2
For each member already initiated in another magical group	+1
For every four members part of the group	−1 (Max −3)
Limited Membership	−1
Material Link	−1
Oath (allowing for individual strictures)	—

For each member there is specific set of individual strictures that the group can establish if the group bond includes an oath. For every two individual strictures taken, subtract 1 from the ritual modifier. Also for each individual stricture, a penalty can be added for breaking any stricture. You must include an individual stricture in the bond in order to add penalties for breaking it. Each penalty has its own cost modifier and, yes, breaking multiple strictures can cause repeated penalties that may result in death.

After the ritual completes successfully, the bond can be seen astrally by any other members of the group. Members also can sense any member who has violated individual strictures (though not how or which ones) with a simple Assensing + Intuition [Mental] (3) Test. Once bonded to a group, the magician cannot bond to another group if any of the strictures conflict with the new group. After the initial creation of the group bond, the group strictures prevent the ritual from completing for new members under any circumstances. Only a majority of members can break the group bond be broken for the entire group (the bonding Karma is lost).

A member may permanently sever his bond to the group by successfully performing a ritual similar to the one used to join the group and paying 1 Karma.

INDIVIDUAL STRICTURES

ATTENDANCE

The group has regular meetings (group rituals, sport practice, trideo games). The magician must be physically present for these specific meetings. Meetings should be planned to take place every one to three months, with a total face time of three hours per meeting. Hiding out because a run went south is no excuse for breaking this stricture.

BELIEF

The group has a specific more or philosophical belief that they all adhere to. This should have at least three tangible rules that can be understood and followed. Any activity that violates the belief breaks the stricture. In all cases, the gamemaster has final say on if an action (or lack of action) breaks the belief.

DEED

All members must periodically perform an action to benefit the group or demonstrate loyalty to the group. Any type of deed may be required, including an astral quest or the gathering specific types of reagents. The frequency of this action being performed should be between one and three months and take between three hours and one week to complete.

DUES

Every month members must make financial payments at the level determined by the group to enable the group to maintain its holdings and services. This would be an additional lifestyle payment made by each member. Missing a payment violates the stricture and may ban the member from using the group's resources for such time until the payment is made.

EXCLUSIVE MEMBERSHIP

The magician cannot be part of any other magical group. If the Awakened character joins with another group, this stricture is immediately broken. If both groups have the exclusive membership, the first group's stricture is broken and the group bond ritual with the second group automatically fails (Karma spent to join is still lost).

EXCLUSIVE RITUAL

The Awakened character can only perform ritual spellcasting with the group as a whole or with other members of the group. This includes performing rituals alone or attempting to bond with another group.

FRATERNITY

Brothers and/or sisters together forever. Members must assist other members when asked. Refusing to help when it is within the Awakened character's means or ability to do so breaks this stricture. It is not necessary to succeed, only to attempt aid.

GEASA

All members must take a geas (p. 142) reflecting the group's purpose or belief. For example, Vigilia Evangelica have a vow of silence.

OBEDIENCE

The group was formed with a hierarchical structure. Rank and status are defined by the group's purpose and number of members. It may have voted in a charismatic leader or the founding members are the council. Ranks in the group may be defined by Initiate grade, years of service, or ordeals taken. Regardless of the structure of the group, lower-ranking members must obey orders from higher-ranking members. Failure to obey violates this stricture.

SERVICE

Members must spend time working on group-related matters. This may include matters relating to running a business (taking inventory, bookkeeping, customer service, etc.) or maintaining the group's resource/lifestyle (housekeeping, security, shopping, etc). The Awakened character must spend twenty hours per month performing such duties. Doing less breaks the stricture.

SECRECY

Rule #1, of [x] group: You don't talk about [x] group! Any discussion involving the group or member's activities for the group with an outsider, or discussions held where an outsider can overhear, violates the stricture. There may be cases of a delay of punishment or forgiveness of this violation if the magician learns later that someone was spying on him and overheard his conversation.

VIOLATING STRICTURES

Violating individual strictures is bad for the group. Because of the bond, the total number of strictures violated by each member participating during any ritual, including the group bond ritual, adds to the opposing

YOU TALKED! TABLE

PENALTIES	MODIFIER	DESCRIPTION
Branding	–1	The person is physically marked through magic in such a way that even those who are not part of the group recognize the person broke some law. Examples are the black spot on the hand, or a branded letter on the forehead. These wounds do not heal and cannot be treated till the broken stricture is atoned for.
Burn	–1	The person suffers elemental damage with a Force equal to the Force of the group bond ritual. This is a visual presentation of "on pain of death," so those not Awakened can see the effect of breaking magic law.
Cripple	–1	The person suffers the effects of detrimental magic, reducing a specific physical attribute by 1.
Magic Loss	–2	The person loses a point of Magic until the breach of stricture is atoned for. This penalty includes the loss of a power point. If there is a mixture of Awakened and mundane individuals bonded together, this penalty acts like cripple to the mundane instead.
Pain of Death	–1	The person suffers direct physical damage with a value equal to the Force of the group bond ritual. The appearance of damage varies.

All penalties are subtracted from ritual-based spellcasting (as a dice pool modifier to Step 7: Seal the Ritual, p. 296, *SR5*) using the group bond as the mystical link. Because of the bond, the magician cannot protect himself with his own wards, counterspelling, or even masking. The penalty occurs instantly as the stricture is broken. For those that do physical damage, it only occurs once. For the rest, the loss or mark remains until the subject atones for the stricture. The loss cannot be countered or removed except by atonement. Breaking the bond permanently by the member removes the obligation of obeying the strictures and healing of marks, but the Magic and attribute lost is permanent.

TATTOO MAGIC

GROUP BOND AND TATTOO MAGIC

There are criminal organizations and adept clans that have found a way to use this group bond beyond a group of wizards looking for magic support. They use this group bond to identify each other through less -than-obvious means, and they can use this bond to enforce loyalty with deadly consequences. While those added to the group this way do not have to be Awakened, the leader must be in order to create the bond. Note that this would be a separate ritual bond from the group bond of magicians.

The benefit of this bond is of instant recognition with Awakened and non-Awakened alike through a physical connection such as a handshake. Adepts with magic sense can perceive the bond to others of the group at a distance of (Magic Rating) meters. Those with astral perception/projection can actually see the bond as described above.

Bonded individuals who do not have the Sorcery skill cannot free themselves of the bond on their own. They would need the help of a magician who knows the group bonding ritual. This can become dangerous if the bond includes strictures such as secrecy.

Adepts who have learned Tattoo Magic can use the Artisan skill as a substitute for Ritual Spellcasting in creating group bonds.

TATTOO MAGIC

The Tattoo Magic technique can be purchased for 5 Karma and learned in two weeks, after which the magician can keep magic viable through tattooing art. This is not a separate skill, but an enhancement to other skills and metamagics. Using the Artificing skill, the magician can create qi and other foci as tattoos. With contractual rituals, Tattoo Magic can be used on mundanes and Awakened alike to reinforce the magical connection and consequences of breaking said magical contract (the group bond). When this is combined with the Quickening and Anchoring metamagics, a magician can tattoo such spells onto a subject.

ALLIANCE

This trait increases the limit (e.g., Accuracy, Handling, or Rating) of an item by the initiate grade when the Awakened uses it. The skill used with the item must be an active skill relating to a physical attribute. This trait applies to items other than attuned items.

BERSERK

This trait is violently aggressive. When a combat situation arises, the Awakened character must make a Simple Charisma + Willpower [Social] (3) Test (wound modifiers apply). Failure means that item's rage has consumed the Awakened character for [Initiate Grade] turns, –1 per hit on the test. When a character is berserk, he goes after his attacker(s) without regard for personal safety. While in a berserk rage, add one half the initiate grade (round up) to the damage value of attacks made with the item. Awakened characters who follow a mentor spirit with a berserk disadvantage stay in the berserk rage longer (increase endurance of the rage by a number of combat turns equal to the initiate grade).

BLOOD THIRST

Weapon foci used as athames (p. 90) can develop this trait. It cannot be imbued unless the Awakened person knows the art of **Sacrifice** (p. 90). If the weapon focus is used in combat and the Awakened tries to not kill their opponent, the Awakened character must make an Opposed Charisma + Willpower vs. the Force of the weapon foci (including traits) Test. If the focus achieves more successes, then the Awakened character must attempt to kill his opponent with the focus during that combat turn. If the Awakened character cannot kill the opponent (including if the opponent escaped or died at the hands of another), the focus "bites" the Awakened character, doing physical damage equal to the Force of the focus in order to be sated.

LOYALTY

The item works only in concert with the will of the one who imbued this trait. Anyone else who attempts to use the item suffers a dice penalty equal to the Initiate grade of the individual who imbued the trait. This affects both physical and magical skills used in connection with foci. If the bonding magician's initiate grade is higher than the Force of the item, then it acts as a non-enchanted item for anyone else. It can only bond to the individual who imbued it.

PERCEPTIVE

Items with the Perceptive trait have a more sensitive link to their owner. It allows the Awakened to use the Observe in Detail (p. 165, *SR5*) to know the location of the item within (10 x Magic Rating) meters from him, even if it's not visible. If the item is actively being concealed (Masking Ward, Invisibility), then it's an Opposed Test pitting Perception + Intuition vs. the Force + Magic attribute of the magician hiding the item. If the calculated Force (Force of item + number of traits) is greater than the Force of a ritual or spell hiding the item, then the Awakened senses the item but does not know its location.

RESPECT

The item, when visible to others and in contact with the Awakened character, reduces social penalties (p. 140, *SR5*) by the Awakened character's initiate grade. It can only reduce penalties to zero; it cannot create bonuses to any Social Tests. Imbuing an item with Respect comes with an additional monetary cost of five percent of the item's value x initiate grade. On its own, the item exudes Respect. Anyone who would steal the item or trash it in a random act of vandalism must make a Composure Test with a threshold equal to (initiate grade + 1). Failure means that the person is unable to take or damage the item.

RECTITUDE

For attuned items that are also qi or weapon foci, this trait gives the item more resistance to being disenchanted or deactivated. When held by the adept, add (initiate grade + 1) to the focus's resistance to being deactivated or disenchanted (p. 307, *SR5*). When it is on its own, add 2 to the Force of the foci for its resistance.

Force when sealing said ritual (and possibly can cause the ritual to fail). To overcome the stigma after breaking a stricture, the magician must succeed in an initiation ordeal to cleanse the bad vibe. For a player, if they have personally violated strictures, they also feel the effects. Besides the ritual spellcasting penalties mentioned (–1 per violation, per member participating), the magician's Magic is affected. Drain from using magical skills is increased by 1 for every structure violated until the magician atones for the violation.

IMBUE ITEM

Items of power can be imbued with various traits. These traits make the item more significant, even gaining its own reputation. An imbued weapon may not be as famous as Excalibur or Kusanagi-no-Tsurugi, but every sword has to start somewhere. Each trait enhances the Awakened's use of the bonded or attuned item. The Awakened character should exercise caution when considering the use of items with powerful traits, as they may affect the Awakened's personality. While altruistic traits are mentioned here, there are also selfish traits that items can incur through darker arts and twisted minds. Imbued traits can stay with the item after the owner's death, even if the item is bonded or attuned to another person. Imbuing ritual force is equal to the hits rolled using the appropriate dice pool on the Object Resistance Table (p. 295, SR5) with a Karmic cost based on the Item Attunement Table (p. 124) upon completion. This ritual takes (Force) hours to complete.

Each trait adds 1 to the Force when calculating bonding cost (if the focus had been previously imbued), the maximum number of active foci, and focus addiction. The maximum number of traits that can be given to an item is equal to its Force (or the highest Force for stacked foci). An item cannot be imbued with the same trait more than once. Attuned items can have 1 trait. For adepts, each attuned item that is imbued is considered Force 1 when calculating addiction. If a focus is disenchanted or the item is destroyed, the imbued traits also are destroyed (Karma spent is lost). If the Awakened individual glitches while performing this ritual, the item may be imbued with a negatively aspected trait. The gamemaster is encourage to make up such negative traits (Demanding, Vindictive, Complaining, etc.).

REMOVING TRAITS

Unless the Awakened character paid the Karma for the imbued trait(s), the item will "resist" the new owner. The Awakened character must remove the trait, spending 1 Karma to cleanse the item of that trait or to attune the trait to him.

KYTHING (ANCHORED)

From the old Scottish word "to make visible," this ritual forces astral beings to become visible. This ritual is most commonly done without a circle, using candles (reagents) to, in the words of one magical tome, "disperse the shadows hiding the invisible." The ritual generates a sphere whose radius is (Force of the ritual x the ritual leader's Magic Rating) meters. Net successes from the ritual become the threshold for the test any astral spirit, watcher, or astral projecting magician that comes in contact with the sphere must make to see if they are forced to manifest. For the test, astral spirits and watchers roll Force + Magic rating of the controlling magician; astral projecting magicians roll Willpower + Magic. Failure results in involuntary manifestation. This involuntary action takes away a service the spirit may own any individual. This manifestation is also taxing on the projecting magician (p. 314, SR5). The astral being (watcher, spirit, magician) must leave the area of the ritual before they can stop manifesting. The Kything ritual takes (Force) minutes to complete and lasts for (Force) minutes after the completion of the ritual. **Requires Sensing**.

FAR SENSING (SPOTTER)

The magician can use this short ritual to expand his metamagic sense ability to cover a greater area. The area of the spell is increased to Force x (sum total of the participants' Magic attributes) x 100 meters. The spell's subject must be present in the foundation during the ritual but may then take his new sense outside the foundation while the ritual participants sustain it for him. This ritual allows the subject to use the **Observe in Detail** action (p. 165, SR5) to sense both positive and negative background count without astral perception or projection. This ritual also allows the participants to readily detect astral phenomenon such as alchea, mana storms, warps, surges, or things similar that are either already present or entering the area of the spell. This ritual takes (Force) hours to complete. **Requires Sensing**.

HOMUNCULUS (MINION)

This ritual is described on p. 298, SR5.

LEECHING (MANA)

Leeching is a great geomantic ritual for short-term gains and long-term consequences in drawing mana energies for immediate use. The minimum Force required equals the positive background count of the area. Leeching cannot be used in an area with a negative background count (mana ebbs or voids). If the aspected background count was created through the Aspect Mana Line ritual, add the Magic Rating + initiate grade of the leader of that ritual to the Opposed Test. If successful, reduce the aspected background by the net successes of the ritual up to a mana ebb (p. 32). Unlike the Manifest Sha ritual, which displaces mana from an area, this ritual allows the magi-

cian to draw it in. The area affected by the ritual is (Force x 2) meters in radius. The immediate effect of the ritual within the area is that of a deathly aura (p. 194). The net successes of the ritual test (to a maximum of the Force of the ritual) can be used in the area as automatic successes in a Magic-related skill test. The successes can be spread across multiple tests, but each success can be used in this fashion only once. This pool of net successes is temporary, lasting (Magic rating x 10) minutes. The long-term consequence is that the area becomes a mana ebb, with a negative background count equal to the net successes of the ritual. The mana in the area takes time to recuperate; the background count increases by 1 per week until it returns to zero. Gathering reagents (p. 317, SR5) in the area is also affected. It takes one week to recovery each reagent (instead of the normal two days) until the background count is back to its original strength.

Leeching takes (Force) minutes to complete. **Requires Geomancy**

LEY SIGHT (MANA)

This ritual enables the magician to see and hear from any point within the aspected domain of a mana line with the exception of areas blocked by wards. Augmented vision or hearing does not apply. Net successes become the limit on any Perception Tests using Ley Sight. Ley Sight can be incorporated into rituals with the spotter keyword, substituting the spotter with performance of Ley Sight, but not as mystical link for spellcasting. Maximum distance that the magician can see is (Force) kilometers along the mana line and can be moved to any point along the line of influence (p. 122). This ritual takes (Force) minutes to complete. **Requires Geomancy**

LIGHT OF DHARMA (ANCHORED)

Based on Buddhism's concept of centering, this ritual allows the magician to channel his inner peace outwardly in a sphere of calm. As the magician completes the ritual, environmental factors (light, noise, wind, etc) (p. 175, SR5) are reduced by the Force of the ritual within the sphere. Noise and wind are muffled and lessen at the boundaries of this sphere, and ambient light emanates from both the magician and the interior surface of the sphere. The magician is the anchor of this ritual and cannot move or perform any action other than speaking or perception. He does not, however, suffer the penalty of sustaining the ritual. The sphere lasts for (net successes x 10) minutes, but the magician can end the ritual at any time. This ritual takes (Force) minutes to complete. **Requires Centering**

LIVING VESSEL PREPARATION (ORGANIC LINK)

To prepare a living metahuman or critter to become a host for a spirit is a complex ritual. Any reagents used in this ritual must be radical in quality. The minimum Force of the ritual is equal to the subject's Willpower. If the subject is unwilling (critters are always considered unwilling), then add the subject's Essence or Magic attribute (whichever is higher) to (Force x 2) of the ritual during the Seal the Ritual step (p. 298, SR5). Note that this does not affect the ritual's actual Force.

Once the ritual is complete, the vessel is astrally marked as being capable of being inhabited by a spirit. This mark is permanent until reversed by a similar preparation ritual of equal Force. This ritual takes (Force) days to complete. **Requires Channeling**

MANIFEST SHA (ANCHORED, MANA)

This ritual allows the magician to temporarily disrupt the power of a mana line or aspected energies of a background count. The minimum Force required is equal to the positive background count. If the aspected background count was created through the Aspect Mana Line ritual, add that leader's Magic Rating + initiate grade to the Opposed Test. If successful, reduce the aspected background by the net successes of the ritual up to a mana ebb (p. 32). Net successes also can be used to increase the duration of the ritual, with each net success adding 1 day. Net successes may be divided between the two functions, but no single net success can perform both functions. The area of the ritual is (Magic Rating x 10) meters in diameter. Any Awakened character in the area or moving through the area is affected by the new background count. This ritual lasts twenty-four hours unless net successes add time. This ritual takes (Force) hours to complete. **Requires Geomancy**

MASKING WARD (ANCHORED)

Though a Masking Ward acts like a basic ward, its main purpose is to conceal magical activity on the astral plane. The ward is transparent so as not to be seen by astral observers. Within the ward, any magical effects (Sorcery, Conjuring, Alchemical preparations) that have a Force less than or equal to the Force of the Masking Ward appear mundane to any observers outside the ward. Since the ward is transparent, it requires an outside observer to come in contact with the barrier or make a successful Assensing + Intuition [Astral] (3) Test. This only makes the observer aware of the ward,

FOOLING WARDS

It is possible to attack a mana barrier or to press through it (p. 315, SR5), but doing so alerts the ward's creator to the action, which is something the magician may want to avoid. A magician may use Flux if they have learned it, or become the astral doppelganger of a person approved to pass through the ward. Crossing the ward using either option requires an Opposed Test of the character's Intuition + Magic + initiate grade vs. Force of the ward x 2. If the individual succeeds in this test, they are able to cross the ward without alerting the ward's creator. If they failed, they cannot cross, but they have not yet alerted the ward's creator. If a material link or spotter was used to generate an astral doppelganger, reduce the ward's dice pool by 4; if a sympathetic link was used, reduce the ward's dice pool by 2.

COMBINING WARD TRAITS

Some magicians can get pretty fancy in constructing a single ward by designing a formula that incorporates attributes of several wards. In these cases, the dice pool of the ward in the Opposed Test is increased by 2 for each additional ward ability. For example, if a magician wants to create a Force 5 Masking ward that is also Obfuscating and Charged, the ritual is treated as if it were Force 9, meaning 18 dice are rolled to seal the ritual. For all other purposes, the ritual is treated as Force 5.

QUICK LIST OF CURRENT SPECIALIZED WARDS:

Alarm	Charged
Circle of Protection*	Cleansing Circle *
Door Ward*	Masking
Obfuscating	Polarized
Trap	

Special wards that can also be combined with permission of the gamemaster.

but not what's behind it. To pierce the illusion of the Masking Ward without passing through or destroying it requires a successful Opposed Test between the Assensing + Intuition [Astral] of the observer and Force x 2 of the ward. If the observer is successful, the ward's concealment does not work for that observer. Failure, however, gives the observer a migraine, resisting Stun damage with a DV equal to twice the net successes of the ward. This ritual takes (Force) hours to complete. **Requires Masking**

OBFUSCATING WARD (ANCHORED)

This ward is similar to the Alarm Ward, but it is designed to block Detection spells. Any Detection spell less than twice the force of the Obfuscating Ward does not detect anything within the area, nor does the magician sense that the spell has been blocked. The magician has to cross the ward in order to detect anything inside the ward. This ritual takes (Force) hours to complete. **Requires Masking (p. 325, SR5)**

POLARIZED WARD (ANCHORED)

A Polarized Ward functions in the same way as a basic ward, with the difference that it is designed to act much like a one-way mirror. Where a basic ward blocks viewing from either side of the barrier, a Polarized Ward appears opaque from one side and transparent from the other. Those on the transparent side must make an Assensing + Intuition [Astral] (3) Test in order to detect the ward. This ritual takes (Force) hours to complete

PRODIGAL SPELL (SPELL, SPOTTER)

This ritual is described on p. 297, SR5.

RECHARGE REAGENTS (GEOMANCY)

This ritual allows the magician to recharge a few reagents quickly by tapping into an aspected mana line aligned to the magician's tradition. This line must be aspected to the magician's tradition in order to work. When the spell is successfully completed, the magician may recharge one depleted reagent per net success up to the current force of the mana line. Once complete however, the mana line's force is reduced by 1 for one week. Cumulative uses can cause a sha effect (p. 35) if used too many times. This ritual takes (Force) hours to complete. **Requires Geomancy**

REMOTE SENSING (SPELL, SPOTTER)

This ritual is described on p. 297, SR5.

RENASCENCE (ANCHORED, SPELL)

This ritual is described on p. 298, SR5.

RITUAL OF CHANGE (MINION)

See Enhancing an Ally, p. 202.

SMUDGING (MANA, MATERIAL LINK)

Smudging is the purification or cleansing ritual for people or places. It often involves the burning of herbal reagents specific to the magician's tradition and culture (mugwart, white sage, etc). Smudging removes psychic imprints left on the astral plane on places and objects. It's frequently used to ward off "evil spirits" that may

be attracted to negative imprints by removing those imprints. Smudging is also used in cleansing objects after a crime for resale (legally or illegally). Some mistakenly believe that smudging can remove spirits such as haunts and bogies, but attempted cleansings of this type only piss them off.

As noted in Psychometry (p. 144), this ritual permanently reduces the psychic imprint by number of success for the ritual. Smudging also reduces the existence of all astral signatures by number of successes within the area (p. 312, SR5). The Smudging ritual cleans an area equal to the ([leader's Magic Rating + initiate grade] x Force) in meters. It takes Force x 30 minutes to complete the ritual. **Requires Cleansing**

SPIRIT PACT (CONTRACTUAL)

The Awakened character has entered into a pact with a free spirit, which uses part of its spiritual essence to augment the character's magical power, stave off Drain, sustain the character's life, and so on. The specific nature of the pact should be discussed with the gamemaster and is subject to his approval. The cost of completing this ritual is in Karma equaling Force x 2 of the spirit. The Force of the ritual must equal to the Force of the spirit. This ritual takes (Force) hours to complete.

SUMMON GREAT FORM SPIRIT (MINION)

A magician can use this ritual to instill more power into bound spirit. The net hits at the completion of this ritual determines the actual effect is has on the spirit. This ritual takes Force hours to complete, with a minimum Force equal to the Force of the spirit Aspected conjurers (who do not perform Ritual Spellcasting) use the Summoning skill instead.. **Requires Invocation**

A magician that knows the Art of **Sacrifice** and **Invocation** may create a truly frightening entity—a great form blood spirit. During the ritual, a metahuman victim must be killed; this is required to fuel the "ascension" of the Blood Spirit.

GREAT FORM SPIRIT

HITS	RESULTS
2	Gain Banishing Resistance (p. 194)
3	Gain an additional optional power (see powers listed by spirit type p. 394, SR5)
4	Gain greater spirit power appropriate to the spirit type
5	Astral Gateway power (p. 194)
6+	Endowment power (p. 195)

SPIRIT PACTS

Free spirits with the Spirit Pact power (p. 205) may enter into magically binding agreements with metahumans. A spirit with this power can usually offer only one or two different kinds of pacts. Negotiating the terms of a pact is pointless, as the first offer a spirit makes is almost always the only offer it will extend. Ending a pact without causing the death of both participants is nearly impossible, as such endeavors are the basis for epic, magical plot devices. Any time a character and spirit have a pact, either party may be used as a sympathetic link (p. 146) to the other.

POSSIBLE PACTS

Gamemasters should carefully consider the balance of her game's dynamics before introducing a spirit pact. A spirit with the Spirit Pact power can enter into any of the following pacts with a metahuman, but gamemasters may also create their own.

Drain Pact: The spirit ties its magical essence to the magician, allowing him to gain a positive dice pool modifier in Drain Resistance Tests equal to the spirit's Edge. Using magic in this way is addictive (see Substance Abuse and Addiction, p. 413, *SR5*), and unlike most pacts, the spirit can cut off the magician at any time. The spirit may demand Karma from the magician to continue supplying him mana.

Dream Pact: The spirit gains control of the character whenever she is asleep. The character's body doesn't sleep, but she is rested when she awakes. While the spirit controls the character, it gains Karma through its actions as if it were the character. The character regains control if her body when she wakes but has no memory of what transpired while the spirit was in control. Note that any damage done to the body while the spirit is in control stays when the character awakes, so they have to deal with it.

Formula Pact: The spirit infuses the character with a copy of its spirit formula. The character gains Immunity to Age (p. 397, SR5), and the spirit cannot be affected by any other copy of the formula for as long as that character lives. The character's aura is visibly tainted by the spirit's signature, and the character may be used (by others or by himself) as the spirit's formula for any purpose.

Life Pact: The spirit's life force is tied to the character's. To keep herself alive, the character may draw upon the spirit's life force at the expense of Karma. She may spend a Complex Action to heal 2 boxes of Physical damage in return for giving the spirit 1 Karma. The spirit doesn't need to be present for this transaction to occur, and it doesn't suffer the healed damage.

Magic Pact: The spirit allows the magician to use its Magic in exchange for the use of the magician's Edge. Once per day, the magician may enhance his Magic attribute by half of the spirit's Magic attribute for (spirit's Force) Combat Turns. In turn, the spirit may spend the magician's Edge for any purpose at any time.

Power Pact: The spirit links its magical abilities to the character. The character may use one of the spirit's powers (except Astral Form, Materialization, Possession, or Inhabitation), and in exchange the spirit may cast one of the magician's spells (if any). This pact lasts only twenty-four hours but can be renewed an unlimited number of times, provided the spirit can be sufficiently bribed into doing so.

GREATER SPIRIT POWER

Air: Storm (p. 199)	**Beasts:** Paralyzing Howl (p. 399, *SR5*)
Earth: Quake (p. 197)	**Fire:** Storm (p. 199)
Guardian: As per the base type of spirit	**Guidance:** As per the base type of spirit
Man: Magical Guard (p. 196)	**Plant:** Regeneration (p. 400, *SR5*)
Task: As per the base type of spirit	**Water:** Storm (p. 199)

TRAP WARD (ANCHORED)

Trap Wards initially function exactly like an alarm ward (p. 122). Once a Trap Ward is triggered and the alarm given, however, it solidifies into a basic ward with solid walls. The intent is slow down the intruder long enough for security to respond. Trap Wards are only triggered by astral forms, not spells. **Requires Anchoring**

WHISPER OF BONES (ORGANIC LINK)

Who says dead men tell no tales? Whisper of Bones is specific type of divination where the necromancer can gain information from a deceased individual. This is not speaking to the dead—the magician is not communicating with a once-living spirit—but it is accessing memories held "within the bones." This divination allows the magician to ask questions about the events surrounding the physical aspects of the body. The questions are answered with images of the subject when alive that may be literal as past events or as vague as some symbolism relating to the Awakened character's tradition. Items and places outside of the body are represented by shadowy figures unless they have some significance (see **Sympathetic Link**, p. 146) to the body. Forensics can use this ritual to help determine events around the person's death, but not necessarily who killed him. Use Divination thresholds when asking questions and getting a response (p. 125). **Requires Necromancy.** This ritual takes (Force) minutes to complete

SECRETS OF THE INITIATES

Scott listened intently as Professor Rockhound lectured on mana lines.

"... and since 2028 we've been using the Typhus-Metzger scale for measuring ..."

"Stupid," Scott heard a voice interrupt from nearby.

"... and various manatropic seeds will 'pop,' as it were..." the professor droned on.

"Idiotic," that nearby voice remarked.

The interruptions were becoming annoying. This was going to be the only time the professor would be able to speak at Montana Tech and Geomancy this year. Scott looked up from the display to see who was in the peanut gallery. Around the terraced seating, he saw similar students watching displays and recording notes.

"The man couldn't find his rear with both ends of a dowsing rod." The voice came from what appeared as a grey wolf sitting in one of the seats two rows back from him. Normally that would've seemed out of the ordinary, but in a classroom of magicians, these things could happen. The wolf looked over at Scott and winked at him.

Scott shook his head. *Who would've brought a watcher to lecture?* he thought.

"Watcher, eh? Hmmph!"

Scott looked over at where the wolf had been sitting, but the chair was vacant. Now that the peanut gallery was gone, he was able to better concentrate on Professor Rockhound's theory on dragon lines.

Later, once it was over, Scott left the lecture hall and was heading across the courtyard to get something to eat at the cafeteria when something bumped him in the leg. He looked down to see that same wolf trotting next to him.

"Hey, Scott," it said, "you know Rockhound's stuff is just scientific mumbo jumbo, right? That's not the way you should learn geomancy."

Scott was a little taken back by the boldness of this strange spirit talking to him. "What do you mean? Even the digital grimoire shows formulas similar to what the professor described."

"Forget formulas, use your gut. Geomancy is getting a feel for the land."

"How's that going to help me figure out how many milli-Typhus-Metzgers various manatropic seeds need to react? I'm getting way overloaded on lab work."

"Wow," the wolf said. "They really have you hermetically hooked. Look. How about this? Geomancy is more hands-on. Why don't you try it my way? If it doesn't work out, I'll help you figure out your milly-whatsit homework. Deal?"

Somehow Scott felt he could trust this spirit. "All right. If you can show me a better way to understand ley lines, we'll try it your way."

The wolf jumped with delight. "Great!" it said as it trotted away behind Scott. "Now, first I want you to find the flow of energies and follow it out of the forest." Then it ran off.

"Forest?" Scott yelled back, wondering what forest, when he ran into something.

It was a tree. Instead of crossing the courtyard for a Nukit burger, Scott found himself lost in the woods. He pulled out his commlink. The NO SIGNAL message scrolled across the interface. He chuckled at the situation as he opened his sight to the astral world. Walking along a game path in the woods, he realized it was not a wolf that was guiding him. It was *Wolf*.

INTRODUCTION

Initiation is a journey toward understanding higher levels of magic, and there are many paths to take. After the chaos of the Awakening, magicians began testing their limits. Once the fundamentals of magic were defined, students of the magical arts explored them in more depth and found new dimensions to the new rules they discovered. Each new discovery further developed and defined metamagics, along with advanced enchantment and alchemical techniques. Whole schools of magical learning were founded, including divination, geomancy, necromancy, psychometry, and so on. Each school includes rituals, metamagics, and enchantment techniques beyond the average magician's understanding. Those who follow these paths are not just called magicians but geomancers, necromancers, sages, and so on. Schools that teach magic offer bachelor's and master's degrees in the Thaumaturgical Sciences or the Thaumaturgic Arts (BTS and MTS, or BTA and MTA), and a Doctor of Thaumaturgy degree, or ThD, is available to graduate students who complete their coursework and initiate.

Presented here are some of the higher arts a magician can initiate into—either alone, through a group, or with a school. Each specific art encompasses a list of rituals, enchantments, and metamagics. When a magician first initiates into the art, he learns one available ritual, enchantment, or metamagic for free, barring any prerequisites. A magician can learn additional advanced rituals and enchantments within that category by spending the same amount of time and Karma as other rituals (5 Karma, see p. 299, *SR5*). For each new metamagical technique, however, the magician will need to initiate to the next grade to gain that new metamagic.

THE INITIATION RITE

Initiation is a milestone of enlightenment in the character's magical or spiritual process. It can take the form of final answers to questions in a greater understanding of magic, a spiritual transformation, or a rite of passage used by the magician's tradition. Many magicians ini-

MAGIC ARTS

Below are some basic information and restrictions for the various magic arts available to initiating magicians and adepts.

RITUALS

These rituals are only available for those who have initiated into this particular school of magic. They cost the same amount of Karma and time to learn as other rituals (5 Karma, see p. 299, *SR5*); no additional initiation grade is needed. These rituals cannot be taught to any other magician unless they too have initiated in this school of magic. Magicians who do not know the ritual can still participate in it as long as the ritual leader knows it (p. 295, *SR5*).

ENHANCEMENTS

For adepts, enhancements represent focused training for one specific adept power, pushing it beyond the traditional limits. The cost in Karma and time is the same as learning a new skill (2 Karma, 1 day). The adept must first have the power before he can augment it. A learned enhancement cannot be taught to another adept unless he or she is initiated into that particular Way.

ENCHANTING

These enchantments are only available for those who have initiated into this school of magic. They cost the normal amount of Karma and time to learn (5 Karma, see p. 299, *SR5*). These items cannot be used by other magicians unless they have also initiated into this school of magic.

METAMAGICS

These metamagics are only available to those who initiate into this school of magic. If more than one metamagic is available, the magician must perform the initiation process, including the Karma and time cost, to learn each one.

tiate into an art on their own instead of going to an institute of higher learning or through a magical group. Prior to 2025, not even universities offered the option to learn such magic.

To get ideas for an appropriate rite and the challenge required to complete it, the gamemaster should start with the beliefs of the character's chosen tradition (see p. 38). The gamemaster can also come up with her own ideas or allow the player to suggest some rites. Examples would be a Lakota shaman completing the Sun Dance ritual to receive a vision quest, a koradji going on a walkabout along the Native Cat Path, or a hermetic mage completing the rites to join a fraternal order. The character's mentor spirit can also play an important role in the rite. As for fraternal orders, group initiation could include completing secret rituals of the mystical group that the magician belongs to or performing tests and writing essays for the university where the magician is studying.

Initiation has a Karma cost, which can be expensive for high initiate grades. Belonging to or creating a mystic group can reduce the cost of initiation. Another option for reducing the cost is to undertake an initiatory ordeal, a grueling mental or physical task that will challenge the magician's determination and ability. A third option is through academic schooling, which costs 10,000 nuyen for five weeks. Group initiation or an initiatory ordeal can further reduce the Karma cost by 10 percent each.

Only one ordeal and/or group can be included per initiation, and these must be chosen before undergoing the initiation rite, as they will help the gamemaster design it.

KARMA COST OF INITIATION

TYPE	COST
Base Cost	10 + (Grade x 3)
Group Initiation	Base cost – 10 percent*
Initiatory Ordeal	Base cost – 10 percent*
Schooling	Base cost – 10 percent*

* These may be combined for a total initiation discount of 30 percent

To receive a group initiation discount, the magician must have successfully completed a Group Bond ritual (p. 129).

INITIATORY ORDEALS

Only one ordeal can be chosen per initiation grade. It cannot be completed prior to initiation; you cannot do an ordeal early just to get it out of the way. Initiation Karma is spent at the beginning of the ordeal. If the magician or adept fails to complete the ordeal, he cannot initiate, but he doesn't lose the Karma spent. The magician or adept can try to complete the ordeal at another time, but she cannot successfully initiate until the ordeal has been completed.

NINE PATHS TO ENLIGHTENMENT

The Nine Paths to Enlightenment are ordeals that subject an Awakened character to physical and mental challenges in the physical or metaphysical world (see **Metaplanar Quest**, p. 140). These can entail finding answers through mediation or strength through suffering. Challenges can encompass arduous tasks, such as carrying a bucket of water up a thousand steps and filling a large tub one bucketful at a time, to more dangerous tasks, like being hung from a tree. Such challenges are up to the gamemaster and should relate to the character's background, tradition, and the magical art he is striving to learn. The time to complete the challenge is twenty-nine days, the period from new moon to new moon. To successfully complete the challenge, the magician chooses one of the nine paths and must succeed in an Opposed Test. Each enlightened path has two attributes; the gamemaster chooses one, and the character takes the other. The player rolls the magician's chosen attribute + current initiate grade, and the gamemaster rolls the magician's other attribute + desired initiate grade. If the character fails, he may try again next lunar cycle. If the character succeeds, that path may not be taken again for a future initiatory ordeal.

METAPLANAR QUEST

A metaplanar quest is a metaphysical ordeal designed to challenge the character. It works best as a metaphor using the character's background flaws and Negative Qualities. The gamemaster should tailor the quest to be appropriately evocative of the initiate's background, belief system, and the magical art the character wishes to attain. As an inspiration, the Nine Paths of Enlightenment are available as suggestions in challenging various character attributes. If the character fails the quest, she may attempt it again until successful, provided she has waited the appropriate interval for re-testing.

Only characters who can astrally project can undertake a metaplanar quest unless they gains access to a spirit's Astral Gateway power (p. 194). Before attempting a quest, the character must prepare herself through a meditation ritual. This simple ritual requires a Force equal

NINE PATHS TO ENLIGHTENMENT

Resilience (Strength, Body): The candidate develops a kinesthetic sense of the body by consciously controlling a sensory withdrawal to isolate the mind. The autonomic functions of the body, such as respiration and circulation, slow down to allow increased endurance of extreme temperatures, hunger, or pain. The character nurtures this ability to fortify his body with the strength of will, allowing greater focus on magic in times of physical stress or pain.

Flow (Willpower, Logic): The candidate develops control over desires and emotions. Once detached from these, the candidate's mind is allowed to wander freely. With practice, the mind settles and begins to flow. This unrestricted stream of consciousness may wax and wane between thoughts of good and evil. As the candidate develops greater control, the intensity of these thoughts diminishes in extent and frequency. The initial goal is to achieve a single thought, then focus on the space and time between thoughts. As the flow calms sufficiently, the true self is revealed.

Balance (Agility, Intuition): The candidate hones coordination between mind and body. Energy is more effectively transmitted between them, enabling the development of agility, intuition, and holistic balance. The candidate is more difficult to rattle, keeping mind and body steady in ways that aid magic use.

Spirit (Willpower, Intuition): This path develops one's spirit. Once the mind is in this spiritual state, it becomes one with the object of meditation, both the concept and name of the object. In combat the *kiai*, or spirit shout, is drawn from this source; the general strength of will a candidate can draw from this path is useful to all Awakened.

Harmony (Body, Charisma): This path controls respiration. The flow of energy through the body is not the consciousness of the spirit but merely the energy the soul uses in its material and astral manifestations. One who can learn to control this energy has the power to bring it to a state of vibration that can be conveyed to others, causing them to vibrate harmonically. A magic user who has abundant energy radiates strength and health.

Instinct (Reaction, Intuition): This path develops the sense of hearing, allowing one to hear her inner voice. Focusing on this path stimulates the proximity sense, which allows one to feel the presence of others. Instinct also serves as the force that separates the astral body from the physical. Meditation on this path leads to the concept of oneself.

Mastery of Time and Space (Logic, Intuition): This path represents the mind's highest level. Meditation on this ideal earns the candidate control over the body's nerve centers. One will also note extraordinary spiritual strength, knowledge, and willpower. This path is the seat of the body's force. The acquisition of the higher voice, or intuitional knowledge and clairvoyance, resides in this path, as does the soul.

Control (Willpower, Strength): This path leads to the marriage of spirit and matter, where the individual and universal consciousness unite. The suffusion of one's consciousness into the Infinite enables the candidate to exercise her will through the elements.

Satori (Charisma, Magic): This is not eternal enlightenment. Rather, it is the goal of meditation and Awakening, a realization of the connections between the mind, body, and spirit as revealed through this path's exercises. A person can have many epiphanies in his or her lifetime yet never achieve eternal enlightenment.

to the initiate grade the character wishes to attain. The ritual takes (Force) hours to complete. Successful completion of this ritual means the character can transcend the physical world and face the Dweller on the Threshold (p. 317, *SR5*). The self-sustaining ritual protects the magician's body with wards while the character is on the journey. Time has no meaning when completing this ordeal. The magician may spend the equivalent of days, weeks, or months in the metaplanes but only hours may pass in the physical world.

ASCETICISM

An asceticism ordeal involves giving up the pleasure of modern technology and conveniences of magic. For a period of at least twenty-nine days, the character must rely on her own skills and talents to accomplish tasks and avoid using any equipment other than basic tools. Forbidden items include electronic devices (commlinks, radios, most firearms, drones), vehicles for transportation (except domesticated animals), fetishes, foci, and spirits (when spirits hear that a magician is taking this ordeal, they are more than happy to oblige and not come when summoned). The character's ordeal must last a number of game sessions as agreed upon by the gamemaster and player. The higher the initiate grade, the more game sessions this ordeal should take. The player must apply the use of several skills during the gaming session. The number of required skill tests per session is up to the gamemaster, but the suggested minimum is (Magic) tests. The emphasis is on the use of skills not the success, though the gamemaster may limit the number of combat skills that can be applied. A character cannot take two asceticism ordeals consecutively.

DEED

A deed ordeal requires the character to perform some difficult task with a specific goal appropriate to the character's background, tradition, mentor spirit, magical group (if he has one), and/or moral code (if he has one). Before starting a deed ordeal, the gamemaster and player should agree on the specific goal and introduce it though roleplaying. Such an ordeal can become a run (or campaign) in its own right, though the run must be personally relevant and appropriate to the character's undertaking. When planning the deed, the gamemaster may want to make the total Karma earned in the course of performing the deed close to the Karma needed to pay for initiation. That way, the candidate can have the Karma needed to initiate when the deed is done, while the deed provided the plot impetus for multiple sessions.

FAMILIAR

This ordeal requires the character to summon an ally spirit (p. 200) at the end of the initiation, and the ordeal consists of the magician discovering what is needed in the spirit formula. This ordeal is available to those who are initiating into the invocation art and would substitute the learning of **Summon Great Form Spirits** with **Ally Conjuration**.

GEAS

To fulfill this ordeal, the character voluntarily accepts a geas, limiting her magic ability. Create an appropriate geas in cooperation with your game master. A geas taken as an ordeal can never be removed.

OATH

The oath ordeal, in which the character swears an oath to obey a given magical group's rules and strictures, is only available to members of such groups (see **Magical Societies**, p. 54). Even if a character swears several oaths during her lifetime, only the first oath qualifies as an ordeal.

HERMIT

A hermit ordeal involves giving up the creature comforts of modern life and devoting oneself exclusively to mental and physical activities that are appropriate to the magician's tradition (subject to the gamemaster approval). The character must abandon her normal lifestyle and adopt a Street lifestyle for a period of at least twenty-nine days. The character must decline all but the most basic of comforts. Comforts such as mooching of another player's lifestyle are forbidden, and characters who already have a Street lifestyle are not eligible for this ordeal. Every seven days, the character must make a successful Survival Test to continue the ordeal; the threshold should be at least 2, but can be higher based on circumstances (and should be higher as the ordeal progresses). Failing any test means the character must start the ordeal over. A character cannot take two hermit ordeals consecutively.

SACRIFICE

Common in many ancient and primitive traditions, a sacrifice ordeal calls upon the magician's resolve to sacrifice or scar a part of her body. Such a sacrifice may never be replaced or hidden through surgery. When the character undergoes this ordeal, she permanently gives up 1 point from an appropriate attribute (e.g., Charisma or Intuition for an eye, Agility for a hand). Examples of sacrifice include ritual scarring of the face, neck, or arms (Charisma), burning the tendons in a hand, arm, or leg (Reaction). The character's natural maximum rating (p. 66, *SR5*) for that attribute is permanently reduced by 1. The character cannot sacrifice a point from a Rating 1 attribute. A rating augmented by cyberware, spells, or adept powers also cannot be sacrificed as part of this ordeal. If this ordeal is taken multiple times, the character must reduce a different attribute before she can reduce a previously reduced attribute again.

THESIS/MASTERPIECE

A thesis/masterpiece ordeal requires the Awakened character to record his insights or create an artistic masterpiece. For those who work toward a formal education, the completion of a thesis for this ordeal has a bonus of a ThD attached to their name (assuming they completed all other academic prerequisites, of course). This ordeal requires the character to create a physical work. A thesis must be written on parchment or printed and bound as a hard copy, and a masterpiece must also have a physical representation (e.g., a musical score, a painting, or a film script). Producing a thesis requires a Logic + Arcana [Mental] (8 + desired initiate grade, 1 week) Extended Test. Producing a masterpiece requires an Artisan + Intuition [Mental] (8 + desired initiate grade, 1 week) Extended Test.

Once completed, the work carries its own aura, which is a copy of the character's at the time of creation. It is also considered a material link to its creator. Physical copies of the work can be made, but each copy is considered a viable sympathetic link. Applicable use of the work (playing the music, creating a trid, referencing the thesis in a magical journal) has no appreciable effect on the magician.

The risk with the thesis/masterpiece ordeal is that if all copies of the work are destroyed, the creator suffers a momentous and metaphysical loss. The character must immediately take on a geas (p. 142) or reduce his initiate grade by 1. If he chooses to lose an initiate grade, this may result in Magic loss if his Magic attribute exceeds 6 + (current initiation grade). Most initiates make at least one backup copy of their thesis or masterpiece to prevent this from happening.

HIGH ARTS

GEOMANCY

Mana is very different from the air that surrounds us. It can vary in concentrations, sometimes forming flows analogous to rivers and streams. These rivers of magic are called mana lines. Most magicians only understand the indirect effects of mana lines, such as the greater concentration of reagents found nearby or the background count of an aspected mana line. Geomancy understands how to subtly affect and manipulate these natural flows of mana to harness that energy for the magician's Sorcery skills.

Practitioners of geomancy can generally be divided into two groups: geomancers and geomasons. This division is similar to that of hermetic and shamanic magic. Geomancy relates to an intuitive view of flowing energies and usually falls into the schooling of feng shui and the books *Kao Gong Ji* and *Lu Ban Jing*, which instruct on construction methods that maximize *qi* energy. Geomancy is older than the books, though; it has been around for over six thousand years, and its fundamental symbolism predates both feng shui and the *I Ching*. This has fueled theories that an advanced culture, much like the Atlanteans, passed on this knowledge in the East. Shamanic traditions tend to follow geomancy.

Geomasonry teaches that logic and freemasonic construction resonate with extraplanar energies. Geomasonry has roots as old as the more intuitive field. The pyramids of Egypt and structures in Amazonia are early evidence of ancient geomasonry. This has added fuel to the theory of an expansive Atlantean civilization, which contributes to the Atlantean Foundation's study of the art. Hermetic traditions tend to follow geomasonry.

Schools like Montana Tech and Geomancy in Butte specialize in teaching both geomantic and geomasonic techniques. (Though MT&G is in the Sioux Nation, its faculty comprises mainly Anglo and hermetic teachers.) Many of the teachings are hands-on out in the field. Students are given dowsing rods and tasked with finding and following the meanderings of a mana line. Other classes progress into manipulation of mana lines with ritual magic and aspecting mana lines toward the magician's tradition, giving the initiate an advantage with other Magical skills. With geomancy, a magician first learns the ritual **Aspect Mana Line** (p. 122). After this initiation, he can further his breadth of knowledge with other rituals. Arthur's foil, dragon's blood, red-capped mushrooms, and other manatropic Awakened plants are the staples of geomancer reagents.

Controlling the few mana lines in an urban environment is a very competitive undertaking, as a mana line works with the feng shui of the building it runs through. Corporations employ geomancers and geomasons to channel these magical energies to fuel physical and as-

tral constructs or to empower rituals. They also hire such talent to subvert or sabotage another corporation's use of mana.

NECROMANCY

Necromancy is not the same as the wizards bringing back the dead as shown in the trids. Only the gamemaster and burning one's Edge can do that. Necromancy is the power and understanding of magic to resonate in human remains and bring forth memories within the bones. The art derives from shamanic rituals for speaking to one's ancestors, but many traditions frown upon it for philosophical and ethical reasons. Necromancy can often be mistaken for blood magic, especially with rituals like Blood Sight and items like the Hand of Glory. However, necromancy is only interested in aspects after life, not to use life as fuel for magic. Regardless, it's not commonly practiced, and few magicians accept practitioners of necromancy. Those who practice necromancy are known as necromancers, though shamanic traditions favor the ancient Babylonian term *manzazuu*, since its sounds less negative.

Only magicians who can summon spirits of man can practice necromancy, as the magician must understand the various virtues and fundamentals of humankind. Law-enforcement officials often have provisions to allow forensic thaumaturgists to follow this path of learning for professional reasons. Necromancy's darker connotations can quickly lead a magician down a path

PROFESSION: FENG SHUI MASTER

All the magic being slung around isn't what's polluting the astral plane and negatively affecting spellcasting. According to this school of thought, the world's misery and psychological problems are responsible. A true feng shui master learns the arts of geomancy and cleansing to not only reduce the background influence but also to adjust the flow of mana to benefit the client. Feng shui masters aspect mana lines, perform smudging, and use Circles of Cleansing to cleanse offices and homes of any negative attitude that's hanging around, allowing wage mages to perform better. The background count reduction may be temporary, but that just helps preserve the feng shui master's job security.

RITUALS

Aspect Mana Line	Recharge Reagents
Manifest Sha	
Ley Sight	

of blood magic, so corporations and law enforcement often require necromancers to take routine psychological evaluations.

Very few schools teach necromantic courses, let alone help students initiate in the art. Loyola University in New Orleans has one of the few official Forensic Thaumaturgy degrees that offers necromancy initiation and certification. Necromancy classes teach a lot of history and human anatomy. At Loyola, students must study human remains and identify the cause of death, both from scientific observation and by speaking with the bones. A knowledge of all aspects of death is key to necromancy. Students learn both past and present burial and funeral ceremonies from across the globe. The first ritual necromancers learn is **Grave Binding** (p. 129) so that the dead can rest in peace. Necromancers commonly use reagents from the nightshade family, which includes belladonna and tomatoes, so this may be why they are mistakenly called *venefici* or poisoners.

PROFESSION: FORENSIC THAUMATURGIST

A forensic thaumaturgist is a magical law-enforcement profession that is not associated with any one tradition (though many mistakenly believe it's a hermetic profession due to the high percentage of hermetic thaumaturgists employed by Lone Star and Knight Errant). Magicians in this profession investigate crime scenes when there is probable cause that the crime was committed with magic. Their skills in Perception and Assensing allow them to find astral signatures in order to identify culprits and review emotional context of the astral plane to help with suggesting motive. The forensic thaumaturgist also has tools to find more clues at the crime scene than mundane investigators do.

Though forensic thaumaturgists arrive at the crime scene after the crime is committed, don't think they're untrained: They go through the same law enforcement and firearm training as their fellow officers. Many forensic thaumaturgists learn necromantic metamagics to more quickly catch criminals in a murder investigation. Law enforcement keeps constant tabs on forensic thaumaturgists, including monthly therapy sessions, to ensure they aren't sliding into darker arts.

RITUALS
Grave Binding
Death Mark
Blood Sight

ENCHANTING
Mortis Optigram
Hand of Glory

PSYCHOMETRY

Face it: Magic is weird, and the astral plane is even weirder. For example, buildings that had some significance to people will still retain some astral shadow, even if the building has been torn down. This is the same for objects that can be used as a sympathetic link. The objects don't gain an aura like living things, but they do resonate with emotions and impressions. Emotions can be associated with objects, similar to the way a sound in the astral world is comparable to the colors of an aura.

Those who initiate into psychometry learn to hear such things. Psychometry schools first teach the class by presenting a number of objects, including one item that has been handled while the rest have not, and students are asked to identify the handled item. Further classes teach how to not only identify the handled item but also the person who handled it. This is about as far as most thaumaturgical schools teach psychometry. This may be due to the stigma of mirroring the sixth-sense pseudoscience of the Fifth World, but it's enough for magicians to use it to their advantage. Those who initiate into psychometry usually first learn **Sympathetic Linking** for rituals.

Further psychometry learning allows the magician to not only recognize this psychometric imprint but also to read it. This allows the initiate to heighten her Assensing skills to interpret lingering emotions and even gain insight.

Oxford Royal College of Magicians is an example of an Awakened school that teaches advanced psychometry. The school educates arcanoarchaeologists and curators to interpret such elements with supposed artifacts in order to identify fakes or search for grave robbers.

PROFESSION: OCCULT PROFILER

While in most cases, law enforcement isn't allowed to use psychometric techniques to hunt down criminals, the same rules don't apply for occult profilers or mystic bounty hunters. Provided the price is right, these magicians can track down people by using psychometry, watchers, and rituals, even when the trail has already gone cold for mundane techniques.

ENCHANTING
Symbolic Link
Mystic Restraints

METAMAGICS
Sympathetic Linking
Psychometry

SYMPATHETIC LINKING

For all links, the object must be small and easily carried by the magician. While a rigger's favorite car could be considered as a sympathetic link, it is too large to carry. Just take the driver's seat cushion.

Using sympathetic or symbolic links in a ritual that normally contains the Material Link keyword is more difficult to successfully complete. When using a sympathetic link, add 2 to the Force of the spell for the opposing test in Step 7: Seal the Ritual (p. 296, *SR5*). With a symbolic link, add 4.

PSYCHOMETRY

Psychometry is like experiencing flashbacks, a flood of senses and emotions that can be uncontrollable. Once the magician develops this skill, the door can be difficult to close. Everything the magician touches generates this kind of feedback. Do you really need to know the life story behind every shot glass and barstool? The magician learns to put up mental shields to filter out distractions from all the input he would get from astral imprints. The magician needs only a few moments to raise or lower his shields to attempt reading an object. To read an object, the magician makes an Assensing + Intuition + initiate grade [Astral] Test; see the Psychometry table for modifiers and results.

When reading an object, the magician has a –2 dice pool penalty to all other actions. Unfortunately, while reading the object, the magician has no control over how long the reading takes, and she cannot stop until the reading is done. It can take 1 minute, 5 minutes, or longer. The gamemaster can roll 1D6 to choose the duration, or he can decide the duration based on the psychometric experience.

SYMPATHETIC LINKING

MATERIAL

A material link is an integral part of the target. For an inanimate object, the material link has to be something that is an essential part of its structure. A brick from a wall would be a material link to that building, but a picture or other piece of decoration in the building would not. If the target is a living being, the material link must be a tissue sample. However, tissue samples decompose eventually and cease being viable as a material link. Blood and other bodily fluids are viable for a few hours, and a finger or larger tissue samples can last a few days before decomposing. A simple Knowledge Test in Biology can give a more concrete estimate of how much time the sample has left. Chemical preservations destroy the sample's viability as a material link.

SYMPATHETIC

A sympathetic link can only be created for sentient beings, as inanimate objects lack sympathy. The object for the link may be something the target uses frequently or that holds sentimental or personal value (a toilet is not a sympathetic object). If an item has been used by the target for more than five minutes (a pen, a wrapper for a McHugh's burger, etc.), then it can also be considered for a sympathetic link.

Sentimental objects can last as a sympathetic link for weeks, frequently worn items are viable for days, and objects constantly used for more than five minutes are viable as a link for twice the amount of time the target held them in the most recent usage of five minutes or longer.

SYMBOLIC

Symbolic links are the weakest possible link for ritual magic. These objects are fashioned into a physical likeness or representation of the target. The risk of using such items is that they can be used as a material link against the magician that created them. See **Symbolic Link** (p. 216).

MAGICIANS AND THEIR MATERIAL LINK

Some people fear magicians because of what they believe magic can do, right? Well, magicians fear other magicians, especially if the latter have a material link that can be used in ritual magic. Trids and mythology push this paranoia of stolen locks of hair or drops of blood by evil wizards, and they're not off base in doing this. The vodou tradition specifically focuses on indirect

PSYCHOMETRY TABLE

SITUATION	MODIFIERS
TIME SINCE IMPRESSION*	
1 day	+0
1 week	–2
1 month	–4
1 year	–6
1 decade	–8
Each additional decade	–2
NATURE OF ITEM	
Nature of item has a strong connection to the impression (wedding ring, beloved toy, etc.)	+2
Initiate had a strong connection to item when impression was formed (friend's toy, school building, etc.)	+2
Impression recorded violence or powerful emotions	+3
Impression recorded violent death	+4
Item is a bonded focus	+ (Rating)**
Item is a place of more than 500 square kilometers	–2
Item carries more than one significant impression	–1 for each
Astral signature has been erased (p. 312, *SR5*)	–1
Cleansing metamagic has been used (Smudging, p. 136)	–Force
Each subsequent attempt to read the item	–2
INFORMATION	

HITS	INFO GAINED
0	None
1	Flashes of insight, superficial and disjointed impressions
2	Longer and deeper insights, though visions are still disjointed
3	Greater details, multiple sensory feedback, more coherence
4+	Lengthy sequences, multiple senses, coherent visions, significant information

* *Items isolated from other auras or from being disturbed (tombs, basements, abandoned towns) can keep their impression for much longer. It is suggested that items within the Gaiasphere—i.e., underground—retain such impressions longer. The gamemaster can reduce the time modifier to that of a week, month, or year for these kinds of items.*

** *Modifier only applies to impressions related to the person to whom the focus is bonded. Stacked foci only grant the highest rating as a bonus.*

ritual magic. Because of this, certain cleaning drones and services designed around the quick disposal of any organic material left behind are labeled as "mage sensitive." Shadow versions of this kind of service even take care of cleaning bloodstains, no questions asked. The Jolly Barber in San Diego, for example, has a dragon-shaped brazier homunculus that eats the sweepings after each haircut. Note that this is different from mana-sensitive services, which are drones and gear that filter pollution or uses less-harsh chemicals to prevent disturbing the magician's feng shui.

DIVINATION

On the astral plane, one can find astral shadows of what physically exists today, shadows of objects and events of the past, and possibly shadows of events of the future. The astral plane is a mingling imprint of emotions, thoughts, and auras of everyone and everything. Divination allows the initiate to peer beyond the mists of time and see some of what fate has in store for a specific subject. Some magicians think they can take a macro view of this to get some semblance of future events associated with a specific person, place, etc. There's no single way to learn divination. This category of magic suffered from an enduring Fifth World stigma of carnival fortunetellers and wildly inaccurate psychics.

IWith regard to the law, all civilized governments and organizations have outlawed using divination to see whether a person will commit a future crime and then arresting the subject for "pre-crime." Using divination on a known criminal to see if he will commit another crime while on parole is admissible, but this is rarely done due to the time and expense of checking every known person with a criminal SIN. Neither Knight Errant nor Lone Star use divination in their investigations because, according to Professor Schwartzkopf in his update of the *Corpus Hermeticum on Divination*, the use of the foreknowledge gained from the Augury ritual can change the actual result, similar in principle to the "observer effect" of particle physics, wherein observing a phenomenon can change the result of the observation. That is to say that particles may be uncertain in their movement and position, but they've got nothing on metahumans.

Education on divination is based on interpreting an object's aura and the mana flowing around or through it. MIT&T's program takes a hermetic approach; to evaluate students' work, computer-generated statistics of an event are compared to the student's augured probability of that same event occurring. More famous and traditional divination schools are the Sibyl private schools in the Italian Confederation, Greece, and other areas around the Mediterranean Sea.

Because divinatory foreknowledge and a magical tradition's interpretation of symbols and imagery can be widely unpredictable, many schools—if they teach divination arts at all—are liable keep such instruction general. Magicians with divinatory knowledge have been called soothsayers, oracles, prophets, or madmen who say that the end is near. A magician learning divination first learns the **Augury and Sortilege** ritual (p. 124).

RITUALS	METAMAGICS
Augury and Sortilege	Danger Sense

DANGER SENSE

A magician can attune himself to a higher awareness of the path he takes in life. This hyperawareness lets the magician sense danger before it occurs. This ability is the same as the adept power of the same name, but substitute the power's levels with magician's initiate grade. The metamagic and the adept power cannot be combined, so a character with both only applies the higher of the two.

SPIRITUAL ARTS

INVOCATION

Conjuring spirits through the power of will is its own skill, but some magicians try to push the limits of what can be brought forth into the world. Invocation teaches the magician to return to the fundamentals of conjuring to understand the relationship between spirit and magician. Schools teaching invocation tend to tailor the studies toward a specific tradition or handful of traditions to narrow the techniques. Not only does MIT&T have one of the top five hermetic libraries in North America, but it is also foremost in teaching many of the spiritual arts.

Magicians' knowledge of the spirit realms continues to evolve. Twenty-five years ago those at MIT&T developed the watcher ritual. The same group also more recently devised the ritual for creating homunculi. MIT&T's invocation studies are specific to the hermetic tradition, though some alumni have started their own invocation courses tailored to Wiccan practitioners.

While still known as a conjurer, a magician who learns invocation focuses his knowledge of ritual magic toward incorporating spirit formulas. Schools start with the conjuring basics; some take trips to the metaplanes to observe spirits that cannot be summoned through normal means. Here they research these spirits and attempt to define the formulas that best fit them. Tests then include ritual calling of said spirits, which is one of the more dangerous parts of education.

After the magician passes these tests, he has a grasp on spiritual traits within their formulas. Those who initiate into invocation often first learn the **Summon Great**

Form Spirit ritual (p. 136), but those undertaking the familiar ordeal (p. 142) must choose the **Ally Conjuration** ritual for their first invocation technique. Ally spirits—also known as familiars, totem companions, and spirit servants—are unique and powerful spirits that support the magician in all his work, not just an aspect of magic or combat. Various traditions see and relate differently to ally spirits. For example, an ally can be a wolf inhabited by beast spirit, a manifested shadowy black cat, or an apparition connected to a human skull.

A few corporations focus on invocation. Security forces often have normal conjurers provide astral security in the form of spirits, but corporations that can afford it maintain a conjurer on standby to invoke great form spirits to deal with shadowrunners.

RITUALS

Ally Conjuration
Summon Great Form Spirit

ENCHANTING

Govi

CHANNELING

Channeling was first understood by traditions that conjure spirits with the ability to possess people and objects. Instead of exploring what can be summoned, these magicians explore the bond between spirit and conjurer. They learn to expand this bond and allow the spirit to share the magician's body while on the physical plane. This metamagic can be learned by any tradition.

While the vodou traditions are most commonly associated with magicians being possessed by spirits (in this case loa), many other traditions explore this concept, including the shamans of Bali who bring hyangs (helpful spirits) into themselves to battle evil influences over people and places.

While MIT&T is the leading school for learning all things spiritual, many choose Loyola University for the atmosphere (Ghede is known to be a party spirit and gets introverts out of the dorm). Being able to share one's body with a spirit's mind is a challenging concept to embrace, as many have difficulty with the psychological therapy and discipline needed to prevent being overwhelmed by the spirit's consciousness.

RITUALS

Living Vessel Preparation

ENCHANTING

Inanimate Vessel Preparation

METAMAGICS

Channeling

CHANNELING

When a magician summons a spirit, she may choose to allow the spirit to possess her instead of allowing the spirit to exist in the astral plane to either manifest (p. 314, *SR5*) or materialize (p. 398, *SR5*). This must be decided at the time of summoning. Treat channeling the same as if the spirit has the Possession power (p. 197), with a few exceptions:

- The magician can use her own skills and has motor control over her body.
- She may relinquish control of her body to the spirit, but at the cost of a service.
- The magician can use the powers of the spirit, but at the cost of a service.
- Because two minds inhabit this same body, Mana spells or powers are resisted by the lowest Mental attribute of the two. Damage from Mana spells or powers is applied to both (no free rides).
- The spirit cannot leave the magician's body until either the services are up, the magician dismisses it, or time expires as per the rules of summoned spirits.

EXORCISM

With knowledge of possession spirits came a rediscovery of how to evict and banish those spirits from their vessels. The shedim's arrival brought both necromancy and exorcism to the forefront of magical studies. Many magicians tied to religious orders looked to the past to deal with such spirits. Schools such as Booth University College hold seminars to teach both magicians and adepts the ability to force a spirit from a vessel without using the Banishing skill.

ENCHANTING

Shofar

METAMAGICS

Exorcism

EXORCISM

Exorcism is a unique form of spirit combat where the magician pulls the spirit from its vessel. The ability requires physical contact with the vessel. A magic user makes an Opposed Test pitting Willpower + Charisma against twice the spirit's Force. A magician with the Banishing skill may add his Willpower to the normal Banishing skill test.

Successfully forcing the spirit from its vessel requires an accumulated total of net hits equal to the spirit's Force. Each exorcism attempt is very taxing: the exorcist suffers Drain equal to twice the number of hits (not net hits) that the spirit achieves in each attempt. Magicians resist this Drain as per their tradition; adepts resist with Body + Willpower. Each exorcism attempt is a Complex Action.

If the exorcism is successful, the spirit loses its corporeal connection and is pushed into astral space. Once in astral space it begins to suffer from Evanescence. Exorcism can only be used against channeled spirits, spirits with the Possession power, or true-form spirits (p. 195) with the Inhabitation power.

PROFESSION: SPIRIT HUNTER

Spirit hunter, aether exterminator, and ghost buster are several titles for those who make a living dealing with astral entities. This normally entails banishing the spirit or defeating it in combat. From bumps and poltergeists to more dangerous insect and toxic spirits, the spirit hunter fights them all—for a varying fee, of course. With a set of banishing foci, the spirit hunter helps homeowners and landlords get rid of the pesky spirits that have taken up residency, or he assists law enforcement with apprehending menacing spirits on the loose in the city. Adepts with Astral Perception may also get into this field and bypass Banishing by using Killing Hands to deliver a good old spirit thumping. Veteran spirit hunters add weapon foci to their arsenal or learn more metamagics like cleansing and exorcism.

UNSEEN ARTS

MASKING

Masking is an art that changes one's astral appearance to be non-magical (mundane) or to adjust one's observed magical strength. For some this may be secondary to hiding bonded foci from other magicians. This art is not taught in any traditional school. More often an individual or a magical group wishes to learn to hide. Example magical orders include the Brothers of Darkness and the rumored Gates of Ishtar. Some clandestine corporate and government schools teach members to disguise themselves and their talents. Those who initiate into masking first learn the **Masking** metamagic.

Masking can be further extended to hide a magician's quickened or anchored spells and alchemical preparations. Other masking techniques can hide works within wards or produce fake magical items that appear real.

RITUALS
Masking Ward
Obfuscating Ward

ENCHANTING
Paper Lotus

METAMAGIC
Masking
Extended Masking

MASKING
This metamagical technique can be found on p. 326, *SR5*.

EXTENDED MASKING
Extended masking extends your masking to include anchored, sustained, or quickened spells; imbued or attuned items; or alchemical preparations that are in the magician's possession. The magician may mask a number of items up to his initiate grade (this is in addition to bonded foci). Each item masked in this way must have a Force less than the magician's Magic attribute. As per the masking rules, an Opposed Assensing test is required to view such items. If the observer fails to gain any net hits, the masked items appear to the observer as normal fluctuations in the background count.
Prerequisite: Masking

FLEXIBLE SIGNATURE
Like other unseen arts, flexible signature is not a traditional school of study. Though normally considered a defensive art, as it temporarily protects from some ritual magic, flexible signature also can be used offensively to bypass wards and other magical defenses. While masking is the passive technique of hiding one's true astral appearance, flux is the active alternative. The magician learns to take control of her own aura and can cause the energies and patterns within to fluctuate. When the magician initiates in to this art, she first learns the **Flexible Signature** metamagic.

RITUALS
Astral Doppelgänger

TECHNIQUE
Astral Bluff

METAMAGICS
Flexible Signature
Flux

ASTRAL BLUFF

When a magician uses Assensing on an initiate possessing this technique, astral bluff allows the targeted character to spend a Simple Action to adjust his aura to give a temporary false impression. These are small adjustments (emotional state, health, etc.), but this change can add weight to a character's disguise or other such falsehoods. The character makes a Con + Magic [Social] (3) Test; if they succeed, they've managed to give the right impression and keep targets from examining their aura too closely. This affect is brief; if the magician's aura stays in visible range of someone who would be inclined to give a closer investigation for longer than five minutes, the jig is up. The target decides that bluff or no, the aura should be inspected, so they take a closer look that is enough to see past any astral bluffs. At this point, if the magician wants to convincingly disguise his aura, he will need to use masking metamagic. The astral bluff metamagic can be used in conjunction with a Con or Disguise test as per teamwork rules (p. 49, *SR5*)

FLEXIBLE SIGNATURE

This metamagical technique can be found on p. 325, *SR5*.

FLUX

With flux, the magician can set his aura in constant flux. While doing so makes his shifting aura stand out in the astral plane, it also temporarily scrambles the mystic link between himself and potential ritual links (material, sympathetic, or symbolic), bonded foci, attuned animals/items, summoned/bound spirits, mana barriers, active spells (sustained, quickened, or anchored), and alchemical preparations (active or command triggered). If the magician casts spells with his aura in flux, the astral signature is also mixed and cannot be read. Any ritual magic that targets a magician in a state of flux has its effective Force increased by 4 + initiate grade for the opposed test in the final step (p. 296, *SR5*). Any attempt to track the target meets a similar problem, increasing in threshold by 4 + initiate grade (p. 315, *SR5*).

A magician with his aura in flux can also attempt to bypass wards (p. 297, *SR5*). Additionally, alchemical preparations with a contact trigger might not activate if touched by a target with his aura in flux. When the magician makes contact with a preparation with a contact trigger, he makes an Opposed Test pitting his Magic + initiate grade against the Force of the preparation; if the magician is successful, the preparation will not activate while the aura is in flux.

The magician can safely keep his aura in flux for (Magic) hours per twenty-four-hour period. While the aura is in flux, the magician cannot command any spirits or watchers that he would normally control, activate foci, or activate any preparations with the command trigger. Excessive use of flux starts to permanently affect the magician. Any use beyond (Magic) in hours in a twenty-four-hour hour period but less than twice (Magic) in hours, unattunes items (foci, fetishes, etc.), which then must be reattuned before they can be used again. Summoned and bound spirits are automatically dismissed. After twice (Magic) in hours, mystic links to items have a fifty percent chance to be permanently broken. This means that foci have to be rebound, magical group bonds have to be redone, etc. An aura in flux for more than eighteen hours in a twenty-four-hour period can cause more permanent problems. These problems are left up to the imagination the gamemaster, but not limited to permanent magic loss or negative magical qualities.

DEFENSIVE ARTS

APOTROPAIC MAGIC

Defensive arts, also known as apotropaic magic, take three different forms: shielding, absorbing, and reflecting an attack. Many magical groups, especially those with rivals, help their members to MCYA (Magically Cover Your Ass) with the **Shielding** metamagic, which is the first and most basic form of apotropaic magic a magician learns when initiating into this art. Only the more militant magical groups or schools continue teaching the second and third forms of magical defenses.

Absorption is the ability to absorb a spell's mana before it materializes, making this the most dangerous of the defensive arts. Like the centering technique, absorption improves the magician's ability to handle mana. While centering allows mana to pass through the magician with less harm to the physical body, absorption allows the magician to hold mana without converting it into a spell. Those who have been on the bad side of a Manabolt spell know holding on to that energy for long is a bad thing. Because of the inherent dangers involved with advanced defensive arts, absorption is largely taught only in military schools such as the Citadel and West Point, where magical combat can be practiced safely. These schools have reinforced combat arenas with thick walls and strong wards to prevent accidental damage. While some would assume students would be involved in so-called wizards' duels like in the trids, combat training assisted by magic is team-oriented and mixes Awakened and mundane combatants.

RITUALS	SPECIAL ACTIONS
Door Ward	Reflect Spell
Charge Ward	Deflect Spell
	Greater Reflection

METAMAGICS
Shielding
Absorption
Reflection

SHIELDING

This metamagical technique can be found on p. 326, *SR5*.

ABSORPTION

Absorption allows the magician to siphon some of the mana away from a spell used against her. This includes triggered preparations and some ritual spells whose ritual includes the spell keyword. With an Interrupt Action (-10 Initiative score), the magician rolls Magic + Counterspelling [Force], where the Force is equal to the spell the magician is defending against. Each success does two things:

- Reduces the Force of the spell by 1.
- Creates a "mana charge" in the magician's aura that the magician can use. The magician can retain this mana charge for 1 + initiate grade Combat Turns and can only retain up to (Magic) in charges.

These temporary charges dissipate when the magician casts a spell. Each mana charge in the magician's aura reduces the Drain Value of the spell he casts by 1 per charge (though the minimum Drain Value of 2 still applies), and then the mana charges are gone. The magician cannot divide the charges among different spells; all stored charges go toward the next spell he casts. If the magician absorbs a number of mana charges greater than the magician's Magic rating, the magician suffers 1 box of Physical damage per mana charge (meaning all stored mana charge, not just the excess), and all stored charges immediately dissipate. Also, if the magician doesn't cast a spell before the mana charges expire, the magician suffers Drain with a Drain Value equal to the remaining mana charges, as they dissipate on their own. The Drain may be resisted as normal. **Prerequisite: Shielding**

Absorption and the Spell Defense Pool: If a magician maintains active spell defense while attempting the absorption technique, the number of hits scored on an absorption roll reduces her spell defense pool by that amount for the rest of that Combat Turn. Resisting damage and spell defense rules occur as normal.

REFLECTION

Reflection is an advanced understanding of shielding metamagic, allowing the magician to turn a defensive ability into an offensive action. If an astrally perceiving magician sees that he or those he's protecting with spell defense are the target of a spell (and note that astral perception is a necessity, not just the knowledge that a spell is being cast), he can access three additional Interrupt Actions that can protect the group instead of using spell defense dice (p. 294, *SR5*). With each Interrupt Action, the magician uses up 1 die from the spell defense dice pool. If no more defensive dice remain, then the Interrupt Action cannot be taken. The three actions possible are: Reflect Spell, Deflect spell, and Greater Reflection. **Prerequisite: Shielding**

REFLECT SPELL

INTERRUPT ACTION
(-7 INITIATIVE SCORE)

With this action, the magician can use Counterspelling + Magic [Astral] versus the caster's Spellcasting Test. If the reflecting magician scores more hits than the caster, the spell is redirected at the caster at half the spell's Force, and the original target takes no damage. Regardless of success, the reflecting magician must resist Drain as if he had used a Reckless Spellcasting action to cast it(increasing the Drain by 3) based on half the Force of the spell being reflected. This reflected spell only affects the caster, regardless of whether it was an area-effect spell. Treat the net hits in reflecting as spellcasting hits, as if the magician had actually cast it. This would add to any net hits from the original Spellcasting Test. If the magician does not get more hits than the caster, then the spell hits as if the magician didn't attempt to defend against it. **Prerequisite: Reflection**

DEFLECT SPELL

INTERRUPT ACTION
(-5 INITIATIVE SCORE, -1 EDGE)

For any indirect spell targeting those the magician is protecting with spell defense, the magician makes a Counterspelling + Magic [Astral] Test against the opponent's Spellcasting Test. Each net hit on the test adds one scatter die to the attack, and the gamemaster determines scatter (p.181, *SR5*). If the magician does not get more net hits than the caster, then the spell hits as if the magician didn't attempt to defend against it. **Prerequisite: Reflection**

GREATER REFLECTION

INTERRUPT ACTION
(-10 INITIATIVE SCORE, -1 EDGE)

This works the same as Reflect Spell but with the option of either sending the spell's full Force back at the caster or as the same version (i.e., if the reflected spell was an Area spell, then the area of effect would be centered on the caster). If the magician does not get more hits than the caster, then the spell hits as if the magician didn't attempt to defend against it. Regardless of success, the magician attempting this action must resist Drain as if he cast the spell himself. **Prerequisite: Reflection**

PROFESSION: ARCANE BODYGUARD

Magic isn't as prevalent as the media presents it, but in the event that you are attacked by magic, the best defense against it is magic. The arcane bodyguard fills this gap by using his knowledge of apotropaic arts to defend others from various spells, rituals, and the occasional preparation.

QUICKENING

Research into self-sustaining magic showed magicians how to quicken a spell by creating an astral linchpin to sustain it. Metaphysicists have used quickening techniques in their attempts to produce manatech. Those initiating into this art first learn the **Quickening** metamagic.

RITUALS	METAMAGICS
Trap Ward	Quickening
	Anchoring

QUICKENING VS. ALCHEMICAL PREPARATION

- Quickening can only be done for spells that can be sustained. Preparations can be done for all spells.
- A quickened spell is fixed to a geographical point or a person, not an object. A preparation is connected to an object.
- A quickened spell has no physical lynchpin that can be destroyed to stop the spell. A preparation does.
- A quickened spell continues to function until it is dispelled or it interacts with an environment that disrupts it (e.g., a change in background count, a person walking through a ward, etc.). A preparation lasts for Potency in minutes or until it interacts with an environment that disrupts it.

QUICKENING

This metamagical technique can be found on p. 326, *SR5*.

ANCHORING

Anchoring metamagic is similar to alchemy but is tied to the foundation rules of a quickened spell. The quickened spell can be attached to a temporary astral construct. This anchor later releases the quickened spell based on a pre-specified trigger. A spell with any duration type can be anchored, and the spell can be triggered by any type of preparation trigger (p. 305, *SR5*), including the background count and Detection spell triggers (p. 219). The trigger's conditions must be defined before the anchored spell is cast.

Once the trigger and its conditions are defined, the magician casts the spell into the anchor and records the number of hits for later reference. The magician must then resist Drain with the added Drain Value cost for the specific trigger.

Because the anchored spell is not tied to a physical lynchpin like an alchemical preparation, creating the spell's anchor requires something a little extra from the magician. To complete the anchor, the magician pays Karma equal to the anchored spell's Force. Anchored spells should be treated the same as quickened spells (p. 326, SR5) with regard to astral intersections (p. 316, SR5), astral combat, and dispelling attempts. Anchored spells retain the spellcaster's astral signature and thus may be used for astral tracking (p. 315, *SR5*) or as a sympathetic link (p. 146).

When the trigger condition is met, the anchor collapses and the spell is released as if the magician just cast it, using the recorded hits achieved. Sustained spells will remain sustained in the same manner as quickened spells. Permanent spells will remain sustained until the effects become permanent, and then the spells end. An anchor may be designed with multiple triggers, if so desired. Triggers may be set to only activate if another trigger condition is met. For example, a contact trigger could be set to activate only when a Detection spell is activated first, so the anchor would be safe to touch until the Detection spell gets a hit. When using multiple triggers, add up all the Drain costs for all of the trigger conditions before casting the anchored spell.

At any given time, an initiate may have a maximum number of anchors active equal to her initiate grade. The magician can end one of her active anchors as a Free Action, letting the spell dissipate without effect. **Prerequisite: Quickening**

See p. 219 for all available triggers.

THAUMATURGICAL ARTS

ADVANCED ALCHEMY/ RITUAL/SPELLCASTING

These are specific arts delving into the formulaic nuances of magic. Many metaphysicists or wage mages in corporate R&D are required to have a degree or two in them. After over fifty years of work, many magical works are developed by corporations. Examples include alchemical compounds like AgHexHex and BDNB and rituals such as Watcher and Homunculus. A lot of time spent learning any of these arts entails research. This research goes into reinterpreting formulas from old scrolls or Matrix searches for Awakened talents. To this end, initiation into advanced magical arts is a deep dive into understanding how raw magical energies convert into magical effects. Many schools offer theoretical concepts in spell design, but it's up to the student to apply them.

ADVANCED ALCHEMY

RITUALS	METAMAGICS
Dispersion	Advanced Alchemy Fixation

ADVANCED ALCHEMY

With advanced alchemy, the magician can prepare magical compounds (p. 218) that can imbue the user with extraordinary powers ... or curse them. The magician can also tailor more specific triggers with preparations (see Advanced Alchemy, p. 218). **Prerequisite: Fixation**

FIXATION

This metamagical technique can be found on p. 325, *SR5*.

ADVANCED RITUAL SPELLCASTING

RITUALS	METAMAGICS	
Imbue	Efficient Ritual	Greater Ritual

EFFICIENT RITUAL

Why sacrifice a whole day standing over a bonfire when twelve hours could do? Magicians who advance their study into rituals can learn to complete a magical ritual faster. Reduce the time to complete a ritual by half for any ritual that the magician is the leader of. The cost of the time reduction is +2 to the Drain Value at the completion step the ritual (p. 296, *SR5*).

GREATER RITUAL

Greater ritual allows the magician to participate in a ritual without adding dice to it. Instead, the magician amplifies the ritual by adding her Magic rating to the ritual's Force for determining its limit, size, and effect. This addition is not included in the completion step of the ritual (p. 296, *SR5*). The magician takes Drain as if she actively participated in the ritual. The magician can be the leader of the ritual and still use greater ritual metamagic, but this adds +2 to the Drain Value when the ritual completes.

ADVANCED SPELLCASTING

METAMAGICS	
Penetrating Spell	Spell Shaping

SPELL SHAPING

This metamagical technique can be found on p. 326, *SR5*.

PENETRATING SPELL

With this metamagic, the magician can choose to increase a Combat spell's AP at a cost of reduced damage before casting the spell. Reduce the DV by 1 for every point of AP increased, up to the Force of the spell. Minimum damage is 1. Drain Value increases by 1 for every point of AP increased. For example, a Force 5 Fireball spell (normally with a DV of 5P and AP –5) is modified to have a DV of 3P and AP –7 before the spell is cast; since the AP was increased by 2, the normal Drain Value is then increased by 2. Net hits are then applied to either increase the Damage Value or reduce scatter, as normal (p. 283, *SR5*).

CENTERING

An amusing analogy of spellcasting is that it's like conducting electricity through a hotdog: too much juice and the magician is cooked. The act of centering lessens the strain of manipulating mana through mental training techniques that are expressed by magicians in many different ways. Thus, magicians learning centering may also take classes in singing, drama, band, or other artistic pursuits. They may even earn a BA degree just in case they burn out their magical talent someday.

As centering is a fairly straightforward technique useful in any field of magic, even schools with a tacked-on magic curriculum teach centering techniques. Classes are a bit eccentric and include activities such as singing show tunes or performing interpretive dance while casting spells. Teachers astrally watch the students cast progressively more difficult and complex spells to assess how Drain affects each student. Magicians who initiate in this art first learn the **Centering** metamagic. Some further their mental practice by learning other techniques for resisting or manipulating mana.

RITUALS	METAMAGICS
Light of Dharma	Centering

CENTERING

This metamagical technique can be found on p. 325, *SR5*.

CLEANSING

Cleansing is the study of mana's psychoreactive properties and the ability to disperse or disrupt those residual imprints on the ambient mana (see **Background Count**, p. 30). Instead of the magician attuning herself to the background count, she learns to proactively neutralize the background in an area. Granted, the neutralization is temporary, but it is useful for a few hours. On a smaller scale, a magician can cleanse the temporary residual imprints caused by an event or use the smudging ritual to remove imprints from an object, similar to how one can wipe away an astral signature.

Through acknowledgment that man has really screwed up the astral world with pollution and human misery, the study of cleansing has found an increase in popularity, and feng shui professionals are in high demand in many cities. For cleansing studies, Williams College has one of the best astral arts programs. Students experience the difficulties of practicing magic around polluted places such as Boston Harbor and learn to see the psychoreactive patterns left on the astral plane.

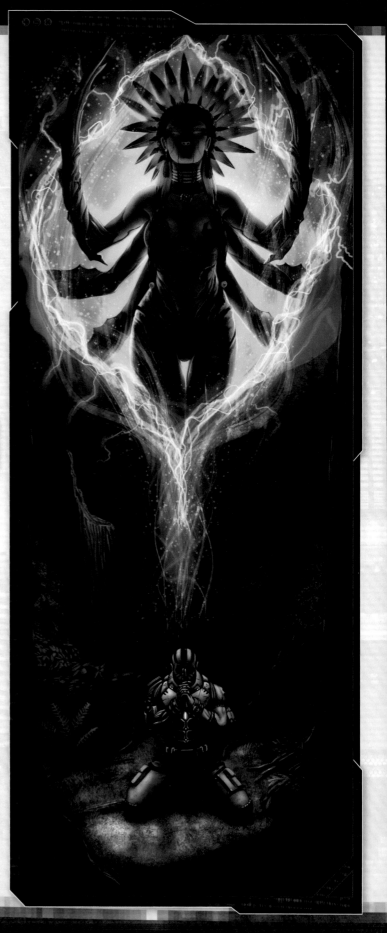

Those who complete cleansing study first learn the **Cleansing** metamagic.

RITUALS
Smudging
Circle of Cleansing

METAMAGICS
Cleansing

CLEANSING

This technique allows the magician to temporarily reduce background count. Cleansing only affects positive background counts such as from a domain (p. 25) or aspected mana. The magician uses a Complex Action and makes an Opposed Test pitting Counterspelling + Magic + initiate grade [Astral] against a dice pool equal to the background count. Each net hit can either reduce the background count by 1 or extend the duration of a previously achieved background reduction by 1 Combat Turn. This background count reduction is temporary and only affects the cleansing magician for (Magic) Combat Turn(s). After the test, the magician suffers Drain with a Drain Value equal to the natural background count. If the background count exceeds the magician's Magic, Drain is Physical. If the background count is greater than twice the magician's Magic, then the magician cannot perform a cleansing action. This action can be done each Combat Turn to further reduce or extend the temporary background count reduction, but the magician suffers Drain equal to the natural background count prior to a second attempt to cleanse the same area.

SENSING

Sensing expands the initiate's ability to become a natural sixth sense. Without peering into the astral, the magician can get a sense of the flow of mana around him as if he were a mundane standing in a breeze. He can feel the topography and elements of the astral space surrounding him. If the magician concentrates, he can sense approaching storms kilometers away.

Many two-year colleges group this study together with centering as their only available magic courses. In Australia however, sensing is a major requirement for practicing mystical arts Down Under. Charles Darwin University has a whole program dedicated to aetherology, the study of astral phenomena, and the curriculum offers initiation into sensing with a degree. If corporations want to do business in Australia, they hire an aetherologist or a magician who has sensing. This magician becomes the corp's astral weatherman, acting as an early warning system to protect corporate assets in the area. Initiation into sensing conveys no title like some of

the other initiatory arts, so magicians occasionally use a professional title after completing a sensing course.

Students learning sensing start by looking for mana lines. However, unlike geomancers, sensing students don't get tools; they have to concentrate on their senses instead. They then progress to identifying events that had occurred in a room by the emotions that flavored the background count. Those who complete the course learn the **Sensing** metamagic.

RITUALS
Kything
Far Sensing

METAMAGICS
Sensing

ENCHANTING
Astral Powder

SENSING

The magician can use the **Observe in Detail** action (p. 165, *SR5*) to learn details of the surrounding area—such as background count, how the background count is aspected, and if background count changes—without having to astrally perceive or project. The magician can also feel a negative background count based on mana ebbs and voids (p. 32) but is more sensitive to them: add +2 when determining the effect of background count. The magician cannot use this ability to sense astral forms, spells, mana barriers, spirits, or foci.

Gamemasters may also give the character a chance to sense some unusual change nearby even if they are not actively using sensing; in this case, the gamemaster should make the Observe in Detail Perception Test in secret to not give anything away. This phenomenon includes noticing alchera (p. 29), mana storms, warps, or surges (p. 34).

PHYSICAL ARTS

Adepts can learn their own metamagics as they progress. As the adept chooses a Way (or chooses not to choose), more improvement options become available. Like the other arts, each Way can have rituals, enhancements, and metamagics to learn. Adepts can always choose items from the Undecided Way even if they follow another Way.

THE UNDECIDED WAY

RITUALS

Attune (Animal)
Attune (Item)
Empower
Imbue

METAMAGICS

Adept Centering
Efficient Ritual
Flexible Signature
Flux
Infusion
Improved Masking
Masking
Qi Sculpt
Power Point

ADEPT CENTERING

This metamagic technique can be found on p. 325, SR5.

INFUSION

ACTIVATION COST: COMPLEX ACTION
When focused, an adept can pull energy from the cosmos and channel it into one of his existing powers. For each level of initiate grade, the adept can add 0.5 PP to an adept power. The total levels of a power enhanced this way cannot exceed the adept's Magic rating. The enhancement will last for (Magic) Combat Turns. Once the power boost ends, the adept immediately suffers Stun damage from this stretch of *qi*. The Damage Value equals four times the total power point cost of the enhanced power (not just the power point boost). In addition to this damage, the adept suffers a temporary loss of a number of power points equal to the power point boost for (Magic) minutes. The gamemaster selects what powers are affected, and the adept should not know a power is inaccessible until he tries to use it. **Prerequisite: Adept Centering**

POWER POINT

This can be found on p. 326, SR5.

QI SCULPT

ACTIVATION COST: COMPLEX ACTION
An adept at peace with herself can adjust her *qi* like wet clay. *Qi* sculpt allows the adept to remove *qi* from one power and temporarily add it to another power in which they already have invested power points. For each level of initiate grade, the adept can shift 0.25 PP of one adept power to another power. The enhanced power cannot have more levels than the adept's Magic rating. This shift of power lasts for (Magic) minutes. Once the shift ends, the adept suffers Stun damage with a Damage Value equal to the four times the power point boost. **Prerequisite: Adept Centering**

THE ATHLETE'S WAY

ENHANCEMENTS

Air Walking

METAMAGICS

Supernatural Prowess

AIR WALKING

The adept can briefly step on air as he would a stone. Add the adept's initiate grade when calculating the maximum jumping distance (p. 134, SR5). **Prerequisite: Light Body**

SUPERNATURAL PROWESS

For any physical action, the adept can substitute a physical attribute for Magic + initiate grade for that test. If done during combat, the substitution affects all physical actions associated to that attribute within a Combat Turn. This metamagic cannot be combined with Attribute Boost. This can be done 1 + initiate grade times per day. Dice pools and Physical limits temporarily change with this action.

THE ARTIST'S WAY

ENHANCEMENTS

Skin Artist

TECHNIQUE

Pied Piper

PIED PIPER

The adept's mastery of the artistic skill becomes an incredible work. His performance of the skill not only mesmerizes the audience, it attracts them. Those who see or hear the performance enter a mild trance. The adept can target a person or a group of people to do nothing else but experience the performance. The adept must have line of sight to the target(s). The adept makes an Opposed Test pitting Performance + Charisma [Magic] against Willpower + Charisma. If multiple individuals are targeted, use the largest dice pool among the defenders and add +1 die per additional target (maximum +5). If the test is successful, the target(s) follow the adept as he performs for (Charisma x 10) minutes. Subjects entranced this way can still have the trance interrupted by significant distractions, such as loud noises or a hard shove. The cost in Karma and time to learn the Pied Piper technique is the same as that of Enhancements (p. 139).

SKIN ARTIST

With this enhancement, an artist's body is her own canvas. The adept possesses even finer control over her skin pigmentation, including formation of more colors (black, red, and blue) from her body. The adept can create a variety of tattoo markings anywhere on her body or change her whole skin tone to an unnatural hue. **Prerequisite: Melanin Control**

THE BEAST'S WAY

ENHANCEMENTS	METAMAGICS
Claws	Apex Predator
	Totem Form (Animal)

APEX PREDATOR

Those on this path have become predatory, and animals sense this. Any animal that attempts to attack the adept (commanded or not) must make an Opposed Willpower + Intuition Test against the adept's Magic + Intuition + initiate grade. Failure means that the animal will not attack the adept, either out of predatory respect or fear of being eaten by the adept, and it will take actions based on that mindset. Awakened critters get a +2 modifier to this test. The animal may attack other people with the adept, just not the adept. If the adept attacks the animal, then the animal may freely counterattack.

CLAWS

The adept taps into his animalistic side and can grow thick, sharp nails like some kind of beast. The Damage Value of his Unarmed Combat attacks increases by 1. **Prerequisite: Keratin Control**

TOTEM FORM (ANIMAL)

Some say there is power beyond earthly *qi*. Others say the energy harnessed is no different than a mage summoning a different spirit. In any case, adepts on this path have found a way to become closer to their animal companion. With this metamagic, the adept taps into that power to become the beast she has bonded.

After a twenty-minute preparation process, the adept shifts into the animal form that matches the animal she is attuned to, with all the abilities of said animal. However, this transformation is not the temporary suspension of human form: it is more akin to a shapeshifter's ability, and many adepts who follow the Beast's Way can be mistaken for a shapeshifter. The adept's Physical attributes and limits become those of the animal, but Mental attributes and skills remain the adept's.

This ability has the drawback of being difficult for the adept to shift back into human form, for the adept's mind slowly becomes more primal in the animal body. After a few days, the adept can become permanently lost in the animal.

The adept needs a successful Arcana + Magic [Mental] (2) test to shift into animal form at the end of the ritual. The adept can stay in animal form for as long as she wishes. Returning to human form requires an Arcana + Magic [Mental] (3) Test. Failure means that the adept must wait another 2 hours to gather her thoughts and override the animal form's increasing instincts. Every twenty-four hours spent in animal form increases the test's threshold by 1. If the threshold exceeds the adept's Mental limit, he becomes the animal permanently. **Prerequisite: Attune (Animal)**

THE BURNOUT WAY

ENHANCEMENTS
Hot *Qi*

HOT QI

As the adept burns out, he normally becomes unable to use some foci because his Magic rating is too low. With the hot *qi* technique, the adept can still use a *qi* focus, but he takes unresisted Stun damage equal to the difference between the focus's Force and his Magic rating each time he makes a test enhanced by the *qi* focus. If the Force of the focus exceeds twice the adept's Magic rating, the damage is Physical. The focus's Force cannot exceed 12. **Prerequisite: Living Focus**

THE INVISIBLE WAY

ENHANCEMENTS   **METAMAGICS**

Shadow Touch   Stillness in the Void

SHADOW TOUCH

Adepts following the Invisible Way can learn to avoid leaving fingerprints on items they touch. This ability can also be used to avoid triggering alchemical preparations that use a contact trigger. The latter ability requires a successful Opposed Test between the adept's Magic rating and the current Potency of the preparation. **Prerequisite: Traceless Walk**

STILLNESS OF THE VOID

An adept who meditates can steel his mind against Detection spells and ritual magic and become as nothing. To enter this state, the adept must remain still and concentrate only on managing his breathing for five minutes; he also cannot speak, gesture, or move. Performing any action, such as being moved or taking any damage, will break the adept's concentration, and he will have to start again. While resisting Detection spells, add 1 + initiate grade to the Opposed test. Items in the adept's possession are also resisted by the adept in this manner to prevent detection (e.g., a Detect Guns spell). Astrally tracking the adept also becomes difficult, adding 1 + initiate grade to the threshold of the Assensing Test for astral tracking (p. 315, *SR5*). The adept can stay in this mental state for eight hours.

THE MAGICIAN'S WAY

ENHANCEMENTS

Digital Celerity   Master of the Nine Chakras

DIGITAL CELERITY

This power allows the adept greater control in the palming or pickpocketing of an object and preventing anyone from noticing the act. This is true sleight of hand that mundane magicians attempt to attain. It imposes an additional -1 Perception modifier per level of Nimble Fingers to anyone observing or being targeted by the adept. **Prerequisite: Nimble Fingers**

MASTER OF THE NINE CHAKRAS

The adept has a better understanding of how magic flows with a person's vital energy. With this power, the adept can strike specific spots of energy concentration, causing a disruption of this flow and temporarily reducing the target's Magic attribute. Refer to Nerve Strike (p. 173), but the attack reduces Magic instead. Magic lost this way has an effect similar to a background count, as the target accumulates dice pool penalties for casting spells or using Magical skills. If the subject's Magic is reduced to 0, the target cannot use any magically related skill or adept power until the attribute recovers. **Prerequisite: Nerve Strike**

THE SPIRITUAL WAY

METAMAGICS

Domain of the Spiritual   Exorcism   Psychometry

EXORCISM

This metamagical technique can be found on p. 148.

DOMAIN OF THE SPIRITUAL

The background caused by domains of religious significance, such as churches, cemeteries, and so forth, doesn't affect those on this path as much as other adepts. Reduce background count penalties by 1 + initiate grade if the background count is aspected toward a religion or spiritual significance.

PSYCHOMETRY

This metamagical technique can be found on p. 144.

THE SPEAKER'S WAY

ENHANCEMENTS   **METAMAGICS**

Silver-Tongued Devil   Fae-Touched
                          Presence

FAE-TOUCHED

Those on this path gain a hauntingly beautiful appearance. An adept may pit his Magic + Intuition + initiate grade against the target's Willpower + Intuition in an Opposed Test. If the opponent fails, then the target believes in an idealized mana-based illusion of the adept. The adept can then substitute Magic + initiate grade for Charisma for all Charisma tests against those who believe the illusion. If the Opposed Test was successful, the illusion lasts twenty-four hours. This can be done 1 + initiate grade times a day. Drain from each attempt equals the target's hits in resisting the attempt (minimum 2).

SILVER-TONGUED DEVIL

An adept of the Speaker's Way can create a longer-lasting impression on subjects when using Commanding Voice (p. 170). If the adept wins the Opposed Test, the target continues to carry out the action for one minute before realizing what they're doing. The Silver-Tongued Devil's verboseness makes it unusable in combat situations. This power comes at a price of mental stress. When using the power, the adept suffers Stun damage equal to the hits (not net hits) from the target's Opposed Test. Damage is resisted by Body + Willpower. **Prerequisite: Commanding Voice**

PRESENCE

The presence of a follower of the Speaker's Way is very palpable, sometimes even visible, when the adept speaks. An adept with this metamagic can add her initiate grade in dice to all tests for one social skill, which is chosen when the metamagic is selected. The metamagic cannot be selected multiple times. The bonus also only applies when the adept is using her skill on others, not when she is resisting social skills of others.

THE WARRIOR'S WAY

ENHANCEMENTS — Barrage, Master of Taijiquan

METAMAGICS — Domain of the Warrior

BARRAGE

A single improvised weapon in the hands of an adept is deadly; a handful is even worse. An adept mastering the Barrage technique can loose a handful of readied, improvised throwing weapons at a target(s). When making the throwing weapon attack, the adept can use the rules for narrow or medium spreads (p. 180, SR5). The adept must have either two or more throwing weapons or a gamemaster-approved handful of improvised weapons readied to use this technique. **Prerequisite: Missile Mastery**

DOMAIN OF THE WARRIOR

Those on this path are not as affected by the background taint of violence and war as other adepts. Reduce background count penalties by 1+ initiate grade if the background is aspected to violence and war.

MASTER OF TAIJIQUAN

While people around the world practice taijiquan—a.k.a. t'ai chi—for its defense-training and health benefits, an adept mastering taijiquan flows like a river in combat, especially with multiple melee combatants. He uses the various attackers' strengths to maneuver their strikes against each other. When the adept successfully blocks a melee attack from one attacker with Counterstrike, he may choose instead to redirect that attack against a second attacker. The second attacker would have to defend against the first attack with the number of hits equal to the adept's Counterstrike test. The base Damage Value is equal to the melee attack from the first attacker. This mastery of kinetic energy only works in combat against multiple melee opponents. You can't make an attacker hit himself, though you can taunt him with the promise to do so. **Prerequisite: Counterstrike**

BUTCHER'S BILL

El Loco Cantina
Key West, Caribbean League
October 21, 2075
1325 Zulu

"Your move, *breeder.*"

Ricky Sharpe just smirked at the burly ork. He knew this street samurai was trying psyche him out, force him to make a mistake. But Ricky didn't spook easily. Many had tried to take him out in one way or another; all had failed.

Outwardly calm, inside Ricky was a spark ready to ignite. His mojo was primed, on-line, and ready to go, waiting for just the right moment to release. Arms casually at his sides, no one noticed that his right hand had drifted two centimeters closer to the wicked combat knife strapped to his thigh. By contrast, the ork seemed agitated and radiated tension; his fingers flexed involuntarily. Ricky was surprised that the ork hadn't already popped 'spurs. Were his augmented reflexes dialed-up too high, or was bravado just a cover for his fear? Ricky didn't know or care. *No one disrespects the king in his court*, Ricky thought to himself. Teaching this tusker a lesson was going to be fun.

Outside the cantina, the remnants of Hurricane Steven hammered away. Lightning flashed, thunder rumbled. Inside was dead quiet, the crowd barely breathing and giving both combatants a wide berth. The moment was almost here.

An extra bright flash of lightning led a deafening blast of thunder. Ricky struck. Too fast for a normal metahuman to see, his left hand seized one of the shot glasses on the table before him. The cantina crowd suddenly went berserk with cheers; the fight was on.

Startled, the ork went for his own glass, but by the time his first shot of tequila went down, Ricky was on number three.

Ricky was in the zone, his movements a prime example of an adept's power and grace while the ork's cheap augmentations made him look clumsy and jerky. Within four heartbeats, Ricky had downed his sixth and final shot as the ork reached for number five. Slamming the last glass to the table, Ricky neatly pivoted and his right hand shot out. At the far side of the cantina, his combat blade buried itself dead-center into a battered dartboard. Fumbling his last shot and operating on pure reflex, the ork let his own dagger fly … handle first into the jukebox two meters low and to the right of the dartboard. The blade bounced off and the jukebox came to life, blasting Johnny Banger's latest hit single "I Do What I Want."

"*Winner!*" called out the elven bartender, pointing toward Ricky. Ricky raised his arms in triumph and basked in the cantina's adulation. The street-sam stood there motionless with his cyber-eyes unfocused, face blank. Then he fell to the floor. In the background, the losers of side-bets surrendered credsticks or wads of local scrip to the victors.

"No one messes with the king in his castle!" Ricky proclaimed as he retrieved his dagger. As he slid the weapon focus home with his right hand, Ricky realized that his left was aching to do the same thing. But the weapon foci's twin was gone, lost during a bad batch of business in South America just a few months ago. It was like a missing limb—he still felt like it was there, still could feel it on him sometimes.

The clanging of an old-fashioned ship's bell mounted at the end of the bar interrupted his thoughts. "Okay everyone, last call!" announced the bartender.

BY R.J. THOMAS

Ricky ignored the order and grabbed a bottle of tequila from the top shelf. He'd stay as long as he wanted, just like he'd done for the past few months. *Ghost, I love this little drek-hole,* Ricky thought.

Throughout the cantina, patrons hurried to pay off tabs or down the remnants of their drinks as the bouncers oh-so-gently encouraged them to get the frag out. Within minutes, the only ones in left was Ricky, the staff—and a lone figure sitting at a back table with a bottle of Maker's Mark bourbon and two glasses.

One of the bouncers, a human male with too many muscle replacements, took offense to Mr. Bourbon's inability to follow directions. "Hey, *omae*, you forget to turn on your ears or somethin'? Or you just too fragging stupid to understand what 'last call' means?"

Expression partially hidden by a black ball cap and pair of dark smartglasses, Mr. Bourbon took another sip. Snarling, Muscle Man stormed over, slammed his palms onto the table, and leaned forward; spittle splattering on Mr. Bourbon's longcoat.

"Listen hoop-licker, I *said…*"

"Heard what you said just fine." Mr. Bourbon calmly interrupted. "Jus' ain't leaving yet, s'all."

Muscle Man smirked. "And why's that?"

"I got some business. With *Ricky.*"

Ricky's head turned toward the sound of his name. He didn't recognize the voice, that odd blend of UCAS Midwestern and CAS Cajun, but there was something about it that got his attention.

From across the cantina, their eyes met for the first time. "Do I know you?"

Setting his glass down gently, Mr. Bourbon straightened up a bit in his seat and filled the second glass. "No, not me. An associate of mine." He pulled a battered machine pistol and set it on the table.

Ricky recognized the weapon, and his blood ran cold.

"Now then, you have an outstanding bill with me. How 'bout we settle up on it?" Mr. Bourbon said.

Ricky kept it frosty. "I don't know what your game is, so how about you just get your sorry hoop out of here. No one's gonna let you ..." He let the thought dangle as his hand strayed toward his blade.

"*Oh contraire,*" Bourbon interrupted. "I think if dey knew 'bout your work in South America, dey'd be the first ones to skin you."

Free City of Bogotá
Zona Centrico
September 29, 2074
1531 Zulu

"Zero-Two to Zero-Six; Major, you got party-crashers inbound, ETA less than two minutes. You need to evac *now!*"

"Still securing the wounded, need at least three. Can you stall them?"

From behind her Desert Strike's scope, Sergeant Major Raina Watkins licked her tusks like a tiger when it smelled prey. "Oh, I'll make them seriously regret their current course of action."

"Copy that. Keep your 'link open and be ready to move once we start exfil."

"Assholes and elbows on your mark, sir."

Within the confines of her perch atop an abandoned apartment building, Raina re-adjusted her shooting position to get a better angle on the hostiles. They were at least platoon strength, sporting light mil-spec armor (with no identifying marks) and standard small-arms. But there were two machine gunners and one trooper packing a Ballista Missile Launcher. Raina scowled. The rescue teams would be sitting ducks when they tried to move with the wounded.

It was a basic rescue mission, skulking into Zona Centrico to get Fifth Team, which had been ambushed attempting to escort a VIP to a safehouse. Raina had been sent ahead to conduct recon and set up overwatch. Until now, the mission had been textbook. But in combat, Murphy was never far away.

Through her scope, she saw the hostiles move with order and discipline. Fire Teams leap-frogged each other to provide covering fire. They must have been tipped off to Fifth Team's location because they headed right for it.

"Sorry, chummers, not today." Raina said to herself. She touched a small pouch on her vest that contained a worn, battered unit patch and recited: "I am the Shepherd, the Wolf-hunter, and none shall harm my flock …"

Magic spread throughout her body in a warm rush, washing away any lingering pain or aches from sitting in the same position for almost a day. Her senses sharpened; the sniper rifle in her hands felt like a true extension of her body. Through her astral perception, she didn't see any magicians. Too bad. They might have stood a chance.

The hostiles were over one hundred meters away, but the Desert Strike's targeting receptacle easily aligned with the side of the rocket trooper's head and then drifted down his back. With squeeze of the trigger, Raina's rifle coughed once. A half-second later, the ammo magazine containing high-explosive rounds exploded like a bomb. Four enemy troops caught in the hellish blast radius fell to the ground. They didn't get back up.

The rest of the hostiles opened up in all directions, desperately trying to lay down suppression fire. But Raina was in no real danger. She smoothly targeted one of the machine gunners; his head exploded in a flash of gore and kinetic energy. Three more times Raina squeezed the trigger, and three more enemy troops died. Their commander ordered a retreat as their discipline started shifting to panic. The survivors popped thermal smoke to cover their egress, but Raina could still see some of them. She could have taken out at least two more, but her mission was complete. She was a solider and a professional, not a murderer.

"Zero-Two to Zero-Six, call me an overachiever, enemy forces bugging out. Now's a good time to get the frag out of there."

"Copy, that Zero-Two. All packages are wrapped and ready to ship. Rendezvous at Rally Point: Alpha in four minutes. Don't miss the bus!"

"You kidding? You owe me a bottle of the good stuff for this, sir!"

Magic still active, Raina rose from her perch and suddenly felt movement behind her. On pure reflex she jerked to the side and felt a sudden, lancing pain in her leg. Falling back down, she saw a throwing dagger buried to the bone in her left thigh. Without thinking, she reached down and pulled it out; a sharp gasp of pain burst from her lips as she realized how stupid that was. Pressing her free hand to the gushing wound, she scanned the area for her attacker and saw nothing, except two more daggers imbedded in the plascrete ledge.

"Damn, you're good," said an unfamiliar voice "No one's been able to dodge any of them before. But I still think I came out ahead on this one."

Raina's head snapped toward the echoing voice just in time to see a human male wearing an Urban Explorer jumpsuit vault himself up and over the building's ledge. With a tight flip, he landed in a crouch, arms crossed over his chest as he glared at her. "And here I thought today was going to be boring. Oh, great shooting by the way, very accurate. Although I have my own preferred method of killing." His arms flared outward, spinning a pair of wicked-looking combat knives in his palm. Raina frowned. Even without her astral senses, she knew another adept and a pair of weapon foci when she saw them. *Frag me.*

"So now, if you'll just hold still, we can get this over with quickly. Or, struggle a bit if you want, but you'll just die tired. Either way, I need wrap this soon to catch *Aztlan Nights* on the trid." He said surging forward with blinding speed.

Melee combat wasn't Raina's forte, but she was far from helpless. As the adept charged, he swiped his blades in a crisscross pattern for distraction just before his right hand struck low toward Raina's femoral artery. Anticipating the move, Raina ignored the display and (barely) blocked the attack with her rifle; the adept was *fast*. She whipped her rifle up, catching the adept in the chin. Stunned, he took a step back. Raina seized the moment, driving the butt stock into his face. There was a satisfying crunch of cartilage as blood spurted from his nose.

The adept staggered back and cried out—not in pain, but pleasure. He shook ecstatically while wiping blood all over his face. Raina had seen this before, and the sudden horrible realization of what the adept was chilled her to the core. She quickly raised her rifle to her shoulder, only to see the barrel was damaged. *Frag me twice!*

The adept quickly regained his composure as Raina quick-drew her Crusader machine pistol and fired. Three rounds struck the adept center-mass and he fell to one knee, but the jumpsuit's armor held. Already feeling the first effects of blood loss, Rania lined up a head-shot, hand slightly shaking. The adept just laughed.

"Not bad at all" he said with gleeful murder painted on his face. "You almost got me! I'm quite anxious to see what you do next." As he spoke, he brought forward a knife, point up. Raina started to dodge when she realized the knife was being used as a pointer. She heard the dull "*whump*" in the distance followed by a tell-tail whistle. Looking up, she saw a spotter drone a mere twenty meters above.

It was time to go. She swan-dove over the side and fell into a pile of garbage four stories below—a pile she'd arranged earlier for just such a circumstance. Above, the first of the artillery shells slammed into the apartment, obliterating the top floor and sending debris flying. Quickly rolling off a safety net she'd hidden, Raina glanced upwards and saw the whack-job adept bounding off the apartment building and its catwalks all parkour-style. She had one option: *run.*

Fueled by magic and desperation, Raina sprinted as fast as her legs would take her. She ran around blasted walls, destroyed vehicles, and mangled bodies. But the adept stayed right on her heels.

"Whoa! Hold up there, sugar-tusks! I don't want to hurt ya. I just want to rip your heart out!" he yelled as he leaped off a pile of bodies. Raina replied with a burst from her Crusader, but the shots went wide.

"I'm starting to think you don't like me!" he yelled, then let three more daggers fly. Unable to dodge, Raina felt two sink into her lower back and one in her injured leg. Stumbling, she dropped her rifle and slammed against the burnt-out hulk of a Devil Rat APC. Leaning heavily against it, Raina raised her Crusader. Injury, blood loss, and exertion had taken their toll; shock was setting in. Her vision swam, and the ARO smartgun receptacle in her smart goggles made her nauseous.

The artillery had stopped, but the adept was slowly advancing on Raina, focus spinning in his hands. Summoning whatever strength she had left, she stood up against the APC and steadied the Crusader with both hands, putting the targeting receptacle right on his face. "Stop," she said.

The other adept chuckled. "So, setting up a final showdown, eh? You're betting—hoping—that you can shoot me in the head before I can sprint over there and gut you like a fish."

"Oh come on, tusker-babe, you're gonna die soon anyway! Why not let me make it quick?"

"*No.* Stop right *now!*"

"Not a chance. You honestly think you can even hit me with that?"

"No, just stalling."

A bit of blood dribbled from her mouth as she nodded upward. The other adept looked up and saw the spotter drone. His eyes went wide. Then he heard the whistle.

Raina didn't know how long she'd lay there. The sound of crackling audio in her earbud brought her back to consciousness. Too weak to move, it was all she could do to roll on her back.

"... is Zero-Six, do you copy!"

Her jaw worked a few times before she croaked a reply "Zero ... Zero ... Two here."

"Raina, I'm still in the area and receiving images, but your GPS is out."

But then a cry of pure rage split the air. Tilting her head, Raina saw the adept about twenty meters away, his jumpsuit burnt and tattered revealing lacerated skin and burnt flesh, shifting through rubble and scrap. He turned toward her, murder etched on his face. "This is *your* fault! It's gone because of you!" He stalked forward, only one blade in hand.

Darkness formed at the corners of her vision, and there was not a thing she could do about it. "Zero ... Nate ... did you get?" she croaked.

"Yeah, mission accomplished. Now give me your damn location or turn on your GPS!"

"Not this time, sir. I'm done. Sorry, Nate. I won't be able to make the big party."

"What? No, Raina, no! Hold on, *hold on!*"

Raina reached up and dislodged her earbud, just as the other adept straddled her abdomen. It might have hurt, but she was already numb. Still, as he leaned in close. Raina met his gaze and decided to hold on for as long as she could.

"Now, what did I say earlier about your heart? Oh yeah ..." The adept thrust his dagger into Raina's chest.

"You know what, I'm sick of this. Bruno, get him *out* of here" Ricky said.

Bruno the over-muscled bouncer smiled as she reached for Mr. Bourbon to show him the door. Abruptly, he collapsed to the floor, unconscious. Mr. Bourbon slowly retracted his arm.

"Anyone else wanna get stupid? This is between me and Ricky, *comprendre?*" Bourbon said.

The cantina workers were frozen in place, unable to speak. So was Ricky. He'd never seen an unarmed strike that fast before; for the first time, he wasn't sure he could take someone. Still, he kept his cool.

The elven bartender who found the courage to speak first. "Please, señor, just go! You have the wrong man! Ricky could not have done the things you said!"

In reply, Bourbon reached into his longcoat and pulled out a long, wicked combat dagger. He gave everyone a good look before he thrust it into the table. "Look familiar?"

The staff gasped at the sight of the blade. It was an exact match for Ricky's.

"How many people did you carve up with these blades, Ricky? Dozens? Hundreds?" Bourbon's fingertips held the blade and casually turned it. Ricky's eyes never left it; he was already turning red, his calm veneer fading.

"Hey look, chum," said one of the other bartenders "You could have gotten that anywhere."

"Maybe. Ask Ricky? He seems interested in it."

Ricky just stood there, hand hanging near his thigh, sweating with its tight group on the blade.

Mr. Bourbon slowly stood. "Want to know where I found this? I was only a half-a-click away. When I got dere, I found dis instead of you. Your trail was easy to follow. Took me two days skulking through an active war zone, but I found your doss. Yeah, I seen what you did to her and da others, or what was left of dem. And the altar. What did the press label you, Butcher of Bogotá?" he said.

"Still doesn't mean anything," said the other bartender.

"Doesn't mean ... they never proved ... found HA!" Ricky suddenly barked, his face a mask of madness and anger as he looked at his other blade with longing. "Ah, fuck it. Give it to me." His voice took on a high-pitched tone.

"Ricky?" said the elven bartender, slowly backing away.

He ignored her; all he cared about was reclaiming what was rightfully his. "Give it to me. *Now*"

"Best you all leave," Bourbon said. The staff quickly complied.

Alone, they stared at each other. Ricky shook with anger, while Bourbon was calm and steady.

"So how'd you find me?" Ricky asked.

"Image link in her goggles. Saw the whole thing. After that it was a simple matter of knowing who to talk to, and how much to pay. A lot of people want you dead."

Ricky chuckled "Nothing new. Just have to change identities again. So what now? We have our little standoff, a duel to see who's better?"

Bourbon just stood there.

"What, suddenly can't speak? Couldn't get you to shut up a few minutes ago and now you won't say a *fucking* thing? And for what? Some fucking worthless *tusker bitch?*!"

Bourbon's right hand drifted toward the Crusader on the table.

"Oh! I see. This is some sort of honor thing, right? You're an 'Avenging Angel' or some drek, huh? Okay, Gumbo-man. I'll play your little game. And tell you what. I'll do the 'honorable' thing. I'll offer you the same terms I offered her. So let's see who's faster, you with that piece of drek gun, or me with my ..."

There was a sudden sharp crack. Ricky's body jerked violently as his brains evacuated the back of his skull. Bourbon stood there, a smoking custom Colt 2066 heavy pistol in his left hand. Ricky stood for a few seconds more, then his eyes rolled into the back of his head. He fell to the floor.

"Honor doesn't apply to rabid animals. They get put down."

It didn't take long to find what he was looking for on Ricky's body. It was in the right chest pocket of his jumpsuit. He pulled it out, along with several other items, including a wedding ring, an earring, an old USA silver dollar, a small plastic dolphin, and a lock of hair in a tiny plastic bag. All were trophies from other victims. He said a quick prayer for all of them, hoping he'd granted them justice as well. He took a moment to gaze at his objective: a battered and worn patch depicting a grim reaper looking over his shoulder, with a stylized "61" at the bottom. He clutched it tight, eyes watering behind his smartglasses. Taking a deep breath, he pulled out two similar patches from his own pocket: his and his father's. Placing the three together, he secured them all as he activated his commlink and walked out of the cantina. The rain had stopped.

"Bravo Zero-Six to Freebird. Mission complete. The bill has been paid."

PHYSICAL MAGIC

Growler's ears twitched and his eyes snapped open when he heard the scream. On pure reflex he rolled from his makeshift "house" and into a combat crouch with nose up, sniffing the air. Immediately he knew that something was wrong.

Despite the odors of garbage and decay, the intruder's scent came to him as another scream sounded. A low, menacing rumble started in his chest, and Growler took off at a full sprint. He heard various sounds in the distance while bounding through the labyrinth of debris, garbage, and assorted junk left behind by Seattle's downtown corporations. Even without his heightened senses, he'd have found these intruders easily.

He skidded silently to a halt next to a rusted dumpster and slowly peered around it. In the alley's dim light he saw a middle-aged human woman wearing a modest business suit with a gleaming NeoNET employee pin on her lapel. She held up a bloody hand as she cradled a teenage boy. Growler recognized the boy—an arrogant corp brat who liked slumming. Damn mongrel finally bit off more than he could chew. Blood streamed down his face as he lay limp against the woman; both were on the ground against a chain-link fence.

Two humans and an ork surrounded the pair. All three wore white and grey synthleathers and sporting the skull facial tattoo of the Dissemblers. Their hands gripped long, curved knives.

"P-Please ... let us go!" the woman pleaded to the gangers as blood dripped from her hand. "I just want to take my son home."

The big ork chuckled. "You here that, chummers?" he said to his companions before turning back to the woman. "Sorry breeder, but this here is a special night. My two boys here got to prove what they got, and to do that proper, we need nice ... fresh ... meat" The three laughed in unison as the woman sobbed.

White-hot fury sparked in Growler. Magic surged through his body, and he started to bark and snarl.

Now centered, Growler charged from behind the dumpster with a speed that belied his dwarven stature, barreling toward one of the humans. Before the wannabe ganger reacted, Growler dipped slightly and smashed a vicious uppercut into his target's groin. The wannabe's eyes went wide as his lower abdomen caved in.

Using his upward momentum, Growler rose to his full height and grabbed the ganger's belt. His senses already told him the ork was attacking. Growler pivoted on his foot and slammed the human into the ork, sending them both to the ground.

After releasing his target, Growler turned and charged the second human. Fear flashed in the wannabe's face as he desperately swung a sweeping blow that Growler easily dodged with a quick sidestep. As the knife and arm swung past him, Growler seized the limb then twisted and yanked the captured appendage in one quick motion. The shoulder joint separated with a wet *shunk* sound, and the human crumpled to the street, screaming in pain.

Growler turned to face the ork who was back on his feet, but the ork just laughed and said, "Halfer, you just fragged up bad. Mr. Grey will pay a nice bonus for your sweet meat!"

At both ends of the alley, several more figures appeared, all wearing white and grey with skull tattoos on their faces. Each of them joined the ork in laughter, swinging clubs, chains, and knives as they advanced.

Growler snarled then turned and bared his teeth. He crouched low as he felt the bones and muscles in his smiling face take on canine features. "Bring it then, because haven't you heard?" he said in challenge "It's not the size of the dog in the fight. It's the size of the fight in the DOG!"

ADEPTS IN THE SIXTH WORLD

"Well, congrats there, Timmy ... you're a physical adept! Try not to kill anyone, okay?" –Anonymous poster, Shadowland BBS, circa 2051.

So what exactly *is* an adept anyway? Go to any city or sprawl and ask John or Jane Q. Wageslave, and you'll likely get something that references the latest episode of the *Karl Kombatmage* spin-off, *Holly Striker: Street Warrior*. While the drones-at-large (meaning people, not the remote-controlled kind) have grasped the basic concept of what an adept is, in reality they have approximately less than a clue about the truth.

PUBLIC PERCEPTIONS

In 2023, adept abilities were officially recognized as a form of magic. Before recognition, these abilities were simply mistaken as exceptional aptitude because they didn't manifest in a way that could be easily identified in the same fashion as spells or conjuring. But this was a double-edged sword for newly minted physical adepts. Those who claimed their abilities were magical in nature were vindicated, but the door of prejudice was now opened.

UNFAIR ADVANTAGES

Because magic is integral to what adept powers are and because the powers work like technological augmentations, many felt adept powers were a kind of cheat. Full magicians, for example, could simply choose not to use their abilities, but adepts couldn't turn their powers off (or so many believed). It also didn't help that adept powers were mostly combat-oriented and most adepts were somewhat aggressive by nature. For every peaceful Zen master, there were several stories of psychos on a magic-fueled killing rampage. The facts were highly exaggerated, but public perception usually wins out over reality, especially when there's profit from stereotypes. As new adept powers began to emerge, the public started to see that adepts weren't just about killing people and breaking things.

ADEPTS: POWERS AND PREJUDICE

Like magicians, adepts faced their share of prejudice and discrimination, but it was subtler.

Because their powers were perceived as unfair or unearned, adepts were excluded from many professions—the one exception being military and security services. Never ones to throw away a good weapon opportunity, governments and corporations actively recruited adepts for their combat abilities. A decently powered adept could (and still can) receive insane pay rates and/or benefits for their services just for signing a nice, legally binding contract.

Not every adept was so lucky. Athletes in particular were affected by prejudicial practices. For many decades, they were banned from professional sports and leagues based on their so-called unfair advantage. In reality, the enhanced abilities or physical attributes weren't the problem: many believed adepts couldn't be regulated or controlled. Technological enhancements were fine because they could be controlled.

As a result, adepts formed their own professional leagues, such as the Gladio MMA organization. Eventually, adepts gradually found acceptance, and closed-off leagues opened up. Some prejudice still remains, however, and adepts still face intense scrutiny.

The answer to what makes an adept is both simple and complicated. Understanding the basic idea of physical magic is the easy part. The hard part is explaining how an adept learns, hones, and utilizes those abilities.

WALKING THE PATH

Like magicians, most adepts manifest their power sometime around puberty. At that point, the question becomes "so what now?" Once an adept's powers manifest, he has several hard choices to make that will determine what kind of adept he'll become. For some, the choice is easy: they know what they want and see magic as a means to make it happen. Others see magic as a spiritual endeavor. For these adepts, their powers are nothing more than another expression of the self, another part of a whole.

Regardless of an adept's personal beliefs, she'll have to make those choices. Within adept circles, this is commonly known and as "finding the Path." In a nutshell, the Path represents the choices the adept makes to develop her abilities and determines what she will become, be it warrior, athlete, artist, speaker, or some other Path yet to be discovered. The Path the adept walks is as unique as the adept herself.

MYSTIC ADEPTS: BLURRING MAGICAL LINES

Just when it seems magic has been figured out, something changes the rules. Mystic adepts fall into this category. Part magician and part adept, these magic users form a class all of their own, as they're able to access both adept powers and use traditional sorcery and conjuring skills.

On average, mystic adepts tend to be less powerful compared to their magicians or adept counterparts. To take advantage of both traditional magic and adept powers, the mystic must split his magical energies and training between the two. In the magical community, mystic adepts are sometimes known as jacks of all trades or "backup magicians." While these labels are unfair, they're not entirely inaccurate. Against a full magician or regular adept of equal magical rating, the mystic adept usually falls short when comparing magical abilities.

What the mystical adept lacks because of her divided magical priorities, she makes up for it in versatility. While not as powerful, the mystical adept's ability to be more of a Swiss-army magician makes her very valuable in a variety of situations. Not every situation needs the best or most powerful ability, as sometimes what the mystic adept offers is just enough get the job done.

ADEPTS IN THE SHADOWS

The one place where adepts have always found a home, for better or worse with no questions asked, has been the shadows. Like governments and corporations, fixers and Mr. Johnsons are always on the lookout for uniquely qualified individuals, and adepts often fit the bill.

On a shadowrunner team, adepts are usually the specialists, the ones who know how to do one or two things very—no, *extremely* well. They may be the expert shooter, the ninja-like infiltration specialist, or the silver-tongued devil who could talk a Knight Errant or Lone Star copper out of their badges. Maybe they can to simply beat the ever-loving drek out of someone without breaking a sweat. And that's just scratching the surface. Adept powers offer great flexibility and allow the physical magician to perform any number of services for their team.

WAYS OF THE OLD MEET THE NEW

Over the past few decades, adepts have expanded their knowledge of how their mojo works. Just like magicians, today's adepts are significantly more powerful than their predecessors. Just a few years ago, some adepts began experiencing a surge in their overall abilities. The exact reason for this is still being debated, but some say the

SYNERGY: BUILDING THE BETTER ADEPT

The idea of a Path isn't just metaphorical fluff; it has real applications when building an adept character. In the *Creating a Shadowrunner* chapter of the *Shadowrun, Fifth Edition* core rulebook (p. 62), Step One is "Choose a Concept." This step is critical because beginning adept characters have a limited amount of Magic to purchase powers from. It's fine to say "I want to build a combat adept," for example, but what kind of combat adept? A gunslinger? A marksman? A hand-to-hand specialist? Players should consider these questions during character creation, and gamemasters should be ready to advise the player if need be.

Once the player chooses a Path, he will need to keep this in mind during the rest of character creation. A gunslinger adept, for example, is going to need decent Agility and Reaction attributes while a brawler adept needs good Strength and/or Body. Certain Positive qualities also help. Players will want to make sure they have enough skill points to pull it all together. For a player building a mystic adept, the number crunch during character creation is even more important because she has to consider Power Points and a Magic Rating.

This does not mean that players have to nitpick over every detail. Rather, these general considerations help new (and even veteran) *Shadowrun* players streamline the character creation process. Not every character is expected (or encouraged) to be one hundred percent optimal. If a player wants to create a utilitarian or support adept with a loose focus and a wide range of powers because that's what the team needs, go for it. The main goal of *Shadowrun* (or any game) is to have fun above all else.

mana spike caused by the return of Halley's Comet back in 2061 was to blame. Others claim more refined training techniques helped adepts optimize their abilities.

Regardless of the reason, a curious phenomenon has gained prominence within the adept community: the adoption of Ways. While the exact details of a Way vary from adept to adept (some include codes of conduct or spiritual trappings), dedication to a particular Way helps adepts further develop a chosen group of abilities based on their chosen Path. For example, an athletic adept may choose to focus her efforts into playing a particular sport and develop abilities to best play that sport rather than focus on general athleticism.

While some dismiss Ways as pseudo-mystical, psycho-semantic junk, researchers have confirmed that Ways do work and began cataloging them. To date, ten Ways have been identified.

ARTISAN'S WAY

The Artisan's Way is the most recent Way to be identified and recognized as such. Most current practitioners were once considered followers of the Artist's Way. With an unusual affinity towards modern technological devices, followers of the Artisan's Way are master technicians and fabricators. They use magic to design, build, repair, and maintain technological devices. What separates them from Artists is they value function over form. With a focus that borders on obsessiveness, Artisans work to get every milligram of performance out of any chosen device. They see technology as an addition to talent (both magical and otherwise), not a replacement. In addition to their technological acumen, Artisans also show a superior level of hand-eye coordination when using certain technology, such as vehicles.

ARTIST'S WAY

Followers of the Artist's Way are creators of wondrous things or master showmen. Their goal and purpose in life is to use their magic and share the beauty they perceive in the world around them (or share the chaos and pain they see, if that's their particular bent). Some do it with a classical artistic medium, such as painting or sculpture. Some tirelessly compose poetry, songs, and stories to capture and inspire the imagination. Others stand before the crowd, feel the ebb and flow of their emotions, and use their magic to play just the right note or sing just the right word for maximum effect. Through their chosen medium, Artists seek to connect with their audiences in a way few know how.

ATHLETE'S WAY

The drive to be the best is what sets the Athlete apart from others. Since the first Olympic games millennia ago, there have always been competitors who wish nothing more than to test the inherent limitations of their bodies in the pursuit of glory. To an Athlete, the challenge is what matters the most. Whether he is an MMA fighter going for the championship, a sprinter going for the gold in the Olympics, or a baseball player going for the home run record, the Athlete uses his magic to enhance his athletic skills and abilities to push himself past his limitations, all for the sake of going one more round, crossing one more kilometer, or gaining one more second.

BEAST'S WAY

Some say the person does not choose the totem, but rather the totem chooses the person. This is true for those who follow the Beast's Way. Like their shaman brethren, followers of this Way have heard and answered the call of an animal spirit, for they have been found worthy of the totem spirit's guidance, wisdom, and power. For these adepts, simply following this Way is not enough because their patrons can be demanding or fickle. The adept must adhere to strict ideas of conduct, less she offend her patron totem and risk having her abilities taken from her. This is usually not a problem, for those who answer this call usually give of themselves freely and embrace their new life.

BURNOUT'S WAY

Considered more of a corruption and aberration than an actual Way, the Burnout's Way represents adepts that have lost or forsaken their magical abilities for technological augmentations. These adepts are often held in contempt or pitied by other magic users. The reasons adepts find themselves on this Way are myriad. Some may have lost Magic due to injury or Essence drain and are desperate to replace it. Others may not have the discipline to properly develop their powers and seek to find shortcuts to personal power, only to find they can't stop. Some may have been driven insane by their talent and wish to excise it like a cancer. Followers of this Way often become mere shells of what they once were.

INVISIBLE WAY

Stealth, silence, and secrecy: these are the objectives of the Invisible Way's followers. Favored by adept assassins, infiltrators, and spies, this Way allows adepts to perfect their ability to go unseen or unnoticed when going about their work. These adepts could be anywhere, at any time. If they have truly perfected their craft, no one will ever know what happened until after the adept is long gone. While this Way is associated with criminal pursuits, not all those who follow the Invisible Way have this intent. Sometimes, remaining unseen is simply the most expedient way to deal with a problem.

MAGICIAN'S WAY

This Way is almost exclusively composed of mystic adepts, and those who follow the Magician's Way strive

to develop both their magician and adept abilities. Because of the tremendous amounts of effort required to fully develop both talents at the same time, most mystic adepts often favor either their adept or magical powers, depending on which Path they have chosen. Followers of this Way also tend to be somewhat more focused or obsessive than other mystic adepts when it comes to training and power development, which is understandable when considering the unique challenges they face.

SPEAKER'S WAY

Sometimes, the Speaker is the nice person you just had an easy conversation with who convinced you of something you normally wouldn't agree with or talked you into doing something you normally wouldn't do. Other times, she stands at the front of the crowd, and her fiery, impassioned, or compelling speech moves the onlookers to direct action. And when it's all over, if she's done her job right, you'll have no idea you've been influenced by magic at all. This is how the Speaker operates. Her voice is her weapon of choice, and her

influencing magic is her ammunition. Of all the Ways, these adepts are the most subtle (and in some ways, the most dangerous), because how many of us can remember *every* conversation we've ever had? How often may we have been subtly influenced without being the least bit aware.

SPIRITUAL WAY

Similar in many respects to the followers of the Beast's Way, those who follow the Spiritual Way have been blessed (or maybe cursed?) with the patronage of a mentor spirit. Spiritual Way adepts seek to follow their path with the guidance of their mentor spirit. Some mentors are very demanding, but the adept's rewards for diligence are significant. Those who follow this Way are said to be more spiritual than most adepts.

WARRIOR'S WAY

As the Athlete pushes her body past its limits for glory, Warriors do the same for victory. The most prolific physical magicians in the Sixth World, Warriors are the ones most associated with the term "adept." From professional soldiers to street fighters and everything in between, Warriors come from countless backgrounds and fight for any number of reasons. In combat the Warrior is truly in her element. Despite what many may think, not all Warriors are bloodthirsty killing machines. In truth some are lured by the bloodlust of battle, but Warriors also count the most honorable metahumans in existence among their number. When the Warrior fights, she fights to *win*.

NEW ADEPT POWERS

The following is an expanded list of powers available for both adept and mystic adept characters. Additional powers can be found on p. 308, *SR5*.

ANALYTICS

COST: 0.5 PP PER LEVEL

Adepts with this power can easily analyze, detect, recognize, and solve ciphers, patterns, or puzzles. This allows them to recognize clues or evidence during an investigation. For every level purchased, Analytics grants a +1 modifier to any test that involves pattern recognition, evidence analysis, observation, puzzle solving, or logic-based problems. It does not add dice to Technological Skill tests except for identification purposes. For example, Analytics doesn't help with repairing a firearm, but it will help the adept recognize a knock-off.)

Analytics is not an immediate or instant solution to every problem. Rather, it's meant to help the adept detect clues and glean information that could be overlooked (gamemaster's discretion).

ANIMAL EMPATHY

COST: 0.25 PP PER LEVEL

This power gives the adept a greater affinity for all non-sentient animals, both normal and paranormal. For every level purchased, the adept gains +1 die to all Animal Handling tests. This power can also be used to intimidate or frighten animals.

BERSERK

COST: 1 PP
ACTIVATION: SIMPLE ACTION

The adept can voluntarily enter a frenzied mental state to increase his physical abilities. While in this state, the adept gains a +1 to all Physical attributes but suffers a temporary loss of –1 to all Mental attributes (minimum of 1; this power cannot be used by adepts with any Mental attributes starting at 1). Note: this also affects the adept's Physical, Mental, Social, and Astral limits. Once activated, the adept remains in this state

for (Magic x 2) Combat Turns or until any enemy targets are down. Adepts can attempt to leave this state early with a Willpower + Charisma (Magic x 0.5) Test. When the power wears off, adepts must resist Drain equal to (Magic x 0.5, rounded up).

BERSERKER'S RAGE

COST: 1 PP
PREREQUISITE: BERSERK
ACTIVATION: COMPLEX ACTION

The adept passes melee berserking and delves deeper into a frenzied mental state. All bonuses and penalties from the Berserker power are increased to +2, and the duration is increased to (Magic x 4) minutes. To exit this state early requires a Willpower + Charisma Test. The threshold is (Magic x 0.5) + 2), with a minimum threshold of 3. If successful, the adept can use her full Mental attributes to resist Drain. Regardless of when she exits this state, the adept will have to resist a Drain Value of (Magic x 0.5). Any Wound Modifiers apply. A glitch on an exit attempt increases the duration to (Magic x 3) minutes.

BLIND FIGHTING

COST: 0.5 PP

Drawing on a special kind of sixth sense, an adept with this power is able to continue fighting even when he is blinded or deprived of vision. It reduces the penalty for Blind Fighting by 1. This power can be combined with the Strike the Darkness martial arts technique for a cumulative reduction of 2 (p. 141, *Run & Gun*).

CLOAK

COST: 0.25 PP PER LEVEL

Using the Cloak power, the adept has an increased chance of avoiding magical detection. For every level of this power, the adept gains a +1 die for opposing a Detection spell being used against her (see p. 285, *SR5*). Cloak does not prevent a magician or mystic adept from reading the adept's aura through astral perception or viewing her from astral space; it just makes it more difficult to zero in on the targeted adept.

COOL RESOLVE

COST: 1.0 PP PER LEVEL

Adepts with this power are extremely confident and self-assured in social interactions. This includes situations such as negotiations with a Mr. Johnson, running a con on the street, staying in-character while undercover, or resisting the tender inquiries of a professional interrogator. Each level gives the adept +1 die in all Opposed Tests involving Social skills, regardless of whether they initiated the action or are resisting someone else's social skills.

COMMANDING VOICE

COST: 0.25 PP PER LEVEL (MAX 3)

Adepts with this power have a knack for convincing people to believe them or do things for them in certain situations. For every level of this power, an adept gains a +1 die to any Opposed Intimidation or Leadership tests that they initiate (normal limits apply). If the adept succeeds, then the target(s) will agree to or follow the adept's next suggestion or command, within reason and depending on the situation. A subject won't normally harm himself for example, but he may be persuaded that the pretty-boy elf over there was making moves on his girl/guy and that punching said elf is a good idea. Or an adept may convince a corporate secretary to give up some dirt on her boss.

To keep this power in check, gamemasters can also grant targets a situational bonus based on how inclined the subject would be to believe the adept. An adept can attempt to use this ability on up to (Charisma) people at a time, with a –1 dice pool for any additional subjects.

COUNTERSTRIKE

COST: 1.0 PP PER LEVEL
ACTIVATION: INTERRUPT ACTION
(–5 FROM INITIATIVE SCORE)

Counterstrike is an extremely potent ability that allows an adept in unarmed combat to redirect an attacker's energy through a combination of skill, intuition, and magical ability. To employ this power, an adept must first use a successful Block action against an incoming attack and spend her next available action to make a melee combat attack. For the adept's next melee combat attack test, add a number of dice equal to her levels in Counterstrike and the net hits from the Block. Engaging in any other action before attacking, even Dodge or Full Defense, negates the bonuses gained from this power. This power cannot be combined with the Counterstrike and Opposing Force martial arts techniques (p. 124 and 139, *Run & Gun*).

ELEMENTAL EFFECTS: NORMAL AND TOXIC

There are several powers this section that allow an adept to deal elemental damage or use an elemental effect, the most common being acid, cold, electricity, and fire. To understand how these elements cause damage, see p. 170, *SR5*.

These aren't the only elemental effects that can be employed. Toxic adepts can use pollutants and radiation instead of normal elemental damage. To understand how these toxic elements work, see the sidebar about elemental effects in this book, p. 105.

ELEMENTAL BODY

COST: 1 PP
ACTIVATION: COMPLEX ACTION
PREREQUISITES: ELEMENTAL STRIKE

An evolved version of Elemental Strike and similar to the critter power Elemental Attack, Elemental Body creates an elemental field that envelops the adept. This field forms approximately three to five centimeters from the adept's body and can be used offensively and defensively.

To activate this power, the adept must spend a Complex Action channeling the desired element. For offensive purposes, treat Elemental Body like the Elemental Strike power, with a DV of (Magic x 2)P and AP –(Magic x 0.5). For defense, anyone or thing coming into contact (melee or unarmed strike) with the adept while Elemental Body is active must resist the same DV and elemental effect as the offensive strike; fast-moving projectiles such as bullets or thrown weapons are unaffected. Items already on the adept's body or held by the adept are not damaged, but they do not gain any elemental effect.

Elemental Body lasts for (Magic) Combat Turns or until the adept is rendered unconscious. This power can be deactivated at will using a Free Action before the time limit expires. Once deactivated, the adept must resist a Drain Value of (Magic x 0.5) + the number of Combat Turns the power was active. Only one effect can be used at a time, and each elemental effect must be purchased as a separate power.

ELEMENTAL STRIKE

COST: 0.5 PP
ACTIVATION: SIMPLE ACTION
PREREQUISITES: KILLING HANDS

Elemental Strike enhances the damage caused by an unarmed Killing Hands strike by channeling an elemental effect into the attack. Activating this power requires a Simple Action and the effect remains active for (Magic) Combat Turns or until the adept deactivates it with. Free Action or is rendered unconscious. While active, the chosen elemental effect wreathes the hand, foot, or other body part the adept uses to strike. Only one effect can be used at a time and can't be combined with any other adept striking power except Killing Hands. Each elemental effect must be purchased as a separate power.

ELEMENTAL WEAPON

COST: 0.5 PP
ACTIVATION: SIMPLE ACTION
PREREQUISITES: WEAPON FOCI

Similar to Elemental or Toxic Strike, Elemental Weapon allows an adept to channel an elemental effect (normal or toxic) through her weapon focus instead of her hands. A Simple Action is required to first channel the desired elemental effect. Elemental Weapon remains active for (Magic) Combat Turns or until the adept deactivates it with a Free Action or is rendered unconscious. Only one elemental effect can be used at a time, and each elemental effect must be purchased as a separate power. This power can also be used with other powers that enhance an adept's Accuracy or skills related to foci.

EMPATHIC HEALING

COST: 0.5 PP
ACTIVATION: SEE TEXT

Used only in the direst of circumstances, the Empathic Healing power allows an adept to literally take on the wounds of another in order to heal them. To accomplish this, the adept rolls a Magic + Willpower Test. For every hit, one box of Physical damage transfers from the wounded target to the adept's damage track. Only Physical damage can be healed in this way.

Subjects with lower than normal Essence, due to augmentations or Essence loss, are more difficult to heal. Apply a negative modifier equal to the subject's lost Essence (6 – current Essence Rating, round down) to the dice pool for the adept's healing test. The test itself requires two full Combat Turns per box of damage to complete, and the healing adept must maintain physical contact during the entire process. Damage modifiers are applied once the adept completes the process.

FACIAL SCULPT

COST: 0.25 PP PER LEVEL
ACTIVATION: COMPLEX ACTION

This power allows an adept to change his appearance by shifting the muscles, bone structure, and cartilage in his face. Each level purchased gives the adept a +1 dice pool modifier for Disguise Tests. The effect can be sustained for (Magic) hours.

Common changes include altering ear shape, changing nose shape, raising/lowering cheekbones, growing tusks, reshaping the forehead, lengthening/shortening facial hair, and so on. Adepts can even change their face to another metatype of they wish, but they can't change their body shape. The time required to change one feature is approximately one minute. Multiple features can be changed simultaneously with a Body + Magic Test, with each hit resulting in one additional change. The adept needs another full minute to undo the changes and return their features to normal.

FLEXIBILITY

COST: 0.25 PP PER LEVEL (MAX 3)

Adepts with the Flexibility power can bend or twist their bodies past the metahuman norm, which allows them to squeeze through openings smaller than the adept (gamemaster's discretion) and escape restraints easier. It also makes and adept harder to subdue during unarmed combat. For every level of Flexibility the adept possesses, the threshold for moving through cramped corners or getting out of restraints is lowered by one. During unarmed combat, if someone is attempting to subdue the adept, the adept gains +1 die per level of Flexibility to prevent being subdued; normal limits still apply.

FREEFALL

COST: 0.25 PP PER LEVEL

This power helps adepts absorb the damage from a fall or jump down for a specific distance. This ability does not help the adept increase the distance he is jumping, such as with the Light Body power. Every level of Freefall allows the adept to fall or jump down 3 additional meters without any adverse effects (beyond the three meters normally allowed). When calculating fall damage past his personal distance threshold, subtract the overall level bonus from the Damage Value of the fall and then apply damage normally (see p. 172, SR5). This means that an adept with Freefall receives no damage from a fall of six meters or less, rather than the typical three meters. Beyond that, if an adept with two levels of Freefall falls 15 meters, the power negates 6 points of damage from the fall, changing the Damage Value of the fall from 15P to 9P (the fall's AP remains unchanged). As long as the adept experiences no damage from the fall (either because the fall was short enough to cause no damage or because they successfully resisted all applicable damage using Body + Armor, the fall counts as a normal move action, and can be combined with an attack. Any other means of dealing with the damage does not allow this opportunity. Longer falls count as a Complex Action.

HANG TIME

COST: 0.25 PP PER LEVEL
ACTIVATION: SEE DESCRIPTION

Adepts with this power receive two benefits. First, for each level of this power, the adept gains a +1 dice pool bonus for all Climbing Tests. Second, the adept can temporarily adhere to surfaces, such as walls. For each level of this power, the adept can attach himself to a surface and hang out for approximately five minutes, provided he remains motionless and keeps physical contact with the surface in question with hands, feet, knees, or elbows. The adept must spend a Simple Action to bond his magical energy with the surface; normal clothing such as gloves or boots does not interfere with this power, but the use of heavy armor (armor with a Rating of 13 or higher) will. Moving the attached body parts on the surface they're adhering to, such as a moving vehicle, breaks the bond, making the adept fall off.

INERTIA STRIKE

COST: 0.5 PP
ACTIVATION: FREE ACTION

This power allows an adept to generate and channel extra energy into an unarmed or melee strike specifically intended to knock a target down. To use this power, the adept must first declare her intention by spending a Free Action before the actual strike to channel the necessary energy. If the adept is successful with the attack, she adds (Magic x 0.5) to her Strength to determine if a knockdown occurs (p. 194, SR5). Inertia Strike does not deal damage. Using this power is considered a Called Shot (see p. 195, SR5). Note: This power cannot be combined with the Imposing Stone Martial Arts Technique (p. 138, Run & Gun).

KINESICS MASTERY

COST: 0.5 PP
PREREQUISITES: KINESICS

An advanced version of Kinesics (p. 310, SR5), this power allows two adepts with this ability to communicate with each other while using solely non-verbal cues, such as body language and minute facial expressions, and natural subconscious cues. While general messages and mental states are easily relayed, those with Kinesics Mastery can relay specific, detailed information such as locations, names, places, or numbers. Communication in this way requires adepts to have direct line of sight and be close enough to read each other's facial features and body language, whether through natural, augmented, or magical means.

LINGUISTICS

COST: 0.25 PP

Through enhanced memory and mimicry, adepts with this power are able to learn new languages after a minimal amount of exposure to it, without spending Karma. To learn a new language, an adept must be exposed to the new language for (12 – Magic Rating) hours, (minimum 1 hour). The adept then makes a Logic + Intuition Test using the Linguistics Table. If successful, the adept gains the language at Rating 1. Further development of the new language requires normal Karma expenditure.

LINGUISTICS TABLE

LANGUAGE	THRESHOLD
Common (English, Japanese, Spanish)	1
Uncommon (Latin, Or'zet, Sperethiel)	2
Obscure (Aramaic, Lapp, Berber)	3

MAGIC SENSE

COST: 0.5 PP

Magic Sense allows an adept to detect the use of magic in her vicinity. Treat this power as the Detect Magic spell (p. 287, SR5) but with a range equal to (Magic x 10) meters. Adepts with the Astral Perception power can also use Magic Sense to detect astral forms while perceiving the astral plane.

MELANIN CONTROL

COST: 0.5 PP

This power allows the adept to change the color of his skin and/or hair to that of another ethnicity/metatype, limited to the colors normally found in metahuman genetic expressions. The shift costs a Complex Action and lasts for (Magic) hours.

METABOLIC CONTROL

COST: 0.5 PP

An adept with this power has the ability to enter a deep meditative state where all metabolic processes are slowed. This has two benefits. The first is to reduce the amount of rest the adept needs. In game terms, for every hour the adept in this state, she increases the interval for taking fatigue damage from sleep deprivation by another three hours (see p. 172, SR5).

The second benefit preserves the adept's life in emergency situations. When the adept goes into Physical overflow damage, he immediately goes into this meditative state. While in this state, the adept only takes an additional box of overflow damage every (Body) hours. An adept can exit this state whenever he wishes, but doing so while severely injured causes all wounds or toxins to immediately take effect unless treated or healed.

MISSILE MASTERY

COST: 1 PP

In the hands of an adept with Missile Mastery, everyday items such as bottles, credsticks, tools, empty clips, flashlights, cooking utensils, and so on can be turned into deadly weapons. Such improvised weapons have a Damage Value of (STR)P with an Accuracy of 3. The adept can also declare whether these weapons do Physical or Stun damage. Additionally, adepts with this ability have a greater affinity for throwing weapons. For ranged attacks with non-explosive throwing weapons, the adept gains +1 die and adds +1 to the weapon's Damage Value.

MOTION SENSE

COST: 0.5 PP

Able to sense movement in her immediate vicinity, an adept with this power becomes a living motion sensor and is very difficult to sneak up on or ambush. Through a combination of natural and magical senses, the adept feels the movement of people, animals, or objects by their displacement of air molecules, changes in ambient barometric pressure, vibrations, or the minute disruption of the local mana field. This feeling alerts the adept to movement around her equal to (Magic) meters and can be used to detect living beings or objects that would otherwise be hidden by normal senses such as sight, sound, or smell. The size of the target also directly affects the adept's ability to sense it.

To use this power, the adept must first make a Perception + Magic [Mental] test. The threshold for this test is based on the size of whatever the adept is attempting to sense; consult the Motion Sense table for results.

MOTION SENSE TABLE

MOVING THING IS	THRESHOLD
Smaller than dog/cat	3
Smaller than average metahuman (dwarf)	2
Average metahuman (human, ork, elf)	1
Larger than average (troll)	Automatic success

NERVE STRIKE
COST: 1 PP
By targeting various nerve clusters in his opponent's body, an adept with this ability can disable or subdue on opponent without causing physical injury or death. To use this power, the adept must first declare his intention to employ it and then make a normal melee attack. If successful, the adept may choose to reduce his opponent's Agility or Reaction (attacker's choice) by 1 per net hit instead of inflicting Physical or Stun damage. If the targeted attribute reaches 0, the target is rendered paralyzed. An attacker must choose only one attribute to target per attack. The target regains lost attribute points with rest: 1 hour of rest recovers 1 lost point.

Nerve Strike works best on metahumans but can also be used against critters. A critter's nerve clusters are more difficult to target, so two net hits are required to lower the targeted critter's attribute by 1; all other normal rules apply. Targets without a functioning nervous system, such as spirits, drones, and so on, are unaffected by this power.

NIMBLE FINGERS
COST: 0.25 PP
Adepts with this ability have exceptional manual dexterity. In game terms, this grants +1 die to Palming

Tests, Performance Tests where the adept plays a musical instruments that requires the use of fingers, or any tests where small tools or items are used (gamemaster's discretion). Additionally, the Simple Actions Change Gun Mode, Insert Clip, Remove Clip, and Use Simple Device are now considered Free Actions.

PAIN RELIEF
COST: 1 PP
Similar to Nerve Strike but nicer, an adept channels mana into qi/chakra points to relieve tension, pain, and muscle fatigue. In game terms, this means removing the effects of Stun damage from a target. To use this power, the adept makes a Magic + Agility Test against a target. Every net hit temporarily removes one box of Stun damage from the target; normal rules for healing patients with implants still apply (p. 208, SR5). This effect only lasts for (Magic) hours or until the actual damage is healed, whichever comes first. The time necessary to complete the process is five minutes per box removed, and the adept must maintain contact with the target. Should the adept lose contact with the target for any reason before the process is complete, all benefits are lost and the adept must repeat the process.

PENETRATING STRIKE
COST: 0.25 PP PER LEVEL (MAX 4)
This ability allows an adept to focus and project an unarmed attack a short distance forward, bypassing armor the target may have or punching through their thick, stubborn hide. In essence, this gives the adept's attack an AP rating equal to the levels she has in this power (maximum 4). This power can be used in conjunction with the Killing Hands power but not Elemental Strike.

PLAGUE CLOUD
COST: 0.5 PP
ACTIVATION: FREE ACTION
This power surrounds the adept in a dense cloud of fumes, insects, or other pollutants or toxins. All ranged attacks made while the power is active (either against or by the adept) are considered to be in at least Moderate Fog/Smoke (see Ranged Attack Modifiers, p. 173, SR5). If anyone makes a successful melee attack against an adept with this power is active, the attacker must resist the damage effects of pollution (see sidebar, p. 105).

RAPID DRAW
COST: 0.5 PP
No longer limited to pistols, the Rapid Draw power can be used by the adept to rapidly and more easily employ a variety of weapons in combat. Any weapon that is properly holstered can be quick-drawn; this includes blades,

pistols, and throwing weapons. To use this ability, the adept makes a standard quick draw test (p. 165, *SR5*) but the threshold for this test is decreased by 1; this is cumulative with the use of a quick-draw holster. Also, with this power, a Quick Draw action is considered a Free Action.

For the purposes of this power, larger weapons such as SMGs, shotguns, or assault rifles attached to slings and/or held in front of the adept at the "low ready" position are also considered holstered and can be quick-drawn as such.

RIPOSTE

COST: 0.5 PP PER LEVEL
ACTIVATION: INTERRUPT ACTION
(–5 FROM INITIATIVE SCORE)

Similar to Counterstrike, Riposte is used during armed melee combat to redirect an attacker's energy against them. To employ this power, an adept must first use a successful Parry action against an incoming attack and spend his next available action to make a melee combat attack. For the adept's next melee combat attack test, add a number of dice equal to his levels in Riposte and the net hits from the Parry. Engaging in any other action before attacking, even Dodge or Full Defense, negates the bonuses gained from this power. Note: This power cannot be combined with the Riposte and Yielding Force Martial Arts techniques (p. 125 and 141, *Run & Gun*).

SKATE

COST: 1 PP

This power is a minor form of levitation that gives an adept the ability to run across a surface that she normally wouldn't be able to, such as thin ice, a fragile structure, or water. The adept pushes off with her first step as she moves across the target surface before she stops. The distance an adept can traverse is equal to her Magic rating in meters. Attempting to traverse further distances requires the adept to find a stable surface or landing area to repeat the process; those who fail to find such a surface fall through whatever they are moving across. An adept attempting an acrobatic move or defensive Interrupt Action while using this power suffers a –3 dice pool penalty to her dice pool for the acrobatic or interrupt test.

SMASHING BLOW

COST: 1 PP

Adepts with this power focus their magic into a single unarmed strike to break through obstacles. Multiply the adept's base DV by 2 when attacking a barrier or other static structure. This applies to both physical and magical barriers.

SPIRIT CLAW

COST: 0.25 PP
ACTIVATION: FREE ACTION

Named by the Beast's Way Sioux adept that discovered it, Spirit Claw allows the adept to temporarily create a small weapon of spiritual energy for use against spirits. While the discoverer's manifestation of this power appeared as a set of oversized claws, others with this power have learned to form whatever weapon they desire—clubs, hammers, daggers, spikes, and so on—based on their particular Way or paradigm. Activated with a Free Action, Spirit Claw adds (Magic x 0.5) to the adept's unarmed DV against spirits (regardless of whether the combat is physical or astral). It remains active for (Magic x 0.5) Combat Turns or when the adept deactivates it with a Free Action or strikes with it. To use Spirit Claw again, the energies must be re-channeled by spending another Free Action. Against spirits, this power can only be combined with the Killing Hands power.

SPIRIT RAM

COST: 0.5 PP
ACTIVATION: SIMPLE ACTION

Similar to Spirit Claw, Spirit Ram creates a temporary, ram shape—horns, ram's head, wedge, spikes, and so forth—in front of the adept for charge attacks against spirits in either physical or astral combat. The Reach of this weapon is (Magic x 0.5), and its DV is (Magic) with AP – (Magic x 0.5). Spirit Ram moves with the adept and remains active for (Magic x 0.5) Combat Turns or when the adept deactivates it with a Free Action or strikes with it. To use Spirit Ram again, the energies must be re-channeled by spending another Simple Action.

STILLNESS

COST: 0.25 PP PER LEVEL (MAX 3)

This power allows an adept to exert control over her body to avoid detection. By slowing her physiological processes (heart rate, breathing, and the need to flex muscles) and entering a relaxed state, the adept becomes completely motionless for a specific amount of time. Her body's heat signature is also lessened, making the adept harder to detect by thermographic means. For every level of this power, the adept can remain in this state for approximately one hour. Anyone using auditory or thermographic means to locate or perceive an adept using this power receives a negative penalty equal to the level of the adept's power. Visual searches or Perception Tests are unaffected by this power. This power is negated as soon as the adept moves.

SUSTENANCE

COST: 0.25 PP

Adepts with this power have exceptional metabolisms and can function with less food and water than normal.

An average metahuman requires approximately three meals per day to maintain normal functions before fatigue damage begins. An adept with this power needs only one meal per day. In game terms, the intervals for hunger and thirst are increased to seven days for hunger and three days for thirst (p. 172, *SR5*).

TEMPERATURE TOLERANCE

COST: 0.25 PP PER LEVEL

This power allows adepts to better withstand the effects of extreme temperatures. For every level in this power, the adept gains a +1 dice pool bonus for resisting damage caused by extreme temperature exposure (p. 172, *SR5*). This also can be used against magical effects such as elemental fire or cold (p. 170-171, *SR5*).

THREE-DIMENSIONAL MEMORY

COST: 0.5 PP

Three-Dimensional Memory allows an adept to mentally record an area he has visited and then later recall it in ultra-clear detail. This ability is favored by adept investigators and recon specialists. To use this ability, the adept in question must use a Complex Action to view the targeted area in detail. This includes what he actually observed, but also any sensations he felt. The range of what the adept can observe is (Magic x Magic) cubic meters. He can record a number of areas equal to his Magic rating.

To recall what he recorded, the adept requires a Perception + Magic [Mental] test. What area he's able to remember depends on what he was actually able to observe—for example, he wouldn't know the contents of a closed cabinet but will remember the cabinet's features in detail—and how long ago he observed the scene. To determine the threshold for the test, see the Three Dimensional Memory Table. If the threshold is reached, the adept can mentally walk through the scene and recall everything he mentally recorded; however, he will be unable to interact with anything in the scene.

THREE DIMENSIONAL MEMORY TABLE

TIME PASSED	THRESHOLD
24 hours	1
1 week	2
1 month	3
1 year	4
Over a year	5

TOXIC STRIKE

COST: 0.5 PP
ACTIVATION: SIMPLE ACTION
PREREQUISITES: KILLING HANDS

Toxic adepts with this power can channel either pollutants or radiation to an Unarmed Combat attack to cause extra elemental damage. The use of this ability follows the same rules and guidelines as the Elemental Strike power (p. 170). Each toxic elemental effect must be purchased as a separate power.

NEW ADEPT QUALITIES: WAYS

Often confused with and thought of as nothing more than magical traditions for adepts, Ways are less a rigid structure system or set of beliefs and more a personal philosophy or code of conduct that physical and mystic adepts adopt or identify with while developing their abilities. The path the adept takes while following a particular Way may differ, but for all adepts there are three basic fundamentals.

An adept cannot follow two Ways simultaneously. While there are many paths an adept can take while following her Way, doing so requires a certain amount of focus and commitment necessary to gain the bonuses a Way grants. Therefore, only one Way can be followed at a time.

The bonuses granted by Ways to purchase adept powers all follow the same rules. For every 2 points in an adept's Magic Rating, that adept may reduce the cost of one level of one power from that Way's list by half. For example, let's say that a player chooses an adept power that costs 1 Power Point. If that power is covered by a specific Way and all prerequisites are met, the cost for that power is reduced to 0.5 Power Points. Likewise, a 0.5 PP power costs 0.25 PP. Adept powers that cost 0.25 Power Points cannot be discounted further. This cost reduction cannot be used multiple times if the power has multiple levels: the reduction applies to only one level, but can be used for different aspects of the same power, such as a different Increased Attribute. The adept then can use the saved Power Points to buy a new power or new levels in an existing power at full cost. If an adept follows a Way and increases his Magic Rating through Initiation, he may use this discount every time he adds two points to his Magic Rating.

Players can amend previously created characters and retroactively purchase a Way. This is per the gamemaster's discretion. See p. 103, *SR5*, for more information about purchasing and paying off qualities.

THE ARTISAN'S WAY

COST: 20 KARMA

In keeping with their affinity for all things technological, adepts of the Artisan's Way are able to alter the standard Adept Centering metamagic ability (p. 325, *SR5*) to grant bonuses for either Active Vehicle skills or Active Technical skills. Bonding a *qi* focus (p. 319, *SR5*) that enhances the adept's Improved Ability (any Technical and Vehicle skill) power costs two Karma less than normal.

Artisans may choose to use their Way discount bonus on the following skills: Analytics, Enhanced Perception, Heightened Concentration, Improved Ability (any Technical or Vehicle skill), Improved Potential (Mental only), Metabolic Control, Three-Dimensional Memory.

THE ARTIST'S WAY

COST: 20 KARMA

Master creators or entertainers, those who follow the Artist's Way channel their energies into inspiring people and showing them the beauty of the Sixth World. As such, they're able to use standard Adept Centering to negate any negative modifiers during a Performance Test for an artistic performance or an Artisan Test for the creation of an artwork. They can also bond a foci that enhances their Improved Ability (Artisan) power for two Karma less than normal.

Artists may choose to use their Way discount bonus on the following skills: Astral Perception, Cool Resolve, Enhanced Perception, Improved Ability (Artisan), Kinesics Mastery, Metabolic Control, Three-Dimensional Memory, Voice Control.

THE ATHLETE'S WAY

COST: 20 KARMA

These adepts focus their energy on only one thing: honing their bodies for maximum performance to become the absolute best at whatever sport, game, or competition they've chosen. As such they receive a +1 effective initiate grade while using the Adept Centering technique for any skill from the Athletics skill group.

Athletes may choose from the following skills for their Way discount bonus: Great Leap, Improved Ability, Improved Physical Attribute, Improved Potential, Pain Resistance, Skate, Spirit Ram, Rapid Healing, Wall Running.

THE BEAST'S WAY

COST: 20 KARMA

Adepts who follow this path are under the guidance of an animal mentor spirit, which they refer to as their totem, similar to some shamans. Through the emulation of their totem, these adepts seek to improve themselves, and like followers of the Spiritual Way, they're considered to be more spiritual than the average adept. As such, they receive all the bonuses and drawbacks associated with their personal totem, without having to purchase the Mentor Spirit Positive Quality.

Because of their unique outlook, followers of the Beast's Way have an above-average rapport with nature and gain a +1 situational bonus to all Animal Handling Tests; however, if the adept's totem is a predatory one, this bonus does not apply against animals that totem would normally consider prey. When dealing with the same animal as their totem, the adept gains an automatic +4 for any Animal Handling Tests involving them.

Followers of the Beast's Way may choose from the following skills for their discount bonus: Astral Perception, Berserk, Combat Sense, Elemental Strike, Enhanced Perception, Killing Hands, Magic Sense, Mystic Armor, Motion Sense, and Traceless Walk. In addition, Beast's Way adepts can also choose another power not in this list for the discount.

THE BURNOUT'S WAY

COST: 15 KARMA (AT CREATION; SEE TEXT FOR COST OF ACQUIRING QUALITY AT OTHER TIMES)

Those who have embraced technology in all the wrong ways or felt the need to take shortcuts to achieve power and performance find themselves on this "Way." Often they become mere shells of themselves. Most do not start as a Burnout; it's usually something that happens to them. To start this path after character creation, the adept must have lost or sacrificed at least 2 points from their Magic rating to any kind of augmentation that lowers essence.

If the Burnout previously had a true Way, then they must pay back any discounted powers by rearranging or sacrificing current powers until the values match the adept's new Magic Rating. They are, however, allowed to keep whatever metamagics they may have previously earned through initiation. To compensate for this loss, Burnouts are considered to be more compatible with augmentations: treat any standard augmentations the adept acquires after burning out as being alphaware grade for purposes of Essence loss, though not for purchase costs. (All other grades function as normal). Note that lost Essence due to new augmentations will reduce Magic as normal (p. 54, SR5).

As long as the adept still has a Magic Rating, he can still continue to initiate and gain more Magic and adept powers. Once he gains two Magic Rating points after taking the Burnout quality, he loses the quality, though he keeps the benefits gained up until that point (meaning the Essence cost of his augmentations do not change).

THE INVISIBLE WAY

COST: 20 KARMA

Master spies, infiltrators, and assassins—all are common followers of the Invisible Way. What more can be said?

Because a follower of this way generally prefers stealth to direct, open combat, bonding a focus that

enhances a physical non-combat skill costs two less Karma than normal.

Followers of the Invisible Way may choose from the following skills for their discount bonus: Blind Fighting, Combat Sense, Critical Strike, Enhanced Perception, Great Leap, Killing Hands, Motion Sense, Nerve Strike, Skate, Three-Dimensional Memory, Traceless Walk, Wall Running.

THE MAGICIAN'S WAY

COST: 20 KARMA

One of the most popular Ways for mystic adepts, the Magician's Way seeks to find balance between physical and magical abilities—or at least find what works best for the adept. Because of the time the adept spends on her sorcery and spellcasting abilities, many feel that she is not truly embracing either aspect. Adepts who practice this Way feel they are simply trying to either make the best of what they have or find the best of both worlds.

Because they do not specialize as much as other adepts (and do not receive a bonus besides the discount on Power Point cost), followers of this Way are able to choose any power they want for the discount, with the exception of Improved Reflexes.

THE SPEAKER'S WAY

COST: 20 KARMA

Often called social adepts, Speakers are some of the best faces in the biz. Adepts of the Speaker's Way are highly talented negotiators, fixers, and motivators. They use words the way a samurai uses his sword, talking themselves in and out of situations that would kill others. When it comes to changing people's minds or getting them to do something, accept no substitutes.

Speakers receive a +1 to their dice pool when using flexible signature and masking metamagical techniques. In addition, the Karma cost for bonding foci that increase their Improved Ability (Social skill) power is two less than normal.

Speakers can apply their Way discount bonuses to the following powers: Analytics, Cool Resolve, Enhanced Perception, Improved Ability (Social skill), Improved Potential (Mental or Social), Kinesics Mastery, Three-Dimensional Memory, Voice Control.

THE SPIRITUAL WAY

COST: 20 KARMA

Those who follow this path are under the guidance of a mentor spirit, similar to shamans. Through the emulation of their mentor spirit, these adepts seek to improve themselves and are considered to be more spiritual than the average adept. As such, they receive all the bonuses and drawbacks associated with their personal totem, without having to purchase the Mentor Spirit Positive Quality.

Because of their more spiritual outlook, adepts of the Spiritual Way have an above-average rapport with spirits, which conveys a +1 situational bonus to all Conjuring Tests. And when dealing with other magicians who follow the same mentor spirit, the adept gains an automatic +2 dice pool bonus for any social tests involving them.

Followers of the Spiritual Way may choose from the following skills for their discount bonus: Astral Perception, Elemental Strike, Elemental Weapon, Enhanced Perception, Killing Hands, Magic Sense, Mystic Armor. In addition, Spiritual Way adepts may choose one power from another Way's list for the discount.

THE WARRIOR'S WAY

COST: 20 KARMA

The Warrior is the type that most mundanes associate with the word adept. These elite combatants dedicate their lives to forging their bodies into lethal weapons or engines of war. Combat is their calling, and they excel at it, accomplishing through skill and magic what others use augmentations to accomplish.

Bonding a weapon focus costs two less Karma than normal for those following the Warrior's Way.

Warriors can choose from the following list of powers for their discount: Blind Fighting, Combat Sense, Counterstrike, Critical Strike, Improved Ability, Improved Potential (Physical), Killing Hands, Missile Mastery, Motion Sense, Rapid Draw.

THE IMMATERIAL TOUCH

It can happen to anyone.

Eidolon's friends consoled him after everything went south, but their words only made things worse. During the drive to his safehouse, their words echoed in his head:

Don't sweat it, chummer.

Maybe you were just tired.

Whatever the cause, it wasn't just "performance anxiety," as Ophelia had claimed. This was far deeper, something elusive just beyond the edge of his peripheral vision.

I am a summoner, Eidolon told himself upon entering his silent doss. *I summon things. That is what I do.*

If that was true, then why had no spirits answered his summons during the run? If Eidolon was *really* a summoner, he would've snagged a fire elemental without a problem, and Faust wouldn't have gotten winged. Then Eidolon could've had the elemental torch the Ming Solutions building's entire security detail. Or he could've ordered the spirit to sustain some of his spells so he could focus on other ones.

But no. Damn things wouldn't obey him. Worse still, the spirits he had tried conjuring during the run just flat-out ignored him. He'd heard old shaman tales about impolite spirits, but any spirit could still be dominated, even impolite ones.

Take a few days off, Faust had ordered once the team had escaped to safety. *Figure this out or we'll find ourselves a new summoner.*

Eidolon shook his head. Maybe he *was* just tired.

But the spirit world called to him. Instead of resting he sat lotus style at his hermetic circle. For hours he wandered astral space until the connection between his body and astral form grew tenuous.

Just as he was about to collapse back into his body, a little wisp in the shape of a newborn babe hovered before him.

Quit whining, the spirit of man said. *If you'll shut up, El Infante will perform one service for you. Deal?*

Eidolon couldn't believe his luck. *Deal,* he said. Intertwining tendrils of astral energy passed between him and the spirit, and he returned to his meat body.

Spirit, he said through their astral link, *why do none of your kind answer my summons?*

You already know why, said El Infante.

No, I don't.

Trust me, you do.

Eidolon scrunched his eyebrows. *Then ... cast a spell to compel truth from me and ask why I cannot conjure your brethren.*

Very well, El Infante said.

Eidolon momentarily felt a sensation of falling as tentacles of mana dug into his aura. The sensation quickly passed, and he shifted to the astral perception to face his accuser.

Summoner, El Infante demanded, *why do my brethren refuse to answer your calls?*

The energy of the spell yanked the words from him: *Because I treat spirits as tools rather than equals, by subjecting them to spiritual discomfort, disruption, and anything else I want. Since I'm a complete and total drekhead to spirits, every inhabitant of the metaplanes knows to avoid me.*

Eidolon gasped and collapsed back into meatspace. The loosening of his own astral presence meant El Infante was departing, the conditions of the service having been met.

Wait! Eidolon shouted into the ether. *Tell me how to fix this!*

Silence answered him. The spirit was gone.

A lot of folks—including chummers with doctorates in thaumaturgy or other impressive line items on their résumés—think they know a lot of concrete facts about spirits and the spirit world. However, none of 'em can hold a candle to Man-of-Many-Names. Believe it or not, he's been in this line of work even longer than I have, and I wouldn't be surprised if he's spent more time in astral space during his lifetime than he has the physical plane. He literally wrote the book on spirits—a number of times.

I don't care whether you know a part-time conjurer or if you've got a few decades of experience commanding astral beings. Unless you fancy being on the business end of a slotted-off spirit or finding yourself in arrears to the spirit world, you owe it to yourself to read what Man-of-Many-Names has to say.

» Bull

THE NATURE OF SPIRITS

POSTED BY: MAN-OF-MANY-NAMES

So you want to know about spirits? For starters, anything you think you might know about spirits or the spirit world—well, you can forget it. Literally. It's probably all wrong anyhow. If you have a printed tome from some dubious institution of so-called higher learning, go ahead and heave it into an incinerator somewhere. If you have Matrix-based books on spirits or conjuration, go ahead and delete them. I'll wait.

Seriously. I'm not kidding. The first step to understanding spirits is letting go of preconceptions and starting over from the ground floor. I once had a copy of *Shamans and the Spirit World*, a textbook first published in 2019 or so. Book's a collector's items these days—it'd fetch a few thousand to the right bidder—but I burned that book to hell when I realized it was time to move on. Since then, I've compiled numerous books about spirits, and I've burned or deleted each and every one of them after something I thought was true turned out to be false (or only occasionally true). In fact, I fully expect this little document you're reading to become obsolete or disproven sometime in the near future.

Does this mean spirits and the spirit world are far more mutable than we ever thought they were? Possibly. But it's just as probable that the spirit world stays exactly the same and it is we who change, that we are the ones unable to see the underlying spiritual workings of the astral plane. The spirit world is like physical matter. At first the Greeks thought the world was made up of the four Aristotelian elements—air, earth, fire, and water—but then scientists discovered molecules, then learned that molecules further divided into atoms. In fact, the term "atom," meaning "indivisible," betrays the hubris of those who named it. Imagine the scientific community's surprise upon learning that the "uncuttable" atom had subatomic parts, and that those subatomic particles could be even further divided into quarks and other drek. The rabbit hole just keeps going and going.

Such is the spirit world. Every time we learn something new and claim some aspect of spirits is "indivisible," we find that the spiritual "atom" can be divided over and over again. This further proves we are indeed children peering into a vast infinity that we will likely never fully comprehend. On the bright side, some of us children are more adult in our understanding than others. I will do what I can to mature your education further.

» Ah, there's the Man-of-Many-Names I know; the whole understandable vernacular thing was beginning to throw me.
» Balladeer

» Always bodes well when someone regarded as an expert in his field admits to us that everything he knows is wrong.
» Clockwork

» *Ipse se nihil scire id unum sciat.*
» Man-of-Many-Names

» *Gesundheit?*
» Slamm-0!

» "I know one thing: that I know nothing." —Socrates
» Man-of-Many-Names

Okay, so you've incinerated, deleted, or otherwise destroyed all of your books filled with fallacies and outright lies about spirits? Good. Now we can get down to biz.

WHAT SPIRITS ARE

Your average "expert" on spirits will likely start off telling you what spirits are. I'm not going to do that because that's like trying to explain color to a blind person. Instead, it'd be more useful to tell you what spirits *aren't*.

Spirits aren't mineral solvents or distilled alcohol—some moron back in the olden days just slapped the term "spirit" on those substances, so we're kinda stuck with it. (The only reason I mention this is because I've known more than a few imbeciles who actually thought getting drunk would help them see into the spirit world. Turned out it did, but not in the way they intended, as they all died from alcohol poisoning. Amateurs.)

Spirits also aren't a cold wind that makes the hair on your neck stand on end, and they're certainly not the sensation that someone walked over your grave. Those are just biological reactions to things playing tricks with your brain. A manifested spirit passing through a meat body can leave someone with a strange sensation, but there aren't any graves involved there, just a spiritual entity sharing physical space with you for a short time. And for the record, most spirits don't like invading the physical space of another if they can help it. Possession is a completely different story, though: if you're an unwilling vessel, then grave-shivers are the least of your worries.

Spirits also aren't ghosts—at least not in the pre-Awakening, haunted-house sense. If you wander a dilapidated house in the middle of the night and see some spectral thing you think looks like someone's great-great-grandpappy or an American Civil War soldier or whatnot, that's not a spirit—at least I don't *think* it's a spirit. There's a pretty big grey area there. Spirit activity can be documented and vetted, whereas most "ghost" activity falls under domain of anecdote and hearsay.

The fact that some spirits claim to be the ghosts of former living beings muddies the water somewhat, but in many instances those spirits have been proven to be liars. If we take away from this the fact that spirits cannot be trusted to reveal the truth of their own nature, then we have at least one valuable lesson.

WHERE SPIRITS COME FROM

Much like what spirits are, defining where spirits come from is a complicated question. So let's take a similar approach and talk about where spirits *aren't* from. A spirit can influence, be influenced by, or inhabit the physical plane, but it does not originate from there. Spirits are astral beings, and astral beings cannot suddenly decide to hop over into the physical plane and remain there permanently, leaving their astral nature

behind. A good indicator of the origin of spirits is they spend about ninety-nine percent of their existence in astral space unless commanded or compelled to do otherwise. A spirit spending too much time out of its plane of origin is like a metahuman spending more than a few hours in the Challenger Deep: it's possible, but metahumans need all kinds of provisions to last at those depths, whereas water-breathing creatures accustomed to the pressure at those depths don't need anything special to survive. Spirits *can* survive for extended periods on the physical plane, but it is not their default state, and such free spirits are the exception rather than the rule.

So spirits are from the astral plane, but what exactly does that mean? There are many schools of thought on the subject, with no one school holding dominance over the others, so maybe they're all right in a sense. Maybe they're all wrong. Maybe they are right and wrong at the same time, depending on your perspective, timing, and current plane of residence.

One such school claims spirits don't really *live* on the astral plane, as least not in the same terms as flora and fauna live in the physical plane. This belief holds that spirits aren't alive at all, that a spirit is simply an astral construct of the conjurer's will made manifest on the astral plane. According to this idea, a conjurer sends out a portion of his will to shape astral space, instilling it with its own kind of "life," which dissipates whenever its services are expended—what proponents of this thinking call "anthropomorphic willpower attenuation." Many support this argument with the contention that materialized spirits belonging to certain traditions always tend to have a certain look about them: Hermetic spirits often appear like the raw element of their favored metaplane, whereas shamanic spirits tend to look more wild or ragged along the edges, and spirits from possession traditions don't even materialize on the physical plane at all. In fact, some claim they can identify the tradition of a spirit's conjurer just by looking at a spirit's aura or materialized form.

The belief that spirits are willpower constructs makes for some interesting dinner conversation, but that's as far as it goes. Think about it like this: if a magician sees his conjurations as manifestations of his own consciousness, then he's basically arguing with himself during a particularly difficult conjuring, he's making friends with himself when he controls a spirit, and when his spirit goes uncontrolled, the poor slot has literally lost his mind. The idea has *some* merit, however, as it explains the differences in spirits conjured by various traditions. Personality or partner? Intellect or entity? This age-old debate probably won't get solved anytime in the near future. I believe shamans conjure different-looking spirits than hermetics because it reflects how metahuman society works. Think of a corp exec: She's not going to be seen in the company of street thugs—at least not willingly—and those same street thugs aren't going to be hobnobbing with the social elite at the opera anytime soon. People's social circles tend to have some degree of similarities of appearance to each other.

Another school of thought believes that spirits are born from the fabric of the metaplanes. I won't get into too much detail about the metaplanes themselves—as I understand, Magister, an old chummer from the Shadowland days, has a forthcoming upload called *Aetherology* about that—but each spirit has an affinity for a specific metaplane. According to this idea, if a spirit has an affinity for, say, the metaplane of air, then the spirit was born from the astral energies of that particular plane. However, a spirit taking a liking to a particular metaplane doesn't mean it was born there, per se: I have never seen a metaplanar womb giving birth to astral entities of any kind. In my own limited experience—for I am but one single man (albeit with many names) with but one lifetime—I believe spirits develop an affinity for a specific plane as they mature or evolve over time. For example, a firefighter is not born a firefighter: She is born metahuman and develops the drive to fight fires and arsonists as she develops. Someone who likes hot springs was not necessarily born in a hot spring.

Then there is the belief—the one I most commonly espouse—that spirits aren't even born at all. They always are, always have been, and always will be. They saw the creation of the manasphere in the First World and will still be around to witness the mana spike that initiates the Two-hundredth World. A disrupted spirit can eventually return to its conjurer after a given time, so as far as I know, if you permanently destroy a spirit in its favored metaplane—well, congratulations: you just destroyed something that witnessed the dawn of time.

But then again, I could be wrong about that too. Like I said, this whole book will probably end up deleted at some point.

HOW SPIRITS BEHAVE

I'll be the first to admit that, aside from a few specifics, the behavior of spirits—what they do and how they do it—baffles me, and given how long I've been in this trade, that should tell you something. I think it's better that I start you from a blank template than I fill you with faux knowledge. Far be it from me to let your expectations get shattered at the worst possible time because an alien being from an alien place with an alien mind had the audacity to do something I did not expect.

That said, there are a number of spirit behaviors that are somewhat predictable in the sense that (most) dogs bark, (most) snakes slither, and (most) birds fly.

LIVING ON THE ASTRAL

Unless ordered otherwise, spirits spend the vast majority of their existence on the astral plane. They can brave the physical plane for as long as necessary, but from what I gather they don't enjoy doing so (though again, there are exceptions), much as being in a space suit in zero G for long periods isn't exactly comfortable for metahumans.

Some spirits, such as watchers, can't even materialize, so they inhabit astral space one hundred percent of the time. On the other hand, spirits unable to inhabit meat space in any way can still manifest. A manifested spirit can't directly affect the physical plane to, say, pick up an object or trip someone with its leg. Of course, materialized spirits are dual-natured beings, so even when they're in the physical plane, their essence remains in astral space.

The most common question I get about spirits is what they do all day in the astral plane. First, "all day" is a misnomer, since time is more malleable and fluid than the worldwide exchange rate for nuyen. Second, spirits don't have to *do* anything. I've seen some drift lazily through the astral and the metaplanes like bits of ocean particulate carried about in a current, but I've also seen spirits moving so fast that they don't even seem to have a destination in mind apart from making undue haste. So the answer to what spirits do on the astral is a resounding "I don't know." Am I starting to sound like a broken audio file yet?

OBEDIENCE

Regardless of what you believe about the nature of spirits, once fact remains true: a spirit who enters into a transaction with a conjurer will be obedient to that conjurer unless something prematurely breaks that connection. Why obedience occurs remains a matter of debate. A hermetic mage will probably tell you spirits are subservient to conjurers due to their belief that metahumanity dominates the spirit world in the metaphysical hierarchy. I prefer to believe that the reason spirits obey orders from conjurers—even orders harmful to themselves—might be due to a couple of different things.

In general, I believe spirits are far nobler creatures than we metahumans. Once a spirit enters into a conjurer's bargain, they stick to the letter of the bargain rather than the spirit of it (no pun intended). A metahuman can break a contract at any time, but a spirit either refuses to or is incapable of doing so. I'm not going so far as to say a spirit can't lie, per se—they can, and I've got a few physical, mental, and astral scars to prove it—but it seems spirits don't want to sink to metahuman levels when it comes to astral transactions. Or they are restrained somehow, compelled to obedience, but that does not align with my way of thinking.

- ⦿ Spirits can lie? Are you sure?
- ⦿ Pistons

- ⦿ A loyal spirit, like a mentor or ally spirit, probably isn't going to, but a spirit not under your control has no obligation to tell the truth. Why do you ask?
- ⦿ Frosty

- No reason. Asking for a friend.
- Pistons

Another possible explanation for spirits showing potentially painful deference to conjurers might be the natural laws of astral space, which magicians are still trying to catalog. Some pre-Awakening stories tell of contracts between people and magical beings, and those contracts were binding regardless of what either party wanted, which usually led to one party getting a "be careful what you wish for" kind of moral to the story. The contracts in those stories are based on the underlying, unbreakable laws of magic. Most of them were fairy tales retold by people with no real conception of magic, but there was still a grain of truth to them, as these same laws often apply to the post-Awakening world as well. However, like any "truth" about spirits, there are still exceptions. A spirit can still attempt to break free when its conjurer is knocked out or killed. When a spirit departs in this way, the spirit is technically in breach of contract but suffers no ill effects. To some this supports the theory that a spirit is simply a manifestation of the conjurer's consciousness, while others say it shows that the conjurer's consciousness exerts some degree of control on the spirit; when the consciousness is gone, so is the control. And the spirit.

POSSESSION AND INHABITATION

Your average spirit is an independent entity that uses its own form as a means of getting around or interacting with meat space, but there are two similar spirit behaviors that provide alternative means of interacting with metahumanity.

Possession is similar to how old flatvids regarding demons and the like portrayed it: A spirit possessing a vessel—either an object or a living being—can control that vessel like someone driving a car. Among conjurers, the two most common suppositions about possession are either A) that certain spirits prefer or require possession of a vessel in order to touch the physical plane, or B) that all spirits are capable of possession and the only ones that evidence that capability are those summoned by possession-tradition conjurers.

Some regard possession as a definitive evil, but the evil's not the procedure—it's in the method. Possessing an object isn't evil in the traditional sense, because it's just a *thing*, but a spirit possessing a living vessel can be construed as evil if the vessel is unprepared—i.e., unwilling or unexpected. But then again, evil is not inherently in the tools; it's in how you use those tools.

Inhabitation, on the other hand, has the capacity to be truly sinister. It's like possession in that it also requires a vessel, but that's about where the similarity ends. Whereas possession treats the vessel like a truck, inhabitation treats a living vessel like a house with someone

BRYAN SYM

already living in it. The spirit inhabits this house by killing the owner and rifling through all of the stuff he left behind. Depending on how the inhabitation procedure went, sometimes the spirit will redecorate the exterior of the house while retaining all of the original owner's mementos. Other times, the inhabitation attempt burns the entire house down—souvenirs and all—resulting in a "normal" spirit capable of materializing. If you run into an inhabitation merge that's more "house" than spirit, you probably won't be able to tell it's a spirit unless you assense its aura (assuming, of course, that nothing is masking its aura). On the other hand, a merge that's more spirit than "house" is probably going to scream "spirit" even at first glance. No matter how you slice it, the essence of the vessel's original occupant is destroyed during an inhabitation merge.

- If you ever cross paths with an "inhabitation merge" that claims to be a friend of yours or spouts some other sympathetic bullshit, run the fuck the other direction. It's a trick. Personalities don't ever survive a merge, no matter what kind of lies the merge tries to tell you.
- Sticks

- If nothing survives the merge, then inhabitation spirits—like bugs—are really good at mimicking part of the original vessel's aura and making the merge look like a true blending of the two.
- Ethernaut

- I wouldn't put anything past them.
- Sticks

WHAT SPIRITS WANT

Conjurers who believe spirits are discrete entities with their own goals and desires realize that spirits don't do anything for free. How many free-of-charge favors would you do for a chummer before you start telling him to slot off? It's not just a case of "Hey, spirit, I want something from you." It's more a case of "Hey, spirit, I'd like you to do something for me, and in return I'll give you this." In any case, like many spirit-related topics, what a spirit wants can change with the tides.

TRANSACTIONS: A GIFT FOR A GIFT

The biggest question that conjuration scholars have attempted for decades to solve is why spirits obey us. What hold does metahumanity—little more than infantile invaders to the astral plane—have over astral beings? Plain and simple, the conjurer-spirit relationship is a symbiotic, two-way relationship. A conjurer needs something he can only get from a spirit, and a spirit needs something it can only receive from the conjurer.

Each attempt at conjuration is in some ways similar to runners meeting with their fixer or Mr. Johnson. They meet at an established location, set forth terms, broker a deal, negotiate a price. Then an exchange takes place, either in terms of money, services, goods, favors, promises, or other intangibles. Experienced conjurers will attest that the same thing occurs when a magician calls upon a spirit: they arrange a "meet" on the astral, negotiate a price, and either seal the deal or walk away.

Whether you realize it or not, every conjurer-spirit agreement in the spirit world utilizes a currency that can only be spent in astral space, and each transaction occurs in the span of a millisecond or less of meat-space time. Some conjurers aren't even aware a transaction takes place: they call a spirit, and the spirit obeys as if that's what it was meant to do. Only foolish conjurers fail to realize the coin they spend to get this favor.

So what does a conjurer give a spirit in exchange for its services? Some religious groups that refuse to conjure spirits would have the general populace believe we conjurers offer up our souls, our firstborn sons, or some other nonsense to make spirits obey us. The answer is far less sensational. Spirits, as astral beings, don't feed in the same way as we meat creatures do, but the law of conservation of energy can be applied to astral space. That means spirits still need to gain sustenance from *somewhere*. Now, I hear what you're thinking: Spirits aren't astral vampires. True, but what we give spirits in exchange for their services are things we won't even miss. For example, a spirit might be content to obey for the astral equivalent of a strand of hair or a clipped fingernail. Don't ask me exactly what an "astral fingernail clipping" is because I really couldn't tell you. It's intangible, even on the astral plane. Whenever I barter with a spirit for its services, my astral form feels infinitesimally lighter, if astral forms can be said to have weight. Bear in mind that some spirits demand steeper prices for their services, such as one's life essence or karmic surplus, but none of those are potentially life threatening unless the conjurer allows them to be.

THE GOLDEN RULE

Okay, so spirits want some form of astral energy in return for performing services. But what *else* do they desire?

A spirit isn't just some mindless, astral-parity machine. Like a kind of loyal pet—although I hesitate to use the term "pet" for *any* spirit—it remains by the conjurer's side regardless of the punishment inflicted upon it. Once the services are expended or the bond dissipates, an abused spirit departs from the conjurer as soon as possible. Some types of spirits—most notably ally spirits or bound free spirits— attempt to flee at the first available opportunity. From this we can infer that spirits in general don't appreciate being mistreated.

The Golden Rule of Spirits is just the same as it is in the Bible, the writings of Confucius, the Mahabharata, and more: treat a spirit how you would like to be treated. You can certainly mistreat spirits if you want—I won't stop you—but bear in mind that karma is a complete bitch, and you deserve everything you get.

There are many ways to cause spirits pain or discomfort. For those arguing that spirits can't feel pain because astral beings lack a nervous system, I challenge you to try one or more of the things in the list below and see whether your life improves. For the record, this list isn't meant to give you ideas so you can go out and find new and inventive ways to be a scourge of spirit world. I'm leaving this list here so that you can *avoid* these things—or prevent others from doing them. This isn't an all-inclusive list, so if you stumble across an item not listed here, be sure to let me know so I can verify it.

- **Disruption:** When a spirit is disrupted by being knocked out in combat or by intersecting an astral barrier that wins the contest, that spirit's astral energies are forcibly returned to its native metaplane. The spirit can return after a few weeks, usually three or four.
- **Post-banishment conjuring:** Spirits get banished all the time. Sever the link between summoner and spirit, and all services owed become forfeit. However, if you banish someone's spirit and then immediately demand services from it, that spirit is going to start out disliking you from the get-go. To a spirit, banishment is like being rabbit-punched. Hit a guy in the base of the skull, and you know he's not going to be happy when you point a gun at his head and demand he do something, even if you offer to pay him.
- **Binding (all types):** Most spirits resist binding attempts, because being bound is a far more complicated astral transaction than a simple gift-for-a-gift exchange, and more often than not, spirits end up on the short end of the stick. Bound spirits obey their conjurers just like an unbound spirit will, but the longer and more often a spirit remains bound, the more restless it becomes. Repeatedly binding the same spirit over and over again is akin to forcibly keeping someone awake for several days on end. The problem gets worse when a conjurer uses long-term binding or "fettering." These types of binding require the magician to sacrifice karmic energies and weave them into the spirit, something deeply distressing for the spirit.
- **Resist Drain:** Having to deal with spellcasting Drain at the wrong time is a huge inconvenience, so it's tempting to pass Drain off to a spirit under your control. Spirits really hate this. When you shunt Drain to a spirit, the mana backlash tears through the spirit's essence without any filter. We metahumans at least have a meat filter with which to absorb Drain, which is why we feel tired or fatigued—or pass out entirely, in worst cases—when Drain hits. If you've ever

been shocked by live electricity for more than a few seconds, then you have at least some idea of what it's like to pass Drain to a spirit.
- **Spell binding:** This is perhaps the easiest way to earn black marks in the spirit world. When you pass the sustainment of a spell to a spirit to maintain for an extended period of time, the spirit must funnel its own astral energies into the spell. This is fine for the short term, but eventually the spirit must permanently invest itself into the spell, causing the spirit to weaken as time passes. The inherent danger of spell binding is that a spirit forced to exhaust all of its astral essence this way dissipates permanently, and no number of metaplanar quests will ever be able to recover it.

๏ One thing Many-Names doesn't list here is corruption. If you expose a spirit to toxic elements, you run the risk of mutating the spirit. Not only are toxic spirits in a constant state of agony, these abominations are incredibly dangerous, especially if they become uncontrolled. And somewhere, deep inside, they completely loathe what they have become.
๏ Winterhawk

๏ From what I understand, mana voids and other negative background counts can also hurt spirits. Once saw a chummer willfully expose a spirit to an area nearly devoid of mana, and even though I'm a mundane, I heard sounds and felt feelings that still give me nightmares. Felt like I was like watching someone drown in the ocean or die of decompression in space.
๏ 2XL

ASTRAL DENIZENS

Spirits can also fall into other categories beyond what metaplane they happen to fancy. Of course, these categorizations are just as much in flux as everything else in these books I write and burn and rewrite. For now, all of the following spirits I'm going to talk about are worth discussion, regardless of whether I'll delete these entries six months from now.

And bear in mind that if you think something's missing from this list, that doesn't necessarily mean I don't believe it exists. It might just mean you and I see it differently (or I might've deleted it awhile back and never got around to re-adding it). The spirit world is changing every day. The magicians of the Sixth World have been conjuring, commanding, and manipulating spirits for sixty-plus years, and don't think that our clumsy efforts and toddler-like muddling haven't changed that plane. Just as we have been growing accustomed to spirits, so spirits have been growing accustomed to us, and it wouldn't surprise me if that familiarity means spirits change how they present themselves to us just to mess with us. So remember: Nothing is set in stone.

GREAT FORM SPIRITS

Regular spirits of the conjured kind suffice for most people's needs. But what about when you have a big, grandiose job? A regular, run-of-the-mill spirit cannot take care of the mammoth tasks you have in store. You want a great form spirit.

Great form spirits are well named, as they are larger than regular spirits in essentially every conceivable way. If you conjure a spirit of water and have it literally rain down on the opposition, then the best your spirit can do is give your obstacles their own personal rain cloud. Now, if you took your rain-cloud spirit and swapped it with a great form spirit, then you could order up a super-cell storm—one of those storm fronts so dark, black, and massive that it feels like the world is coming to an end when it slowly rolls overhead. Granted, you can always scale back the supercell to something more manage-able, but you get the idea. To reiterate: When you want to light a fireplace or a bonfire, you conjure a normal fire spirit, but when you absolutely *must* burn down an entire forest, you want a great form fire spirit.

A great form spirit results from an initiate using Invo-cation metamagic to let a normal spirit use mana to mul-tiply its own astral energies like a magnifying glass. Since only initiates can conjure great form spirits, I wouldn't worry so much about your average wage mage sudden-ly summoning a hurricane from the depths of their own mediocrity or triggering a 9.1-Richter-scale earthquake in the middle of a firefight. On the other hand, great form spirits can be difficult to control, so if you acciden-tally burn down or flood your whole neighborhood, use your last moments to reflect on the flaw of hubris. We all have to learn our lessons.

MENTOR SPIRITS

Ask most magicians what the most important spirit is, and mentor spirits will rank pretty high among the an-swers. Mentor spirit, totem, spirit guide—all of them are essentially the same, no matter what magical path you follow. Not all magicians have mentor spirits, but those who do tend to have more focus regarding their magic. Mentors can represent many different things—a force of nature, an ideal, a mission—but all of them lead their adherents down a specific path, sometimes both figuratively and literally.

Mentor spirits are difficult to pin down. They appear when and however they wish, they leave no trace of their passage on the astral, and in most cases none but the adherent can see them. A magician cannot directly control his or her mentor, and just what the mentor gets out of the relationship is unclear, but the magician re-

ceives the advantages —and accompanying disadvantages—all the same.

Don't believe me about control? Try to conjure your mentor spirit right now. Go on; I'll wait. You can't? No surprise. Or maybe try to banish your mentor, send it back to where it came from. Oh, you can't? Well then. That's because a mentor never offers to performs services, and it never owes services to anyone, so it cannot be banished.

Many researchers doubt mentor spirits are real. They say that they are a figment of a magician's subconscious, or that astral space is molding itself to the magician's mind. Here's what I have to say about that: The ocean can't grow a mouth and tell you what its salinity or pH is. A mound of rock isn't going to tell you whether it's hiding gold or gems. You cannot commune with yourself and tell yourself things you do not currently know—yet mentor spirits reveal such things to magicians all the time.

My belief is that mentor spirits are all-encompassing astral entities who have lived so long they know how to transcend the laws of astral space and appear to have abilities that no other spirit possesses.

AVATAR SPIRITS

Ever been walking down a street and seen something or someone out of place that reminded you of your totem or mentor spirit? Ever had a strange spirit lead you to something important? That was probably an avatar spirit.

Avatar spirits walk a very strange line. At times they exhibit qualities of mentor spirits, free spirits, or summoned spirits, sometimes all at once. Every avatar I've seen or heard about takes a shape familiar to one's mentor spirit. They can also appear and disappear at whim like mentors, and they cannot be conjured or banished like normal spirits.

Many see avatars as an astral extension of one's mentor or a magician's subconscious shaping of spirit energies. On the other hand, it's just as likely that an avatar spirit is subservient to a mentor spirit, and the reason it cannot be conjured or banished is because it owes the mentor an infinite number of services.

FREE SPIRITS

People have a lot of misconceptions about free spirits. Thanks to sensationalized newsvid stories and trid productions that err on the side of ridiculous, your average mundane thinks free spirits are bogeymen that could be masquerading as her best friend or could appear out of nowhere and drag her soul to hell or some other such nonsense. In all honesty, free spirits aren't all that special when compared to normal spirits. The main difference between conjured spirits and free spirits is a free spirit decided not to return to its favored metaplane after fulfilling its services or being freed via banishment, disruption, or otherwise.

All free spirits have some reason—whatever it may be—for wanting to stay and interact with the physical plane. Free spirits can and do act like any other spirit, yet they are beholden to no master but themselves. Since free spirits are indeed free in the conjuring sense of the word, they can spend as much time in the physical plane as they want.

Now, you may be asking, why don't non-free spirits show up in droves in meat space? The truth is, no one knows for sure. Since astral space is a spirit's native domain, free spirits are like the Jacques Cousteaus of the spirit world, exploring the depths of the physical plane. Once certain spirits have a taste of our native plane, they want to stay and have a look around.

The problem with free spirits is they're remarkably difficult to get rid of. If you want to make a free spirit leave a particular area, first you need to study the spirit long enough to determine its metaplanar affinity. This isn't as easy as it sounds; many free spirits know how to mask their auras, and when accessing their favored metaplane, they often take paths we don't know. Second, you have to discover the spirit's true name, which is an abstract representation of the spirit's essence. This involves either traveling to the spirit's metaplane and undertaking a metaplanar quest (difficult), or attempting to discover the true name from observing the spirit (more difficult). A true name, once learned, can be turned into that spirit's formula, and anyone who holds this formula can bind that spirit.

To permanently prevent a normal disrupted spirit from ever reappearing again, you need to destroy it in its favored metaplane. To permanently destroy a disrupted free spirit, however, you need to destroy a copy of its spirit formula and hope that does the trick. Sometimes it works, sometimes it doesn't. Hard to tell unless that spirit shows up again later seeking revenge, a partnership, or some mix of the two. Free spirits are often difficult to understand.

That said, I currently group free spirits into four rough categories.

HELPFUL

Few free spirits are reliably supportive of metahumanity, I'm afraid. **Warden spirits** are helpful only under certain conditions and they are the only spirits in this category. These types make protecting the earth's environment their primary goal, so woe be to any toxic or corrupted magicians that stand in their way. If you're an eco-activist or are fighting against some known polluter—be it metahuman or corp—then you might be able to convince a warden to help you. But if you're the opposite, you'd better hope your affairs are in order.

Also keep in mind that twisted versions of warden spirits do exist, and they protect their corrupted, toxic environment just as fiercely as non-corrupted wardens do.

- Every warden spirit I've encountered wouldn't give me the time of day at first. If you want to help a warden or gain its support for anything, be prepared to make a good-faith demonstration of your commitment to the warden's mission, or you can forget it. And wardens have a pretty big imagination as to what constitutes an acceptable demonstration.
- Ecotope

HARMFUL

Unfortunately, there are far more hurtful free spirit types than anything else. Some might sound scary to mundanes, but just make sure you've got some spirits or able sorcerers watching your back.

Shadow spirits are like the serial killers and sociopaths of the spirit world, interested solely in malevolence. Now, I like to think of myself as a very pro-spirit person, and I give weird spirit behavior a lot of leeway, but I have no desire to drift down the same astral roads, or even astral planes, as these monstrosities. Shadows are like a disturbed child who snaps a small dog's neck and sneers while watching the light go out of its eyes. I'd rather bind a toxic spirit than deal with shadows, because toxics can at least be reasoned with (sort of). Most free spirits tend to have some grasp on morality, but shadows do not have a moral compass of any kind.

If you encounter a shadow, I suggest one of two things: either run away as far as you can—which probably won't work—or find a magician capable of discovering the free spirit's true name and destroying that abomination for good.

- Shadows get a BTL-like rush out of pain and suffering, so sometimes they employ metahuman agents to bring them victims. I once uncovered an extensive underground slave trade that was designed solely for providing victims for the spirit. The most disturbing thing about that particular shadow was it literally scared all of its victims to death.
- Winterhawk

Trickster spirits, on the other hand, only partially belong in the harmful category. These types of spirits see the physical world and its inhabitants as a playground. Problems occur when a particular spirit's sense of amusement takes a turn for the macabre. I've seen the whole gamut of tricksters in my day, and their behavior can range from mostly benign—chasing dogs around the park, making odd sounds to confuse passersby—to deadly—flicking people off the tops of dangerous precipices, scaring slightly inebriated drivers into driving into utility poles—and everything in between. Your average, non-lethal trickster is merely a nuisance, but even nuisance activity can turn deadly if the spirit plays pranks when you've got bullets flying at you.

A trickster's particular brand of humor might not make sense to you, and vice versa. If you want to try reasoning with one, find someone with a darker sense of humor than yours.

- I once saw a trickster spirit at a comedy club's open-mike night. Man, that thing absolutely *killed*—and I don't mean that in the stabby clown sense.
- Slamm-0!

Vanguard spirits are the first line of defense against anything that threatens other spirits. Anywhere you find a concentrated population of spirits, odds are a vanguard or three is among them. Some believe vanguards are scouts for a future spirit invasion of the physical plane, going so far as to trick us into conjuring more spirits or twisting other spirits for their own ends, but that's just the conspiracy theorists talking.

Vanguards don't give two figs about metahumanity, so approach them with caution. They'll give even spirit-friendly people the cold shoulder because these spirits place the needs of spiritkind above all else, even if it means proactive, belligerent behavior.

VARIABLE

Animae/animi are free spirits that closely identify with metahumanity in one way or another. They generally take the materialized form of a man (an animus) or woman (an anima), and depending on the situation, they might present a different metatype than you saw them wear on a previous occasion. I have also encountered free spirits that assumed aspects of both genders—don't ask me what to call these. The important factor here is these spirits explore our society like mapmakers would explore an unknown wilderness.

Because of their connection to metahumanity, animae and animi can be just as moral or immoral as any random person, so they can be helpful, harmful, or completely indifferent to a particular metahuman plight. To help them understand their obsession, most animae/animi take on a personal crusade, which can be small or big in scope, depending on the spirit. If you share a particular spirit's crusade, it might agree to join forces with you, but woe betide he who opposes a spirit's mission.

Your average anima/animus has an unmistakable spiritlike look to it even when materialized, but there are notable exceptions. For example, a Yamatetsu shareholder named Buttercup managed to hide her identity for *eight years* before she outed herself back in late 2050. So if you think someone you know might be a free spirit, maybe they are …

Mimic spirits also walk the razor's edge between being helpful or dangerous due to their desire to copy specific aspects of metahuman behavior, particularly vices. A mimic who appreciates food is harmless compared to, say, one driven by bloodlust or carnal predation. No one is quite sure what these spirits gain from their behavior, as—strictly speaking—materialized spirits that aren't possessing or inhabiting a living vessel lack taste buds, endocrine or reproductive systems, central nervous systems, or any of the other things a metahuman needs to indulge in and enjoy various activities. Most mimics go through the motions rather than actually enjoy the vice in question, so it's more a case of "monkey see, monkey pretend."

Now, some mimics emulate more admirable metahuman traits, such as love, compassion, and justice, but sadly these are the exception rather than the rule. Even among spirits, depravity holds a far stronger attraction than nobility.

BENIGN

Observer spirits are a new curiosity of mine. They do little more than watch the physical plane and that's it. They don't report to any other spirits, interact with the physical plane, or get involved with metahuman affairs—at least not in any observable way. An observer spirit simply plants its astral recliner, sits back, and watches without even the courtesy of inviting you to share an after dinner sherry.

If you want to try getting an observer spirit to acknowledge you in any way, you clearly appreciate impossible challenges. Might as well pull up your own recliner, because you won't be going anywhere for awhile.

* So that explains the weird, seemingly catatonic spirit I stumbled on not too long ago. It just lingered near the fringes of this burnt-out forest, like it was … waiting for something. Creepy as hell.

  Make no mistake, if you poke one of these "observers" hard enough, they will retaliate.
* Jimmy No

ALLY SPIRITS

Ally spirits are akin to familiars from old fairy tales: the cat that follows the witch around, the raven that sits on the witch doctor's shoulder. An ally can take many different forms, depending on the conjurer's needs, magical tradition, and so forth. Allies can have normal, materializing-spirit behavior, or they can possess or inhabit vessels. For example, in my day I've seen an ally that possessed a magician's fedora, so she always carried her ally around. I've also seen dogs, cats, wolves, eagles, bears, and even Awakened critters possessed by ally spirits. The sky is literally the limit.

Shaping and conjuring an ally is a time-consuming process. First, the initiate must specify the spirit's potency, appearance, and abilities; from this he can create the ally's spirit formula. Next, he begins conjuring the spirit. During the ritual, the magician must offer the spirit an amount of Karma in order to bind it in a way far deeper than any other binding method. If the ritual is successful, the ally springs into existence under control of the conjurer. Its services are effectively unlimited, and it begins its partnership with a state of absolute loyalty to its summoner.

Although an ally starts out like a lost puppy willing to do anything for its master, it is just like any other spirit in the long run. Treat it as a partner, and it'll follow you until you send the old watering pail flying with your boot. However, if you abuse your ally too much, the next time you get knocked unconscious, it will likely try to escape your control.

* Be nice to your allies, people. I once watched a guy mistreat his ally, and after he got nearly beaten to death in a bar fight one day, his ally broke free and decided to stick around as a trickster spirit just to get some revenge. Damn thing would scare the living daylights out of him in the middle of the night. When he tried to destroy the thing, it backfired. I never heard from him again.
* Sunshine

OTHER SPIRIT PHENOMENA

In the spirit world, not everything fits into neat little boxes. Some things just don't make sense, regardless of how anyone else tries to explain them. I'm at that age where trying to explain something that defies explanation just isn't worth it, so take these things at face value. A list of spirit phenomena could fill a whole library, so I'll just mention a few.

ASTRAL ECHOES

Hackers commonly swap stories about "e-ghosts"—digital personalities of people who became trapped in the Matrix during the Crash of '64. . Astral echoes are, for lack of a better definition, the spirit analog of e-ghosts. These echoes tend to focus on one specific concept ad nauseam, be it an emotion, a person, an event, and so on. Good luck trying to get one of these to owe you some services, because they're not all put together. These things probably resulted from mundanes that went through an astral rift and got lost in astral space until only these echoes remained.

GHOSTS

In any form, ghosts look like a stiff breeze might disrupt them. They appear faint, like tenth-generation copies of a spirit, but they pay no heed to summoners trying to conjure them. Could they be astral representations of the dead? Maybe. Maybe not. No matter how long I've looked, I've yet to find my grandfather in astral space.

WILD SPIRITS

Sometimes spirits manifest or materialize on the physical plane without being summoned, but they don't have a strong enough aura to be considered free spirits. These wild spirits wander about, sometimes in search of something, sometimes slack-jawed as though they've been donkey-kicked. Many think wild spirits just wandered across the planar barrier by accident, like whales who got themselves washed up on a beach and have no idea how to get back to the ocean. Others think that they might have originated from some plane we don't even know about, which would explain why some of these spirits believe that *we* are figments of *their* imaginations.

SELLING
ONE'S SOUL

Runners are chock-full of pithy sayings about how we should go about our affairs. "Never deal with a dragon." "Never trust an elf." I would like to suggest an addition: "Never negotiate with a spirit."

You're certainly welcome to try, but spirits know how the world works better than we do, and they're far more patient than the boulder that bathes in the moving stream. When a spirit gives you an offer, it knows it can wait until you give in to its demands. So, if a spirit offers you something and the exchange sounds favorable, it probably isn't, but your chances of getting an improved second offer are nil.

Spirits can offer someone anything, but here are a few things that recur frequently.

KARMIC EXCHANGE

The exception to spirits offering unfavorable terms applies to Karma, that intangible that makes the world go 'round. Free spirits *love* Karma, and they'll do anything they can to get it, even if it means having to steal it. Karma is like a wondrous and rare delicacy that a spirit cannot obtain for itself. So when a spirit asks for part of your karmic essence, know that it's a seller's market. On the other hand, if you drive up the price of your virtue too high, the spirit will just leave and find someone else. So, if you really want what the spirit is offering, it's better to go ahead and take it rather than risk running the spirit off with a bad counteroffer. There are always hundreds of thousands of other magicians on the planet that the spirit can ask.

SPIRIT PACTS

Spirit pacts are the closest one can get to a proverbial deal with the devil. These go far beyond simple Karma bartering and can result in the gain of incredible abilities. Of course, everything in the Sixth World—even intangibles—comes with a price tag attached, and spirit pacts have a high markup.

A spirit pact involves a free spirit intertwining its spiritual essence with a metahuman's; this essence sharing results in both parties being inextricably linked at the astral level. So, if the spirit is permanently destroyed, the metahuman connected to it also dies, and vice versa. I believe it may be possible—but unlikely—to undo a spirit pact without killing both the spirit and its partner, but such a feat would require steps not even I am privy to. If you didn't follow my advice about never negotiating with spirits and you find yourself living on borrowed time because you're trapped in a spirit pact, I am not one who can rescue you from your self-crafted fate.

BALANCING THE SCALES

Let's say you've been selfish when it comes to spirits you command, and you've treated them like mere animals or tools over and over again. Eventually, those spirits you mistreated are going to gossip among other spirits, and at some point getting any inhabitants of astral space to listen to your conjuration attempts will be like trying to get Aztechnology to publicly reveal their most powerful magic rituals.

So, if you've fragged up bad enough that you have trouble summoning normal spirits, a spirit *will* respond to a request to balance your karmic scales. If you do the Atonement ritual right, you can bribe a spirit with enough Karma, reagents, and whatever else it asks for in exchange for spreading beneficial gossip amongst the spirits back home. Of course, frag up and ask for forgiveness too many times in a row, and the spirits will label you insincere and demand increasingly higher bribes for clearing your name.

GAME
INFORMATION

NEW SPIRIT RULES

This section provides rules and options for using spirits and conjurers in *Shadowrun*.

ASTRAL MOVEMENT

Every spirit has an affinity for one particular metaplane, known as its native plane, and may instantaneously travel to that metaplane with a Complex Action. Mana barriers do not prevent this movement.

Also, by using metaplanar travel, a spirit may bypass a dual-natured mana barrier by traveling to their native metaplane and then reappearing on the other side of the obstacle. However, a spirit may only bypass the barrier in this way if its conjurer is on the other side of the barrier or if the spirit is familiar with what lies beyond the barrier.

DISRUPTION

Spirits don't die, at least not in the traditional sense. When Physical or Stun damage fills up a spirit's Condition Monitor, that spirit is disrupted and immediately returns to its native metaplane. Spirits possessing vessels are only disrupted if the vessel's Condition Monitor suffers a lethal amount of overflow damage (see **Exceeding the Condition Monitor**, p. 170. *SR5*).

A disrupted spirit cannot appear outside its metaplane for a period of 28 days minus its Force, with a minimum time of 24 hours. If you're on a deadline and desperately need a disrupted spirit back before that time expires, you must undertake a metaplanar quest (see p. 140) to the spirit's native metaplane and retrieve the spirit. To retrieve a possession spirit, you must already have a prepared vessel awaiting the spirit, regardless of whether the quest was successful.

Disrupted spirits still count against a conjurer's limit of spirits, but a conjurer may choose to release a disrupted spirit at any time.

SPIRITS AND VESSELS

Some spirits temporarily interact with the physical plane with the Possession power (p. 197) instead of Materialization. Others permanently take over a physical body by using Inhabitation (p. 195). Possession may be facilitated by preparing a vessel (see **Vessel Preparation**, p. 135) for the spirit; Inhabitation, however, requires a prepared vessel. Possessed/inhabited vessels are dual-natured (p. 395, *SR5*), and only one spirit may occupy a vessel at a time.

A magician's body is always considered a prepared vessel for any spirit he conjures, so no special preparation is necessary. Also, an astrally projecting magician's empty body counts as an available vessel.

The spirit itself controls the possessed vessel, and the host's mind is either suppressed (via Possession) or destroyed (via Inhabitation). However, if a magician's body is controlled by a spirit he summoned, he retains awareness of the spirit's actions, he can perceive through his own body, and he can give the spirit commands (much like a rigger remote-piloting a vehicle). Also, an initiate can use the Channeling metamagic (p. 148) to gain further control of his body while possessed.

SPOTTING SPIRITS IN VESSELS

Noticing materialized spirits is easy, but spirits using Possession or Inhabitation are harder to detect. To spot a spirit possessing/inhabiting a vessel, an observer must succeed in a Perception + Intuition [Mental] (6 – spirit's Force) Test. Success also reveals clues as to what the spirit really looks like. At the gamemaster's discretion, the use of a spirit's powers may create an effect similar to a shamanic mask, thus adding a +2 dice pool modifier to the Perception Test.

NEW SPIRIT OPTIONS

Conjurers can use the following options to gain more flexibility with their spirits.

LONG-TERM BINDING

Sometimes you just can't trust anyone but a spirit with an prohibitively long task. If you want to assign a bound spirit to a lengthy task, you can pay an amount of Karma equal to the spirit's Force to have that spirit perform a service or a set of services for up to a year and a day. All other services are lost, and the spirit no longer counts against the conjurer's spirit limit.

A spirit that is disrupted while performing a long-term service automatically returns to its task after 28 days minus the spirit's Force.

FETTERING

Attempting to rebind a spirit during a firefight just isn't practical, but sometimes you end up using a bound spirit's final service at an inconvenient time. One solution to worrying about services is to bind the spirit in such a way that it obeys commands without using up any services. This process is known as fettering.

To fetter a spirit, a conjurer must perform a Binding ritual (see p. 300–301, *SR5*). In addition to the normal expenditure of reagents and time, the magician must give the spirit Force x 3 Karma and 1 point of his Magic attribute. In return, the spirit gains the Banishing Resistance power (p. 194). If the spirit breaks free (see *Losing an Ally*, p. 202), or is banished, destroyed, or voluntarily released, the conjurer regains his 1 point of Magic. On the other hand, if a magician with a fettered spirit loses the last point of his Magic attribute for any reason, the fettered spirit automatically departs and takes the last of the magician's talent with it; the magician is then considered burned out and does not regain the 1 point of Magic the spirit borrowed.

A fettered spirit counts against the magician's spirit limit, and a magician may only fetter one spirit at a time. For purposes of this one-at-a-time restriction, an ally spirit is considered a fettered spirit. Thus, a magician with an ally may not fetter spirits unless he first loses or releases his ally spirit.

RECKLESS CONJURING

Conjuring a spirit works like a careful transaction between conjurer and spirit, but—like a fence needing to ditch stolen goods before the heat catches him—sometimes a conjurer doesn't have the luxury of making a sound bargain with a spirit.

A magician may make a rushed attempt to conjure a spirit by spending a Simple Action instead of a Complex Action. Make a standard Summoning Test but reduce the Limit by 2 after all reagents have been expended; also, add 3 to the Drain Value.

A magician may only use Reckless Conjuring once per Action Phase.

NEW SPIRIT TYPES

Beyond the six spirit types previously mentioned, there are four other spirit types that several other traditions can conjure. These spirits follow the general rules for summoning (p. 300, *SR5*) and astral forms (p. 394, *SR5*).

GUARDIAN SPIRITS

Peerless warriors and staunch protectors, guardian spirits can embody anything from fierce marauders to holy avengers.

B	A	R	S	W	L	I	C	M	ESS	EDG
F+1	F+2	F+3	F+2	F	F	F	F	F	F	F/2

Physical Init.	((F x 2) + 1) + 2D6
Astral Init.	(F x 2) + 3D6
Skills	Assensing, Astral Combat, Blades, Clubs, Counterspelling, Exotic Ranged Weapon, Perception, Unarmed Combat
Powers	Astral Form, Fear, Guard, Magical Guard, Materialization, Movement, Sapience
Optional Powers	Animal Control, Concealment, Elemental Attack (summoner chooses element during summoning), Natural Weaponry (DV = F + 2), Psychokinesis, Skill (choose any Combat skill)

GUIDANCE SPIRITS

You want to know what lies in your future? The mysterious advice from a guidance spirit might be the ticket.

B	A	R	S	W	L	I	C	M	ESS	EDG
F+3	F–1	F+2	F+1	F	F	F	F	F	F	F/2

Physical Init.	(F x 2) + 2D6
Astral Init.	(F x 2) + 3D6
Skills	Arcana, Assensing, Astral Combat, Counterspelling, Perception, Unarmed Combat
Powers	Astral Form, Confusion, Divining, Guard, Magical Guard, Materialization, Sapience, Search, Shadow Cloak
Optional Powers	Engulf, Enhanced Senses (Hearing, Low-Light Vision, Thermographic Vision, or Smell), Fear, Influence

PLANT SPIRITS

From the smallest blade of grass to the mightiest giant sequoia, plant spirits represent all facets of the plant kingdom.

B	A	R	S	W	L	I	C	M	ESS	EDG
F+2	F–1	F	F+1	F	F–1	F	F	F	F	F/2

Physical Init.	(F x 2) + 2D6
Astral Init.	(F x 2) + 3D6
Skills	Assensing, Astral Combat, Counterspelling, Exotic Ranged Weapon, Perception, Unarmed Combat
Powers	Astral Form, Concealment, Engulf, Fear, Guard, Magical Guard, Materialization, Sapience, Silence
Optional Powers	Accident, Confusion, Movement, Noxious Breath, Search

TASK SPIRITS

Task spirits: for when you absolutely need something to make your shoes—or what have you—overnight while you sleep.

B	A	R	S	W	L	I	C	M	ESS	EDG
F	F	F+2	F+2	F	F	F	F	F	F	F/2

Physical Init.	((F x 2) + 2)+ 2D6
Astral Init.	(F x 2) + 3D6
Skills	Artisan, Assensing, Astral Combat, Perception, Unarmed Combat
Powers	Accident, Astral Form, Binding, Materialization, Movement, Sapience, Search
Optional Powers	Concealment, Enhanced Senses (Hearing, Low-Light Vision, Thermographic Vision, or Smell), Influence, Psychokinesis, Skill (choose any Technical or Physical skill)

NEW SPIRIT POWERS

The following new powers are available to spirits in addition to those found in *SR5*.

ANAPHYLAXIS

Type: P   **Action:** Complex
Range: Touch   **Duration:** Instant

Anaphylaxis is a massive systemic reaction induced by a concentrated burst of pollutants from a toxic spirit. Treat this as a toxin attack with the following ratings:

Vector: Inhalation
Speed: Immediate
Penetration: 0
Power: Force
Effect: Physical damage, anaphylactic shock
Anaphylactic Shock: If the damage is not completely resisted, the victim enters anaphylactic shock, result-

ing in muscle spasms and systemic failure, and eventually death if the problem is not addressed or treated. The victim takes 1 box of damage each Combat Turn until he dies from cardiovascular breakdown, unless he is treated with a First Aid + Logic [Mental] (2) Test with appropriate drugs (such as from a medkit) or an Antidote, Detox, or Heal spell.

ASTRAL GATEWAY

Type: M   **Action:** Complex
Range: LOS (A)   **Duration:** Sustained

The spirit can open an astral rift (p. 28), which forces all nearby objects to become dual-natured and allows even mundanes to astrally project. An astral rift can open to any metaplane the spirit can visit.

AURA MASKING

Type: M   **Action:** Free
Range: Self   **Duration:** Sustained

Sometimes a spirit doesn't want someone to assense its natural aura. This power functions like Masking (p. 326, *SR5*) and Extended Masking metamagics. Use the spirit's Edge in place of its initiate grade. The spirit can also hide its own use of powers on itself within the mask; only a magician who pierces this mask can see the spirit using such powers. A spirit can mask itself to look like another astral being, but it cannot try to pass itself off as a mundane being unless it is attached to a physical body or has the Realistic Form power (p. 198).

BANISHING RESISTANCE

Type: M   **Action:** Auto
Range: Self   **Duration:** Special

When resisting a Banishing attempt (p. 301, *SR5*), treat the spirit as if it owes a number of services equal to its Edge; these refresh every sunrise and sunset and are cumulative with any services the spirit may actually owe a conjurer.

DESIRE REFLECTION

Type: M   **Action:** Complex
Range: LOS   **Duration:** Sustained

Desire Reflection finds the greatest desire of a single target within line of sight and evokes a full-sensory illusion keyed to the desire in the target's mind. Certain spirits use this power to draw in potential victims. The spirit itself can appear as a harmless or pleasing aspect of the illusion at will. To use this power the critter must succeed in an Opposed Test pitting its Magic + Intuition against the target's Willpower + Intuition. If it scores any net hits, the victim falls for the illusion. Otherwise the power fails to affect the victim.

Left to their own devices, victims act as if their de-sire were real and right in front of them. If the victim is attacked, injured, slapped, and so on, he may make another Opposed Test to resist the illusion; if the attack or what have you comes directly from a component of the illusion, add +2 to the dice pool. Each hit reduces the spirit's net hits on the original Opposed Test. If the spirit's net hits are reduced to 0, the victim breaks free of the illusion. Those who fail are lost and entranced, caught up in the fulfillment of their desire.

DEATHLY AURA

Type: P   **Action:** Simple
Range: Special   **Duration:** Sustained

The spirit radiates an aura of fear and decay, which taints the surrounding environment. For an area with a radius of (Force) meters around the spirit, the temperature drops by (Force x 2)°C. Also, organic material in this radius decays at a faster rate, aging by a factor equal to the spirit's Force. This effect is not fast enough to noticeably damage metahumans and other large critters, but the aura withers plants and kills small creatures such as insects or mice. This aura fills living creatures with unreasoning terror. Someone who wishes to voluntarily enter an affected area must succeed in an Opposed Test between their Charisma + Willpower and the spirit's Force x 2 or else they are compelled to flee until they are out of sight of whatever caused the aura.

DEVOURING

Type: P   **Action:** Complex
Range: Touch   **Duration:** Sustained

Insect spirits use the Devouring power to consume all biomaterial (e.g., crops, wood, vegetation) and most non-living objects. Some flesh-form and hybrid-form spirits seem to derive sustenance from this consumption, whereas others regurgitate the material for constructing parts of their hive. The spirit makes an Opposed Test, using the spirit's Force x 2 against the Object Resistance (p. 295, *SR5*) of all possible materials/objects within (Magic) meters (to save time, the gamemaster may choose to roll once for the spirit and then roll Object Resistance for each object or object type). If the spirit gets any net hits against a particular object, that object is devoured. While this power is sustained, barriers lose 1 point of Structure Rating and vehicles take 1 box of damage per Combat Turn. Living critters and characters are unaffected.

DIVINING

Type: M   **Action:** Special
Range: Special   **Duration:** Special

This power functions like the Divination metamagic (p. 147), except the spirit uses Magic + Intuition to divine meaning instead of Arcana + Logic.

ELEMENTAL ATTACK (POLLUTANT)

Type: P   **Action:** Complex
Range: Special   **Duration:** Instant

This attack follows the rules for Elemental Attack (p. 396, *SR5*) but with the following modifications.

Pollutants can take many forms, including biological waste, industrial runoff, biohazardous materials, and so on. Pollutant attacks have a DV of (Magic x 2)S with an AP of –(critter's Magic). Additionally, once the pollutant has worked its way into the character's system (that is, after the interval determined by the toxin's Speed), he must resist a toxin with the following stats:

Vector: Contact, Inhalation, Ingestion
Speed: 12 hours
Penetration: 0
Power: critter's Magic x 2
Effect: Stun damage, disorientation, nausea

ELEMENTAL ATTACK (RADIATION)

Type: P   **Action:** Complex
Range: Special   **Duration:** Instant

This attack follows the rules for Elemental Attack (p. 396, *SR5*) but causes radiation elemental damage, which results in radiation burns, radiation poisoning, and other serious side effects.

Radiation damage is treated as Physical damage and ignores Armor; however, the affected character may add the rating of a hazmat suit or other radiation-resistant gear when making a Damage Resistance Test against radiation damage. Radiation poisoning may also cause nausea (p. 409, *SR5*), headaches, blindness, or other central nervous system impairments (per gamemaster's discretion).

ENDOWMENT

Type: M   **Action:** Complex
Range: Touch   **Duration:** Sustained

The spirit grants the use of one of its powers to the target. The spirit may still use the power while the target uses it, and the spirit can grant a power to a number of targets equal to twice its Magic. No character may gain more than one power from a spirit at a time.

ENERGY DRAIN

Type: M   **Action:** Complex
Range: Touch or LOS   **Duration:** Permanent

The Energy Drain power is used by a number of dangerous critters and spirits in different ways. Each version of this power is slightly different, depending on the entity using it. Similar to the Essence Drain power (p. 396, *SR5*), Energy Drain allows the creature to suck life energy from a victim, be it Karma, Force, Magic, or Essence. For some creatures, such as blood spirits, shedim, or insect spirits, this power is Touch range, so a resisting victim must be subdued first or drained unwittingly. Other beings, such as shadow spirits, merely require line of sight for this power, allowing the critter to feed off its victims from afar.

Draining a point of Karma, Force, Magic, or Essence requires a Willpower + Magic [Mental] (10 – target's Essence/Force, 1 minute) Extended Test. If the critter is disturbed or interrupted before this test ends, the point is not drained. If the Extended Test is completed, the critter drains one point of the specified energy, adding to its own or converting the energy to an appropriate rating point at a 1:1 ratio. Some critters, such as astral bacteria or insect spirits, use the drained energy to reproduce, as noted in their individual descriptions. Drained points are permanently lost.

In addition to the drain, victims suffer 1 box of damage for each point drained. Depending on the critter, this may be Stun damage (shadow spirits, astral bacteria) or Physical damage (blood spirits, shedim). Victims who take Physical damage appear drained, withered, and hollow, and are sometimes marked permanently (white hair, hair loss, wrinkles, premature aging, or other strange markings).

If a character's Magic is reduced to 0, he burns out and becomes mundane. If a critter's Magic is reduced to 0, it dies. If a spirit, sustained/anchored/quickened spell, focus, or mana barrier's Force is reduced to 0, it is destroyed. If a victim's Essence is reduced to 0, they die.

HIVE MIND

Type: M   **Action:** Auto
Range: Special   **Duration:** Always

All insect spirits of a given species controlled by a shaman or a queen/mother possess a constant telepathic bond with one another. Insect spirits may send a telepathic message to one or more spirits in the hive and/or the shaman as a Free Action. The shaman or queen/mother can also use this link to experience any of the hive's insect spirits (or switch to another spirit) with a Simple Action, similar to the Sense Link power (p. 198) but without range limitations.

The constant buzz of insect spirits in an insect shaman's mind can be distracting, especially if the hive is agitated. When this occurs, the shaman must succeed in a Magic + Willpower [Mental] (2) Test in order to suppress the background hum and concentrate on something, such as fighting or spellcasting.

INHABITATION

Type: P   **Action:** Auto
Range: Self   **Duration:** Special

Most spirits can only affect the physical world by materializing or possessing a vessel. A spirit with Inhabitation exists on the physical plane continuously after it has merged with a prepared vessel. The spirit cannot be separated with Banishing, and the spirit cannot voluntarily leave the vessel. An inhabiting spirit is only disrupted when its vessel is either destroyed or killed from Physical damage overflow (p. 209, *SR5*). If the inhabited vessel is living, the spirit gains complete control of the body and access to some or all of the vessel's memories. During merging, the vessel's original spirit is consumed (if present) and that character is lost (though gamemasters may decide otherwise, if appropriate to their stories).

To inhabit a vessel, a spirit requires a prepared vessel (p. 135) in a magical lodge with a Force at least equal to the spirit's Force. Once the vessel has been enchanted, the spirit may use Inhabitation on it. The Inhabitation process takes a number of days equal to the spirit's Force. At the end of that period, the spirit makes an Opposed Test using its Force x 2 against the vessel's Willpower + Intuition. The spirit's conjurer (if any) may influence the result by adding his Binding skill to either dice pool. If the spirit is attempting to inhabit a nonliving vessel, the spirit rolls Force x 2 against the vessel's Object Resistance dice pool (p. 295, *SR5*). The number of net hits determines the resulting form. If the spirit gets a critical glitch, the merge is unsuccessful, and the vessel is immune to further inhabitation attempts by that spirit.

The Inhabitation process is trying for both spirit and vessel. If the vessel is removed from the magical lodge before the merge is complete, the spirit and host generally die (though the gamemaster is entitled to make exceptions for hosts). At the end of the inhabitation period, the spirit takes full control over the host; the type of form depends on the Opposed Test results, as follows:

- **True form:** A true form results when the spirit rolls 2 or more net hits or the vessel gets a critical glitch. The vessel is irrevocably destroyed or consumed during the process. The spirit takes form on the astral plane and gains the powers of Astral Form and Materialization (p. 394 and 398, *SR5*). The true form bears no resemblance to the vessel and retains only the knowledge, skills, and attributes of the spirit alone. A true form can persist on the astral or physical planes indefinitely without being tied to a conjurer or a spirit formula. Once disrupted, the spirit can only return by inhabiting a new vessel.
- **Hybrid form:** A hybrid form results when neither spirit nor vessel roll 2 or more net hits. Both vessel and spirit become a single, dual-natured entity (p. 395, *SR5*). The hybrid form's physical attributes are enhanced by the spirit's Force. The spirit retains all of the host's natural abilities but only some of its memories and none of its skills (the spirit retains its own skills, however). A hybrid gains Immunity to Normal Weapons (p.

397, *SR5*) but loses the ability to assume an Astral Form (p. 394, *SR5*). The inhabited body exhibits signs of the takeover, as the merge warps the vessel with signs of the spirit's nature (see Spotting Spirits in Vessels, p. 192). The spirit is under no obligation to return to its native metaplane if its services are banished away, and it may persist indefinitely as an uncontrolled spirit. Unlike Possession spirits, hybrid forms can operate a direct neural interface, and the vessel's cyberware (if any) continues to function for the spirit.
- **Flesh form:** A flesh form results when the vessel rolls 2+ net hits. A perfect combination between spirit and vessel, the flesh form retains all of the vessel's abilities, knowledge, and skills (except Conjuring skills), and its appearance is virtually indistinguishable from the original vessel. A flesh form gains the following powers: Aura Masking (p. 194), Dual-Natured (p. 395, *SR5*), Immunity to Normal Weapons (p. 397, *SR5*), and Realistic Form (p. 198).

MAGICAL GUARD

Type: M　　　　**Action:** Free
Range: LOS　　　**Duration:** Instant

A critter with the Magical Guard power can use the Counterspelling skill and provide spell defense and dispel spells the same as a magician's ability (p. 294, *SR5*).

MIND LINK

Type: M　　　　**Action:** Simple
Range: LOS　　　**Duration:** Sustained

A critter with the Mind Link power can open and maintain telepathic communication with another sapient creature. The spirit can maintain a number of simultaneous mental links equal to its Magic attribute. If multiple sapients are engaged via Mind Link with the same spirit, they may communicate freely with each other as well as with the original spirit.

MUTAGEN

Type: P　　　　**Action:** Complex
Range: Self　　　**Duration:** Sustained

A being can use the Mutagen power to magically enhance its physical body at the expense of its mental abilities. While using the power, it can shift a maximum of (Magic) attribute points from Mental to Physical attributes. This power can be used by possessing spirits, shifting Mental attribute points from the spirit to the vessel's Physical attributes. Shifting in or out of mutated form requires a Complex Action. Instead of shifting attribute points, a gamemaster may choose to use this power to generate a new physical feature, like a tail, claw, or new eye.

PESTILENCE

Type: P **Action:** Auto
Range: Touch **Duration:** Instant

The critter carries non-magical, contagious infection that may infect characters that come in contact with it (or its secretions). Treat this disease as a toxin (p. 408, SR5) with the following attributes:

Vector: Contact
Speed: 1 day
Penetration: –2
Power: 8
Effect: Stun damage, disorientation, nausea. Disease effects last 1 full day. Each day the disease Power increases by 2 and the character must make another Toxin Resistance Test, until the disease's Power is reduced to 0.

POSSESSION

Type: P **Action:** Complex
Range: Touch **Duration:** Special

Some spirits are incapable of materializing, so they must possess vessels in order to interact with meat space. During a possession attempt, the spirit uses the vessel's aura as a temporary conduit to the physical plane. The spirit makes an Opposed Test by rolling its Force x 2 against the vessel's Intuition + Willpower for living vessels or the Object Resistance dice pool of an inanimate vessel. A prepared vessel (p. 135) gives the spirit a +6 dice pool modifier. If the spirit fails, it is forced back to the astral plane. If the spirit succeeds, both spirit and vessel are considered a single dual-natured entity (p. 395, SR5) for the possession's duration.

A possessing spirit may be forced back to the astral plane with a Banishing Test (p. 301, SR5). If the possession attempt fails or the spirit is banished, that spirit cannot attempt to possess that vessel again until the next sunrise or sunset.

The following rules govern Possession spirits:

- **Living Vessels:** While possessing a living vessel, the spirit allows the vessel to reduce the Wound Modifier (p. 169, SR5) by 1 die for every point of the spirit's Force, to a maximum Wound Modifier of 0. Also, for any Physical attributes where the spirit's Force is higher than the vessel's Physical attributes, the vessel's Physical attributes are increased by half the spirit's Force (rounded down). While possessed, the spirit's Mental and Special attributes are used (which means a possessed technomancer cannot access Resonance), with Initiative modified accordingly (use the spirit's Initiative Dice). The spirit also uses its skills, as it cannot access the knowledge and skills of the host. Possession does not allow the spirit to operate AR or cybernetic interfaces, and the spirit cannot gain benefits from any augmentations that would require active control.

- **Dead/Inanimate Vessels:** While possessing a nonliving vessel, the spirit adds half of its Force to the vessel's Structure and Armor Ratings (p. 197, SR5), Object Resistance dice pool (p. 295, SR5), or Physical attributes, depending on the situation and/or vessel type. The combined entity uses its enhanced attributes (or the spirit's, if the vessel lacks attributes) to calculate Initiative, and it uses the spirit's Initiative dice. The spirit can use any of its powers through the vessel itself, but it can only move the vessel in ways the vessel can normally perform. For example, a spirit possessing a gun can fire the gun but cannot move the gun or access any smartgun functions. Generally, spirits can only control mechanical functions, not anything that requires complex electronic, DNI, or wireless control.

- **Possession and Services:** Like Materialization, Possession itself doesn't use any of the services a spirit owes its conjurer, but once the spirit completes its services, it abandons the vessel and returns to astral space. The vessel reverts to its prior state but keeps any damage incurred. The spirit also abandons the vessel and returns to astral space on the summoner's command, even if the spirit still owes services.

- **Roleplaying Possession:** A magician possessed by a spirit she conjured is fully aware of what the spirit is doing and is still able to give it commands and direction. To prevent a player feeling sidelined, gamemasters are encouraged to allow a player of a possessed magician to roleplay the spirit that she commands and is controlling her body. Gamemasters may also consider extending this to characters who are possessed by a "friendly" spirit. This still does not give the spirit direct access to the host's knowledge or skills.

- **Damage:** If the spirit or the vessel has already sustained damage, that damage sticks around upon successful possession, but only the greater set of the combined Wound Modifiers applies (modified by the spirit's Force, for living vessels). Physical damage incurred during possession is recorded as a single track, and both vessel and spirit retain the full amount of this damage when possession ends, which is cumulative with any previous damage. When possession ends, the vessel's Physical attributes return to normal while the damage stays in place, so this damage can have potentially lethal side effects.

QUAKE

Type: P **Action:** Complex
Range: Special **Duration:** Instant

The spirit can create earthquakes with potentially devastating effects. The quake affects an area with a radius of (Force) kilometers, and the shaking persists intermittently for (Force) minutes. Areas especially vulnerable to earthquakes are usually not areas that receive them frequently, as people in vulnerable areas tend to build dwellings with earthquakes in mind. The spirit makes a Magic + Willpower Test and the number of hits represents the magnitude of the quake, as noted on the Quake Table.

QUAKE TABLE

While the effects of an individual quake are highly dependent upon the conditions of surrounding soil, the quality of engineering, and the preparedness of the surrounding citizenry, the following guidelines can be used (generally, a quake includes the effects on the line for its number of hits as well as all the other effects for a smaller number of hits):

HITS	EFFECTS
1	Motion detectors useless for the duration; sleeping people awaken.
2	Top-heavy objects fall; unlatched doors and windows swing open or shut.
3	Furniture shifts; objects fall off shelves in bulk; drivers of land vehicles must make Vehicle Tests.
4	Ordinary buildings damaged; doors jam; minefields detonate.
5	Furniture overturns; windows break; entire area considered difficult ground.
6	Freestanding fences, walls, and trees sag or fall over; gas lines are unsafe.
7	Roadways become impassable; some buildings collapse.
8	Many buildings collapse, crevasses appear in pavement and open ground.

REALISTIC FORM

Type: P **Action:** Auto
Range: Self **Duration:** Special

A spirit with Realistic Form can be mistaken for a normal physical creature or object when it materializes, or it appears unremarkable when joined to a vessel. A spirit that appears as a metahuman would have a heartbeat and a regular breathing rate. A spirit that appeared as an object mimics the object's normal functionality; for example, a toaster could be plugged into the wall to toast bread (though it would have no Matrix link, making it an antique toaster). The spirit is in no way disguised from the astral plane, but to physical observation appears to any senses to be a natural part of the physical world.

Note that spirits with the Materialization power normally only have one materialized form. Materializing spirits with this power can choose to appear using Realistic Form or their normal materialized form. A fire elemental can still appear as a column of angry flames but might also be able to appear as a beautiful woman.

REINFORCEMENT

Type: P **Action:** Complex
Range: Touch **Duration:** Special

This power strengthens the resistance of natural and constructed materials. To fortify materials, the spirit must take a Force x 2 [Force] (square meters, 1 hour) Extended Text. If successful, the spirit's Force is added to the Structure and Armor Ratings. Multiple applications of Reinforcement are not cumulative, and only the highest effect counts. Once the reinforcement is in place, it is permanent.

SENSE LINK

Type: M **Action:** Simple
Range: Special **Duration:** Sustained

A critter with the Sense Link power can share sensory data with its summoner (and vice versa). The summoner experiences the critter's emotions (at a low level) and can send simple commands, which the critter may not understand or follow, especially if the command places them in danger. An Intuition + Charisma Test, opposed by the critter's Willpower + Intuition, may be used to persuade the critter to obey. In addition, the summoner can experience one of the critter's senses with a Simple Action; with each Simple Action expended, the summoner can choose which sense to experience. Augmented senses (whether they are magically augmented or otherwise) in the summoner do not work through the critter. The range of this power is equal to (Magic x 50 meters). If the critter is hurt while the link is intact, the summoner must resist Stun damage equal to the damage inflicted on the critter with a Willpower + Magic Test.

SHADOW CLOAK

Type: P **Action:** Free
Range: Self **Duration:** Sustained

This power allows a creature to envelop itself in utter darkness, making it appear to be a shadow. Shadow Cloak is useless in full daylight and unnecessary in complete darkness; other lighting conditions make it difficult to see the creature using this power. Apply a -2 dice pool modifier to Perception Tests for detecting the creature in Partial Light, -4 dice pool modifier in Dim Light, and a +1 dice pool modifier in Glare conditions.

SILENCE

Type: P　　　　**Action:** Complex
Range: Special　　**Duration:** Sustained

　　A creature with this power can surround itself in a sphere of silence with a radius equal to the creature's Magic in meters. Sounds from within the area are muffled, and sounds entering the area are harder to hear by the creature or anyone else. Sound-based Perception Tests and the Damage Value of sound-based attacks are reduced by the spirit's Magic.

SONIC PROJECTION

Type: P　　　　**Action:** Complex
Range: Special　　**Duration:** Sustained

　　This power affects everyone within earshot—except for spirits of the same type—and creates a deafening and distracting buzz. The spirit makes an Opposed Test using its Force x 2 against each target's Willpower. Sound dampers and spells like Hush/Silence provide additional dice to the defender equal to their Rating or the hits the caster scored. Each of the spirit's net hits provides a negative dice pool modifier on all tests for as long as the buzzing is sustained.

STORM

Type: P　　　　**Action:** Complex
Range: Special　　**Duration:** Special

　　A spirit with this power can send a massive, destructive elemental storm against a targeted area. Icy rain, bolts of lightning, gale-force winds, and more strike the area. The affected area's radius equals the spirit's Magic x 100 meters. The spirit makes a single Unarmed Combat + Magic [Force] Test, and all characters, creatures, and objects in the area are considered subject to Suppressive Fire (p. 179, SR5). The storm's base Damage Value is (Force)P.

NEW QUALITIES

The following qualities can be applied to spirits or conjurers. If the quality does not have a Karma cost or bonus, it can only be applied to spirits.

RESTLESS

Some spirits are just meant to be free, and a restless spirit tries to break its chains at any opportunity. When a conjurer performs a binding ceremony on a spirit with the Restless quality, the spirit gains a number of free hits equal to its Force divided by 3 (rounded up), in addition to the hits it rolls for the test.

　　When making a test to see if an ally breaks free (see *Losing an Ally*, p. 202), a Restless ally spirit gains a number of additional dice equal to 6 minus its current Loyalty rating.

SERVILE

Though most spirits find serving metahumanity a form of imprisonment, a servile spirit wants nothing more than to answer a summoner's call with gusto. When summoning a spirit with the Servile quality, a conjurer receives one free hit on his Summoning Test and on any Binding Test performed on this spirit.

SPIRIT CHAMPION

COST: 14 KARMA

Something you did had a lasting, positive effect on the astral plane, and the whole spirit world is talking about it. Characters with this quality may spend (Force x 5) drams of reagents when performing a Summoning Test to receive a +1 dice pool modifier, in addition to any reagents spent to set the limit for the test. Also, Binding Tests require only (Force x 20) drams of reagents, and the summoner receives a +1 dice pool modifier.

SPIRIT PARIAH

BONUS: 14 KARMA

Something you did slotted of the spirit world something fierce, so spirits *really* don't like you. In order to even get their attention, you must make additional offerings to get spirits to show up. A character with this quality must expend (Force x 5) drams of reagents in order to make a Summoning Test; reagents spent to increase the test's limit do not count toward this amount. If the character cannot expend enough reagents, the test automatically fails. Also, Binding Tests require (Force x 30) drams of reagents, and the summoner receives a –1 dice pool modifier.

NEW MENTOR SPIRITS

BERSERKER

Those who follow the path of Berserker love fighting just for the sake of fighting, be it with words, fists, or spells. He is the greatest of all warriors, capable of wading into battle without fear, and he will wage his war singlehandedly if necessary.

ADVANTAGES

　　All: +2 dice pool modifier for Composure Tests
　　Magician: +2 dice for Physical-type Combat spells, preparations, and rituals
　　Adept: 2 free levels of Mystic Armor or Pain Resistance, or 1 free level of each

DISADVANTAGES

Berserker's followers have very short fuses. Whenever someone strongly disagrees with you (gamemaster's discretion), you must pass a Charisma + Willpower (3) Test to keep from striking out against the offender. If the test fails, the attack can be in any form you choose (fist, spell, etc.), but it must have the intent to cause damage.
Similar Archetypes: Warrior, Warmonger

CHAOS

Adherents of Chaos seemingly do things at random and love to start arguments or barroom brawls just for kicks, often through random trickery. While most people have a rather fixed sense of right and wrong, a Chaos follower's moral compass points in a different direction from moment to moment.

ADVANTAGES

All: +2 dice pool modifier for Con Tests
Magician: +2 dice to Illusion spells, preparations, and rituals
Adept: 2 free levels of Improved Potential (can be 2 levels for the same limit, or 1 level apiece to affect 2 different limits)

DISADVANTAGES

You are an inveterate gossip trying to stir up trouble, especially between friends, and thus cannot keep damaging secrets to yourself. Also, anytime you encounter a public situation deemed too quiet or stable (gamemaster's discretion), make a Willpower + Intuition (3) Test. Failure means that you are compelled to stir the pot in any way you desire, be it attacking, telling lies, or throwing a drink on someone nearby.
Similar Archetypes: Trickster, Troublemaker

PEACEMAKER

Deep down, all Peacemaker wants is for everyone to get along, even if they are currently mortal enemies. She believes every argument can be solved in some way; on the other hand, she knows some arguments require force or bodily harm in order get one's point across.

ADVANTAGES

All: +2 dice pool modifier for Negotiation Tests
Magician: +2 dice to Detection spells, preparations, and rituals
Adept: 2 free levels of Enhanced Perception

DISADVANTAGES

You see even enemies as potential friends and go out of your way to keep from hurting anyone unless the situation truly warrants it. At the very beginning of

combat, you must pass a Charisma + Intuition (3) Test; failure means you are unable to take actions that cause Physical damage for the duration of combat. At the beginning of a new Combat Turn, you may choose to retake the test if you failed the first time and you or a member of your team suffered damage in the previous Combat Turn.
Similar Archetypes: Mediator, Pacifist

ORACLE

Past, present, and future—Oracle knows all and sees all. She peels back the veil of mystery and reveals what has been, what is, and what will be. Nothing escapes her notice, and things that are hidden do not remain hidden for long.

ADVANTAGES

All: +2 dice pool modifier for Arcana Tests
Magician: +2 dice for Detection spells, preparations, and rituals
Adept: Free Astral Perception

DISADVANTAGES

You hate mysteries with a passion and can disappear for days trying to track down the answer. When confronted by a particularly haunting question (gamemaster's discretion), you must take a Willpower + Intuition (3) Test. Failure means you must undertake an Intuition + Logic [Mental] (5, 1 hour) Extended Test to try researching the answer. Completion of the Extended Test does not necessarily mean you found the answer, but it at least silences the question in your mind for the time being.

When a follower of Oracle becomes a Grade 1 initiate (p. 324, *SR5*), she must choose Divination (p. 147) for her first metamagic rather than a Power Point or any other benefit.
Similar Archetypes: Teacher, Mystic

ALLY SPIRITS

An ally spirit can be a great boon to an initiated magician. To conjure an ally spirit, a magician needs to either craft or find an appropriate spirit formula. Once the magician has the proper formula, she may attempt to conjure and bind the spirit.

ALLY SPIRIT FORMULA

An ally's spirit formula is a physical representation of the spirit, similar to an initiate's thesis (see p. 142). A magician can obtain this formula in one of two ways:
- The conjurer (or a trusted third party) can create the formula from scratch by making an Arcana +

Logic [Mental] (Force x 5, 1 day) Extended Test. Be aware that having someone else design your spirit formula means the creator might keep a copy for themselves.

- By undertaking a metaplanar quest (p. 140) to the chosen metaplane, an initiate can locate a formula that matches her needs.

To perform the summoning ceremony, the conjurer needs a physical copy of this formula. For allies requiring a vessel, either the original or a copy of the spirit formula must be carved into the prepared vessel.

CREATING AN ALLY SPIRIT FORMULA

To create a spirit formula and determine the Karma costs for conjuring an ally spirit, perform the following steps:

Step 1: Choose Force: The base cost of an ally spirit is 8 Karma times desired Force.

Step 2: Choose Form(s): The ally spirit may have only one of the following powers: Inhabitation (p. 195), Materialization (p. 398, SR5), or Possession (p. 197). Materialization allies have a base form that usually applies to the conjurer's traditions. Allies can have additional forms at the cost of 2 Karma each; an ally can switch between forms using a Complex Action. Inhabitation allies must have a prepared vessel for them, but they can only have multiple forms if a true form results from the merge. Possession allies have no material form of their own, but vessels can be prepared for them.

Step 3: Choose Powers: Ally spirits start with Astral Form (p. 394, SR5), Banishing Resistance (p. 194), Realistic Form (p. 198), Sapience (p. 400, SR5), and Sense Link (p. 198). Each ally also receives one additional power per point of Force, chosen from any powers of spirits appropriate to the conjurer's tradition. Beyond this, further powers appropriate to the conjurer's tradition may be chosen at the cost of 5 Karma per power. If the conjurer chooses the Elemental Attack, Energy Aura, or Engulf powers, she must specify what form the power takes.

Step 4: Choose Skills: Allies start with the skills of Assensing, Astral Combat, Perception, and Unarmed Combat. Additional skills that the conjurer knows or that may be needed for the spirit to use one of its powers (such as Exotic Ranged Weapon for Elemental Attack or Counterspelling for Magical Guard) cost 5 Karma each. Allies may never possess skills from the Conjuring group, and they may only be given the Flight skill (p. 394, SR5) if it fits the spirit's form.

Step 5: Choose Spells: An ally spirit can be taught any spells the conjurer knows for 3 Karma each or ones the conjurer doesn't know for 5 Karma each (spell formulae are still required).

CONJURING AN ALLY

The ritual for summoning an ally must be performed in a magical lodge with a Force at least equal to the ally being summoned. Follow summoning rules (p. 300, SR5). Immediately after summoning, the spirit must be bound using standard binding rules (p. 300, SR5). Calculate Drain as if summoning and binding a spirit of the ally's Force.

If the binding succeeds, the magician pays an amount of Karma as outlined in the ally's spirit formula. If the binding generates succeeds, the magician pays an amount of Karma as outlined in the ally's spirit formula. If the necessary amount of Karma cannot be paid, the ritual fails.

If the ally has the Inhabitation power, the conjurer must already have a prepared vessel. After the spirit is bound it must immediately use its Inhabitation power on the vessel. As per the Inhabitation power (p. 195), the conjurer may choose to influence the outcome of the Inhabitation Test. Inhabitation takes a number of days equal to the spirit's Force and is considered part of the ritual; thus the magician must continuously attend to the vessel during this time.

ALLY SPIRIT ABILITIES

Ally spirits follow standard spirit rules, with the following exceptions:

AID SORCERY AND AID STUDY

When using Aid Sorcery and Aid Study services, an ally spirit is considered appropriate for every spell category.

ATTRIBUTES

An ally's Physical and Astral attributes equal its Force. However, allies start with an Edge attribute equal to the Edge of its conjurer. Inhabitation allies follow the rules for the Inhabitation power (p. 195) to determine physical attributes.

LOYALTY

Allies are more loyal than normal spirits because that loyalty is part of the spirit's formula. Because of this, an ally will serve a character until their master's death (or near-death) frees them. Unlike normal spirits, an ally might go out of its way to assist its master or volunteer helpful information. On the other hand, a mistreated ally can potentially turn on its master. Allies are considered to start with a Loyalty rating of 6 (see p. 55, SR5), but a master's particularly callous behavior toward her spirit or other spirits can potentially lower this. See **Ally Spirit Loyalty**, p. 207.

MAGIC SKILL USE

Every ally spirit is considered a full Magician (see p. 69, SR5) and can be designed with any magical skills known to its summoner, except skills in the Conjuring group. Allies also may not initiate, and an ally inhabiting a vessel may not astrally project.

NATIVE PLANE

An ally's native metaplane is specified by the spirit formula and can be used to destroy the spirit by making a metaplanar quest (p. 140) to that plane.

OPEN-ENDED SERVICE

An ally's services are never exhausted, and the ally can perform any unbound or bound spirit service (see p. 302, SR5) an unlimited number of times, including Resist Drain (see below). Ally spirits do not count against a magician's limit of bound spirits.

RESIST DRAIN

A magician casting a spell may choose to have her ally spirit take the spell's Drain instead. This can be done in two different ways. Either use the ally's Magic attribute to determine if Drain is Physical or not and have the spirit resist the Drain as normal, or the magician may buy one extra hit on her Drain Resistance Test in exchange for her ally suffering one box of Physical damage (which the ally cannot resist). Regardless of the method, using this service is incredibly painful for the spirit and will foster hatred in the spirit if abused.

SENSE LINK

Ally spirits have the power of Sense Link (p. 198), which let them share sensory data with their conjurers at a limited range. The conjurer may not target spells through this power.

ENHANCING AN ALLY

Sometimes you want to give your ally spirit a little more oomph—add new forms, powers, skills, or spells or increase the spirit's total Force. This enhancement requires first modifying your ally spirit's formula. Modifying the formula requires either an Arcana + Logic [Mental] (Force x 5, 1 day) Extended Test or a metaplanar quest.

The rebinding ritual, known as a Ritual of Change, must be performed in a magical lodge with a Force equal to or greater than the ally. Spend the usual amount of binding reagents, and pay Karma equal to all the relevant changes to the spirit. However, increasing an ally's Force with a Ritual of Change requires 16 Karma per point of Force beyond the spirit's initial Force.

An Inhabitation Test is not necessary for inhabiting allies, but the conjurer may choose to provide a new vessel for the spirit to merge with.

LOSING AN ALLY

A magician who routinely mistreats his ally spirit is just asking for it to eventually turn on him. Also, a magician who is overly dependent on his ally or regularly endangers it can risk making the ally resentful, which may cause it to seek freedom. An ally can only break away during a Ritual of Change or if its master is knocked out by Drain or by Physical damage, and it will only make the attempt if it feels it has been wronged in some way.

When an ally attempts to break free, it makes a Force x 2 [Force] test against the magician's Binding + Magic [Mental]. If the spirit generates any net hits, it goes free and may become a free spirit (gamemaster's discretion).

If an ally successfully breaks free during a Ritual of Change, the ritual fails: the reagents and time are spent, but the Karma remains unspent. The magician must also resist a Drain Value equal to twice the number of hits the spirit got on its test. If the magician is incapacitated by the Drain, the ally immediately goes free.

AVATAR SPIRITS

In game terms, avatars are powerful free spirits that can act as a magician's spirit guide. Attacking or using magical skills against an avatar is usually futile, as it can result in the magician being transported to the metaplanes, unable to use magic for a time, or some other consequence of the gamemaster's choosing. If in danger, an avatar spirit will instantly vanish to the metaplanes.

Avatar spirits are intended to be used for roleplaying opportunities. They can act as a warning of impending doom or they can play devil's advocate. In any case, an avatar spirit should never be something players can exploit.

FREE SPIRITS

The following rules offer guidelines for using free spirits in a Shadowrun game.

BORN FREE

Whenever a spirit becomes uncontrolled, the gamemaster decides whether it becomes a free spirit. Bound spirits with a Force of 6 or higher tend to become free spirits due to a long association with metahumanity and the natural world, but lesser spirits, especially unbound ones, tend to return to the metaplanes.

To randomly determine whether a spirit goes free, have the spirit make an Edge [Force] (3) Test. If successful, the spirit becomes free and has a starting Edge of 1. Every net hit increases the spirit's Edge by 1. Failure means the spirit departs to the metaplanes. Unbound spirits generally do not go free and suffer a –4 dice pool modifier for the test. On the other hand, spirits that have had memorable or frequent encounters with metahumanity receive a +2 dice pool modifier.

NEW POWERS

Every free spirit gains the Banishing Resistance power (p. 194) and is considered a full Magician (p. 69, SR5) with the exception that they may never have skills in the Conjuring group and may not astrally project from an inhabited vessel unless it has the Astral Projection power (p. 204). Also, when a spirit becomes free, it gains a number of new powers equal to its Edge attribute. After that, each time the spirit's Edge increases, the spirit also gains another new power. New powers can be chosen from any of the following:

- The original spirit type's list of optional powers.
- One of these spirit powers: Astral Gateway, Aura Masking, Divining, Energy Drain (Essence), Materialization, Possession, or Realistic Form.
- Any metamagic technique available to metahuman initiates (except those from the Spiritual Arts, p. 147). Free spirits use Edge instead of initiate grade. Free spirits may also possess metamagics currently unknown to metahumanity, which can provide gamemasters with a unique opportunity to introduce a new metamagical technique.
- A unique power chosen from the list under Free Spirit Powers on p. 204.

FREE SPIRIT SERVICES

A free spirit does not normally owe services to anyone, but it can perform any service a bound spirit can perform (p. 302, SR5) if it wishes to. A free spirit can be bound by its spirit formula (see below) and compelled to perform services, but it does not return to the metaplanes when the services are exhausted or its master dies.

TRUE NAMES

The true name of a spirit is a complex, arcane formula that represents the sum total of the spirit's essence and nature. Although intricate and abstract, an identified spirit formula can be transcribed by the Arcana skill into recognizable symbols and terms. Anyone who possesses a copy of a spirit formula can command the free spirit that the formula represents. Because of this, few free spirits are willing to allow multiple copies of their spirit formulas to exist.

LEARNING THE SPIRIT FORMULA

A spirit formula can be learned via several different methods:

- **Find Physical Location:** A spirit's true name can be physically imprinted on an object, a person, or even a place that was near the spirit when it first broke free, but free spirits often relocate any object imprinted with its true name at the first opportunity. The true name itself is similar to an astral signature and can be identified with an Assensing + Intuition [Astral] (3) Test. Translating the true name into a spirit formula requires an Arcana + Logic [Mental] (spirit's Force x 5, 1 day) Extended Test. A bound spirit can assist in this task as an Aid Study service, regardless of the spirit's type. The spirit formula takes a form appropriate for the spirit's tradition: a thaumaturgic formula for a hermetic mage, a totemic statuette for a shaman, and so on.
- **Metaplanar Quest:** An initiate may learn a spirit's true name by undertaking a metaplanar quest (p. 140) to the spirit's native metaplane. A spirit's metaplane can be obvious or obscure. Without obvious clues, a magician must either succeed in an Assensing + Intuition [Astral] (2) Test if observing the spirit directly or an Assensing + Intuition [Astral] (5) Test if assensing an astral signature. A metaplanar quest for a spirit's true name should be an appropriately harrowing and difficult undertaking, and it might require a spirit guide to reach the necessary plane. A successful quest etches the true name in the initiate's mind; at any time thereafter, he can translate it into a spirit formula with an Arcana + Logic [Mental] (spirit's Force x 5, 1 day) Extended Test.
- **Design Formula:** If a magician directly observing the spirit succeeds in an Assensing + Intuition [Astral] (5) Test, she can attempt to design a functional spirit formula from scratch. Doing so requires an Arcana + Logic [Mental] (spirit's Force x 10, 1 day) Extended Test.

SPIRIT FORMULA COPIES

A spirit is instinctively aware of the location of all copies of its spirit formula—where any of them are when they are created, moved, or destroyed—no matter how many astral barriers exist between the spirit and the formula. If a new copy is made, the spirit automatically becomes aware of its location.

FREE SPIRITS AND KARMA

Free spirits need Karma to grow in power, but unlike characters, they cannot earn it for themselves. A free spirit must receive Karma as a freely given gift from a metahuman; it cannot take Karma for itself unless it has the rare Energy Drain (Karma) power (p. 205). Negotiate a deal with a free spirit, and it will likely ask for Karma as payment; some spirits may ask for services, contacts, unique enchantments, or even material wealth, but generally Karma is what they value above all else.

FEEDING THE FREE SPIRIT

Giving a free spirit Karma requires either a spirit pact (p. 205) or a ritual involving the spirit's formula. Although a spirit needs Karma, allowing metahumans access to its spirit formula places itself in a vulnerable position. This means the spirit's best interest is to keep donors happy—or dead. The ritual to give Karma takes 1 hour per point of Karma given.

USING KARMA

A free spirit can use Karma to improve itself in the following ways. See **Character Advancement**, p. 103, *SR5* for more details.

- It may improve its attributes separately. Each attribute begins at the Force the spirit had when it went free. Free spirits have no racial maximum.
- It may improve or purchase new skills.
- It may initiate as a magician does, but doing so grants a new spirit power per grade rather than a metamagical technique.
- It may increase its Force by 1 point at a time by paying Karma equaling the new Force x 10. Raising Force increases all of the spirit's attributes and powers that are based on Force.

BINDING A FREE SPIRIT

The inherent power of a true name allows anyone, even mundanes, to summon and bind a free spirit.

SUMMONING A FREE SPIRIT

To call forth a free spirit, the summoner must possess the spirit formula and concentrate on the spirit. The spirit will be drawn to the formula and manifest nearby, usually with a bad temper. This summoning generates no services, but no roll is required, and the summoner suffers no Drain. Also, magic cannot prevent this action from occurring. Even a spirit possessing a vessel must abandon the vessel and appear if summoned this way. A spirit inhabiting a vessel is resistant to this pull since its essence is anchored to the physical plane, but it must travel toward the summoner by the fastest physical means possible. If the summoner moves before the inhabiting spirit arrives, the spirit is no longer drawn toward the summoner.

THE BINDING RITUAL

If the summoner chooses to bind the spirit, the presence of the spirit's formula prevents the spirit from harming the summoner during the binding ritual. The ritual to bind a free spirit requires (Force x 25) drams of binding reagents. The ritual itself may be conducted anywhere—no magical lodge is needed—and it takes a number of hours equal to the spirit's Force. At the end of the ritual, the summoner makes an Opposed Test by rolling his Binding + Willpower [Mental] against the spirit's Force + Edge. If the character wins, the spirit owes a number of services equal to the number of net hits. This ritual also produces no Drain.

The spirit cannot harm the summoner until its services are exhausted, but the spirit can still plot to put its master in harm's way. The spirit can also be re-bound with another binding ritual an unlimited number of times. If the master glitches on the rebinding test, the spirit gets 1 Combat Turn to do anything it wants before the binding takes effect and places it back under the master's control. If the master critical glitches the test, all services owed are lost and the spirit becomes free once again.

BANISHING A FREE SPIRIT

Free spirits can be banished just like any other spirit (p. 301, *SR5*), but all of them possess the Banishing Resistance power (p. 194). Since a free spirit is usually unbound and owes no services that can be banished away, each net hit the banisher receives reduces the spirit's unspent Edge (bound free spirits add their Edge and services together). A free spirit whose Edge is reduced to 0 in this way is temporarily disrupted and vanishes to its native metaplane. It may return when its Edge replenishes.

A free spirit that has been banished or disrupted can be prevented from ever returning if the banisher immediately destroys a copy of the spirit's formula and succeeds in an Opposed Test between her Banishing + Willpower [Mental] and the spirit's Force + Edge. Unfortunately, there's no way to tell whether this succeeded or not, unless the spirit later returns. The banishing attempt may be repeated, but this requires another copy of the spirit's formula.

FREE SPIRIT POWERS

The following powers are only available to free spirits.

ASTRAL PROJECTION

Type: M   **Action:** Complex
Range: Self   **Duration:** Special
   The spirit can astrally project, just like a magician (p. 313, *SR5*). This power is only available to spirits with the Inhabitation power. A spirit that does not return to its body after (Force x 2) hours is disrupted.

MUTABLE FORM

Type: P   **Action:** Auto
Range: Self   **Duration:** Special
   Spirits normally materialize with the same form every time, but Mutable Form allows the spirit to appear

differently each time. The spirit's aura is unchanged, however. If the spirit also has the Realistic Form power (p. 198), add the spirit's Force to any Disguise Tests (p. 133, 136, SR5) it makes to impersonate someone. This power is only available to spirits with Materialization.

PERSONAL DOMAIN

Type: M **Action:** Auto
Range: LOS **Duration:** Sustained

The spirit leaves its personal mark over an area of astral space, up to 10,000 square meters per point of Force. Over time this area accumulates a background count aspected toward the tradition the spirit represents (p. 30). The gamemaster determines how quickly the background accumulates, but the process should take months or longer, and the background count should not exceed the spirit's Force / 2.

REGENERATION

Type: P **Action:** Auto
Range: Self **Duration:** Always

Similar to the critter power of Regeneration (p. 400, SR5), this power only applies to the spirit's materialized, possessed, or inhabited form. If the spirit possesses or inhabits a formerly living vessel, the vessel slowly regenerates back to its living form. For example, a wooden homunculus begins to grow new leaves, and a corpse regains a semblance of life.

SPIRIT PACT

Type: M **Action:** Special
Range: Special **Duration:** Special

A spirit with this power can enter into one or more spirit pacts (p. 137). The gamemaster has the final say on what pacts a spirit can enter into. For rules about conducting a spirit pact, see *Spirit Pact (Contractual)*, p. 136.

GREATER POWERS

Greater powers are so dramatic, unusual, or powerful that they can often define an entire encounter with a spirit. Gamemasters should keep these powers rare and limit a spirit to only one of them.

HIDDEN LIFE

Type: P **Action:** Complex
Range: Touch **Duration:** Permanent

The spirit uses this power to permanently place its life force in a creature, place, or object. As long as the hiding place remains safe, the spirit cannot be permanently banished or destroyed by any means. The spirit is able to return after a year and a day if banished with its spirit formula, but a character holding the spirit formula may call the spirit sooner.

The hiding place gains Immunity to Normal Weapons with a Magic equal to the spirit's and Immunity to Age (p. 397, SR5). If the hidden life holder is destroyed, the life force returns to the spirit, and the spirit is treated normally.

ENERGY DRAIN (KARMA)

As described on p. 195, with a Range of Touch and causing Physical damage.

VESSEL TRADING

Type: P **Action:** Complex
Range: Touch **Duration:** Instant

A spirit with Possession may choose to evict the life force of a living vessel, either by ejecting the victim's life force as an astrally projecting creature or putting the victim's life force in the spirit's old vessel. If the old vessel already contains a life force that was subdued by Possession, the victim is forced to astrally project instead. Follow the standard rules for the Possession power (p. 197). Victims placed into a living or nonliving vessel cannot control the vessel like a possessing spirit and are trapped there. The only possible methods of escape is if a free spirit with this power switches them back, the victim can astrally project, or the vessel is exposed to an astral rift or an entity with the Astral Gateway power (p. 194). A victim trapped in an inanimate vessel or astral space will feel his life force ebbing away, and he will die after (Magic or Essence) x 2 hours.

WEALTH

Type: P **Action:** Complex
Range: LOS **Duration:** Special

A spirit with this power can generate precious metals, jewels, and other rare items of great value. Where these items come from is a question no spirit has answered. Once per month, the spirit may make a Magic + Edge [Force] Test. Every hit generates 10,000 nuyen worth of mineral alchemical reagents, usually precious metals or gems. These permanent creations indefinitely carry the spirit's astral signature. The markets being what they are, characters may find it difficult to sell magical gems.

A spirit with this power may also create a similar amount of temporary wealth each day, but the next time the suns sets or rises, these valuable items vanish or transform into dirt or other worthless substances. Because of this, savvy businessmen are reluctant to purchase magical gold.

GREAT FORM SPIRITS

The rules for great form spirits can be found under **Summon Great Form Spirit (Minion)** on p. 136 and **Invocation** on p. 147.

REPUTATION IN THE SPIRIT WORLD

Conjurers interact with the spirit world on a regular basis, and odds are they might purposely or unwittingly perform actions that endear the spirit world to them a bit more or less than usual. Word travels fast through the spirit world, so if you have trouble getting spirits to answer or obey you, maybe it's time to take a good look in the mirror.

Actions have consequences, and nowhere is this more true than when dealing with spirits. To reflect how the spirit world regards a character, the gamemaster may choose to use the Spirit Index and Astral Reputation.

ACCRUING SPIRIT INDEX

The following actions increase a character's Spirit Index by the listed amount:
- Disrupting a normal spirit: 1
- Destroying disrupted spirit in its native meta-plane: 5
- Banishing then conjuring the same spirit: 2
- Rebinding: 1 per Binding Test beyond the first
- Binding a Free Spirit: 5
- Permanently Banishing/Destroying a Free Spirit: 5
- Long-term Binding: 10
- Fettering: 20
- Using Resist Drain power: 5
- Using Spell Binding spirit service: 20
- Exposing spirit to toxicity/corruption: 1 per hour
- Exposing spirit to mana void: (Background Count) per hour
- Losing an ally spirit: 20

The gamemaster is encouraged to keep a character's Spirit Index secret until its effects begin to impact gameplay.

A character can negate accruing Spirit Index for his actions in one of two ways. First, any action—regardless of its Spirit Index value—that is deemed helpful to the spirit world (gamemaster's discretion) does not accrue Spirit Index. Examples include using a Spirit Index action to disrupt a magical threat, such as a blood, insect, or toxic spirit. Second, by expending ([Astral Reputation + 1] x [Spirit Index value of action]) drams of radical reagents (p. 210), a character may prevent accruing Spirit Index points for any action worth 5 or fewer Spirit Index points. Unfortunately, no amount of reagents can offset the immediate damage of more heinous crimes against spirits. Those kinds of actions require slightly more contrition to erase.

ASTRAL REPUTATION

A character's Astral Reputation begins at 0. For every 25 points of Spirit Index a character accumulates, his Astral Reputation increases by 1. When performing Summoning, Binding, or Banishing Tests or when conducting interactions with spirits that require using social skills, a character incurs a negative dice pool modifier equal to his Astral Reputation.

ASTRAL REPUTATION

RATING	EFFECTS
0	Spirits either don't know who you are, or you've atoned for all your spiritual crimes.
1	You've only manage the rock the spirit boat a little, but who hasn't? Spirits are relatively obedient.
2	Some spirits suspect you don't have their best interests in mind. Other give you the benefit of the doubt.
3	The jig is up. Powerful spirits rarely speak to you, but weaker spirits aren't yet wise to your game.
4+	You've rightfully earned the spirit world's enmity. Only desperate spirits answer when you call.

ALLY SPIRIT LOYALTY

Ally spirits usually begin with a Loyalty Rating of 6. In addition to a master's actions that might reduce her ally's Loyalty (gamemaster's discretion), a magician's Astral Reputation ties directly into how loyal the ally is. If a magician attempts to summon a new ally, reduce the ally's Loyalty rating by the summoner's Astral Reputation. If this results in a Loyalty of 0 (or lower), the ritual automatically fails and the ally vanishes before it can be bound.

After summoning and binding an ally, the ally's Loyalty rating decreases by 1 each time the summoner's Astral Reputation increases by 1. Likewise, if the summoner's Astral Reputation ever decreases, the ally's Loyalty rating increases to reflect the spirit's newfound esteem.

SETTING THINGS RIGHT

When your reputation among spirits has reached a point that it's negatively affecting your conjuring abilities, it might be time to balance the karmic scales. There are two different ways to work oneself back into the good graces of the spirit world, and neither of them are easy.

Conjuring Geas: As a sign of contrition, the conjurer may choose a geas (p. 142) that restricts their summoning and apply it to any action that uses the Conjuring skill group. Example geasa would be: only conjuring spirits during the day (time geas); only performing Conjuring group actions at one's personal lodge (location geas); or only summoning spirits of three selected types. Each different geas taken reduces the conjurer's Astral Reputation by 1. Like any negative quality, a geas may later be removed by spending Karma (see **Qualities**, p. 106, *SR5*). Removing a geas with Karma does not affect Astral Reputation. Treat geas as if it provided a 5 Karma bonus.

Atonement: The character may also spend Karma to lower her Astral Reputation. For the ritual to repay one's debt to the spirit world, see **Atonement (Contractual)**, p. 123.

TURNING LEAD INTO NUYEN

"Welcome to the Phoenix's Nest," chirps a holographic assistant at the talismonger shop in Cheyenne. "How may I help you?"

Helix looks up from the deck in her hand and gives the hologram a wink as it fades away.

The shelves are lined neatly with "fair trade" reagents from around the world, including telesma and fetishes organized and alphabetized by tribe—though the Sioux have a conspicuously larger end cap.

Finally noticing the hologram's silence, a heavy-set man with a neatly trimmed beard looks up from his commlink and straightens his short coat. "Um, can I help you find something?"

Helix makes eyes at him from behind her iridescent blue lashes. "Sure thing, sugar. My client is looking for a few hard-to-find reagents for his work. Some say you have frankincense for sale."

The proprietor looks at her. "This way then. The area over here is for our more potent reagents. We also offer distillation services if these products don't meet your client's requirements." He leads her to a back room where a rainbow of colored-glass bottles are stored alongside lined boxes holding various stones carved to convey a semblance of power. "And here is the frankincense."

As Helix chews her gum and looks around the room, her brother Knotingham strolls into the store, wearing the clichéd outfit of a black duster and cowboy hat. She spoofs the alarm at the door to prevent it from going off as her brother enters.

"I'll be with you in a moment," says the flustered proprietor, as he isn't used to having to talk to people. "We're having some technical difficulties."

Helix brings out a little perfume bottle and smiles as she sprays some on her exposed neck. In a fluid motion, she sprays the back wall of stones and frankincense. The proprietor gasps; fingerprints appear to glow a burnt orange along the shelves and corner. It appears the shelf can move based on the position of the fingerprints.

"Tsk, tsk, sugar," she says. "Looks like someone has been naughty. And a false door? Shall we take a look at what's behind it?"

As Helix pushes on the shelf where the fingerprints are, the proprietor tries to use his commlink. "I don't know who you are," he says, "but I'm calling the cops." He discovers his commlink OS is locked and turns to leave the building, but finds Helix's brother blocking his way. Before he can react, a stun baton touches his chest.

Knotingham catches the unconscious proprietor and places him behind the counter. "Target One is out."

"System is under my control," says Helix. "Store is now closed and the room is located."

"Good," says a voice over their earpieces. "Brogan is coming to you."

The door handle jiggles as Helix unlocks it. Just beyond is a wicker man made of wood bundles and plastic trash. Brogan walks past Knotingham into the room. The room contains racks of foci in various states of completion, a table with a pouch of what looks like gold dust, some liquid-filled vials, and four partially wrapped jade disks that looked as if they had just arrived. A hermetic circle is painted on the ground.

Brogan stops at the circle. "Helix, would you mind pouring out one of those vials onto the circle? Be careful not to get any on you."

Helix does as he asked, and the paint and even the concrete starts to smoke and burn. Brogan then crosses the circle, picks up the bag of gold and the jade disks, and stuffs them into the wicker man's chest before leaving the store.

"Knotingham," Helix says, "leave the gift and escort Brogan to his next stop."

Knotingham leaves a glass egg on the counter before and Helix leave the store. "Where to next, Boss?" he asks.

"I have business in Butte Below," Brogan replies.

Minutes later, the proprietor wakes up disoriented from the shock. He sees the glass egg on the counter. A second later his attention is focused on the shadowy figure on the other side of the counter. Then the egg explodes in magical flames.

INTRODUCTION

The ideals of alchemy have been around for a long time. It gained popularity as a pseudoscientific attempt to change mundane metals into precious ones. Transmutation and elemental magic have their roots in alchemy. Since the Awakening, alchemy has also been used for retrieving reagents. Enchanting skills have progressed from foci and fetishes to other permanent magical items and the pairing of magic and technology known as "manatech." More than sixty years of dabbling and esoteric research have produced a wide variety of items, with some presented in *Shadowrun, Fifth Edition* (pp. 304–306, *SR5*) and here.

ALCHEMY BASICS: THE PREPARATION

From potions to flying carpets to scrolls containing words of power, legends have told of miracles wrought through the skills of the enchanter. Since the Awakening, such items can be created in the Sixth World as preparations. Preparations, like almost all magic, require a lynchpin, which channels magical energies from the astral plane to the physical plane. With preparations, the lynchpin is not only the words and images used but also the object that accompanies them. Anchored spells and foci contain a lynchpin that acts as the conduit for magic; when casting a spell, the magician himself is considered the lynchpin. And like geeking the mage, destroying a lynchpin breaks the magic. Damage to a preparation, even a scratch, can destroy the object's lynchpin properties and release the magic within. The object itself may still be functional, but the prepared magic is gone. This is a preparation's primary weakness.

Many alchemists have attempted to use a preparation as "manatech" weapon. They soon discovered that bullets and other high-velocity projectiles make poor preparations as they or the natural materials used in the preparation are scratched, heated, and/or deformed when fired. Low-velocity projectiles like arrows and knives have better success. Usually a command trigger is used: the magician's partner fires the projectile, and the magician activates the preparation's trigger. Contact triggers carry inherent risk to the projectile's firer, and if the projectile misses, odds are it will be too damaged to act as a lynchpin or will remain live and potentially trigger when a friendly or a bystander touches it. With a command trigger, even a prepared shot that misses can still be effective if it's connected to an area-effect spell.

Alchemical preparations are not as smart as anchored spells (p. 152). Once the trigger condition has been met, the preparation (not the magician) sustains the spell for a finite duration, which cannot be stopped unless a magician dispels the spell early. The advantage of preparations is they remain in a suspended state that allows them to be transported through wards (see p. 297, *SR5*). Preparations are a single-use spell. Once the spell has been triggered, the preparation must be re-prepared to cast the spell again with the same trigger. Compared to traditional spellcasting, repeated use of preparations is impractical.

Basic preparations a magician learns represent objects inscribed or decorated with their tradition's formula for the alchemical spell. However, the idea of potions and poultices as preparations is not lost to alchemists. Studying advanced alchemy is required for learning how to combine ingredients into a preparation (see p. 218) or magical compounds.

ORICHALCUM, THE STANDARD OF REAGENTS

According to Platonic legend, the priest-kings of ancient Atlantis discovered orichalcum, but by Plato's time it was known only by name. This orange-gold alloy is utterly absurd from any metallurgical standpoint, as only alchemy can create it. For a brief time during the passing of Halley's comet, orichalcum could be found in the earth. This came as a surprise to alchemists and parageologists who believed orichalcum could not occur naturally. The orichalcum rush was short-lived, however. After Halley's comet passed, the minable veins of orichalcum disappeared. Some suspect that the ore's discovery was coincidental to the passing of

QUICK ANSWERS TO QUESTIONS ABOUT PREPARATIONS (PP. 304–306, SR5)

- A preparation sustains the magic for the spell through the lynchpin (p. 304, SR5).
- A preparation that is not active is considered a sympathetic link (p. 146) to the magician who created it.
- Only one preparation can be activated per Combat Turn, using a Simple Action.
- When the preparation activates, it rolls Force + Potency [Force] as though its spell was just cast. Reagents do not change the limit for the preparation's activation; they only increase potency during creation.
- Preparations become dual-natured only when active, so they cannot be triggered from the astral plane.
- A preparation can be disenchanted through contact with the object.
- Once the prepared spell is triggered, it can be dispelled or resisted like any other spell.
- A preparation can only handle one alchemical spell at a time.
- Once triggered, a preparation's magic is released.
- Preparations with a contact trigger affect the magician and opponent alike after the magician completes the preparation and stops touching the preparation. This is similar to the delay from a hand grenade.
- As with a successful touch attack, the subject of a contact-triggered preparation cannot dodge the attack and can only resist the effect.
- If the preparation takes even a single box of Physical damage, the magic potential is lost.
- Once triggered, the spell cannot be stopped unless it is dispelled or its duration ends.

CREATING ORICHALCUM

At the end of the circulation, the magician must make an Alchemy + Magic [Astral] (3) Test. Failure to meet the threshold of this test consumes the reagents but results in alchemical slag (unusable for magic purposes). Success produces one dram of orichalcum.

With a failure, the magician must make a Body + Magic (3) Test to resist the detrimental effects of radical lead vapors. Failing this test means the character suffers the occasional effects of disorientation (p. 409, SR5) from hallucinations. Each net deficit results in eight hours of hallucinations. This disorientation isn't continuous, but it occurs during stressful or long events in that time period; exactly how this madness plays out is up to the gamemaster. Every subsequent failure to create orichalcum permanently adds an additional eight hours to the next orichalcum-creation failure. This represents the slow spiral into alchemical madness.

Halley's comet and miners had actually unearthed archeological remnants of a very old age.

Scientific examination is difficult because spectroscopic analysis breaks orichalcum down into its component mundane metals. Orichalcum possesses many of the physical properties of gold, such as being dense and highly malleable. It alloys easily with iron, making it preferred for weapon foci construction. Aqua regia dissolves orichalcum, but the magical metal can be reclaimed.

A magician can create a single dram of orichalcum with the Alchemy skill. It takes thirty drams of radical reagents: ten of gold, ten of copper, and ten of cinnabar. The reagents circulate in an alchemical lab for an average of twenty-eight days, with different traditions adding or subtracting a day or two. Hermetics tend to have formulae relating to the orbit of the moon, which is twenty-seven days, while most shamanistic traditions adhere to a full twenty-nine-day lunar cycle—from new moon to new moon. Regardless of the time, this circulation involves the slow heating, cooling, blending, and precipitation of the reagents; any faster and the magic is lost. The magician must tend the circulation by checking the process and adjusting things every ten hours or so. Again, hermetic mages and more modern traditions tend to adopt the industrial revolution's work shift of eight hours, while shamanistic traditions follow a twelve-hour schedule and tend to the circulation at sunrise and again at sunset. After the circulation time, the magician completes the cool-down process, which results in one coin-size dram of orichalcum from the gases and ashes of the reagents. Note that the amount of orichalcum is small compared to the amount of materials used in its creation. Magicians have attempted to collect and condense the remaining vapors into more orichalcum, but this is just as hazardous as failing to create orichalcum in the first place. Failure to create orichalcum presents a risk of magical and neurological damage from alchemical lead vapors produced by the slag.

CREATING REFINED AND RADICAL REAGENTS

A magician can use the Alchemy skill to distill raw reagents into refined reagents and radical reagents. Refined reagents are a step up from raw reagents collected from the field. Radical reagents are powerful, at least for reagents. Refined and radical reagents open more options for the Enchanting skill.

To distill a batch of raw reagents into refined reagents, the alchemist must circulate ten reagents in an alchemical lab for around ten hours. Again, hermetic and modern traditions have adopted the industrial eight-hour work shift for their formulae, while shamanistic traditions have a slower, twelve-hour process tied to sunrise and sunset. At the end of this circulation, the alchemist makes an Alchemy + Magic [Astral] (3) Test. Success results in one dram of refined reagents, and the raw reagents' magic is used up. Failure to meet the threshold means that some of the reagents' magic escaped. The failure difference to the threshold is how many raw reagents were consumed and have to be replaced when trying again. A critical glitch in this test means that all the raw reagents were wasted and the magician needs a new batch to start over.

Refined reagents can be distilled into radical reagents by using the same method: every ten full drams of refined reagents distill into one dram of radical reagents.

TALISMONGER SHOP (ALL SALES FINAL!)

Besides the usual reagents and foci, all sorts of products can be created by a magician skilled in enchanting. While all these products can be used by any magician, those produced with the Artificing skill must be attuned before they can be functional. This is an Intuition + Magic [Astral] (5, 1 hour) Extended Test. An attuned item is considered a sympathetic link to the magician when used in ritual magic (p. 121). The base Potency of purchased items is 6.

AQUA FICTUS

A fool's gold solution that can be used to make false reagents or make an object such as an alchemical preparation or a ritual circle appear to be magical. Aqua fictus looks like a swirling metallic solution that emits occasional flashes of light. Any item coated with aqua fictus appears to glow with a concentrated-mana aura like that of reagents. This trick is difficult to detect. A successful Alchemy + Magic [Mental] (3) Test lets a magician notice the false magic coating on a mundane object. Sales of such items are hit or miss because of the variety of reagents required, and the coating fades entirely after twelve hours. This solution is used in the creation of fake magical items, such as a paper lotus (p. 215).

AQUA FORTIS

This substance detects traces of orichalcum and other true elements. An eight-ounce spray bottle can cover one square meter. Any traces of orichalcum left behind, such as from spilled aqua regia, glow gold. Other Awakened elements glow violet. Aqua fortis allows the user to Observe in Detail (p. 165, SR5) to see if orichalcum or other Awakened elements are present. The gamemaster determines the threshold of the test.

AQUA REGIA

This solution can dissolve orichalcum without damaging the metal's magical properties. This makes the material very easy to transport discreetly. Eight ounces of aqua regia can dissolve 1 dram of orichalcum. Aqua regia is a corrosive acid (p. 170, SR5) capable of dis-

MISPLACED MAGIC ITEMS

There are days when you'll find yourself drunk at a bar and your misplaced wand ends up being used by the brew master as a fruit skewer in some lady's cocktail. So how does that affect practicing magic with that wand? Besides the odd citrus smell, there is a chance that the ambient mana levels caused discord in the item, which forces the magician to re-attune the item in order to use it again. He does not, however, need to re-spend Karma. In general, if the attuned item is not in the magician's possession or at a location where he has an active lodge or circle, the gamemaster should make a daily test of Background Count x 2 (3) (for more information on background counts, see p. 30). If successful, the item is no longer attuned to the magician.

Adept-attuned items (p. 124) and foci may also feel discord if lost or left behind, and such items will lose their attunement bonuses until they are re-attuned. Adepts re-attune items the same way magicians do.

MAGICIANS' CURRENCY

While nuyen is always accepted, such transactions are easy to track, and some unlicensed or unregistered magicians prefer an alternative currency that is accepted by all practitioners of magic. To fill this need, small vials of aqua regia containing a single dram of orichalcum are often used in bartering for magical goods. Half vials are rare but acceptable for smaller exchanges. While orichalcum cannot be used as a reagent in this state, it can be used by anyone with magic talent once it has precipitated from the solution.

solving any metal. The base Damage Value is 14P with an AP of –4.

To extract orichalcum once it has been dissolved in aqua regia, the magician must subject the solution to near-freezing temperatures. This breaks down the formula and neutralizes the alchemical properties. Once the neutralization begins, the orichalcum begins to precipitate. The aqua regia then vaporizes into yellowish green smoke and dissipates.

AQUA VITAE

More of an alchemist's joke, aqua vitae is an alcoholic distillation created through alchemical means. Since soy is the prevalent food staple in the Sixth World, alchemists have worked out ways to distill liquor from just about anything (which gives "hair of the dog" a whole new mean-

PROFESSION: BREW MASTER WITCH/WARLOCK

With trids propagating the myths of love potions and good luck charms, alchemists are constantly approached to provide such items to mundanes. Unfortunately, magic doesn't work exactly that way. The positive that grew from this myth is the alchemists' Guild of Brew Masters. A brew master witch or warlock learns how to use alchemy to create his or her own alcoholic beverages and how to be a bartender, serving mixed drinks akin to mythical potions.

Several upscale bars hire brew master witches or warlocks to provide harmless entertainment with contact-triggered magical drinks. Love Potion Number Nine and Potions of Healing or Wishes are names for mixed drinks that the witch or warlock makes for the average Joe in the bar.

Guild members also learn how to brew more exotic aqua vitae. These brews have different magical properties than normal formulas. Such brews include Tir Alamestra, Japanese Toso, and Mediterranean Styx. These may not bring good luck, but to high-paying clientele, the end result is worth the price.

FLUORESCING ASTRAL BACTERIA

Science has had some success in cultivating mana-sensitive bacteria strains as part of astral security. Three strains exist: FAB I, FAB II, and FAB III. The first strain dies when an astral form or magical force such as a spell passes through it. In death the bacteria release a chemical that can be seen with UV light. The second strain is dual-natured, making it difficult for astral forms to pass through it, and the displacement can be seen physically. The third strain was a mutation that actively seeks out and feeds on astral forms and can be lethal to dual-natured creatures.

ing). Such brews are more potent than standard alcohol. Aqua vitae has an Addiction Rating of 4 (p. 414, SR5)

ASTRAL POWDER

Astral powder, also known as fairy dust, is attracted to sustained magic like static cling. Astral powder was developed as an alternative to using FAB (fluorescing astral bacteria) to detect astral entities, since some consider FAB an environmental hazard regardless of the genetic variant. Astral powder clings to spirits, astrally projecting beings, wards, and sustained or quickened spells. This allows non-Awakened characters to use an Observe in

Detail action (p. 165, SR5) on such things, though the observer will not know exactly what the object is. For example, a person targeted with an Invisibility spell would look no different under astral powder than an astrally projecting magician would. The dispersal device is a paper sphere preparation, which is learned as part of astral powder's formula. This sphere detonates after being thrown, and the astral powder contained within disperses a cloud with a three-meter radius.

Since astral powder is physical, it cannot move through other physical objects. If an astral spirit coated in astral powder goes through a wall, the powder stops at the wall. If a sustained spell is dropped, the powder also drops to the floor. Astral powder doesn't glow like FAB, so visibility modifiers apply. Other conditions, such as rain, wash off the astral powder after a few minutes. **Requires Psychometry (see p. 144).**

FETISH

An alchemist can create a magical device that reduces Drain when cast with a spell suited to fetishes (p. 212). Such spells have to be learned specifically with the fetish, meaning that a character would have to learn a spell twice if he wants to cast it both with and without a fetish. An alchemist needs 1 dram of radical reagents to make the fetish functional for magical use. A magician casting a fetish spell either through Spellcasting or Ritual Spellcasting can reduce the Drain Value by 2 (to a minimum of 2).

GOVI

In the vodou traditions, govi are specially prepared clay pots to hold work loa (watcher spirits). The houngan shapes clay into a pot, etches it with images of their mait-tete, and paints it. Since 2057, govi have been created from glass bottles or other modern containers properly designed with vevers (symbolic images of the loa). Other traditions have taken up creating their own versions of govi to contain watchers. These brooches and talismans are marked with spiritual symbols of the magician's tradition and incorporate a small compartment to contain the watcher.

A govi is created like other preparations, with the govi's Force determining the Force of the watcher it can contain. To determine Drain for the preparation, roll (Force of watcher x 2) test; the hits are Drain, plus any modifications for the trigger (p. 305, SR5). Roll separately to resist Drain for the Watcher Ritual Spellcasting. Potency reduces by 1 point of Force per week, instead of the customary 1 per hour. The magician can offer (Potency x 25) drams of reagents after creation to prevent the govi's Potency from reducing for half a year. This offering can be done every six months. After creation, a watcher is created specifically for that govi. Only one spirit can be connected to a govi at a time. In the case of a watcher, the govi keeps the entity suspended within it, allowing the magician to break

up the watcher's allotted time. It also allows for quick use of a watcher without having to perform the ritual. Releasing a watcher from a govi is a Simple Action.

If a govi is destroyed, the watcher associated with it is also destroyed, whether it was residing in the govi or not. Govi can be found, but the watcher within can only be commanded by the magician who created it. A magician can attune a found govi, but the watcher associated with it is dispelled. **Requires Invocation (see p. 147).**

HAND OF GLORY

The Hand of Glory is an alchemical formula found in the banned witchcraft book *Compendium Maleficarum*. This preparation's lynchpin is the hand of a talented, deceased individual (the formula romanticizes this as the hand of a hanged criminal, but any hand will do). This unique alchemical preparation allows the magician to use the remembered talent of the individual when performing a task. In game terms, the Hand of Glory is tied to one physical Active skill known by the previous owner. The skill is limited by the Force of the ritual instead of

any other limit, including Accuracy. Reagents used must be refined quality or better. When triggered, the magician can use the skill for a number of minutes equal to the Potency. The Hand of Glory, once created, is bonded to the magician and cannot be unbound until the Hand is destroyed or used. It also doesn't lose Potency.

The Hand of Glory can be reused without re-preparing the item, but this requires the magician's blood (and thus leads down the path to blood magic). Normally an object used in an alchemical preparation can be re-prepared if it hasn't been destroyed, but the Hand's talent fades twenty-four hours after being used. In order for the Hand to remember its talent, the magician must take Physical damage with a DV equal to the preparation's Force, then transfer his blood to the Hand to recharge it. This wound cannot be healed by magic.

The *Compendium Maleficarum* warns of trying to own more than one Hand of Glory, saying that the Hands may seek vengeance on their creator if not used—idle hands being the devils tools and all that. **Requires Necromancy (see p. 143).**

INANIMATE VESSEL PREPARATION

Preparing a vessel requires a number of radical reagents equal to five times the Force of the spirit that will possess or inhabit the vessel. Preparing a vessel is done in the same way as a standard preparation, with a minimum Force equal to the Force of the spirit that will enter the vessel. This creation is challenging to craft, as the magician's Alchemy test must exceed the vessel's Object Resistance (p. 295, *SR5*) or Force, whichever is greater. Time to complete is ten days minus the net hits from the Alchemy test (minimum of 1 day). Failure means that a number of reagents equal to the hits from the Opposed Test are lost and the magician has to start again. **Requires Channeling (see p. 148).**

DEAD VESSELS AND SPIRITS

While a corpse can be prepared for inhabitation, most spirits don't like the concept of being confined to such a thing. Necromancers say "the bones rub them the wrong way." Some mages find that the spirit inhabiting a corpse will do or say odd things as they channel some of the memories of the previous owner. Such is the risk of creating zombies or *corps cadavres*.

MANA-SENSITIVE FILM PLATE

Modern magicians have updated the ancient process of daguerreotype photography, exchanging the essential chemical actions with an alchemical process. The layers of chemicals used are mana-sensitive, derived from various Awakened plants and animals, allowing auras, spirits, and even background count to be recorded on the plate. Mana-sensitive film plates are used with mortis optigrams and quicksilver cameras.

MORTIS OPTIGRAM

According to an old, oft-ignored theory, in death the eyes record the last moments of life. Necromancers have found good reason to believe this theory, and they can photograph such images on astral film by using a mortis optigram and the eyes of the deceased. The eyes are positioned to face the plate in the camera. As the magician takes the picture, the last thing the eyes saw is captured on the mana-sensitive film plate. The process takes twenty minutes to complete.

The practice of using the mortis optigram varies greatly, as does the use of such an item as legal evidence. In a criminal case, Tír Tairngire treats a mortis optigram no differently than any physical evidence. The UCAS and CAS permits law-enforcement forensic thaumaturgists to create mortis optigrams as part of an investigation, but the image is considered a valid lead rather than evidence. NAN governments don't allow the creation of mortis optigrams in any instance due to claims that the process is an aberrant ritual. Amazonia is mixed, depending on the severity of the crime.

The mortis optigram is not always a reliable source of information, as the eyes may be closed at the time of death. Other issues include drugs or cybernetics. Note that cybereye replacements cannot be used in a mortis optigram. The resulting image is almost realistic and oddly three dimensional on the mana-sensitive plate. If the deceased suffered from hallucinations, even ones induced by drugs, those hallucinations can appear on the plate. If the deceased had the ability to astrally perceive, astral space may also appear on the plate (see **Quicksilver Camera**, p. 215). Astral photos from a mortis optigram are not pretty since they are tainted with echoes of pain and emotional turmoil. **Requires Necromancy (see p. 143).**

MYSTIC RESTRAINTS (CUFFS/MASK/JACKET)

For confining petty Awakened criminals, law-enforcement officers use cuffs and hoods that distract the incarcerated with lights and sounds or use electric shock to keep twitchy fingers in line. For the hardened criminal magicians, however, police use individually tailored mystic restraints. The shape of these restraints acts like acupuncture that restricts the magician's access to magic. Mystic restraints (cuffs, masks, or jackets) have to be crafted with the Artificing skill, using the same Force requirements as crafting a symbolic link. Permanently creating the restraint requires 1 Karma.

Net hits from the Artificing Test determine the Force of the restraint, and the Force of the restraint reduces the Magic rating of the Awakened individual (including adepts). Adepts restrained this way temporarily lose Power Points associated with Magic loss; they may choose which powers are affected. There are many pressure points to use, but each restraint is limited to how much Magic it can it restrain. While restraints are made for a specific individual, an existing restraint can be attuned to another individual, but it will be half as effective. This requires an Intuition + Magic (5, 1 hour) Extended Test and requires either assensing the subject or having a material link of the subject to be used in attuning the restraints.

Mystic cuffs are made of steel or titanium and can have a maximum Force of 8; they are ineffective if the subject has one or more cyberarms. Masks are made of steel and leather or ceramic and have a maximum Force of 12. Similar to a straitjacket, a mystic jacket can have embedded brass studs on the inside and woven symbols on the outside. A mystic jacket can have a Force up to 18.

If the subject has the Flux metamagic (p. 150), he can reduce the effectiveness of the mystic restraints by his initiate grade while his aura is in flux.

PAPER LOTUS

Not all talismongers are nice or play fair. The ability to falsify magical material for financial gain is a strong motivator. Besides the few pre-Awakening artifacts that have shown up, "paper lotus" is a general term for using the Artificing skill (p. 306, *SR5*) to create a counterfeit magical item. These magical items are indistinguishable from the real thing unless an observer passes a Perception Test (see below), but they cannot be used for any magical purpose. These magical items are considered to have the Counterfeit quality (p. 197, *Run & Gun*). If the item can be bonded, the bonding will fail when attempting to spend Karma, and the item will be exposed as counterfeit. Fake reagents don't do anything when expended. In both cases, the illusion eventually expires, so any magician can see that the object is fake.

When the Artificing ritual is complete, the number of net hits becomes the threshold for an observer determining if the item is a fake through a Perception Test. The Force of the Artificing ritual determines how many days the item appears to be magical. Paper lotus creators run the risk of someone detecting their items as a fake and then using them in ritual magic as retribution against the artificer. These items are sympathetic links while the illusion lasts. **Requires Masking (see p. 149).**

QUICKSILVER CAMERA

The quicksilver camera is a handheld camera with a built-in collapsible tripod. It can hold five mana-sensitive film plates, with only one being exposed at a time. This camera can take an astral photograph in two minutes.

Early astral photography required several hours of exposure, but six years ago, technology and thaumaturgical research reduced the exposure time to only thirty minutes per mana-sensitive plate. These plates allowed

MAGECUFF AND MAGEMASK

Magecuffs are crafted with glomoss (a form of bioluminescent plant that glows in response to magic or astral entities) and a light-triggered shock device. If the cuffs detect spellcasting or astral projection, the cuffs subject the incarcerated individual to a 15S electrical attack (p.170, SR5).

A magemask is a plastic hood and gag that cuts off the incarcerated individual's line of sight and produces a combination of light and sounds that disorient the magician and deters astral projection. Attempting astral projection while wearing a magemask requires a Willpower + Intuition (4) Test.

anyone to take a picture of the astral world, and while beautiful enough to have a gallery at the MoMA in New York, they capture a very blurry view of astral space. Astral space is very dynamic, so it cannot sit still for thirty minutes. Also, the mana-sensitive plate could be overexposed since mana isn't tied to light exposure, and whole sets of plates could be ruined if an astral entity moved through the camera during exposure.

To improve the process, alchemists altered the plates so that the Awakened photographer acted as the plate's catalyst. To take a photo, the photographer removes the cap to expose the plate to visible light and activates the plate's chemicals to record the astral world. Once activated, the exposure process cannot be stopped, and it completes in two minutes. Moving the camera before the full exposure time ruins the photograph (astrally and visibly). One the exposure time has elapsed, the astral photo automatically develops with a secondary alchemical process.

FAKE MAGIC ITEMS

ITEM	MINIMUM FORCE OF ARTIFICING RITUAL	UNITS OF AQUA FICTUS REQUIRED
Reagent (10 drams)	2	1
Fetish	4	1
Refined Reagent (10 drams)	4	2
Quicksilver Camera	5	1
Radical Reagent (10 drams)	5	4
Alchemical Preparation	6	1/2 Force
Focus	8	1/2 Force
Artifact	*	*

Gamemaster should decide the Force of the ritual required, as artifacts are unique. In many cases, additional requirements/reagents are needed in falsifying an artifact.

Physically the image is in color as seen with a normal camera but with iridescent marks overlaying the image. These swirls and spots represent the alchemical reaction to recording the astral plane, not what mundanes believe are auras and spirits captured on film. Viewing the picture astrally reveals another image: a snapshot of the flow of astral energies at that point in time. This astral image captures astral signatures, background count levels, and the auras of wards, sustained spells, Awakened individuals, spirits, critters, preparations, and bonded foci. The photograph can be replicated through alchemical means. The auras in the photo can only be read and recognized through astral perception.

Characters may attempt to use Assensing to analyze any astral being, aura, or signature captured in an original astral photo; the threshold for an Assensing Test is 2 more than normal, and the limit for the test is fixed at 4 due to the camera's limitations. Astral entities or objects that pass through the area while the photo is being taken show up as ghostly images, but no information can be gleaned from them. Copies of astral photos also lose a level of detail, making the fixed limit for the Assensing Test 3.

Since astral photographs capture auras, the plate can serve as a sympathetic link (p. 145) to any entity or object that remained in the shot for the duration of the exposure. Duplications of the original photograph can be used as a symbolic link (p. 216), with the photograph meeting the "Creator has met the target" condition. An original astral photograph's aura can be wiped through smudging (p. 136). The wiped photograph is treated the same as a copy, though the photograph is considered to have a Force 12 psychic imprint.

SHOFAR

The shofar, which is a more impressive name than "the horn that scares spirits," derives from the Judean tradition of exorcism. The shofar's sound causes spirits to be shaken and leave the area. When using it, make an Opposed Test pitting the spirit's Force + Willpower against the shofar's Force x 2. Materialized or manifested spirits that fail the Opposed Test stop what they are doing and retreat back to astral space, wasting the service they are in process of fulfilling. Materialized or manifested free spirits attempt to leave the area as if affected by the Fear power for a number of Combat Turns equal to the shofar's Potency. Spirits inhabiting a living or non-living vessel are only distracted by the noise and suffer a -2 dice penalty to all actions for that Combat Turn. The shofar effect is instantaneous, but after activating it, the item disintegrates. The shofar has a longer shelf life than other compounds, as its Potency reduces by 1 per week. **Requires Exorcism (see p. 148).**

SYMBOLIC LINK

From effigies to drawings, a symbolic link is a representation of a spell's target. The most notorious of symbolic links are voodoo dolls, which a magician can use to inflict curses upon the individual the doll represents. The magician uses the Artificing skill to create a symbolic link, but the required Force depends on how well the magician knows the subject. The symbolic link is viable for a number of days equal to the net hits in the Artificing Test. The downside to symbolic links is that the object contains the creator's astral signature while the link remains viable. This means that a voodoo doll can be used as a material link against the creator. **Requires Psychometry (see p. 144).**

SYMBOLIC LINK CREATION

CONDITION	REQUIRED FORCE
Creator knows the target intimately or has a material link	2
Creator has assensed the target or has an original astral photograph	4
Creator has a copy of an astral photograph of the subject	8
Creator has met the target	12
Creator is personally unfamiliar with the target	16

MAGIC ITEM PRICE INDEX

ITEM	SKILL	THRESHOLD	BASE TIME	MATERIAL COST	AVAILABILITY	PURCHASE COST
AgHexHex	—	—	—	—	8	Force x 500¥
Aqua fictus	Alchemy	3	10 hours	850¥	8	1,000¥
Aqua fortis	Alchemy	3	10 hours	43¥	4	50¥
Aqua regia	Alchemy	3	10 hours	85¥	5	100¥
Aqua vitae	Alchemy	3	4 hours	13¥	1	15¥
Astral powder	Alchemy	4	2 day	70¥	4	120¥
BDNB	—	—	—	—	8	Force x 500¥
FAB I	—	—	—	—	10	50¥ per cubic meter
FAB II	—	—	—	—	16R	Force x 50¥ per cubic meter
FAB III	—	—	—	—	20F	Force x 25,000¥ per cubic meter
Fetish	Artificing	2	1 day	1,700¥	4	2,000¥
Govi	—	—	—	—	Force	Force x 50¥
Hand of Glory	—	—	—	—	(Force x Force) R	Force x 1,500¥
Lot's Curse	—	—	—	—	14F	Force x 1,000¥
Magecuff	—	—	—	—	5	1,000¥
Magemask	—	—	—	—	2R	200¥
Mana-sensitive film plate	Alchemy	4	3 days	21¥	4	25¥
Mortis optigram	Artificing	4	1 week	2,550¥	6	3,000¥
Mystic cuff	—	—	—	—	(Force)R	Force x 200¥
Mystic jacket	—	—	—	—	(Force)R	Force x 500¥
Mystic mask	—	—	—	—	(Force)R	Force x 400¥
Quicksilver camera	Artificing	4	1 week	2,125¥	4	2,500¥
Sage	—	—	—	—	(Force x 6)R	Force x 800¥
Shofar	—	—	—	—	Force	Force x 800¥
Spirit strength	—	—	—	—	(Force x 6)R	Force x 3,000¥
Symbolic link	Artificing	—	1 day	—	—	—
Witch's moss	—	—	—	—	(Force x 6)R	Force x 1,600¥

FORBIDDEN KNOWLEDGE

There are several magical books that law enforcement tries to keep out of public hands. These are similar to guides on how to get away with murder or how to make a dirty bomb, but for questionable magical activity. Legal actions vary for those caught with one of these tomes, but consequences can involve the magician's license to practice magic being revoked or being added to a security watch list. They aren't exactly instructional guides on how to do blood magic. Instead they're like a gateway drug that gives the magician a little taste of the dark stuff.

COMPENDIUM MALEFICARUM

The *Compendium Maleficarum* is a handbook on necromancy and other dark rituals. The *Maleficarum* was originally published in Italy in 1608, and a magician named Lopiccolo partially revised the tome in 2041, applying modern black-magic terminology and techniques in his translation. Lopiccolo did not complete his revision, unfortunately; he died horrifically while attempting to revise the ritual on page 251 of the tome.

DE PRAESTIGIIS DAEMONIUM

This is a handbook on witchcraft—the bad kind. Originally published in 1563, it was first translated from Latin to English in 1928, and no one revised it for the Sixth World until 2028. *De Praestigiis Daemonium* discusses curses, potions, and avoiding being drowned or burned at the stake.

MORTUUS MALUM

First bound in the twelfth century, *Mortuus Malum* collects Roman accounts from Gallic, Celtic, and other tribal rituals as the Roman legions conquered Europe from 60–33 BC. These rituals didn't involve your garden-variety free spirits: they were meant for calling down demons to disembowel the Roman army. Demons didn't actually attack the Romans during their conquest of Europe; however, like many mystical items, scholars believe there's a grain of truth to *Mortuus Malum*'s rituals.

99 BOTTLED DEMONS ON THE WALL

Published circa 2058, this modern neo-anarchist book covers using alchemy and ritual sorcery for terrorist activities. A similar book is *The Neo-Anarchist's Guide to Street Magic* from 2065, which offers tips and tricks for using sorcery and conjuring for crime and profit.

ADVANCED ALCHEMY

Initiation into the advanced alchemy metamagic (p. 152) allows the magician to create more specific triggers, including a delayed timer and specific target contact, to be added. It also allows the magician to create magical compounds with unique properties.

MAGICAL COMPOUNDS

Some preparations are very unique in design, requiring specific reagents in its creation. While they can be similar to other alchemical preparations, these magical compounds require specific refined reagents to create and, if the magician wishes, to improve Potency. For example, a magician creating the sage compound must have at least 1 refined dram of lichen reagent. If he prepares the sage at Force 4 but wants a Potency of 8, he must add an additional 8 drams of refined reagents. Magicians who know the formula for these preparations are leery of giving up such secrets, so starting characters are not allowed to learn these formulas. Magical compounds still use alchemical preparation rules in their creation (p. 304, *SR5*).

While inactive, a magical compound can be dispelled like any other alchemical preparation. When active, these compounds are trickier to dispel. The magician must be in contact with the compound and can use the Disenchant skill to resist or reverse the compound's effect. The compound can resist with twice its Force. Each net hit against the magical compound reduces its Force. If the Force is reduced to 0, the compound no longer functions, and its aftereffects begin. For other compounds, the secondary effects still apply for the compound's complete duration until healing is applied. Magical compounds have an active duration that lasts (Potency x 10) minutes. Inactive magic compounds degrade slower, reducing Potency by 1 every day.

EMPOWERED MAGICAL COMPOUNDS

These compounds give the subject a spell-like ability or critter power, which the magician can turn off with a Simple Action. The power lasts for either (Potency x 10) minutes or until it has been dispelled. When the subject uses an ability, the test uses the preparation's Potency in place of Spellcasting and the preparation's Force in place of Magic, with the usual Force for the limit.

Every time the spell is activated after the initial activation, the subject feels strain from the spell's Drain Value based on the Force of the preparation. For critter powers, Drain equals the preparation's Force. The magician resists the Drain Value with Willpower alone or per

TRIGGERS FOR PREPARATIONS AND ANCHORED SPELLS

COMMAND (P. 305, SR5)

Anchored Version: A magician can trigger this spell with a Simple Action, regardless of range or line of sight. If the preparation is out of sight, then the magician cannot chose the target of the activated spell.

Advanced Command (Delay Timer): When the magician sets up a Command trigger, he can choose to delay its activation for up to 60 seconds. The length of the time delay must be chosen when the preparation is created. This trigger adds 2 to the Drain Value of the preparation's creation.

CONTACT (P. 305, SR5)

Anchored Version: This trigger can be activated either when a living aura, a previously assensed aura, or any aura not belonging to the spellcaster comes into direct physical or astral contact with the anchor. Note that without the lynchpin, the anchor is invisible on the physical plane and takes up space equal to the caster's size.

Advanced Contact (Target-Specific): Creating a preparation with this contact trigger requires a material link to the subject. After successful creation, the preparation only activates on contact with the person associated with the material link. This trigger adds 1 to the Drain Value of the preparation's creation. Such a preparation can be used as a sympathetic link to both the preparer and the subject it was created for. This trigger is for preparations only.

Advanced Contact (Gender/Metatype-Specific): This contact trigger allows the preparation to only trigger when touched by someone of either a specific gender (which includes a full range of genders rather than the traditional binary two; people should be treated as the gender with which they identify) or metatype. This trigger adds +3 to the Drain Value of the preparation's creation.

TIMED (P. 305, SR5)

Anchored Version: A timed trigger can range from 1 Combat Turn up to (Force) months before the spell activates.

BACKGROUND COUNT (ANCHORED SPELLS ONLY)

This trigger activates if the background count of the area is modified in any way: raised, lowered, or undergoes an aspected change (see **Background Count**, p. 30). At the gamemaster's discretion, any magic use in the area may create sufficient minor, temporary background fluctuations to trigger the construct. This trigger adds 1 to the Drain Value of the anchored spell.

DETECTION SPELL (ANCHORED SPELLS ONLY)

If a Detection spell is part of the anchor, the triggered spell can only target someone or something in direct physical or astral contact with it. In addition, if a Detection spell serves as the trigger, this spell can aim the anchored spell at any valid target it detects within range. This second spell must be quickened (p. 326, SR5) and linked to the anchor. This trigger adds +1 to the Drain Value of the anchored spell.

---

the magician's tradition. If the subject is sustaining the spell or the power is considered always on, he suffers a –2 penalty to all actions. At the end of the spell's duration or when it is dispelled, the compound's aftereffects take effect. This aftereffect lasts for an equivalent original duration (not the duration before it was dispelled) and cannot be treated even by magic.

Other magical compounds have a negative effect instead of benefitting the user. These magical compounds either target a subject with a spell, or the compound reduces an Awakened creature's ability by the compound's Potency. While this negative effect is active, the secondary effect is untreatable.

Magical compounds unfortunately don't function well in combination with augmentations. When used on such a subject, reduce both the compound's Force and Potency by the amount of Essence the subject has lost to augmentations.

AGHEXHEX

AgHexHex, more formally known as silver hexamagnohexaphosphate, is a magical alchemical compound found to have a detrimental effect against Awakened creatures capable of transforming into vapor particles (Mist Form), keeping them corporeal.

Trigger: Contact

Effect: Once in contact, if the Potency exceeds the target's Magic attribute, the Mist Form power is negated completely for the duration of the compound. If the target is using Mist Form when sprayed by AgHexHex, the target forcibly reverts to solid form for that Combat Turn regardless of Potency, causing (Force + 4) Stun damage.

Aftereffect: Nauseated side effect

Required Reagent: Refined silver

MAGICAL COMPOUND SIDE EFFECTS

This is a list of side effects that can be applied to the user/target of a magical compound.

BLINDED

One eye: –4 all actions involving sight. Two eyes: –8 on all actions, no vision-based Perception tests allowed.

STUNNED

Subtract 10 from Initiative score at the beginning of the Combat Turn while the effect is active.

DEAFENED

One ear: –2 all actions involving hearing. Two ears: –4 on all actions involving hearing, no hearing-based Perception tests allowed.

UNABLE TO SPEAK

The target loses the ability to form understandable speech. He can mutter, gesture, groan, and drool, but everything they try to speech comes out as gibberish.

BLEED OUT

The target suffers 1P damage, unresisted, for every action she performs that does not use the First Aid skill.

ONE-ARMED BANDIT

The target's arm is ineffective, and he is unable to perform any actions with that limb.

WEAK SIDE

The target suffers a –2 dice penalty on all melee Defense Tests while the affected arm is ineffective.

BROKEN GRIP

The target is unable to maintain her grip on anything, and she suffers a –1 dice pool penalty per injured arm for all Subduing or Clinching attacks. Any item in her hand drops.

FATIGUED

The target makes a Damage Resistance test using Body against a DV of (Potency)S. This is a one-time side effect.

WINDED

The target is unable to perform Sprint actions.

NAUSEATED

Make a Body + Willpower (4) Test. Each hit less than the threshold causes the target to double over and begin vomiting for one Combat Turn. A vomiting target suffers a –4 dice pool penalty to all actions.

SLOW DEATH

Physical Damage only; causes internal injury. Target suffers unresisted 2P damage every 1 minute.

SLOWED

The target's movement, both Walk and Run rate, is halved.

BDNB

Also known as "Bad Dog! No Biscuit!," this compound is commonly used for hunting Awakened game.

Trigger: Contact

Effect: Reduce the subject's Magic attribute by the Force of the compound when the subject uses the Paralyzing Howl power (p. 399, *SR5*). If the Force exceeds the target's Magic attribute, the power is negated completely for the duration of the compound.

Aftereffect: Unable to Speak side effect

Required Reagent: Refined hell hound's tongue (*Cynoglossum magiofficinale*)

LOT'S CURSE

Lot's Curse is a poison made from the Awakened Gomorrah tree, whose fruit causes calcification of flesh and death when eaten.

Trigger: Contact

Effect: The target is subjected to a Petrify spell. Even if the target resists the immediate petrification, the secondary effect is still petrifying the target from the inside. Upon the target's death, the petrification becomes permanent. If the victim is still alive at the end of the duration, they return to normal.

Aftereffect: Slow Death side effect

Required Reagent: Refined Gomorrah apple

SAGE

Trigger: Contact

Effect: The target is empowered with the Detect Magic, Extended spell.

Aftereffect: Both eyes suffer the Blinded side effect

Required Reagent: Refined *Cladonia stellaris* lichen from the North American tundra

SPIRIT STRENGTH

Trigger: Contact

Effect: The target is empowered with the Hardened Mystic Armor power (p. 397, *SR5*).

Aftereffect: Reduce the target's Physical limit to 1 for an equivalent duration.

Required Reagent: Refined teonanácatl mushroom from Aztlan

WITCH'S MOSS

Trigger: Contact

Effect: The target is empowered with the Paralyzing Touch power (p. 400, *SR5*).

Aftereffect: Both arms suffers the Broken Grip and Weak Side side effects.

Required Reagent: Refined barghest blood

THE LIFE OF A TALISMONGER

The charging piasma swung its massive claw at the chest of its target—a troll runner called Hammer. Moving faster than the Awakened bear, the cybered troll shifted his body to the right, narrowly avoiding the violent blow. With the silver-haired bear drawn into a vulnerable position by its own inertia, the runner put all his weight behind the swing of his axe, burying it into the back of the enraged bear. The bear roared ferociously in pain as blood splattered everything nearby, including the troll. The piasma staggered backwards, and after a second or two, aggressively charged again at its prey, razor-sharp tusks lowered and ready to swing up and into vulnerable flesh.

"Chummer, are you sure this is the only way to collect this pelt? This seems a bit extreme to me," gasped Hammer as he scrambled to get out of the way of the piasma's massive maw as the bear snapped at him.

"Quite sure," replied the calm voice of the human onlooker, standing just inside the camp. "You're no good at using bows. And simply shooting the beast using a gun would contaminate the pelt with gunpowder residue and metallic residue. Enchanting with it after that would simply be impossible for me. Same thing goes with tranquilizers and other drugs. This animal must be killed with a properly prepared melee weapon per United Talismonger Association regulations, which in this case is the axe you are wielding."

"How about magic?" the female elf called Silver asked. "I could simply stun this bear out with a spell, and make this a simple kill for him."

"I'm sorry, my dear," the talismonger replied. "Your astral signature could also affect the pelt's aura negatively, potentially ruining the specimen for me. This needs to be a clean kill. If you want to be paid, this is how it needs to go down."

The piasma charged once more at the troll. This time, the piasma connected with its claw, ripping into Hammer's left shoulder with its claw and slamming the troll to the ground. Despite the obvious gash in his arm and shoulder, the troll rolled away from the bear towering over him on its hind legs and scrambled back to his feet with blood trickling liberally down the left arm of his body armor.

"And I'm sorry, there's nowhere on that bear that I can jack into. So I'm pretty much useless here," chimed in the team's hacker, Megapulse. "Sorry, Hammer."

"That's all fine and good, but I also don't want to see my chummer get killed," Silver replied, simply ignoring their decker. After a few seconds, Silver asked, "Well, what if I were to cast on *him*? Would an armor spell on Hammer be out of the question?"

The talismonger thought about it for a few seconds. "No, I don't see how that would screw things up."

Without waiting for further explanation or permission, Silver cast her spell, enveloping the troll in a blue, translucent energy field, just as the bear swatted the troll again with its paw, this time connecting with the troll's center mass. The troll once again went skittering along the forest floor, getting a mouthful of dirt in the process. But this time, the claws did not penetrate the troll's flesh.

"ARGH ... THAT FUCKING HURT," roared the troll, grabbing at his ribs. It was likely at least a couple of them were broken from the mighty blow. Rising once more to his feet, Hammer swung furiously at the piasma. Swing after swing the troll struck the silver bear, drawing greater amounts of blood on the blade of the axe. Unrelenting, the very pissed-off troll swung his axe at the bear again and again until the bear fell before the Hammer's feet, dead.

"There's your fucking pelt," growled the Hammer, throwing down the talismonger's axe in rage. Looking at the female elf standing next to Mr. Johnson, Hammer grimaced, "First Cheyenne and that wonderful job that got both of our asses kicked, and now this! You certainly have a way of picking the crappy jobs for us! Never again will I go on one of these excursions where I get mauled! Contrary to popular belief, trolls are not meant to pick fights with Awakened bears!" The blood-stained troll started to move past the onlookers, heading toward his tent where he could patch up his shoulder and attend to his ribs. Glaring down at his chummer, Hammer looked down at his torn up shoulder and then back up to Silver. "And by the way, elf, you owe me a new set of armor."

POSTED BY: LYRAN

It is no exaggeration to say that talismongers are a magic user's best friend. Talismongers provide access to reagents; reagents that runners would have to take time away from their runs to hunt down and collect themselves if talismongers were not available. Many urban shadowrunners would lack the skills, experience, and the proper gear to adequately undertake these excursions into remote and uninhabited parts of the world where some of the best reagents exist. In many hostile environments, if you don't know precisely what you're doing, your inexperience will get you killed.

Once the reagents have been gathered, suitable telesma have been acquired. With their broad knowledge of the arcane, talismongers undertake the complicated enchanting process to combine all these elements and turn them into powerful foci and alchemical preparations of all varieties. These can be invaluable to your typical shadowrunner at the street level, particularly when a runner team is going up against a potent magic-based threat such as a corporate wage mage or a toxic shaman who may have their own foci and other magical gear. In short, a quality talismonger can turn any magic-using slot with a small amount of talent into an elite, magic-using shadowrunner over time. This is an asset that no magician or adept should ever be without. Talismongers' services can, and very often do, keep a magic user alive, even when the rest of the world may want him dead.

⊘ Talismongers: the magic fixers of the world. Not only do they enchant foci, but they run their own networks for obtaining hard-to-get reagents, often times bartering and leveraging favors for the items they need among each other. Many times, these established networks will save talismongers time and effort. Why go out and harvest the reagents yourself, when another talismonger you know in the network has extra reagents they can sell you, or trade you for something you have that they need? Most talismongers are also best friends with smugglers and poachers, often to be able to bypass customs with some of their less-than-legal acquisitions. And many times, talismongers will act as Johnsons, hiring runners to help them obtain the items that they can't obtain on their own.

And also, they need runners to keep them safe from other talismongers out in the wild that might see them as easy prey for robbery.
⊘ Stone

⊘ So, how does that make talismongers any different from talisleggers?
⊘ Lone Rider

⊘ Legitimate talismongers, although we will bend the rules on occasion to acquire some illegal stuff for their clients, will, as a general rule, follow the vast majority of legal restrictions for the materials they collect imposed on them by the various governments. This means carrying legal-ish permits and licenses for gathering reagents. Talismongers also (more or less) adhere typically to the talismongering guidelines as laid out by the United Talismongers Association. So if the UTA says, "Hey, this is dangerous and you should not do it," a talismonger frequently follows that practice. Or if the message is "Hey, this animal is near extinction, don't hunt it," a reputable talismonger heeds that advisory, or at the very least acts responsibly by not hunting and killing pregnant female specimens of the paranormal critter. A talislegger basically says "fuck you" to the authorities and will do anything and everything they want for a profit. Also, talismongers tend to be more independent, or if they work for someone, they work for a legitimate organization such as an UTA-affiliated magic group. Talisleggers, on the other hand, tend to work for organized crime.
⊘ Lyran

⊘ Like you and the Koshari?
⊘ Ma'fan

⊘ That's different. They're a client, not my employer. I have also been contracted to do jobs for the Yakuza and the Triads. I am independent, and I follow my own path.
⊘ Lyran

⊘ You can add the "not using dragon reagents" to the list of things that legitimate talismongers will not do any more, and for good reason. Seeing as though a vast majority

THE ROLE OF THE ARTISAN SKILL AND ENCHANTING

Outside factors, including background counts, emotions, and environmental destruction are well known to influence the conditions of reagents. And so, too, when a talismonger is crafting a focus, emotions that a talismonger invest in the enchanting process can either make things easier to create a focus—or more difficult. Crafting a focus as a work of art, and infusing it with creativity and passion, is one way talismongers can influence the enchanting process and make it easier. Prior to making the Enchanting Test, a talismonger may elect to make an Artisan + Intuition [Mental] (5, 1 Day) Extended Test. Net hits represent the creativity and the passion the talismonger is infusing into his work. If a mystic adept has an adept power that can influence their creativity, such as Pied Piper, they may choose to use that power and make that test instead. The character may only make this test if the focus they are constructing is being individually made and is not being mass produced. Taking one's time to craft a focus instead of merely assembling one requires an investment of time. The character decides how much time they have put into crafting the focus, with a minimum time being 1 day. Some talismongers will take several days working on one focus, much like a sculptor or painter does on their art forms, while others take weeks and some take months to add artistic flourishes to their work, from engravings and inlaid jewels to elegant drawings. Some very rare talismongers sometimes takes a year or longer crafting the telesma before making the final Enchantment Test. The net hits from the Artisan Test are then used as bonus dice for the Enchanting Test, in addition to any enchanting focus they may be using. The maximum amount of bonus dice that can come from this process equals the ranks in the skill used as part of the Extended Test.

Alternatively, negative emotions can have a detrimental impact on the design of a focus. If the character is mentally distracted or is emotionally distraught in some way while they are making an enchantment, the gamemaster make call for a Composure Test (p. 152, SR5) with a threshold of 2, higher if the emotions involved are especially intense. A successful test allows the character to keep their emotions in check while they are designing a focus. A failure imposes a –2 dice pool modifier to the final Enchanting Test, and a glitch means a –4 dice pool modifier. A critical glitch causes the character to make a critical mistake, which ruins the entire enchantment and wastes the reagents.

of talismongers that participated in that practice are no longer in business today.

> ● Jimmy No

> ● Or alive.
> ● Slamm-0!

Talismongers, because of the nature of their work, will work out of a physical shop. A talismonger needs tools, some place to store their reagents, and a proper work area to enchant (also commonly referred to as their magic lodge). This would typically be a storefront known as a lore shop, which most reputable talismongers prefer as it makes it easy for their clients to find them. Alternately this could be the back of a van or other type of vehicle, as some talismongers prefer to remain mobile and harder to find, while also keeping the location of their permanent magic lodge secret. It is a lot harder to steal from a mobile talismonger when you're not sure where they're ever going to be. You should not judge a talismonger based on how they conduct their business, however. Instead, you should judge talismongers based on the quality of their work as well as their street cred. Some talismongers do not engage in fine craftsmanship; choosing instead to mass produce foci, and turning anything and everything into a focus, from crappy cigarette lighters to ugly, cheap-ass rings that cost no more than twenty nuyen, with no sense of quality control or aesthetics. From my perspective, those crappy talismongers are no different than these megacorporate subsidiaries that approach talismongering and enchanting as a "one-size-fits-all" operation and lack any individuality, subtly, or soul in their work. Honestly, I fail to see how they can do their jobs without infusing even a small amount of passion and creativity into their work. Others, such as myself, are true artisans, and will spend a lot of time and effort getting the aesthetics perfect on a particular focus. We're quite particular in what we will enchant and how we will enchant it. Talismongers like myself know no limits when it comes to our art. Craftsmanship is something we take great pride in, and we go to great lengths to satisfy the customer, no matter how far we must travel or what remote parts of the world we must visit to gather various unique reagents for the purpose of creating just the right custom focus for our customers. Even if it means tossing out our first or second attempts at enchanting a focus, we'll do it, if only to make sure our art form is perfect and our reputations as true artisans are preserved.

So what does it take to be a talismonger? It really depends on who you ask. I would say the first and foremost quality of being a good talismonger is possessing a fundamental knowledge of alchemy, herbalism, metallurgy, geology, geography, and of course thaumaturgy. You have to be able to identify which herbs, plants, metals, gems, and paranormal critters are good for enchanting and which ones possess the highest-grade qualities

for enchanting purposes. You also need to know how to determine whether a specimen is of good quality or whether it has become tainted by environmental factors and is unusable. A good talismonger is always looking for ways to perfect their techniques and will frequently barter and haggle with other talismongers for tips on how to refine their enchanting process. In remote areas, such as in South America and Africa, there is a lot more fluidity with governmental forces. One day, you may be working with one government, and in the next, you have a different government with new rules breathing down your neck. You need to be adaptable to change. This also means there could be new government officials to bribe. So keeping up with current events in geo-political hot spots is also crucial for the success and the long-term survival of a talismonger.

- Making sure you have goods you set aside to use in bribes— it's just as important as having ammunition for your guns. In remote areas, soldiers are not going to be interested in your cred sticks and electronic accounts. Those things are useless in places where wireless connectivity is limited. Instead, they'll be interested in gemstones, silver, gold, or other valuable commodities. In many third-world spots, be prepared to lose approximately fifteen percent of the reagents that you harvest to these opportunistic sons of bitches in the form of bribes.
- Traveler Jones

- Yes, this is why I will still harvest crappy reagents when I come across them. The things that I can't use but still look like they are worth a lot of nuyen, I will pass off to the uninitiated. What's not valuable to me might be valuable to them. And the best thing about it is they probably will never know the difference.
- Lyran

The best places to visit for harvesting reagents tend to be remote locations that are difficult to access and less likely to have been impacted negatively by metahuman contact. Amazonia is perhaps one of the best locations for finding pristine specimens of fauna and paranormal critters for your enchanting needs, particularly in the heart of the Amazon Rainforest. However, with Aztlan's encroachment into the northern parts of the rainforest, you need to stay away from the northern areas where Aztlan has moved in since the Azt-Am War, as the Azzies are not treating the area gently. Also remember that there are many dangers to be found in the Awakened rainforest, including carnivorous trees (which can provide powerful reagents if they don't kill you first), the ghost cartels, deadly insects, and venomous paranormal critters, some of which have yet to be classified by today's science. Africa continues to be another popular spot for reagent gathering. But again, rapid urbanization of wilderness areas, irresponsible poaching, and strip mining operations continue to whittle away at sources of radical-quality reagents. Asia also suffers similar problems, particularly with the rapid loss or wilderness.

One part of the world that does not suffer as much metahuman intrusion is Australia. With all the wild magic, mana storms, and highly venomous Awakened paranormal critters, Australia's outback is one of the best places in the world to harvest untainted reagents. In North America, there are still a few locations that are ideal for harvesting reagents. Mount Shasta, despite being devastated by the events surrounding the climax of the Great Dragon Civil War, still has locations that are ideal for talismongering. The Mohave Desert is also known for its exemplary reagents. The main drawback, besides the unbearable temperatures during the summer months, is you might just have to endear hostile spirits, resulting in many talismongering expeditions disappearing into the desert and never being seen again. And the NAN nations, particularly the Sioux Nation and the Pueblo Corporate Council, have territory that has been protected

from metahuman abuse, making them ripe for reagent hunting. The downside of these locations should be obvious: these lands are generally restricted, meaning only talismongers belonging to the tribes that are native to those nations can enter. Even then, there are tight restrictions on what they can and cannot harvest. Talismongers from outside find it difficult at best to work in these areas without overtly breaking the law. Many talismongers find that they have no choice but to break the law to make a living in these areas, even if they would prefer to remain law-abiding.

- Yes, talismongers have it rough. Not only do they have to worry about governments and all the dangers associated with doing their jobs properly, they also have to worry about the criminal syndicates. Some will just try and kill you outright for competing for their resources. Those that don't will try to intimidate you into giving up a share of your reagents for the privilege of staying in business. And many will give in to those shakedown demands, 'cause it's better to be alive than dead.
- Hard Exit

Talismongering has become much more complicated thanks to the dragons. Talismongers typically have locations that they have staked out and have claimed as their own territory for prime reagent harvesting. Due to prime specimens of reagents being so hard to come by, talismongers are very protective of the areas that produce decent reagents. Independent talismongers regularly hire runners to help defend their turf. Talisleggers wil generally have the muscle of the syndicate they are working for to keep rival operations out of their way, in order to protect syndicate profits. Don't expect a rival talismonger to be willing to negotiate for rights to use

HIGHLIGHTED FOCUS: COMBAT KNIFE FROM THE UNITED STATES' CONFLICT AGAINST NATIVE AMERICAN NATIONS IN 2016

In the Museum of Sioux History in Cheyenne lies a combat knife used during the Native American Nations' battle for independence against the United States Government. According to historians, this combat knife is among the first weapon focuses used during that conflict, and it is believed to have belonged to War Chief Ossiolachiih from the Muscogee tribe. The blade was used for sixteen confirmed kills of United States military personnel during that conflict. What is interesting about this combat focus, beyond its historical significance, is the fact that after nearly sixty years, the enchantment on the weapon focus retains a significant amount of its power nearly sixty years later. Typically in those early years, enchanting was very rudimentary, and enchantments rarely survived past ten years. The quality of this enchantment speaks to the talent and skill

of Ossiolachiih as a master enchanter. The Museum of Sioux History also holds three other weapon foci recovered from that conflict: a tomahawk and two combat axes, all of which have had their enchantments break over time. Currently there is a great demand from collectors looking to acquire artifacts from that era. At various battle sites within the Native American Nations, valuable relics may remain, waiting to be unearthed by the right hunter. However, many battle sites from that conflict are off limits to outsiders, and anyone who violates these tribal laws could end up serving lengthy prison time. Some see the risk worth it for hunting these historical relics, and for the nuyen they can net. Examination of War Chief Ossiolachiih's combat knife suggests that it was likely a very powerful focus in its day, but has lost perhaps half of its potency.

the land. Your intrusion into their territory threatens their livelihood, and they are more than likely willing to take you out than share their turf.

When the dragons extracted their vengeance on the talismonger population for using dragon reagents, they shook up the balance of power within the talismonger community. Many of these optimal locations that were previously claimed by veteran talismongers have since gone abandoned. Ever since the conclusion of the Great Dragon Civil War, there have been power grabs by talismongers and talisleggers over this newly unclaimed territory all around the world, while criminal syndicates have been trying to shore up the operations they have already established and take over areas where rival operations were devastated by the dragons' intervention. So far, the fighting over land use has been bloody. The shifting territories have yet to be resolved, and each day new talismongers are looking to use the chaos to muscle in on the more lucrative territories. If you intend to make talismongering your life, you better watch your back. There's going to people gunning for it, trying to get their hands on the same reagents that you'll be looking for. Life for a talismonger will remain tough for the foreseeable future, until a new pecking order amongst the talismonger community is all sorted out.

TALISMONGERS AND REAGENTS

The enchanting process is a delicate one. Any number of variables can enter the process at any step, causing unintended flaws in the product and perhaps ruining cause the focus. It is because of this the United Talismongers Association recommends that when a talismonger is collecting materials, they should only use properly prepared tools in gathering reagents. The UTA has approved the sell of a cleanser that, using an industry-recognized process, can eliminate a vast amount of impurities from a talismonger's tools (ranging from chisels, pickaxes, scalpels, and knives to melee weapons, which are handy if you're collecting pelts of paranormal critters), and prevent cross-contamination between reagents. The last thing you would want, for example, is for flecks of dried blood from the pelt of a phoenix from your last kill to end up on the pelt of a horned bear that you just collected. Or a trace amount of diamond dust ending up in an enchanting that does not need it. It may seem like minimal contamination, but it would not be a minor detail later if the focus' enchantment breaks due to the adulteration of the two materials. This is perhaps the easiest part of a talismongers' jobs—keeping their tools immaculately clean and ready for the next batch of reagents. Unfortunately, I know of too many talismongers who are lazy or who overlook this step, risking contamination for the sake

of expediency. They claim it makes no discernible difference in their work, but I can tell you there is a significant difference in the way the focus is constructed and how well crafted (or shoddy) that enchantment is. There have been stories of enchantments randomly shattering on a runner because of how it was made. So if you are looking to be a talismonger and excel in this field, learn to do the right thing at the start of your career, practice proper habits and keep your tools and workspace clean. It may save you a lot of wasted reagents later on. And if you are a runner looking for a talismonger, always pay attention to the street rep of a talismonger. Just like there are shady fences out there who will sell you modeling clay for explosives, so too are there shady talismongers out there that will cut corners to increase their profit margins.

Keep in mind talismongering is never as easy or as glamorous as the trid movies make it out to be, especially when it comes to gathering reagents. You don't just go out to a remote area and spend time looking around on the astral. You have to actively search for them. This means hiking, climbing, sifting and panning rivers, tracking, and digging. This is often tedious and grueling work. Depending on the kind of reagents you are looking for, you could easily spend weeks, if not months, outside of modern civilization. Trust me, the lifestyle is not for everyone. Living inside tents, wearing bulky or burdensome environmental suits, being filthy without the possibility of hot showers for weeks on end, living off of pre-packaged, dehydrated food, encountering exotic diseases that make your life a living hell, and living in extreme temperatures without hardly any modern conveniences are all things that talismongers have come to expect in their line of work. This on top of the risk of always stumbling into dangers that are not natural, but instead, are metahuman-caused. Minefields are the most common threat in my line of work, but so are chemical spills that someone "forgot" to report, as well as radioactive hot spots and toxic waste spills that have been covered up.

If the living conditions and dangers were not enough to discourage you from the lifestyle, you might want to consider the frustration that comes from the realization that not all specimens of reagents share a uniform quality. You could be stuck in the middle of nowhere, chasing a vein of gold to mine, only to find that the vein of gold you finally stumble upon has been contaminated by a chemical spill from MCT, and any gold you unearth will be unusable to you, as the gold no longer contains any trace of magic potential. Or you could wind up spending all your time looking for a paranormal critter specimen when it turns out that it has become mutated or turned toxic by its environment. There is nothing more frustrating than having to start your search all over again when you invested dozens of hours or more on your current search, only to find out that the pot of gold you have been chasing is nothing more than a cauldron of toxic sludge. But that is a reality of today's talismongers: you encounter failure and more failure before you finally strike success.

Experienced talismongers have come to accept there are variations in the quality of reagents. Besides those that have been contaminated to the point of being worthless, there are other reagents that have been severely damaged but can still be used with a lot of effort. Other specimens are only moderately damaged and can be used with less effort; usually these are considered to be "inferior" specimens. And there are still others that are only considered "subpar," meaning they only have moderate imperfections due to various health and environmental factors. If you are lucky, you will stumble across what are called baseline specimens. These are the specimens which are meant to be the normal expressions of the species. In my opinion, the lowest grade of reagents you should ever consider using for enchanting are your baseline specimens. Anything else and you risk ruining the focus by interjecting flaws into the enchantment process. The flaws from these poor specimens can still carry over to the finished product even after the reagents have been turned into refined or radical reagents. Also, the more damaged the specimen of reagent is from various environmental factors, the less you can harvest to use for your enchantments. A vein of silver containing ten drams of material might only be able to produce six drams if it is considered to be of inferior quality. If the severity of the contamination exceeds the amount of drams a source of reagents can produce, than nothing can be harvested and you have wasted your time. So it is more worth your time seeking out higher quality reagents and to get more for your effort than settling for subpar materials.

HIGHLIGHT FOCUS: GUNGNIR

Anyone who is a history buff and is familiar with the events of the Second Matrix Crash may have heard of Gungnir. Gungnir was the weapon focus belonging to the Winternight cult leader known as Wednesday. Wednesday used a number of foci during his day, but none were as well known or as visible to his movement as Gungnir, a weapon focus, enchanted into the form of a spear. No one truly knew how powerful this weapon focus was, as Wednesday kept it masked most of the time. Reports and rumors suggested it was quite powerful, possibly a Force 12 weapon focus. When Europol captured Wednesday, they learned that it was a Force 8 weapon focus, decorated with Norse runes and inscribed in gold lettering. Europol also confirmed that it was a toxic weapon focus. For nearly a decade, it was left in an evidence locker room. In 2073, when someone went to destroy the weapon focus, Europol learned that the spear had vanished. They still have no idea when it disappeared. They believe that remaining Winternight cells or other, newer neo-Winternight groups, may have been responsible for its theft. Its location is still a mystery. There is a 25,000 nuyen bounty on its recovery, as well as the capture of anyone behind the theft. So far, there are still no good leads as to where this toxic weapon focus has gone.

REAGENT QUALITY AND AMOUNT THAT MAY BE HARVESTED

QUALITY	AMOUNT HARVESTED
Unusable	No reagent can be harvested from source
Tainted	–6 drams
Inferior	–4 drams
Subpar	–2 drams
Baseline	No modifier, all drams that the source of material is capable of producing can be harvested
Superior	No modifier, all drams that the source of material is capable of producing can be harvested
Prime	No modifier, all drams that the source of material is capable of producing can be harvested

Superior and Prime specimens take less time to refine into refined and radical reagents. Reduce the time it takes to convert Superior reagents into refined and radical reagents by 25 percent (round up). Reduce the time it takes to convert Prime specimens into refined and radical reagents by 50 percent (round up).

An Assensing + Intuition [8, 10 minutes] Extended Test before the talismonger collects the reagents will inform him of the quality of specimen.

If you are prepared to spend a lot more time hunting reagents, it is possible to gather reagents from superior and prime specimens of plant, mineral, or animal life. These specimens are extraordinarily hard to come by in this age of ground, water, and air contamination, so if you have your heart set on acquiring these types of reagents, be prepared to spend even longer periods of time hunting for them. However, the qualities of these superior and prime specimens allow for a higher quality of focus to be made, and will allow the enchantment on the focus to last much longer. This is why I generally stick to using superior and prime specimens for my reagents, and choosing to only use baseline-grade reagents when I absolutely have to. The location where you harvest is key to your success at locating superior and prime specimens. If you are harvesting in places like Amazonia, you have a much greater chance of locating superior and prime specimens that have not been tainted by pollution or toxins. However, if you try talismongering in places like Aztlan, which still has a problem of excessive mana warps, or Tsimshian, which

has become the poster child for toxic waste dumps the world over, all you're going to find are severely tainted and unusable reagents. This is why finding a good place to harvest and protecting it from other talismongers and talisleggers is key to your success.

As a talismonger, it is also important to keep in mind that the methods you use to gather reagents can impact the quality of the specimen of reagent, particularly with paranormal critters. The way you choose to collect animal pelts may either be neutral and does minimal damage to the pelt, or can be recklessly applied and cause severe harm to the pelt of the creature that it actually degrades its quality. Talismongers early on realized that shooting an animal up with bullets is a bad thing, as there's a chance of contaminating the pelt with metallic and gunpowder residue that can fuck with the enchantment process. Not to mention that gunshot wounds inflict traumatic damage on the body of a paranormal critter, causing you to lose potential drams of reagents. To minimize damage to a specimen, the UTA recommends using a basic bow and arrow if you are hunting an animal at a distance. Both the bow and the arrow should be properly treated and prepared using the approved UTA cleanser to avoid contamination of the specimen from foreign particulates. Using tranquilizers and other drugs on a specimen also has a negative reaction on the specimen and degrades its quality. Combat spells cast on paranormal critters have been known to adversely affect reagents that are harvested from their bodies. If you cannot use a bow and arrow, the next best thing to collecting material is engaging the paranormal critter in melee combat with a treated melee weapon. Any other method risks damaging the pelt, and risk damaging the reagents you are looking to preserve.

TOOL CLEANSERS

ITEM	AVAILABILITY	COST
Tool cleanser (15 uses)	10	50¥

For each tool a talismonger uses, they make an Artificing + Magic [4, 10 minutes] Extended Test to properly clean each tool and get it ready for harvesting reagents. If improperly cleaned tools are used to harvest reagents, roll 1D6; on a 1, the reagents have their quality downgraded by one line (e.g., going from baseline to subpar, or subpar to inferior). Tools that use lasers or produce flame to cut or melt reagents, or otherwise do not allow for cross contamination of reagents, do not need to go through this process.

IMPORTANCE OF INDIVIDUALIZING A FOCUS FOR A SPECIFIC USER

Due to how reagents work, talismongers must take the person that they are building the focus for into consideration. This also includes their mentor spirit. During the enchantment process, if a talismonger uses at least one reagent that has a direct connection with the mentor spirit (or totem), such as the use of eagle feathers as reagents for a focus for a follower of the Eagle totem, the person buying that focus will find it easier to bond to that focus. In game terms, the character receives a –1 reduction to the Karma cost that the character has to pay to bond to that focus. If all reagents used for a focus are related to the individual's mentor spirit, that reduction increases to a –2 to the bonding Karma cost. For example, if a talismonger constructs a focus for a follower of the sea totem and uses nothing but coral reef, naturally grown pearls, and conch shells as reagents, that bonus becomes a –2. This bonus is only available to individuals that have mentor spirits.

There is a price, however, for this Karma reduction. Using reagents that hold a connection to a mentor spirit gives the mentor spirit power over that focus. This typically is not a big deal, but should the follower upset the mentor spirit, in addition to taking away certain bonuses the follower receives for upsetting the mentor spirit, the mentor spirit could also turn off any focus where this connection was established and where the follower took advantage of this Karma reduction. If a follower chooses not to take the Karma cost reduction for bonding to the focus and chooses to pay full value, however, this connection is not established with the mentor spirit, which means the mentor spirit has no control over the focus.

Also, should the follower ever decide to change their beliefs and follow a different totem or mentor spirit, the connection with that mentor spirit is severed, and the focus becomes inert until the character spends the full Karma cost to re-bond to the focus—provided the character wants to re-bond to the focus that was basically dedicated to the purpose of their former totem. Bonding to an old focus that was dedicated to an old mentor spirit could be perceived by the current mentor spirit as a slight against them and could risk the anger of the new mentor spirit.

There are questions that persist as to whether a runner who wishes to use a higher rated focus than the one they currently using must purchase a brand new focus or if they can simply upgrade it. The truth is, foci can be upgraded under the right circumstances. The main restriction on upgrading any focus is that it must be done by the same talismonger who forged the focus in the first place. A focus cannot have the astral signatures of two talismongers interwoven into its tapestry. Attempting to do so automatically shatters the enchantment. This means that foci taken from other magicians and you do not know who enchanted them cannot be upgraded. Also, the focus must simply be upgraded to the same, stronger version of itself. It may not be repurposed as another type of focus. A power focus may not be upgraded to become a sustaining focus.

UPGRADING AN EXISTING FOCUS

The talismonger will need to add regents to the enchantment equal to difference in karma costs for bonding the old focus and bonding the upgraded version. For example, if a character wishes to upgrade a Force 3 Spell focus to a Force 5 Spell focus, the talismonger will need to use 4 reagents to upgrade the focus (10 being the new cost for bonding the focus, 6 being the cost of bonding to the Force 3 focus). The talismonger will need to make another Enchanting Test to re-forge the focus. They may, if they so choose, make another Artisan + Intuition test to rework the aesthetics of the focus to incorporate the changes into its design. Because the character was only bonded to the previous version, they will only need to pay 4 Karma to fully bond with the upgraded focus.

THE BUSINESS SIDE OF TALISMONGERING

There is no doubt about it: there are a lot of downsides to the life of a talismonger. However, there are a lot of upsides as well, including the potential for making a lot of nuyen. Talismongers are able to sell raw, refined and radical reagents to consumers, as well as focus formulae, spell formulae, and alchemical preparations. Although the market sets the prices for what talismongers can charge, many of the prices already have a descent amount of profit already worked into the pricing. It is also important to note that not all talismongers will offer formulae or foci at the market value, some will charge as much as 20 percent more for their goods, while others will offer discounts of up to 10 percent on their wares for their "regular customers." It is important for runners to establish solid bonds with their talismonger contacts in order to take advantage of these potential discounts, and to avoid being taken advantage of by high prices.

When costs for a particular, special ordered focus exceed the standard market value that is when negotiations come into play. For a well crafted focus that required a lot of artistic design, a talismonger will likely ask for at least a 1,000 nuyen above the fair market value for the focus. This can increase greatly, depending on the talent and reputation of the talismonger, and also what went into creating the customized focus for the client. In my business, I can regularly ask for ten thousand nuyen above the normal cost of a focus. My reputation for quality and my craftsmanship easily justify such an asking price. Experienced talismongers with similar reputations can charge similar amounts, and can expect to get it. And of course, talismongering is an industry where tipping your talismonger is not only recommended but expected. After all, talismongers are busy metahumans, and those who tip well tend to end up at the top of their "to do" lists, while those that don't find themselves waiting long periods of time to have their requests processed. So do yourself a favor, chummers, and tip your talismongers well.

HIGHLIGHTED FOCUS: JOHNNY "SHOCKY" BYRNES' ARES PREDATOR

What has to be the most gaudy and tasteless focus I have ever seen is a gold-plated Ares Predator II belonging to famed mobster Johnny "Shocky" Byrnes from the 2040's. "Shocky" Byrnes was a made-man with the Bigio family starting in the early 2040's. Back then, the mafia frowned heavily on magic users, so Byrne's hid his magic talent for most of the time he was a made-man. He relied heavily on his Ares Predator (his "signature" piece) to enforce the will of the Bigio family. Little did the family know he had secretly had his gold-plated Ares Predator turned into a focus; a spell sustaining focus, by adding silver-laced initials to the grip of his pistol. It is widely believed Byrnes used this focus to sustain either an Armor spell or a Detect Enemies spell. This spell apparently did Byrnes no good, as he would die in 2053 in a car bomb, believed to have been the work of the Yakuza. Although Byrnes did not survive the explosion, his focus somehow did. Byres' Ares Predator now hangs in the Mob History Museum in Las Vegas.